Smart STEM-Driven Computer Science Education

Vytautas Štuikys • Renata Burbaitė

Smart STEM-Driven Computer Science Education

Theory, Methodology and Robot-based Practices

Vytautas Štuikys
Department of Software Engineering
Kaunas University of Technology
Kaunas, Lithuania

Renata Burbaitė
Department of Software Engineering
Kaunas University of Technology/Panevėžys
Juozas Balčikonis gymnasium
Kaunas/Panevėžys, Lithuania

ISBN 978-3-030-08710-4   ISBN 978-3-319-78485-4   (eBook)
https://doi.org/10.1007/978-3-319-78485-4

Printed on acid-free paper

This Springer imprint is published by the registered company Springer International Publishing AG part of Springer Nature.
The registered company address is: Gewerbestrasse 11, 6330 Cham, Switzerland

Preface

At least in this decade, the acronym STEM (Science, Technology, Engineering, and Mathematics) was among dominating terms and themes in the literature on educational research and practice. In recent years, however, the interest in STEM education has grown even more intensively in both schools and universities, as well as among responsible bodies and organizations, including governments. The signs of that are many reports, the ever-growing stream of supporting initiatives in the USA, Europe, and research activities worldwide in the field. This interest arises from the urgent need to respond to the economic, social, and technological challenges of the twenty-first century. The rapid development of science and technology raises new challenges for labor markets and education. Nowadays, as never before, the modern economy requires the workforce to be equipped with the interdisciplinary knowledge based on using high-tech equipment and methodologies. STEM is, in fact, an interdisciplinary approach to learning. It brings rigorous academic concepts coupled with real-world lessons and tasks as students apply science, technology, engineering, and mathematics in contexts that make connections between school, community, work, and the global enterprise. That enables the development of STEM literacy and with it the ability to compete in the new economy.

The other important research stream focuses on the efforts to improve Computer Science (CS) education. It is difficult to overestimate the role of CS in the twenty-first century as leading science, because practically all sciences use CS approaches. The educators and scientists commonly agree that CS education in high school must consist of two parts. The first part should focus on learning knowledge and skills of ICT and its devices. Typically, we define that as *Digital Literacy*. However, these skills are short-living knowledge, because they are changing with technology. The second part should focus on learning the fundamentals of CS that are essential to understanding our digital world that advances extremely rapidly. This field is also known as *Informatics*, especially in Europe, and brings the long-living knowledge, which lasts forever and does not change with technology.

There is yet another exciting research area the concepts of our book deals with directly, i.e. educational robotics. Robots play an extremely significant role in education due to their "smart functionality" and the ability to engage students in the learning process directly. It is so because robotics entails the possibility to demonstrate various tasks and situations taken from the real world and in this way to enforce the motivation to learn. Indeed, educational robots are smart devices and therefore are so widely used in the field. Robots are able to perform mechanical jobs with little to no human interference. On the other hand, robots contain units to perform computations and control tasks to support mechanical actions. Therefore, it is possible to treat the robot as a dedicated computer with memory and processor, the main units of a conventional computer. For a long time in education, computers have been in use in the mode *use-as-is* (except perhaps specific electronics courses). Similarly, in many cases, we use educational robots in that mode. However, typically robots have a modular structure enabling teachers and students to assemble the whole architecture from the available parts. This activity, in fact, means the use of the pedagogical approach known in the literature under a generic term *learning-by-doing*, though there are other terms such as a *constructivist* approach or *inquiry-based learning* in terms of STEM.

The above-mentioned fields, i.e. STEM, CS education, and educational robotics, are highly heterogeneous in their own rank. Now a myriad of approaches exits to deal with those paradigms separately. However, we still know little about how it would be possible to combine those paradigms seamlessly into a coherent methodology in order to gain the synergistic benefit of all. This book is just about that. The basic idea we discuss in this book is how to project the extremely high variability of STEM pedagogy, STEM and CS-related content onto high school CS curricula, using modern technologies of two types. The first type is educational robotics used as direct facilities of learning in a high school. The second is supporting technologies to enable achieving goals of automation in the preparation, design, and use of the content and learning processes. The supporting technologies include high-level modelling and feature model transformations using meta-programming techniques. Note that we are able to integrate seamlessly those technologies with the conventional software.

In this book, we present the approach that distinguishes from known ones by the following attributes. Firstly, we focus on integrative aspects of the STEM by introducing it into the CS education courses, such as Programming, at the high school level. Secondly, we apply robotics as the relevant means to CS and STEM education. Thirdly, we introduce smart approaches to support this integration. By smart approaches, we mean those that rely on automation, generativity, context-awareness, automated adaptation, and application of knowledge-based approaches such as agent-based in designing and use of the learning content and scenarios. Finally, we present the overall material as a coherent methodology that covers methodological aspects, theoretical aspects, and practices. The latter includes multiple use cases, evaluation procedures, and figures taken from the real teaching setting at the one high school.

This monograph is a result of our intensive research in the field of automation of the educational processes and approaches. To some extent, this book is a continuation of the previous one published by Springer in 2015 (we mean "Smart Learning

Objects for Smart Education in Computer Science: Theory, Methodology and Robot-Based Implementation"). Though it has the same theoretical background as this one (i.e. high-level feature-based modelling, and transformation of those models using heterogeneous meta-programming), this book presents new findings. The novelty of this book covers multiple aspects. Firstly, it includes the explicit integration of STEM concepts into CS courses. This integration requires a new vision, new frameworks, and extended approaches, we have described in this book. Secondly, the book presents a new vision and models of representing smart content and smart scenarios. Thirdly, this book provides new concepts of the Personal Generative Library and Smart educational environments. Finally, this book discusses the relationship of STEM education with emerging paradigms such as the Internet-of-Things and MOOC.

What is the structure of this book? We have divided the content into five parts. Part I is the introductory part and, in fact, is the wide context of the remaining parts. Part II represents the methodological and theoretical background. Part III deals with the design and use of the smart content to support STEM and CS education. Part IV deals with the infrastructure of our approach. Part V extends the vision of our approach.

Part I includes Chaps. 1, 2 and 3. Chapter 1 is about the challenges of STEM-driven Computer Science (CS) education. Chapter 2 discusses a vision for introducing STEM into CS education at school. Chapter 3 deals with educational robotics and smart devices as a way of obtaining the interdisciplinary knowledge.

Part II includes Chaps. 4 and 5. Chapter 4 focuses on learning variability as a methodological background of STEM-driven reuse-enhanced CS education. Chapter 5 provides a theoretical background consisting of feature-based modelling to specify and represent the STEM learning variability and basics of heterogeneous meta-programming to implement the proposed STEM-driven approaches.

Part III includes Chaps. 6, 7, 8 and 9. Chapter 6 presents a vision for understanding smart learning objects (SLOs) for STEM-driven CS education. Chapter 7 describes the design and redesign of STEM-oriented generative learning objects (GLOs). Chapter 8 deals with the design of STEM-oriented smart learning objects (SLOs). Chapter 9 describes agent-based smart learning objects for the STEM.

Part IV includes Chaps. 10, 11, 12 and 13. Chapter 10 presents the concepts and implementation of the personal generative library for STEM-driven educational resources. Chapter 11 deals with the design of STEM-driven generative scenarios for CS education. Chapter 12 analyses the smart STEM-driven environment for smart CS education at high school. Chapter 13 summarizes the educational practices of smart STEM-driven CS education at one high school.

Part V includes Chaps. 14 and 15. Chapter 14 introduces the Internet-of-Things (IoT) vision in CS education and gives an idea for the remote STEM-driven environment. Chapter 15 provides a finalizing discussion, outlines other educational paradigms (such as MOOC and STEM for universities), and formulates open issues.

Who could be the potential reader of the book? We dedicate the book in the first place to the researchers in STEM-driven CS education, CS researchers, especially to those who are interested in using robots in learning and teaching, course designers, and educational software and tools developers. The CS teachers should also be highly interested not only in reading, but in studying the adequate chapters as their advanced teaching material. We hope that the content of the book will be understandable to anybody who has enough skill in programming. Therefore, students studying CS-related courses, especially master-level and PhD students, are also potential readers. As the book includes the wider context (e.g. reusability aspects in technology-enhanced learning and the educational research activities in STEM and CS), the other e-Learning community members might be interested in reading the book as well (especially the modelling of CS education and the integrative aspects of technology and pedagogy).

How should one read the book?

There is no specific algorithm for selecting and prioritizing the chapters for reading. Our writing priority was to present the content so that it would be possible to read a separate chapter independently from others. Nevertheless, some selecting and sequencing seem to be helpful for a deeper understanding. This depends on the reader's status, previous knowledge, and his or her intention. The title of a particular chapter, for example, can be an indicator to make a selection. Our recommendation is the following scheme. The senior researchers and policymakers should first read Chap. 1 and, perhaps, all introductions in each chapter and then to move to the ending sections in each chapter. After that, the readers will have the possibility to make the relevant choice for the in-depth studies of the full material within the chapters. Experts and knowledgeable researchers first could read the introduction and concluding parts of each chapter, or some selected chapters depending on the reader's flavor. If they will find interesting ideas, they could study a particular chapter more intensively. The readers who will select some material for their own research topic should also go through the relevant references.

What about the CS teachers and students? Those readers might use the book's content differently. Chapters 12 and 13 are mainly dedicated to the secondary (high) schoolteachers and students. For example, Section 13.4 presents *the full scenarios* on how to use smart LOs and smart educational robot-based environments to teach and learn STEM-driven CS topics at the school level. The university-level educators and students should use the book content with regard to their teaching/learning topics. For example, Chap. 4 is relevant to teach and learn the feature-based modelling methodology. Chapters 5, 6, 7, 8, 9, 10 and 11 better fit for teaching and learning topics related to model transformations. The educators of CS teachers' should use the book entirely.

We hope that the book will be the beneficial methodological instrument (due to the use of multiple illustrative examples and case studies) for those educators who are ready to provide the innovative models and methods in CS education on the STEM paradigm.

Kaunas, Lithuania   Vytautas Štuikys
Kaunas/Panevėžys, Lithuania   Renata Burbaitė

Acknowledgments

Firstly, we look at the prehistory of writing this book. We could hardly have written this monograph without the aspiration we have experienced in preparing the EU project-proposal on similar topics in 2015. This activity has brought to us a clear understanding of how topics on STEM and CS education are important for huge communities worldwide. The next impact was our continuing research and accumulated practice of the second author in teaching CS based on using robotics in the real setting. Researching and working from day to day in the classroom with students from 2011 onward, we have accumulated a tremendous amount of educational data. The teacher was able to discuss the issues with students, to evaluate, and to carry out the research work in the classroom, as well as to enforce and present the outcomes for a wider audience. Students' contribution to the activities and outcomes in collecting and generalizing data was noticeable. We would like to thank them all. Some of the students became apprentices of the teacher. Especially we would like to mention Adomas Paulauskas, a winner of the special prize of the best computational project in the EU contest of young scientists in Tallinn, in 2017.

We also thank our team members, especially professor R. Damaševičius, and the administration of Informatics faculty at Kaunas University of Technology and the administration of Panevėžys Balčikonis Gymnasium (Lithuania) for promotion and support in writing this book. Finally, we thank anonymous reviewers for their comments on the fragments of the manuscript.

We dedicate this book to the prominent date – the centenary jubilee of restoration the State of Lithuania. On the 16th of February 1918, the Council of Lithuania proclaimed the Act of Reinstating Independence of Lithuania...

Nowadays we believe in the talent and creativity of our young generation and the rest of the world. We hope this book will enrich by new ideas the educational researchers, schoolteachers, students, and other creators of our digital future.

Contents

Part I Introductory Part: Motivation, Challenges, and Conceptual Vision of STEM-Driven CS Education Based on Robotics

1 Challenges of STEM-Driven Computer Science (CS) Education ...   3
   1.1   Introduction   3
   1.2   Motivation of Our Approach   5
   1.3   Smart Education and STEM   9
   1.4   Ten Top Challenges in STEM Education   10
   1.5   CS Teaching Challenges Without STEM Context   13
   1.6   Challenges of STEM-Driven CS Education   15
   1.7   The Book's Objectives and Research Agenda   20
   1.8   The Topics This Book Addresses   21
   1.9   Summary and Concluding Remarks   23
   References   23

2 A Vision for Introducing STEM into CS Education at School   31
   2.1   Introduction   31
   2.2   Related Work   33
          2.2.1   STEM-Based Education Challenges   34
          2.2.2   The Role of CS in STEM-Oriented Education ..   34
          2.2.3   The Role of Smart Devices and Educational Robotics in STEM-Driven CS Education   35
          2.2.4   The Role of Context in Analysis and Design of Educational Systems   36
   2.3   A General Description of Our Approach   38
          2.3.1   A Conceptual Model of STEM-Driven CS Education ...   38
   2.4   A Framework to Implement the Proposed Conceptual Model   42
   2.5   Basis for Implementing Our Approach: A Process-Based Vision   45

2.6   STEM-Driven Learning Processes as a Problem Domain   48
2.7   Summary, Discussion and Overall Evaluation   50
2.8   Conclusion   52
References   52

3   **Smart Devices and Educational Robotics as Technology**
     for STEM Knowledge   57
3.1   Introduction   57
3.2   Related Work   58
3.3   Introducing Robotics in STEM-Driven CS Education   61
3.4   Educational Robot Generic Architecture   64
3.5   Conceptual Model of STEM-Driven Environment   65
3.6   Discussion and Conclusion   66
References   66

Part II   **Methodological and Theoretical Background of**
           Approaches to Implement the Proposed Vision

4   **A Methodological Background for STEM-Driven Reuse-Enhanced**
     CS Education   71
4.1   Introduction   71
4.2   Related Work   73
       4.2.1   Variability Research in SWE   73
       4.2.2   Variability in Learning   77
4.3   Explicit Representation of Variability: A Motivating Example . . .   81
       4.3.1   Capabilities of Feature Diagrams in Learning Object
                Domain   85
       4.3.2   Limitations of Feature Diagrams in Learning Object
                Domain   86
4.4   A Framework to Implement Learning Variability in STEM
       Paradigm   86
4.5   Motivation of STEM-Driven Research Topics   88
4.6   Two Approaches of Dealing with Variability in STEM   89
4.7   Summary, Evaluation and Extended Discussion   91
4.8   Conclusion   94
References   95

5   **Theoretical Background to Implement STEM-Driven**
     Approaches   99
5.1   Introduction   99
5.2   Motivation and Methodology of Describing the Background   100
5.3   Related Work   102
5.4   Background of Feature-Based Modelling   107

        5.4.1   A Vision for Researching STEM-Driven
                CS Education 107
        5.4.2   Basics of Feature Modelling 108
        5.4.3   Formal Definition of Features and Constraints 111
        5.4.4   Static and Dynamic Feature Models 112
        5.4.5   Mechanisms to Support Dynamicity for STEM 114
    5.5 Meta-programming as Solution Domain 116
        5.5.1   Meta-program of Type 1 119
        5.5.2   Meta-program of Type 2 121
        5.5.3   Meta-program of Type 3 123
        5.5.4   Meta-program of Type 4 124
    5.6 Data Transfer Modes Formal Definition 126
    5.7 Summary, Evaluation and Conclusion 126
    References 128

Part III   Design, Re-design, and Use of Smart Content for
           STEM-Driven CS Education

6   Understanding of Smart Content for STEM-Driven
    CS Education 135
    6.1 Introduction 135
    6.2 Related Work 136
    6.3 GLO/SLO Evolution Curve 138
    6.4 A Framework to Define and Understand SLOs 140
        6.4.1   Learner's Vision 141
        6.4.2   Teacher's Vision 144
        6.4.3   Designer's Vision 145
    6.5 SLO Evolution Vision: Researcher's Perspective 148
    6.6 Summary, Evaluation and Conclusion 152
    References 153

7   Model-Driven Design and Redesign of Smart STEM-Driven CS
    Content 157
    7.1 Introduction 157
    7.2 Related Work 159
    7.3 Two Conceptual Models and Two Approaches to Design SLOs .. 161
    7.4 Problem Statement for STEM Content Design and Redesign 162
    7.5 Model-Driven Framework to Design CS-Based SLOs 165
        7.5.1   Understanding of Context in Our Approaches 167
        7.5.2   Model-Driven SLO Design at the Top Level 169
        7.5.3   SLO Design at the Intermediate Level 173
        7.5.4   SLO Design at the Low (Coding) Level 176
    7.6 Theoretical Background of the Approaches 177

7.7   Generic Transformation Rule........................ 180
       7.7.1   Generic Rule............................... 181
7.8   Summary, Overall Evaluation and Conclusion............. 183
References.. 185

8   Stage-Based Smart Learning Objects: Adaptation Perspective 189
8.1   Introduction..................................... 189
8.2   Related Work..................................... 191
       8.2.1   Context-Related Issues in TEL................. 191
       8.2.2   The Term Stage and Relevant Methodologies........ 192
       8.2.3   Adaptation in e-Learning..................... 193
8.3   Motivation of the Approach.......................... 194
8.4   Categories of Learning Objects to Support STEM........... 195
8.5   A Framework and Tasks to Develop SB GLOs............. 197
8.6   A Background of the Approach........................ 198
       8.6.1   Basic Assumptions.......................... 198
       8.6.2   Definition of Basic Terms..................... 199
       8.6.3   Basic Properties............................ 200
8.7   Staging and Context Awareness....................... 203
8.8   Integration of STEM Concepts into SB Model............. 204
8.9   Case Study...................................... 206
8.10   Stage-Based Adaptation Processes and Scenarios........... 207
8.11   Analysis of Capabilities of the SB Model................ 210
       8.11.1 Designer's Perspective....................... 210
       8.11.2 Teacher's Perspective........................ 211
       8.11.3 Student's Perspective........................ 212
8.12   Summary and Concluding Remarks..................... 213
References.. 214

9   Agent-Based GLOs/SLOs for STEM 217
9.1   Introduction..................................... 217
9.2   Related Work..................................... 219
9.3   GLOs and SW Agent Domains Analysis: Problem Statement 220
9.4   Robot-Oriented Agent-Based Educational Environment:
       Architecture and Processes........................... 223
9.5   Implementation of Software Agent: A Case Study........... 225
       9.5.1   How to Integrate Technological Agent into Our
               Vision of STEM?........................... 225
9.6   Evaluation and Conclusion........................... 227
References.. 227

**Part IV Infrastructure to Support STEM-Driven CS
          Educational Practice**

**10 Personal Generative Library for STEM-Driven Educational
     Resources** 233
     10.1   Introduction 233
     10.2   A Concept of Personal Generative Library and More 234
     10.3   Related Work 236
     10.4   Tasks in Creating PGL for STEM-Driven Education 239
     10.5   Basic Idea of the Approach 239
     10.6   Background of the Approach 240
            10.6.1   Definitions of Basic Terms and Relationships 241
     10.7   A Detailed Description of the Approach 244
     10.8   A Methodology of Experiments and Case Study 246
            10.8.1   Results of Modelling 246
            10.8.2   A Case Study: Results Obtained by the Generated
                     Programs 247
     10.9   Adaptation of PGL Concept to STEM Library 248
     10.10 Summary, Discussion and Evaluation 252
     10.11 Conclusion 253
     References 254

**11 A Methodology and Tools for Creating Generative Scenario
     for STEM** 259
     11.1   Introduction 259
     11.2   Related Work 261
            11.2.1   Part A: STEM Context Issues 261
            11.2.2   Part B: Educational Scenarios Review 263
     11.3   Research Tasks and Methodology 265
            11.3.1   A Framework for Creating Scenarios 265
            11.3.2   Architectural Aspects 267
            11.3.3   Design Processes to Develop Generative Scenario 270
     11.4   Methods Used 272
     11.5   Discussion and Summarizing Evaluation 273
     11.6   Conclusion 276
     References 276

**12 Smart STEM-Driven Educational Environment for CS
     Education: A Case Study** 279
     12.1   Introduction 279
     12.2   Related Work 281
     12.3   A Framework for Creating Smart Educational Environments:
            Principles and Requirements 285
     12.4   Part 1: Architectural and Functional Aspects of STEM-Driven
            SEE 288

12.5   Part 2: Main Features of the STEM-Driven SEE
       for CS Education   289
       12.5.1   Communication Processes: A User Perspective   291
       12.5.2   Structure of the Server Part   293
12.6   Part 3: Evaluation of Smart Educational Environments   294
12.7   Discussion, Summary and Conclusion   296
References   300

13   Practice of Smart STEM-Driven CS Education at High School   305
13.1   Introduction   305
13.2   Related Work   306
13.3   Curriculum of Programming Basics to Support
       Our Approach   307
13.4   Case Studies   312
       13.4.1   Case Study 1   313
       13.4.2   Case Study 2   314
       13.4.3   Case Study 3   317
13.5   Evaluation   321
13.6   Conclusion   323
References   324

Part V   An Extended Vision to STEM-Driven CS Education

**14   Internet-of-Things: A New Vision for STEM
       and CS Education**   327
14.1   Introduction   327
14.2   Related Work   328
       14.2.1   Stream A   329
       14.2.2   Stream B   330
14.3   An Architecture of IoT System for STEM-Driven
       CS Education   334
14.4   A Framework to Consider Educational Tasks
       in Relation to IoT   337
14.5   Case Study: Line Following Task   339
14.6   Summary and Conclusion   342
References   343

15   A Finalizing Discussion and Open Issues   347
15.1   Introduction   347
15.2   A Summary and Evaluation of the Proposed Approach   348
       15.2.1   Capabilities of Smart Learning Objects   350
       15.2.2   Capabilities of Generative Learning Scenario   351
       15.2.3   How Does Our Approach Support Computational
                Thinking?   353

15.2.4 Drawbacks of the Proposed Approach 355
15.2.5 Difficulties from Teacher's Perspective 355
15.2.6 Drawbacks from Learner Perspective 356
15.3 Applicability of the Approach at the University Level 357
15.4 STEM in Industry: A New Way 357
15.5 MOOC and STEM-Driven CS Education 359
15.6 Open Issues 361
References 363

Glossary 365

Index 367

Part I
Introductory Part: Motivation, Challenges, and Conceptual Vision of STEM-Driven CS Education Based on Robotics

Part I is the introductory part. It includes three chapters. Chapter 1 introduces readers with challenges of STEM-driven education in general and those challenges caused by the use of this paradigm in Computer Science (CS) education in particular. We analyze challenges, as they are understood by authorities in the field, aiming to motivate our approach we discuss throughout the book. Chapter 1 also formulates objectives, research agenda, and topics this book addresses.

*The **objectives** of the book are, in a wider context, to discuss the concepts and approaches enabling to transform the current CS education paradigm into STEM-driven at the school and, to some extent, at the university. We seek to implement this transformation through the integration of the STEM pedagogy, the Smart STEM content, and the Smart devices into STEM supporting environment, using reuse-driven approaches taken from software engineering and CS.*

Therefore, the objectives are to focus on STEM-driven CS education by applying the reuse-based concepts and approaches as much as possible. The aim is to enhance and win effectiveness through automation. We seek for automation at all levels, i.e. in designing and using the STEM content, the STEM scenario, and the STEM infrastructure. Chapter 2 presents a vision on how we are able to introduce STEM into CS education at the secondary (high) school level and fulfill foreseen objectives. It gives a general understanding of our approach. The basis for that are the introduced framework, conceptual model, and process-based vision. The framework and conceptual model explain the interdisciplinary nature of the approach by introducing STEM-driven robot-oriented scenarios to deliver the knowledge components defined as S-knowledge, T-knowledge, E-knowledge, M-knowledge, and I-knowledge (meaning integrative knowledge). The process-based vision provides readers with the top-level aspects of the functionality of our approach. Here, we describe STEM-driven learning (educational) processes as a problem domain. Finally, Chap. 3 introduces basics of smart devices, mainly robotics, as a core source of the primary interdisciplinary knowledge that includes components covering the fields (Science, Technological, Engineering, and Mathematics) shortly known as STEM.

Chapter 1
Challenges of STEM-Driven Computer Science (CS) Education

Abstract Based on the thorough analysis of the literature, Chap. 1 introduces readers with challenges of STEM-driven education in general and those challenges caused by the use of this paradigm in computer science (CS) education in particular. This analysis enables to motivate our approach we discuss throughout the book. Chapter 1 also formulates objectives, research agenda and topics this book addresses. The objectives of the book are to discuss the concepts and approaches enabling to transform the current CS education paradigm into the STEM-driven one at the school and, to some extent, at the university. We seek to implement this transformation through the integration of the STEM pedagogy, the smart content and smart devices and educational robots into the smart STEM-driven environment, using reuse-based approaches taken from software engineering and CS.

1.1 Introduction

The rapid development of science and technology raises new challenges for labour market and education. Perhaps the most important one is to educate students in *Science, Technology, Engineering and Mathematics* (STEM) who, after graduating, could be able to join the modern labour market of the twenty-first century as fluently and easily as possible. Therefore, the STEM-oriented education has received an increasing attention over the past decade worldwide, especially in the USA. For example, the urgency to improve the achievements in STEM education in the USA is evident by the massive educational reforms that have occurred in the last two decades within these STEM education disciplines. The earlier initiatives include [AAA89, AAA93, ABE04, ITE00, ITE03, NCT00, NCT89]. The more recent initiatives include [NRC11, NRC12].

Typically, STEM is defined as "an interdisciplinary approach to learning where rigorous academic concepts are coupled with real world lessons as students apply science, technology, engineering, and mathematics in contexts that make connections between school, community, work, and the global enterprise enabling the development of STEM literacy and with it the ability to compete in the new economy" [SPS09].

© Springer International Publishing AG, part of Springer Nature 2018
V. Štuikys, R. Burbaitė, *Smart STEM-Driven Computer Science Education*,
https://doi.org/10.1007/978-3-319-78485-4_1

Many reports emphasize the importance of STEM education and predict that the demand for the STEM-based workforce will be growing continuously in the twenty-first century. For example, according to a report by the website *STEMconnector.org*, by 2018, projections estimate the need for 8.65 million workers in STEM-related jobs. The manufacturing sector faces an alarmingly large shortage of employees with the necessary skills – nearly 600,000. The field of cloud computing alone will have created 1.7 million jobs between 2011 and 2015, according to the report. The US Bureau of Labour Statistics projects that by 2018, the bulk of STEM careers will be:

Computing – 71%
Traditional engineering – 16%
Physical sciences – 7%
Life sciences – 4%
Mathematics – 2%

The other report [STEM16] describes the six interconnected components of STEM 2026 and the challenges and opportunities for innovation related to converting these components into widespread practice. The components range from *"Engaged and networked communities of practice"* to *"Societal and cultural images and environments that promote diversity and opportunity in STEM"*.

Therefore, STEM-oriented education becomes well timed and extremely significant now and for the future. On the other hand, the increased demand and requirements as well as the internal reasons cause many challenges and issues. They require of better understanding in order we could be able to manage them adequately. Among others, they include (i) motivating and engaging students to participate in STEM-oriented learning [AEM+14, AGM+15, KKY+14] and (ii) integrating STEM-oriented aspects in the school curriculum [Rob15, GMB+14]. The others include (iii) selecting adequate technological tools, pedagogical methods and activities for the paradigm [DHL+14, Rob15] and (iv) providing students' research and introducing real problem solving to enforce critical and computational thinking, to develop collaborative learning skill for modern workforce market [AEM+14, GMB +14, HB17, DGL+14, DHL+14, FMT14, Hol14, NLS16, SAB+17, SGW16].

In response, there are many calls for greater emphasis on these fields, as well as for improvements in the quality of curricula and instruction. As a result, numerous reports, new instructional materials and programs and even specialized schools are emerging. For example, the report prepared *by the Committee on Integrated STEM Education* [HPS14] formulates the following agenda for action and research.

> *Despite the rise in interest in providing students with learning experiences that foster connection making across the STEM disciplines, there is little research on how best to do so or on what factors make integration more likely to increase student learning, interest, retention, achievement, or other valued outcomes. Recognizing the need for a more robust evidence base, the National Academy of Engineering (NAE) and the Board on Science Education of the National Research Council (NRC) convened a committee to examine current efforts to integrate the STEM disciplines in K–12 education and develop a research agenda that, if carried out, could provide the data needed to inform such efforts going forward..*

Having this situation in mind, the Committee has developed a descriptive framework. The framework aims at providing a common perspective and vocabulary for researchers, practitioners and others to identify, to discuss and to investigate specific integrated STEM initiatives within the K–12 education system of the United States. The Committee has excluded four high-level features that focus on *goals*, *outcomes*, *nature of integration and implementation*. To motivate our goals and tasks, we need to provide some details on this framework.

Goals, as defined in the framework, indicate creating "STEM literacy and 21st century competencies; developing a STEM-capable workforce; and boosting interest and engagement in STEM".

Outcomes, on the other hand, include considering "learning and achievement; STEM course taking; STEM-related employment; development of 'STEM identity'; and the ability to transfer understanding across STEM disciplines". As for *the nature and scope of integration*, the framework addresses the following issues: "which subjects are connected; which disciplines are dominant; and the duration, size, and complexity of an initiative".

Finally, the *implementation* focuses on "instructional designs involving problem-based learning and engineering design; the type of educator supports present, such as pre- and in-service professional development and the development of professional learning communities; and adjustments to the learning environment, such as extended class periods, extended lesson planning, team teaching, and partnering between STEM educators working in and outside of schools".

In summary, the Committee has formulated three broad categories of research questions: (i) outcomes of integrated STEM education, (ii) the nature of integrated STEM education and (iii) design and implementation of integrated STEM education. However, the conclusion made by the Committee states the following:

> *The level of evidence gathered by the committee is not sufficient to suggest that integrated STEM education could or should replace high-quality education focused on individual STEM subjects.*

The statement that focuses also on "individual STEM subjects" encourages us and gives a primary impulse to motivate our approach. The topics we discuss throughout the book is just about STEM-driven CS education at school using smart STEM pedagogy, STEM- and CS-oriented scenarios, technology-enhanced generic (generative) content and smart devices and robotics.

1.2 Motivation of Our Approach

What is STEM? We start our discussion with this question because there is no uniform understanding of what, in essence, the STEM paradigm is with multiple definitions proposed so far. The STEM, as addressed in [DH16], is not the traditional silo disciplines of study but rather a *pedagogical strategy* – an integrated approach to the teaching of Science, Technology, Engineering and Mathematics – referred to from henceforth as integrated STEM. According to [GA14], "STEM pedagogy is rooted in the interdisciplinary application of knowledge. STEM Education is *a philosophy* designed around a cooperative effort to provide students with a comprehensive, meaningful, real-world learning experience". Sanders [San09] notes that "integrative STEM education includes approaches that explore teaching and learning *between/among any two or more of the STEM subject areas*, and/or between a *STEM subject and one or more other school subjects*" (p. 21). Indeed, STEM focuses on integrative aspects of four disciplines into the curriculum. *STEM integration* is "the intentional integration of content and processes of science or mathematics education with the content and processes of technology or engineering education along with explicit attention to technology or engineer learning outcomes and science or mathematics learning outcomes as behavioural learning objectives" [Asu14].

On the other hand, the STEM integration mechanisms as stated in [NSW+13] "remain largely underspecified in the research and policy literatures, despite their purported benefits". This paper provides a key mechanism of STEM integration by producing and maintaining *cohesion* of central concepts across the range of representations, objects, activities, and social structures in the engineering classroom. The STEM integration into the curriculum, in fact, is "*an interdisciplinary teaching approach*, which removes the barriers between the four disciplines" [WMR +11]. According to Huntley [Hun99], an interdisciplinary approach to teaching implies that "the teacher(s) makes connections between the disciplines only implicitly". In other words, instruction involves "explicit assimilation of concepts from more than one discipline" and is "typified by approximately equal attention from two (or more) disciplines" during a learning episode. Jacobs [Jac89] identifies *interdisciplinary teaching* as the approach that "consciously applies methodology and language from more than one discipline to examine a central theme, issue, problem, topic, or experience".

The STEM paradigm has also its roots in *problem-based* and *project-based learning* [Bar10] as it practiced in K–12 engineering and science curricula. In this regard, representation of concepts is essential [NSW+13]. In these approaches, students must learn to perceive the continuity of central concepts in science and math via a variety of representations, such as equations, graphs, diagrams, models and simulations. The range of representational forms is sufficiently vast that scholars in the sociology of science often combine any manner of externalized drawing, writing and graphical notational system used in the service of intellectual activity under the general term *inscriptions* (e.g. [RG98, NSW+13]).

The major element of the STEM curriculum *is* the incorporation not only of *problem-based learning* (PBL) but also of *inquiry-based learning* (IBL). Constructivist theory becomes the backbone that supports both PBL and IBL. The student needs to incorporate their current and prior understanding while discovering new knowledge and should be continuously assimilating and accommodating knowledge, reflecting on it and their experiences [Nua10]. The inquiry process can provide students with opportunities to explore and understand the natural world by themselves. In this way, they become independent critical and creative thinkers. In PBL, teaching students to become inventive problem solvers has long been a goal of science education.

The basis in STEM education is the application of IBL. According to Barell [Bar10], *inquiry* is "the driver of the complex thinking during the problem solving processes". This approach depends on the students' prior knowledge to construct the new knowledge by themselves. Therefore, the student is supposed to be able to act as an autonomous learner and the teacher as a facilitator or mentor. The teacher scaffolds the students by frequently reminding them to reflect, collaborate, ask themselves questions and justify their conclusions. Inquiry processes occur through the development of cognitive, meta-cognitive, psychomotor and social skills. When the students carry out experiments, they apply different inquiry skills such as asking questions, raising a hypothesis, planning an experiment to test the hypothesis, accessing and analysing data, making inferences, drawing conclusions and reporting and writing a research report. Students also apply meta-cognitive skills by engaging in reflective thinking throughout the learning stages.

There are five essential features of inquiry as follows from (National Research Council, 2000):

- *Learners are engaged by scientifically oriented questions.*
- *Learners give priority to evidence, which allows them to develop and evaluate explanations that address scientifically oriented questions.*
- *Learners formulate explanations from evidence to address scientifically oriented questions.*
- *Learners evaluate their explanations in light of alternative explanations, particularly those reflecting scientific understanding.*
- *Learners communicate and justify their proposed explanations.*

With regard to obtaining the knowledge in the cognitive sense, the following observation given by Bruning et al. [BSN+04] resonates with integrative STEM education:

- *Learning is a constructive, not a receptive, process.*
- *Motivation and beliefs are integral to cognition.*
- *Social interaction is fundamental to cognitive development.*
- *Knowledge, strategies and expertise are contextual.*

Science, Technology, Engineering and Mathematics are indeed very broad and heterogeneous fields. Therefore, it is not surprising that there are quite different views and approaches to deal with STEM education. One specific view relates to the role of computer science (CS) in STEM-based education. Gander [Gan15] observes that CS is the leading science of the twenty-first century. Similarly to mathematics, practically all sciences use CS approaches. According to the author, it has to be a part of general knowledge in education. On the other hand, *Informatics Europe* and *ACM Europe* convincingly state that CS education in the school must consist of two parts. The first should focus on learning to make good use of ICT and its devices, also called as *digital literacy*. These skills are short-living knowledge, because they are changing with technology. The second should focus on learning the fundamentals of

CS that are essential to understanding our digital world. This is *informatics*. The latter brings "long living knowledge which lasts forever and does not change with technology".

The aim of this book is to discuss the approach on how to introduce the STEM paradigm into the CS course at the school level. Two basic attributes predefine the essence of our vision on STEM. The first is the use of educational robots and other smart devices for CS education at the secondary (high) school. The second is the use of the robot-oriented teaching content that we represent in a specific way. One type represents the so-called smart learning objects [Štu15] adapted for the STEM needs (meaning meta-programming-based generative learning objects (GLOs) with extended features and possibilities). The other type represents component-based LOs such as tutorials, quizzes, etc.

Both attributes, when implemented, require a wide range of interdisciplinary knowledge to define and integrate STEM components (S, T, E, and M) into CS education. In our model, STEM components represent the following items. The component S covers CS and partially physics topics, i.e. those topics that relate to understanding of robotics functionality. The component T covers a variety of technologies, including the Internet, educational software tools, communication, etc. The component E covers constructing of an educational robot system from available parts, designing of the educational environment and testing it and robot's functionality through modelling. We are also able to introduce the engineering aspects through dealing with real-world tasks or their prototypes. The component M is implicit in our model. Either it appears in the task dedicated to the robot, or it appears within the algorithm to specify the robot's functionality. In our model, the component S stands for the root while the remaining ones are supplementary to define the STEM paradigm within the CS teaching curriculum. Therefore, we consider such a paradigm that integrates STEM within the single teaching course (i.e. CS course also known as informatics).

Note that our previous book [Štu15] has focused on the concept of smart learning objects (LOs) for CS education using robotics too. By smart LOs, we mean generative learning objects with enhanced features and capabilities, including those for generative reuse, adaptability and automation. In this book, we have substantially enlarged this experience by introducing new concepts. We have extended the previous concepts and introduced new ones (such as smart LOs as software agents, generative STEM scenario, personal generative library, etc.) so that we could be able to develop the smart STEM-driven educational environment to support integrative teaching and learning of single CS courses. What are the main drivers of this new vision?

The first and foremost important motivating aspect is the international context, i.e. recognition of the importance of a single course in STEM education as stated in [HPS14]: "*It is not sufficient to suggest that integrated STEM education could or should replace high-quality education focused on individual STEM subjects*". The second is the role of the CS course in education in general as stated previously. The third is the capabilities of robotics to reveal the STEM potential. Finally, the previous research and learning experience in using robotics to provide CS education at school [ŠB15a, ŠB15b] is a good starting point to deal with STEM-driven CS education from the perspective of research, development and practice.

1.3 Smart Education and STEM

The rapid development of technology introduces new capabilities for learners and educators. Now technology enables educators to introduce pedagogical approaches motivating learners to learn in a variety of ways and to manage the whole process more effectively and flexibly. Learners, on the other hand, are able to learn more efficiently and comfortably. In the digital age, education therefore becomes smart. *Smart education* is a relatively new concept that has gained an increased attention in recent years. This concept has many meanings. It covers a variety of aspects, such as smart pedagogy, smart learner, smart content, smart learning device, smart educational environment, etc. So far, there is no unified definition of smart education, though discussions on the topic are intensive and wide.

The paper [Gwa10], for example, proposes a concept of smart learning that discriminates the approach from others by two key attributes: (i) enlarged focus on learners and content rather than on the devices and (ii) effectiveness and intelligence, i.e. smart learning also focuses on the advanced IT infrastructure. Therefore, the technology plays an important role in supporting smart learning, but the focus should not be just on the utilization of smart devices. The papers [SB10, Hwa14] consider smart learning as a context-aware ubiquitous learning. The study [KCL13] considers smart education as a combination of social learning and ubiquitous learning with the focus on learner-centric and service-oriented educational paradigms, though the technology is on the account too.

The book [Štu15] discusses smart learning objects and smart education in computer science based on using robotics. Smart learning objects (SLOs) are about the generic content enriched by the following attributes: (i) deep integration of pedagogical-social and technological aspects within the content, (ii) context awareness for adaptation and (iii) automated generation of content instances on demand and technological support for design and use. Smart education in this context focuses on using SLOs within the robot-based educational environment.

In summary, smart learning is a multidimensional term that reflects the essential attributes as follows: self-directed, motivated and adaptive learning, formal and informal learning, social and collaborative learning and resource-enriched and technology-enhanced learning, to name a few. This is the main reason why it is difficult to define the term precisely. In this context, there is the need to define the term and interpret its possible meaning using some well-defined frameworks.

In this regard, the paper [ZYR16] provides an extensive research and presents a conceptual model to define smart education from a wider perspective. The model, for example, includes a four-tier framework of smart pedagogies and ten key features of smart learning environments to foster smart learners who need to master knowledge and skills of the twenty-first-century learning. The paper defines smart pedagogy as a compound of the following attributes: (i) class-based differentiated instruction, (ii) - group-based collaborative learning, (iii) individual-based personalized learning and (iv) mass-based generative learning. Learners utilize smart devices to access digital resources. Additionally, the paper defines a tri-tier technological architecture that emphasizes the role of smart computing.

The smart computing and smart education are two sides of the same coin. Often, researchers and practitioners understand the smart computing as intelligent technologies such as cloud computing, smart intelligent devices, intelligent environments, Internet-of-Things, big data, etc. Shifting of educational paradigms to smart education would be impossible without advanced technologies with the capabilities of smart computing. Many topics related to smart computing are those computer science education focuses on. Smart education, in terms of identified features, is relevant to STEM education too. It is especially true with regard to CS education using STEM. Using robot-based educational environments (in many cases, they are indeed smart) and SLOs in CS classes, for example, it is possible to achieve the objectives of smart pedagogy. Indeed SLOs embedded into adequate STEM scenarios enable to differentiate instruction, to provide group-based collaborative learning and to introduce personalization and, to some extent, generative learning in terms of its theory relationship to constructivism. The theory brings together our understanding of learning processes (i.e. gaining knowledge and its meaning) and the design of external stimuli or instruction. In other words, the theory of generative learning focuses on selecting appropriate, learner-centric instructional activities for the learner.

1.4   Ten Top Challenges in STEM Education

In this section, we present ten top challenges in STEM education defined by NMC Horizon Project [JAE+13]: "Technology Outlook for STEM+ Education 2013–2018" aiming to identify the fact to which extent they are relevant to STEM-driven CS education we address throughout the book. We have selected this source, because (i) it relies on careful analysis of the topics and uses the experience and knowledge of STEM experts, i.e. the advisory board; and (ii) it covers a wide spectrum of problems. The advisory board rank the challenges in the order of importance. We accept this source as a starting point to formulate challenges of STEM-driven CS education in the subsequent sections.

1. *The demand for personalized learning is not adequately supported by current technology or practices.*

The increasing demand for education, which focuses on customization to each student's unique needs, is driving the development of new technologies that provide more learner choice and control and allow for differentiated instruction. Technology can and should support individual choices regarding access to materials and expertise, amount and type of educational content and methods of teaching. **The biggest**

barrier to personalized learning, however, is that scientific, data-driven approaches to facilitate personalization effectively have only recently begun to emerge.

2. *Appropriate metrics of evaluation lag the emergence of new scholarly forms of authoring, publishing and researching.*

Traditional approaches to scholarly evaluation, such as citation-based metrics, are often hard to apply to research that is disseminated or conducted via social media. New forms of peer review and approval (such as reader ratings, inclusion in and mentioning by influential blogs, tagging, incoming links and retweeting) are arising from the natural actions of the global community of educators, with more and more relevant and interesting results. **These forms of scholarly corroboration are not yet well-understood by mainstream faculty and academic decision-makers**, creating a gap between what is possible and what is acceptable.

3. *Most academics are not using new and compelling technologies for learning and teaching, nor for organizing their own research.*

Many researchers have not had training in basic digitally supported teaching techniques and do not participate in the professional development opportunities that would provide them. Many think a cultural shift will be required before there is widespread use of more innovative organizational technologies or believe that they will get in the way of the learning. **Often, however, the exploration of emerging technology enables adoption of progressive pedagogies.** Some educators are simply apprehensive about working with new technologies. Many educators feel that an attitudinal change among academics is imperative.

4. *Faculty training still does not acknowledge the fact that digital media literacy continues its rise in importance as a key skill in every STEM discipline and profession.*

This challenge is exacerbated by the fact that **digital literacy is less about tools and more about thinking**, and thus skills and standards based on tools and platforms have proven to be somewhat ephemeral.

5. *Cross-institution authentication and detailed access policies are needed to allow sharing of online experiments among institutions.*

While teachers are more equipped than ever to produce online experiments, what they are creating is rarely scalable. **Too many institutions are recreating the same types of experiments repeatedly. Quality standards may improve the reuse of federated designs and experiments**, but institutions also need to consider standards that would allow students from collaborating institutions to access data and tools across security domains.

6. *New models of education are bringing unprecedented competition to the traditional models of higher education.*

Institutions are now looking for ways to provide a high quality of service and more learning opportunities. For example, MOOCs are at the forefront of these discussions, enabling students to supplement their education and experiences with increasingly rich, and often free, online offerings. As these new platforms emerge, however, there is a need to evaluate the models and determine how to best support collaboration, interaction and assessment at scale. Simply capitalizing on new technology is not enough; **the new models must use these tools and services to engage students on a deeper level.**

7. *MOOCs need to be rethought as open ongoing connectivist communities for open teaching and open research.*

Connectivism refers to a model of learning where social and cultural interactions are the focus, and individuals bring their own personal work experience and knowledge to the environment to add to a continuously expanding ecosystem of learning. While this approach of open learning is already established, open teaching and research are new concepts that could leverage this notion of crowdsourcing and collective intelligence to build new pedagogies and practices, along with gaining new findings and insights for science studies. **Learning materials can be created within these communities and used in classrooms all over the world**.

8. *There is still much to be done before we are teaching STEM not as a set of facts but instead as a way of knowing.*

Traditional forms of demonstrating newly acquired STEM knowledge have been through assignments where students are often just reciting facts. This is in contrast with the arts and humanities, where there is generally an opportunity to creatively interpret the subject matter. In a world, where scientific concepts are constantly changing as new evidence is discovered, simply memorizing facts does not contribute to fostering curiosity among students to continuously explore these changes as they arise. **Similar to more creative disciplines, new interpretations in science should be welcomed discourse in institutions.**

9. *Our organizations are not set up to promote innovation in teaching.*

Innovation springs from the freedom to connect ideas in new ways. Our schools and universities generally allow us to connect ideas only in prescribed ways – sometimes these lead to new insights, but more likely, they lead to rote learning. **Current organizational promotion structures reward research instead of innovation and improvements in teaching and learning.** The major consequences of student evaluations on teaching, as well as the direct impact on promotion and career options, translate to big risks associated with the failure of innovations and leave little space for experimentation.

10. *Math needs to be re-designed, and teaching coding should be a major part of that new learning course.*

Many view current math curriculum as stagnant, with students still solving equations and problems in the same manner. According to Code.org, there will be more than 1.4 million computer jobs in demand in 2020; **there is a need for math students to acquire computer science skills. Programming is being incorporated into many institutions as elective courses, but only a few schools have integrated coding directly in math and other disciplines.**

The presented challenges and excluded aspects among them have a direct or indirect association with our topics and context.

1.5   CS Teaching Challenges Without STEM Context

Computer science (CS) is among those fundamental courses within schools' curricula that provide students with the basic knowledge needed for the twenty-first century. There are also other names of the course, such as informatics and computer programming. The latter indicates that basic topics of CS are, in fact, about computer programming. For many students, it is a difficult course. In this section, therefore we focus on analysis of *those challenges* that appear in teaching CS or programming. Here, we ignore the STEM context.

Many reports and research papers announce difficulties in teaching programming for novices. Based on thorough literature studies, we have categorized the following interrelated groups of problems: *pedagogical, cognitive, learning content and technique.*

Pedagogical problems include, for example, the use of learning models that do not correspond to the learner's needs [LY11, SSH+09]. Often it is difficult to personalize learning [GM07]. There are problems of selecting the relevant teaching context [CC10, KS08, Pea10]. The learner's motivation is also a major problem [AG13, CTT10, GGL+12, JCS09, KPN08, SHL13].

Cognitive problems include the use of high-level abstractions that hinder the understanding ability for students with a lack of computational thinking [GM07, Chu07, CMF+09, CTT10]. The need to keep trade-offs between the theoretical knowledge and practice may reduce the cognition level [GM07, LY11, CMF+09, PSM+07, RRR03, SPJ+11, SSH+09]. Among other factors, there are differences in programming paradigms such as structural and object-oriented ones [MR02, SH06, CMF+09, CTT10, RRR03, Sch02]; in most cases, the syntax of programming languages is oriented to the professional use [GM07, CMF+09, CTT10]; also there is the need for the enhancement of creativity in learning programming [KR08].

Learning content problems include the following. Often there are used static learning materials, though programming is a highly dynamic course [GM07, NS09, PSM+07, VBH13]. There are some difficulties in a content adaptation to the learner's context [AG03, GA03, AHH12, LYW05]. In addition, content visualization is a major issue. Though visualization increases the learning performance, the move from textual to visual representation of programs is a complex task [MV07, AHH11, Chu07, KPN08, Röß10].

Technical problems are related to the lack of adequate tools, for example, those that provide adaptation and generalization [AG03, CMF+09, PSM+07]. In addition, traditional learning management systems (LMS) do not cover all contexts needed for teaching programming. Interactive learning in programming has many obstacles due to pedagogical and cognitive problems and lack of technical support [BB09, GC06, GM07, MV07, APH+11, BBC04, CAC12, CMF+09, DAB12, LLY10].

Learning Models Among many others, motivation model stands for the most essential and complicated argument to describe human behaviour aspects of teaching. On the other hand, there is a common understanding in the domain that the models are also the most influential factors to achieving learning performance and efficiency. Here, we consider only those models that, in our view, to the largest extent correspond to the aims of Chap. 1. They include:

- *Pedagogical frameworks* combining the theory and practice of teaching in CS [Sch02]
- *Game-based learning models* [JCS09, SHL13]
- *Program behaviour visualization models* [Chu07, Pea10]
- *Pair-programming models* [DSS+08, SMG11]
- *Robot use-based models* [HS12, CAC12, Tou12]

Educational Environments for Teaching in CS One needs to know the main characteristics that define an effective educational environment (EEE) for teaching in CS. The paper [GM07] indicates on four aspects. Firstly, the EEE should support the identification of the learner's knowledge level and identification of dominating learning style to make learning more personalized. Secondly, the EEE should provide models and facilities to construct programs. Thirdly, it should contain elements of gaming to enforce capabilities in problem solving. Finally, there should be dedicated tools within those environments that support constructing of algorithms.

Kelleher's and Pausch's taxonomy [KP05] categorizes programming and language environments into two categories: (1) *teaching systems* and (2) *empowering systems*. The first aims at taking the support for learning programming per se; usually those systems contain programming kits that highlight the essential aspects of the programming process. Teaching systems have many common or similar features with *general-purpose languages* and relate to *mechanics of programming* (such as a simplification of programming language, automatic repair of syntactic errors, presenting of alternatives for coding, learning support, networked interaction, etc.). The second group focuses on the learner-computer interaction to make the process of developing of a program easier.

There are also mobile environments to support *m*-learning. Researchers, however, take the exclusive role of the robot-based educational environments in teaching CS and other related topics. The main reasons for that are as follows:

- Possibility to transform the abstract items (such as a data structure, algorithm, program) into physically visible processes, enabling to better understand the essence of programming and its practical benefits.
- The paradigm introduces the way for interdisciplinary teaching.

- There is the support of real (physical) visualization through robots moves and actions.
- Educational robots can be also treated as gaming tools to significantly enforcing the learner's motivation to learn and the engagement in the process.
- There is a wide room for the experimentation and exploratory learning.
- All these can be easily connected with learning styles and models.

1.6   Challenges of STEM-Driven CS Education

The State of the Art and Objective   Today we are working in the modern technological surrounding – the multiple smart devices integrated within networks are a commodity of our lives now. Soon not only humans and computers but also everyday life items will be interconnected to create the new computing infrastructure – *The Internet-of-Things* (IoT). This move from the "interconnected computers" to the "interconnected things" is a great challenge for the information communication technology (ICT) workers, computer scientists and society in the whole [AIM10, PZC+14]. It is most likely that there will be the need for changes in computer science (CS) curricula to open the *new CS research tracks* [HSB17, Sta14], in order to provide the adequate knowledge to support the development of new applications and services. Today, as never before, the interdisciplinary research and teaching becomes of the paramount importance.

The research directions for the IoT are dealt with from various perspectives in multiple publications [GBM+13, PZC+14, SEC+13, Sta14, STJ14]. For example, the papers [SEC+13, Sta14] consider IoT as the "human in-the-loop" systems with the new challenges in both social and technology domains. In the paper [PZC+14], the IoT is treated as the context-aware systems with the framework and taxonomy for the IoT proposed. The papers identify the context-aware modelling is the biggest challenge in creating the IoT applications. There is the low-level and a high-level dynamic context modelling [PZC+14]. For the high-level context variability modelling, the feature-based models are at the focus now [ABB+15, CHD15]. Typically, the high-level domain models are to be transformed into the executable specifications to support the functionality of the systems to be created [CH06].

   From the CS research perspective, the IoT, dynamic context modelling and model transformation approaches are treated as a solution domain. Now we focus on the problem domain understanding. As the title of the book states, the problem domain is the STEM-based (Science, Technology, Engineering and Mathematics) approach in CS education. The first thing is clearly understanding at all levels what is happening in the field and around the related areas such as research in STEM, in the IoT as related to the CS research and education. If we look at the separate fields (e.g. STEM, education in CS, IoT) and take into account the recent initiatives in the Europe and worldwide on advanced teaching and learning in CS, it is possible to state that this understanding already exists, but perhaps not yet at all levels and not to the needed extent.

Next, the real breakthrough in advanced CS learning and teaching is hardly possible without the new concepts, especially in that part of pure CS research which is highly influential on the modern education-related software tools, such as modelling, model-driven transformation, knowledge-based generation of the content and processes, innovative methodologies and better understanding of both the pedagogical and technological issues. The currently existing capabilities of technology are not yet exploited in e-Learning as fully as that could be. Even in the separate fields (e.g. STEM, education in CS), there is still a big gap between technological capabilities and pedagogical approaches. The seamless integration of both technology and pedagogy should be seen as the primary concern with advancing CS education and research. The situation, however, is changing dramatically if one has the goal to combine (i.e. research in adequate subfields of CS relevant to the STEM, IoT and STEM-based education in CS) into the *new coherent system*. In this way, we could be able to deal with the challenges that have never arisen before, to discover the innovative solutions and approaches in the twenty-first century.

Today the CS education, in both schools and universities, encounters with multiple *challenges and implications*. The reasons relate to the insufficient understanding of the CS role in the society today and in the near future. Indeed, CS is the fundamental part of ICT that drives the progress of the society, because CS brings the essential knowledge for many separate fields, such as software engineering, hardware engineering, game industry and educational technology, to name a few. Therefore, the understanding of the interplay among those technologies and education becomes of great importance.

In addition, there is the need to better understand the computing trends and technology-enhanced learning. That is so because it *"reflects an evolution from individual toward community learning, from content-driven learning toward process-driven approaches, from isolated media toward integrated use, from presentation media toward interactive media, from learning settings depending on the place and time toward ubiquitous learning, and from fixed tools toward handheld devices"* [Low14]. This understanding and realization of that in practice, even partially in some concrete setting, could be treated as a contribution to smart learning using the STEM paradigm.

Partovi [Par15], the CS educator, in his recent discussion of STEM and CS education indicates: *"Unfilled jobs are in computer science; the biggest area of economic growth is in computer science; the foundational field that isn't being taught in our schools is computer science. When you hear 'STEM,' try focusing the conversation on 'computer science.' That's where the opportunity lies"*. In the context of ITC advances, we need also to understand the following issues. There is the e-Learning paradigm shift from traditional e-Learning to *m*-learning and *u*-learning (meaning mobile and ubiquitous learning) [LH10]. CS education and research play a specific role. The discipline stands for the fundamental piece of knowledge and can be aligned along with the natural sciences, such as mathematics, physics or chemistry [BEP+09].

The other reasons relate to the CS structure and topics themselves. CS-related courses are provided at the different levels at both schools and universities; there is a need of the broad-spectrum knowledge, skills and competencies bringing the additional challenges. The wideness of the CS topics tends to be continuously enlarged (e.g. with ever-extending research in the IoT). Therefore, that results in the need of the cross-disciplinary views and approaches. The audience to be educated is extremely large and diverse that includes (i) technology-literate citizens for the twenty-first century, (ii) cross-disciplinary engineers and scientists working in the variety of fields and (iii) CS professionals responsible for the further enlargement of the IT sector.

The CS content is abstract in nature; thus, it requires various forms of transformations (social, pedagogical, technological) to acquire knowledge in the field. The rapid technology advances stimulate the need to continuously reconsider, renew and re-evaluate the content, teaching approaches and methodology [FL09]. As a result, there are the challenges of integrating technologies for learning [ECE+10]. In addition, there is the need for changes in attitudes to accept innovations in CS teaching (inspired by the ICT and educational theories) at all levels: government politics, administrative (institutional), teachers and students. There is a gap between educational theories and teaching methodologies and ever-increasing capabilities of technologies. There is a contradiction between the tendency of the enrolment decrease to study CS and the demand increase of CS-oriented specialties [CSTA08]. There is the need for more extensive research in CS education and more effective educational methods due to the stated challenges and the ever-growing market pressure.

Because of the technological revolution, there are evident signs of the extremely rapid growth of the application system *diversity* and *complexity* and *software content increase* within the systems, especially in the context of the embedded system sector and IoT applications. Therefore, the demand of CS workplaces, perhaps, will grow adequately. According to estimates [MSD13], the field of computer and mathematical sciences is expected to grow dramatically through 2018. The Bureau of Labour Statistics in the USA, for example, projects that there will be a 25.6% increase in demand in this field. Today there is also an evident shift in learning paradigms: from the *teacher-centred learning* towards the *student-centred learning*. There is an extremely high interest in the interdisciplinary teaching based on the STEM concepts.

The understanding of STEM benefits and the progress and efforts in the field are evident now (first of all in such countries as Australia, USA, UK). In the UK, for example, there is the National STEM Centre [NSC15] that provides wide-scale activities (support for schools, support for colleagues, promoting STEM careers, etc.). Nevertheless, little is known (1) about STEM in the relation to CS education and research. There is a big gap between available methods, approaches that could be able to support the research oriented to CS. Especially it is true with respect to the interplay among different components of STEM and CS using educational robots as nodes of the IoT. There is a great gap between the conceptual level of the STEM paradigm and systemic evidence-based practice in exploring the approach in the real

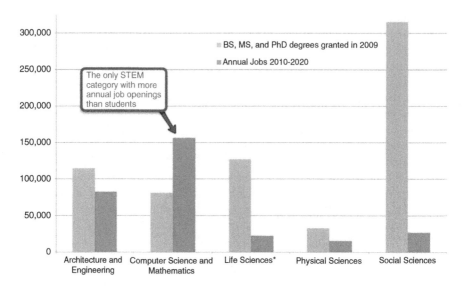

Fig. 1.1 Annual job openings and professionals with degrees available in the USA (Sources: Bureau of Labor Statistics, National Science Foundation)

settings. There is a lack of the technologically sound methods, approaches and tools to support the STEM-CS as a compound field of research and education. Therefore, CS is the only *STEM* field where there are more jobs in the USA as the diagram shows (Fig. 1.1).

However, on the other hand, there is a great disproportion in funding the STEM. On this account, Partovi [Par15] provides the following observation: *"This subcategory of STEM gets <1% of the educational funding, and isn't even available in 90% of schools. Yet it is responsible for the growth and opportunity in STEM. The charts below show that if you remove computer science from STEM, what would remain is: too many students, not enough jobs, and a predominantly gender-balanced or even slightly female-dominated field"*.

The other big challenge is the lack of knowledgeable teachers able to provide STEM-based teaching. In this regard, Williams in CS education week to support STEM [Wil14] writes: *"As long as we continue to enable the idea that teaching falls outside the realm of respected STEM careers, we will struggle to get the most passionate and knowledgeable teachers into STEM classrooms"*.

Challenges Formulated by ACM at the K–12 Level The Association for Computing Machinery (ACM) strongly supports the stated goal of many policymakers and reports that science and mathematics education should be a national priority in K–12. The ACM report [ACM17] states: "We believe that computer science education should be an integral part of our education system and wish to work with national leaders to ensure that the computing field's voice is heard".

ACM therefore has committed to strengthening and improving computing education across the entire educational landscape. Similarly, as other scientific societies, ACM also strongly supports efforts to increase the participation in and retention of students in STEM (Science, Technology, Engineering and Mathematics) fields. The ACM focus is on CS education, which faces special challenges, particularly at the K–12 level.

The outlook for CS-related jobs remains strong despite the extraordinary economic challenges. That is so, because CS underpins the technology sector, which has made tremendous contributions to the US economy and worldwide as well as numerous other sectors that depend on innovative, highly skilled CS graduates. The ubiquitous nature of computing has spread its reach into everyone's daily lives. Numerous issues, such as securing our cyber-infrastructure, making our energy infrastructure more efficient, ensuring better healthcare and many others, highly depend on computing. However, with the percentage of undergraduates majoring in CS and interest at the K–12 level falling, the pipeline supplying the necessary workforce is shrinking.

Today's students are required to make decisions about their educational and career pathways often as early as middle school. Studying CS in K–12 alerts them to the fact that CS is an exciting educational discipline and provides a pathway to a rich choice of careers. CS also brings an important skill set for students entering any career area, including other sciences where innovation and breakthroughs increasingly depend on the contributed knowledge of computer scientists.

Therefore, there is a common opinion that a fundamental understanding of computation and computational (algorithmic) thinking is increasingly important to success in the digital age. Computing education will benefit all students, not just those interested in pursuing CS or ICT careers. CS develops and extends logical thinking and problem-solving skills needed in the twenty-first century.

"Students who participate in high school computing classes and have previous experience with technology demonstrate improved readiness for post-secondary studies", the report states.

According to ACM [ACM17], among the many challenges to educate students in CS are:

(i) *Courses in the fundamentals of CS often count only as a general elective, not as a college-preparatory elective, at the secondary level. Given the demands on college-bound high school students, it is unlikely that these students can afford to explore CS.*

(ii) *As schools have increasingly stepped up the need to integrate, use and teach information technology, the distinctions have blurred between what is called CS and what is, in fact, information technology literacy and the use of technology to support learning.*

(iii) *Certification requirements for high school CS teachers vary from state to state in the USA. In some cases, no computer science certification is available and CS teachers must be certified in some other additional discipline; in others,* teachers are required to demonstrate knowledge in some discipline other than CS (e.g. business or technical applications) to teach computing courses.

(iv) Because of the confusion between CS and technology education, lack of certification standards and the narrow focus by policymakers on core courses tested under the No Child Left Behind Act, professional development programs for CS teachers and research initiatives in CS education have lagged behind other fields.

(v) Participation rates by women and minorities in computer science are among the lowest of any scientific field. In 2008, only 17% of AP CS test-takers were women, even though women represented 55% of all AP test-takers Participation in CS AP tests among underrepresented minorities has increased in the past 10 years but is only at 11%, compared to 19% of all AP test-takers.

Though some of the stated challenges are specific to the USA, e.g. (iv) and (v), the others are common to other countries too.

1.7   The Book's Objectives and Research Agenda

There is the urgent need of extensive research and efforts in STEM-driven CS education, because now it is a roadmap for the twenty-first-century education to address existing and emerging multiple challenges. Therefore, it is possible to state the following.

*The **objectives** of the book are, in a wider context, to discuss the concepts and approaches enabling to transform the current CS education paradigm into the STEM-driven at the school, and to some extent, at university. We seek to implement this transformation through the integration of the STEM pedagogy, the Smart STEM content, the Smart devices into STEM supporting environment, using reuse-driven approaches taken from software engineering and CS.*

Here, by "smartness" we mean the use of innovative methods to design the teaching content for STEM as effectively as possible, i.e. through automation. By the teaching content for STEM, we mean smart LOs, personal generative library for STEM and smart scenario. As the term "smart" has many meanings, we define it more precisely in each context of use. To achieve the objectives, the common task we consider throughout the book is on how *to integrate into the CS high school curricula the STEM pedagogy and STEM content wrapped into robotics and other modern technologies seamlessly.* This common task includes a set of numerous subtasks we consider in the subsequent chapters. The title of a particular chapter, in general terms, also outlines the formulation of an adequate subtask or subtasks. Each subtask relates to some research object such as a smart STEM-driven content, generative scenario, personal generative library, smart CS educational environment, etc. The research tasks and subtasks along with researching objects pertaining to them form the research agenda discussed in this book. The result of this research is a methodology that includes a set of approaches to solve the indicated subtasks to achieve the anticipated objective.

Below we formulate our research agenda as a set of tasks (here, we treat them as subtasks of the common task, i.e. STEM-driven CS education at the secondary school).

Task 1: Definition of the domain "STEM-driven CS education at the secondary school using smart devices, including educational robots". Shortly, we identify the domain under investigation as "STEM-driven CS education".

Task 2: The development of a framework and conceptual model on how to introduce STEM knowledge into robot-oriented CS education.

Task 3: Feature-based analysis and *STEM learning variability modelling* with the focus on not only statistic but also on context awareness and dynamic modelling.

Task 4: Enhancement of reusability and adaptability aspects of STEM-oriented content with the focus on automated, i.e. semi-automatic, generation and adaptation.

Task 5: Developing the adequate approaches and tools for integrating learning variability aspects of different nature taken from heterogeneous sub-domains to support needs for STEM-driven CS education.

Task 6: Creating of the STEM-oriented smart educational environment for CS education at the secondary school based on following components: generative smart learning objects, smart generative scenario and personal generative libraries (for teacher and students).

Task 7: Providing an extensive research by exploring, assessing a variety of processes within the platforms, obtaining bottlenecks, suggesting recommendations for a wider community, formulating new problems, etc.

The educational processes related to the defined domain are themes for research. The main objective in researching the domain is automation. We introduce that through technology-enhanced approaches. We try to use them in a variety of contexts. Our aim is to add more functionality and to make educational processes more effective.

1.8   The Topics This Book Addresses

This book is about the novel approach on how to educate secondary (high) school students in STEM-driven CS course using educational robots. The approach is two-sided. Firstly, we focus on the preparatory work in designing objects, processes and facilities, i.e. creating the infrastructure to support smart CS education using STEM paradigm and educational robotics. In designing components of the infrastructure, we seek to introduce the automation as widely as possible. We can do that, because we apply modern analysis and modelling methods (e.g. feature-based ones) and supporting technologies such as meta-programming, model transformation, agent-based, etc. that enable and support automation. Secondly, we aim at introducing and using those components in the real teaching setting, i.e. at the high school. In doing that, we apply an evolutionary approach, i.e. we have started from the simpler solutions and gradually have introduced the more advanced solutions in terms of functionality and capabilities of automation.

The book is, in fact, a monograph, in which we have presented a methodological and theoretical foundation, as well as the learning experience in using the approach. The research questions we deal in this book include three main clusters: (1) analysis of the domain identified as STEM-driven robot-oriented CS education; (2) modelling, design and implementation of the domain and its sub-domains; and (3) learning experiences and outcomes in using the approach.

What is the structure of this book? We have divided the content into five parts. Part I is the introductory part and, in fact, is the wide context of the remaining parts. Part II represents the methodological and theoretical background of our approach. Part III deals with the design and use of the smart content to support STEM and CS education. Part IV deals with the infrastructure of our approach. Part V extends the vision of our approach. We included abstracts at the beginning of each chapter for easing the independent reading and better understanding.

Part I includes Chaps. 1, 2 and 3. Chapter 1 is about the challenges of STEM-driven computer science (CS) education. Chapter 2 discusses a vision for introducing STEM into CS education at school. Chapter 3 deals with educational robotics and smart devices as a way of obtaining the interdisciplinary knowledge.

Part II includes Chaps. 4 and 5. Chapter 4 focuses on learning variability as a methodological background of STEM-driven reuse-enhanced CS education. Chapter 5 provides a theoretical background consisting of feature-based modelling to specify and represent the STEM learning variability and basics of heterogeneous meta-programming to implement the proposed STEM-driven approaches.

Part III includes Chaps. 6, 7, 8, and 9. Chapter 6 presents a vision for understanding of smart learning objects (SLOs) for STEM-driven CS education. Chapter 7 describes the design and redesign of STEM-oriented generative learning objects (GLOs). Chapter 8 deals with design of STEM-oriented smart learning objects (SLOs). Chapter 9 describes agent-based smart learning objects for STEM.

Part IV includes Chaps. 10, 11, 12 and 13. Chapter 10 presents the concepts and implementation of the personal generative library for STEM-driven educational resources. Chapter 11 deals with the design of STEM-driven generative scenarios for CS education. Chapter 12 analyses the smart STEM-driven environment for smart CS education at high school. Chapter 13 summarizes the educational practices of smart STEM-driven CS education at one high school.

Part V includes Chaps. 14 and 15. Chapter 14 introduces the Internet-of-Things (IoT) vision in CS education and gives an idea for the remote STEM-driven environment. Chapter 15 provides a finalizing discussion, outlines other educational paradigms (such as MOOC, STEM for universities) and formulates open issues.

1.9 Summary and Concluding Remarks

In this introductory chapter, we have discussed the context for writing this book. The context, largely, includes the analysis of the role and challenges of the educational paradigm known as STEM (Science, Technology, Engineering and Mathematics), as well as the role and challenges of computer science education in the digital age. In addition, the context covers the initiatives and actions taken by famous organizations and responsible bodies worldwide in order it would be possible to respond to those challenges adequately. We have identified a large number of initiatives and actions (along with frameworks and approaches) directed to make improvements in STEM and CS education as separate research topics. By analysing this context, we have identified a few significant findings. The first is the urgent need to move to interdisciplinary education based on STEM predefined by many factors (e.g. modern economy requires interdisciplinary skills and knowledge, there is a gap between the motivation to learn in those fields and the demand of STEM and CS-oriented workforce, etc.). The second is the evident appeal for intensifying research efforts in those fields. The third is that we were able to define a niche for our research. So far, we still know little about how it would be possible to combine both fields into a coherent methodology if one wants to get the benefits of this integration. Therefore, this context enabled us to motivate our approach we will discuss in this book.

On this basis, we have formulated the research agenda to our approach, i.e. objective (motivation), research tasks and research methodology. The basic idea and distinguishing feature of our approach is on how to integrate into the school's CS curricula the STEM pedagogy, the STEM and CS content wrapped together with modern technologies of two types. The first relates to robotics as direct facilities used for smart STEM-driven CS education. The second relates to supporting technologies that bring the possibility of automation in preparing, designing, testing and using smart content, smart scenario and smart environment. Therefore, we have formulated the research agenda and enlisted the content of each subsequent chapter to provide and implement this agenda.

References

[AAA89]   American Association for the Advancement of Science (AAAS) (1989) Science for all Americans. Oxford University Press, New York
[AAA93]   American Association for the Advancement of Science (AAAS) (1993) Benchmarks for science literacy. Oxford University Press, New York
[ABB+15] Almeida A, Bencomo N, Batista T, Cavalcante E, Dantas F (2015) Dynamic decision-making based on NFR for managing software variability and configuration selection. ACM
[ABE04]   ABET Engineering Accreditation Commission (2004) ABET criteria for accrediting engineering programs. ABET, Baltimore
[ACM17]   (2017) Computer Science in K-12 STEM education critical for 21st century skills and knowledge. ACM. www.acm.org/public-policy/Case_For_Computing_final.pdf

[AEM+14]   Arshavsky N, Edmunds J, Mooney K, Thrift B, Wynn L, Center S, Samonte K Janda L
           (2014) Race to the top STEM affinity network. http://cerenc.org/wp-content/uploads/
           2014/12/FINAL-STEM-final-report-12-4-14.pdf
[AG03]   Adamchik V, Gunawardena A (2003) A learning objects approach to teaching pro-
           gramming. In: Proceedings of the international conference on information technology:
           computers and communications. IEEE Computer Society, pp 96–100
[AG13]   Anderson N, Gegg-Harrison T (2013). Learning computer science in the comfort zone
           of proximal development. In: Proceeding of the 44th ACM technical symposium on
           Computer science education. pp 495–500
[AGM+15]   Ardies J, De Maeyer S, Gijbels D, van Keulen H (2015) Students attitudes towards
           technology. Int J Technol Des Educ 25(1):43–65
[AHH11]   Alharbi A, Henskens F, Hannaford M (2011) Computer science learning objects. In:
           IEEE International conference on e-education, rntertainment and e-management. pp
           326–328
[AHH12]   Alharbi A, Henskens F, Hannaford M (2012) Student-centered learning objects to
           support the self-regulated learning of computer science. Creat Educ 3:773–783
[AIM10]   Atzori L, Iera A, Morabito G (2010) The internet of things: a survey. Comput Netw
           54:2787–2805
[APH+11]   Alharbi A, Paul D, Henskens F, Hannaford M (2011) An investigation into the learning
           styles and self-regulated learning strategies for computer science students. In: Pro-
           ceedings ascilite 2011 Hobart. pp 37–46
[Asu14]   Asunda PA (2014) A conceptual framework for STEM integration into curriculum
           through career and technical education. J STEM Teach Educ 49(1):3–15
[Bar10]   Barell J (2010) Problem-based learning: the foundation for 21st century skills. In:
           Bellanca J, Brandt R (eds) 21st century skills: rethinking how students learn. Solution
           Tree Press, Bloomington, pp 175–199
[BB09]   Bygholm A, Buus L (2009) Managing the gap between curriculum based and problem
           based learning: deployment of multiple learning strategies in design and delivery of
           online courses in computer science. Int J Educ Develop Using ICT 5(1)
[BBC04]   Boyle T, Bradley C, Chalk P (2004) Improving the teaching of programming using a
           VLE enhanced with learning objects. In: Proceedings of the 2nd international confer-
           ence on information technology research and education ITRE 2004, June 28 2004,
           London Metropolitan University, London, UK. pp 74–78
[BEP+09]   Berglund A, Eckerdal A, Pears A, East P, Kinnunen P, Malmi L, McCartney R,
           Mostrom J, Murphy L, Ratcliffe M, Schulte C, Simon B, Stamouli I, Thomas L
           (2009) Learning computer science: perceptions, actions and roles. Eur J Eng Educ
           34(4):327–338
[BSN+04]   Bruning RH, Schraw JG, Norby MM, Ronning RR (2004) Cognitive psychology and
           instruction. Pearson, Columbus
[CAC12]   Costa CJ, Aparicio M, Cordeiro C (2012) A solution to support student learning of
           programming. In: Proceedings of the workshop on open source and design of com-
           munication. pp 25–29
[CC10]   Cooper S, Cunningham S (2010) Teaching computer science in context. ACM Inroads
           1(1):5–8
[CH06]   Czarnecki K, Helsen S (2006) Feature-based survey of model transformation
           approaches. IBM Syst J 45(3)
[CHD15]   Capilla R, Hinchey M, Díaz FJ (2015) Collaborative context features for critical
           systems. In: Proceedings of the ninth international workshop on variability modelling
           of software-intensive systems. ACM, p 43
[Chu07]   Chudá D (2007) Visualization in education of theoretical computer science. In:
           CompSysTech'07. p IV.15-1-IV.15-6

[CMF+09]   Castillo JF, Montes de Oca C, Flores ES, Elizondo PV (2009) Toward an approach to programming education to produce qualified software developers. In: IEEE 22nd conference on software engineering education and training, pp 101–104

[CSTA08]   Ensuring exemplary teaching in an essential discipline: addressing the crisis in computer science teacher certification. Final Report of the CSTA Teacher Certification Task Force, September 2008

[CTT10]   Corney M, Teague D, Thomas RN (2010) Engaging students in programming. In: Proc. 12th Australasian Computing Education Conference (ACE 2010), Brisbane, Australia. pp 63–72

[DAB12]   Dillon E, Anderson M, Brown M (2012) Comparing feature assistance between programming environments and their "effect" on novice programmers. JCSC 27 (5):69–77

[DGL+14]   Dutta-Moscato J, Gopalakrishnan V, Lotze MT, Becich MJ (2014) Creating a pipeline of talent for informatics: STEM initiative for high school students in computer science, biology, and biomedical informatics. J Pathol Inform 5

[DH16]   Dixon RA, Hutton DM (2016) STEM and TVET in the Caribbean: a framework for integration at the primary, secondary, and tertiary levels. Caribb Curric 24(2016):1–26

[DHL+14]   Duran M, Höft M, Lawson DB, Medjahed B, Orady EA (2014) Urban high school students' IT/STEM learning: findings from a collaborative inquiry-and design-based afterschool program. J Sci Educ Technol 23(1):116–137

[DSS+08]   Dorairaj SK, Singh J, Shanmugam M, Shamini S (2008) Experimenting with industry's pair-programming model in teaching and learning programming. In: Proceedings of the 4th international conference on information technology and multimedia at UNITEN (ICIMU' 2008), Malaysia

[ECE+10]   Eshet-Alkalai Y, Caspi A, Eden S, Geri N, Tal-Elhasid E, Yair Y (2010) Challenges of integrating technologies for learning: introduction to the IJELLO special series of Chais conference 2010 best papers. Interdiscip J E-Learn Learn Objects 6:240–244

[FL09]   Fletcher GHL, Lu JJ (2009) Human computing skills: rethinking the K–12 experience. Commun ACM 52(2):23–25

[FMT14]   Freeman B, Marginson S, Tytler R (2014) Widening and deepening the STEM effect, The age of STEM: educational policy and practice across the world in Science, Technology, Engineering and Mathematics, 2014. p 1

[GA03]   Gunawardena A, Adamchik V (2003) A customized learning objects approach to teaching programming. ACM SIGCSE Bull 35(3):264

[GA14]   Gomez A, Albrecht B (2014) True STEM education. Technol Eng Teach 73(4):8–16

[Gan15]   Gander W (2015) Informatics–new basic subject. Bull EATCS 2(116)

[GBM+13]   Gubbi J, Buyya R, Marusic S, Palaiswamin M (2013) Internet of Things (IoT): a vision, architectural elements, and future directions. Future Gener Comput Syst 29:1645–1660

[GC06]   Gulatee Y, Combes B (2006) Identifying the challenges in teaching computer science topics online. In: Proceedings of the EDU-COM 2006 international conference. Engagement and empowerment: new opportunities for growth in higher education, Edith Cowan University, Perth Western Australia

[GGL+12]   Goldberg DS, Grunwald D, Lewis C, Feld JA, Hug S (2012) Engaging computer science in traditional education: the ECSITE project. In: Proceedings of the 17th ACM annual conference on Innovation and technology in computer science education. pp 351–356

[GM07]   Gomes A, Mendes AJ (2007) An environment to improve programming education. In: CompSysTech'07:-IV.19–1-IV.19–6

[GMB+14]   Gamse BC, Martinez A, Bozzi L, Didriksen H (2014) Defining a research agenda for STEM corps: working white paper. Abt Associates, Cambridge, MA

[Gwa10]   Gwak D (2010) The meaning and predict of Smart Learning, Smart Learning Korea Proceeding, Korean e-Learning Industry Association, 2010

[HB17]   Hasan A, Biswas G (2017) Domain specific modeling language design to support synergistic learning of STEM and computational thinking. Siu-cheung KONG The Education University of Hong Kong, Hong Kong, 28

[Hol14]   Holmquist S (2014) A multi-case study of student interactions with educational robots and impact on Science, Technology, Engineering, and Math (STEM) learning and attitudes, University of South Florida

[HPS14]   Honey M, Pearson G, Schweingruber H (2014) STEM integration in K-12 education: status, prospects, and an agenda for research. Committee on integrated STEM education. The National Academies Press, Washington, DC

[HS12]   Hamada M, Sato S (2012) A learning system for a computational science related topic. Procedia Comput Sci 9:1763–1772

[HSB17]   He JS, Ji S, Bobbie PO (2017) Internet of Things (IoT)-based learning framework to facilitate STEM undergraduate education ACM SE '17, April 13–15, 2017, Kennesaw, GA, USA

[Hun99]   Huntley M (1999) Theoretical and empirical investigations of integrated mathematics and science education in the middle grades with implications for teacher education. J Teach Educ 50(1):57–67. https://doi.org/10.1177/002248719905000107

[Hwa14]   Hwang GJ (2014) Definition, framework and research issues of smart learning environments: a context-aware ubiquitous learning perspective. Smart Learn Environ 1 (1):1–14

[ITE00]   International Technology Education Association (2000) Standards for technological literacy: content for the study of technology. International Technology Education Association, Reston

[ITE03]   International Technology Education Association (2003) Advancing excellence in technological literacy: student assessment, professional development, and program standards. International Technology Education Association, Reston

[Jac89]   Jacobs HH (1989) Design options for an integrated curriculum. In: Jacobs HH (ed) Interdisciplinary curriculum: design and implementation. pp13–24

[JAE+13]   Johnson L, Adams Becker S, Estrada V, Martín S (2013) Technology outlook for STEM+ Education 2013–2018: an NMC Horizon Project Sector Analysis. New Media Consortium

[JCS09]   Jiau HC, Chen JC, Ssu KF (2009) Enhancing self-motivation in learning programming using game-based simulation and metrics. IEEE Trans Educ 52(4):555–562

[KCL13]   Kim T, Cho JY, Lee BG (2013) Evolution to smart learning in public education: a case study of Korean public education. In: Tobias L, Mikko R, Mart L, Arthur T (eds) Open and social technologies for networked learning. Springer, Berlin, pp 170–178

[KKY+14]   Kim C, Kim D, Yuan J, Hill RB, Doshi P, Thai CN (2015) Robotics to promote elementary education pre-service teachers' STEM engagement, learning, and teaching. Comput Educ 91(2015):14–31

[KP05]   Kelleher C, Pausch R (2005) Lowering the barriers to programming: a taxonomy of programming environments and languages for novice programmers. ACM Comput Surv 37(2):83–137

[KPN08]   Kasurinen J, Purmonen M, Nikula U (2008) A study of visualization in introductory programming. PPIG, Lancaster

[KR08]   Knobelsdorf M, Romeike R (2008) Creativity as a pathway to computer science. In: ITiCSE'08, June 30–July 2, 2008, Madrid, Spain

[KS08]   Knobelsdorf M, Schulte C (2008) Computer science in context – pathways to computer science. In: Seventh Baltic Sea conference on computing education research (Koli Calling 2007), Koli National Park, Finland, November 15–18

[LH10]   Liu GZ, Hwang GJ (2010) A key step to understanding paradigm shifts in e-learning: towards context-aware ubiquitous learning. Br J Educ Technol 41(2):E1–E9

[LLY10]   Kris MY, Law KMY, Lee VCS, Yu YT (2010) Learning motivation in e-learning facilitated computer programming courses. Comput Educ 55:218–228

[Low14]   Lowyck J (2014) Bridging learning theories and technology-enhanced environments: a critical appraisal of its history. In: Spector M, Merrill D, Jan M, Bishop E (eds) Handbook on research on educational communitiesand and technology. Springer, New York

[LY11]   Lau WWF, Yuen AHK (2011) Modelling programming performance: beyond the influence of learner characteristics. Comput Educ 57(1):1202–1213

[LYW05]   Lee MC, Ding Yen Ye DY, Wang TI (2005) Java learning object ontology. In: Proceedings of the Fifth IEEE international conference on advanced learning technologies (ICALT'05)

[MR02]   Milne I, Rowe G (2002) Difficulties in learning and teaching programming – views of students and tutors. Educ Inf Technol 7(1):55–66

[MSD13]   McGill MM, Settle A, Decker A (2013) Demographics of undergraduates studying games in the United States: a comparison of computer science students and the general population. Comput Sci Educ 23(2):158–185

[MV07]   Mierlus-Mazilu I, Vaduva MA (2007) Learning objects for programming. In: ICTA'07, April 12–14, Hammamet, Tunisia, pp 167–172

[NCT00]   National Council of Teachers of Mathematics (NCTM) (2000) Principles and standards for school mathematics. The Council, Reston. http://www.standards.nctm.org. National Governors Association

[NCT89]   National Council of Teachers of Mathematics (NCTM) (1989) Commission on standards for school mathematics. Curriculum and evaluation standards for school mathematics. The Council, Reston. http://www.standards.nctm.org

[NLS16]   Nelson TH, Lesseig K Slavit D (2016) Making sense of STEM education in K-12 Context. NARST International Conference, At Baltimore, MD April 2016. https://doi.org/10.13140/RG.2.1.2380.0725

[NRC11]   National Research Council (NRC) (2011) Successful K-12 STEM education: identifying effective approaches in science, technology, engineering, and mathematics. National Academies Press, Washington, DC

[NRC12]   National Research Council (NRC) (2012) A framework for K12 science education: practices, cross cutting concepts, and core ideas. National Academies Press, Washington, DC

[NS09]   Narasimhamurthy U, Shawkani KA (2009) Teaching of programming languages: an introduction to dynamic learning objects. In: International workshop on technology for education (T4E), Aug 4–6, 2009, Bangalore, pp 114–115

[NSC15]   National STEM Centre. What is STEM? http://www.nationalstemcentre.org.uk/stem-in-context/what-is-stem, view on 20/04/2015

[NSW+13]   Nathan MJ, Srisurichan R, Walkington C, Wolfgram M, Williams C, Alibali MW (2013) Building cohesion across representations: a mechanism for STEM Integration Journal of Engineering Education VC 2013 ASEE. http://wileyonlinelibrary.com/journal/jee January 2013, Vol. 102, No. 1, pp 77–116, https://doi.org/10.1002/jee.20000

[Nua10]   Nuangchalerm P (2010) Engaging students to perceive nature of science through socio-scientific issues-based instruction. Eur J Soc Sci 13:34–37. http://www.eurojournals.com/ejss_13_1_04.pdf

[Par15]   Partovi H (2015) What % of STEM should be computer science? https://www.linkedin.com/. Released on 18/05/2015 (viewed on 20/04/2015)

[Pea10]   Pears AN (2010) Enhancing student engagement in an introductory programming course. In: 40th ASEE/IEEE frontiers in education conference, October 27–30, Washington, DC

[PSM+07]   Pears A, Seidman S, Malmi L, Mannila L, Adams E, Bennedsen J, Devlin M, [Pat07] Paterson J (2007) A survey of literature on the teaching of introductory programming. ACM SIGCSE Bull 39(4):204–223

[PZC+14]   Perera C, Zaslavsky A, Christen P, Georgakopoulos D (2014) Context-aware comput-
           ing for the internet of things: a survey, communications surveys & tutorials. IEEE 16
           (1):414–445
[RG98]   Roth WM, McGinn MK (1998) Inscriptions: toward a theory of representing as social
           practice. Rev Educ Res 68(1):35–59
[Rob15]   Robertson C (2015) Restructuring high school science curriculum: a program evalu-
           ation. http://scholarworks.waldenu.edu/dissertations/270/
[Röß10]   Rößling G (2010) A family of tools for supporting the learning of programming.
           Algorithms 3(2):168–182
[RRR03]   Robins A, Rountree J, Rountree N (2003) Learning and teaching programming: a
           review and discussion. Comput Sci Educ 13(2):137–172
[SAB+17]   Swanson H, Anton G, Bain C, Horn M, Wilensky U (2017) Computational thinking in
           the science classroom. Siu-cheung KONG The Education University of Hong Kong,
           Hong Kong. 17
[San09]   Sanders M (2009) Integrative STEM education: a primer. The Technology Teacher, 68
           (4):20–26
[SB10]   Scott K, Benlamri R (2010) Context-aware services for smart learning spaces. IEEE
           Trans on Learn Technol 3(3):214–227
[ŠB15a]   Štuikys V, Burbaitė R (2015) Robot-based smart educational environments to teach
           CS: a case study. In: Smart Learning Objects for the Smart Education in Computer
           Science: theory, methodology and robot-based implementation. Springer
[ŠB15b]   Štuikys V, Burbaitė R (2015) Smart education in CS: a case study. In: Smart Learning
           Objects for the Smart Education in Computer Science: theory, methodology and robot-
           based implementation. Springer
[Sch02]   Schulte C (2002) Towards a pedagogical framework for teaching programming and
           object-oriented modelling in secondary education. In: Proceedings of SECIII 2002
[SEC+13]   Schirner G, Erdogmus D, Chowdhury K, Padir T The future of human-in-the-loop
           cyber-physical systems. IEEE Comput 46(1):36–45
[SGW16]   Sochacka NW, Guyotte K, Walther J (2016) Learning together: a collaborative
           autoethnographic exploration of STEAM (STEM+ the arts) education. J Eng Educ
           105(1):15–42
[SH06]   Sajaniemi J, Hu C (2006) Teaching programming: going beyond "Objects First". In:
           Romero P, Good J, Acosta Chaparro E, Bryant S (eds) Proc. PPIG 18. p 255–265
[SHL13]   Schäfer A, Holz J, Leonhardt T, Schroeder U, Brauner P, Ziefle M (2013) From boring
           to scoring–a collaborative serious game for learning and practicing mathematical logic
           for computer science education. Computer Science Education, (ahead-of-print), pp
           1–25
[SMG11]   Salleh N, Mendes E, Grundy JC (2011) Empirical studies of pair programming for
           CS/SE teaching in higher education: a systematic literature review. IEEE Trans Softw
           Eng 37(4):509–525
[SPJ+11]   Saeli M, Perrenet J, Jochems WMG, Zwaneveld B (2011) Teaching programming in
           secondary school: a pedagogical content knowledge perspective. Inform Educ 10
           (1):73–88
[SPS09]   Southwest Pennsylvania STEM network long range plan (2009–2018): plan summary.
           http://business-leadershipcoaching.com/wp-content/uploads/2013/08/SWP-STEM-
           STRATEGY-Final-Report-Summary-July-2009.pdf
[SSH+09]   Sheard J, Simon, Hamilton M, Lönnberg J (2009) Analysis of research into the
           teaching and learning of programming. In: ICER'09, August 10–11, 2009, Berkeley,
           California, USA. p 93–104
[Sta14]   Stankovic JA (2014) Research directions for the internet of things. IEEE Internet
           Things J 1(1):3–9. February
[STEM16]   STEM 2026: a vision for innovation in STEM education. Department of Education
           (US). innovation.ed.gov/files/2016/09/AIR-STEM2026_Report_2016.pdf

[STJ14]   Singh D, Tripathi G, A.J. Jara (1014) A survey of internet-of-things: future vision,
          architecture, challenges and services. In: Internet of Things (WF-IoT), 2014 I.E. World
          Forum. p 287–292
[Štu15]   Štuikys V (2015) Smart learning objects for smart education in computer science:
          theory, methodology and robot-based implementation. Springer, New York
[Tou12]   Touretzky DS (2012) Seven big ideas in robotics, and how to teach them. In: Pro-
          ceedings of the 43rd ACM technical symposium on Computer Science Education. pp
          39–44
[VBH13]   Vincenti G, Braman J, Hilberg JS (2013) Teaching introductory programming through
          reusable learning objects: a pilot study. J Comput Sci Coll 28(3):38–45
[Wil14]   Williams T (2014) Computer ccience education week: support STEM and the hour of
          code.   www.teachforamerica.org/blog/computer-science-education-week-support-
          stem-and-hour-code. December 8, 2014
[WMR+11] Wang HH, Moore TJ, Roehrig GH, Park MS (2011) STEM integration: teacher
          perceptions and practice. J Pre-Coll Eng Educ 1(2):1–13. https://doi.org/10.5703/
          1288284314636
[ZYR16]   Zhu ZT, Yu MH, Riezebos P (2016) A research framework of smart education. Smart
          Learn Environ 3(1):4

Chapter 2
A Vision for Introducing STEM into CS Education at School

Abstract This chapter aims at showing on how it is possible to introduce and integrate the STEM paradigm into CS education by presenting a vision of the whole approach. We define this vision through the STEM-driven conceptual model and model-driven processes. The model includes the use of robot-based scenarios to deliver the interdisciplinary knowledge pieces defined as S-knowledge, T-knowledge, E-knowledge, M-knowledge and I-knowledge (meaning integrated knowledge). Model-driven processes define the vision on how to implement the conceptual model. We consider two kinds of processes, i.e. *designing processes* to create STEM resources in advance and *usage processes* to use the predesigned resources in the real STEM-driven educational setting.

2.1 Introduction

With this chapter, we start considering our approach. We aim at showing on how it is possible to introduce and integrate the STEM paradigm into CS education. Here, we present a vision of the whole approach. We define this vision as a STEM-driven conceptual model. We will describe the implementation details of this model in subsequent chapters. Note that we wrote this chapter taking some material from our published paper [ŠBB+17]. Note also that we have accepted a writing manner to present the material in each chapter so that it would possible, to some extent, to read one chapter independently from others. Therefore, the attentive reader can find some repetition of ideas from the previous chapter (in our view, most important, such as motivation and literature review).

Educators and scientists define STEM (Science, Technology, Engineering and Mathematics) as *an interdisciplinary approach to learning.* In this approach, *"rigorous academic concepts are coupled with real world lessons as students apply science, technology, engineering, and mathematics in contexts that make connections between school, community, work, and the global enterprise, enabling the development of STEM literacy and with it the ability to compete in the new economy"* [SRS+09].

© Springer International Publishing AG, part of Springer Nature 2018
V. Štuikys, R. Burbaitė, *Smart STEM-Driven Computer Science Education*,
https://doi.org/10.1007/978-3-319-78485-4_2

As discussed in Chap. 1, researchers and policymakers predict that the demand for the STEM-based workforce in the twenty-first century will be growing continuously. Therefore, STEM-oriented education becomes well timed and extremely significant, though there are many challenges and issues that require better understanding to manage them adequately. Among others, they include (1) motivating and engaging students to participate in STEM-oriented learning [ADG+15, AEM+14, KKY+15] and (2) integrating STEM-oriented aspects into the school curriculum [GMB+14, Rob15]. The others include (3) selecting adequate technological tools, pedagogical methods and activities for the paradigm [DHL+14, Rob15] and (4) providing students' research and introducing real problem solving so that to enforce critical and computational thinking, to develop collaborative learning skill for modern workforce market [AEM+14, DGL+14, DHL+14, FMT15, GMB+14, Hol14, MBS15, NLS16, Rob15, SGW16].

As Science, Technology, Engineering and Mathematics are highly broad and heterogeneous fields, there are quite different views and approaches to deal with STEM education. One specific view relates to the role of computer science (CS) in STEM-based education. Gander [Gan15] observes that CS is the leading science of the twenty-first century. As in case of mathematics, practically all sciences use CS approaches. According to the author, it has to be a part of general knowledge in education. On the other hand, *Informatics Europe* and *ACM Europe* convincingly state that CS education in the school must consist of two parts. The first should focus on learning to make good use of ICT and its devices, also called as *digital literacy*. These skills are short living knowledge, because they are changing with technology. The second should focus on learning the fundamentals of CS that are essential to understanding our digital world. This is *informatics*. The latter brings "long living knowledge which lasts forever and does not change with technology".

Two basic attributes predefine the essence of our approach, i.e. (1) the use of educational robots and other smart devices for CS education at the secondary (high) school and (2) the use of the robot-oriented teaching content that we represent in a specific way. One type represents the so-called smart learning objects [Štu15] adapted for the STEM needs (meaning meta-programming-based generative learning objects (GLOs) with extended features and possibilities). Another type represents component-based LOs such as tutorials, quizzes, etc. Both attributes, when implemented, require a wide range of interdisciplinary knowledge to define and integrate STEM components (S, T, E and M) into CS education. In our model, STEM components represent the following items. The component S covers CS and partially physics topics, i.e. those topics that relate to understanding of robotics functionality. The component T covers a variety of technologies, including the Internet, educational software tools, communication, etc. The component E covers constructing of an educational robot system from available parts, designing of the educational environment and testing it and robot's functionality through modelling. We are also able to introduce the engineering aspects through dealing with real-world tasks or their prototypes. The component M is implicit in our model. Either it appears in the task dedicated to the robot or it appears within the algorithm to specify the robot's functionality. In our model, the component S stands for the root, while the remaining ones are supplementary to define the STEM paradigm within the CS teaching curriculum. Therefore, we consider such a paradigm that integrates STEM within the single teaching course (i.e. CS course also known as informatics).

Our approach has multiple new capabilities. (1) It focuses on the wide-scale analysis as a context to build the smart educational environment for STEM-driven CS education at school. (2) It covers the full life cycle processes ranging from constructing/testing of the robot itself to the development and use of robot control programs, scenarios and STEM library for the CS education based on the concept of personal generative library. (3) The STEM knowledge is explicit and integrated within the processes and content and, therefore, it is easy to extract and to present the content for learning. (4) When implemented, our approach exploits the advanced technologies such as feature-based modelling and meta-programming, enabling to introduce systemization and generalization and to achieve a higher extent of reuse through automation, though we present those aspects here as a by-product only. The reader will receive the evidence on those new capabilities gradually moving through subsequent chapters.

The remaining part of this chapter includes the following topics. In Sect. 2.2, we discuss the related work. In Sect. 2.3, we present a general description of our approach that includes a conceptual model to describe the basic idea that contains possible scenarios of gaining STEM knowledge. In Sect. 2.4, we discuss a framework to implement the conceptual model. In Sect. 2.5, we provide a process-based vision of our approach with the focus on the development of STEM-driven content and its use in CS education. In Sect. 2.6, we introduce STEM-driven learning processes as a problem domain. In Sect. 2.7, we summarize the capabilities of the approach and identify some difficulties. Finally, in Sect. 2.8, we provide the conclusion and links with other chapters.

2.2 Related Work

We categorize the related work into four streams with regard to the aims of this chapter as follows: (A) STEM-based education challenges, (B) the role of CS in STEM education, (C) smart devices and educational robotics in STEM education and (D) the role of context for educational systems. Note that so far there is no uniform definition in the literature, of the term STEM. We have presented one in the introduction; however, the following definition is more relevant to our context. According to [FMT15], STEM is "learning and/or work in the fields of Science, Technology, Engineering and Mathematics, including preliminary learning at school prior to entry into the specific disciplines".

2.2.1 STEM-Based Education Challenges

We have already enlisted some challenges in the introduction. Here, we extend a discussion on the topics. Many researchers identify the *learner's motivation and engagement* as the most important issue in STEM education. Therefore, there are many suggestions and approaches on how to deal with the issue. We classify those approaches as follows: (1) using technological toys (i.e. Lego, Knex) [ADG+15, Hol14, KKY+15], (2) increasing the role of the teacher as a mentor in STEM classes [DG16, ADG+15, AEM+14, GHV15, GMB+14], (3) introducing after-school activities related to STEM [CML16, GHV15, GMB+14] and (4) focusing on active learning-based courses [EE14].

The next challenge is the *integration of STEM-oriented aspects into school curriculum*. That covers (1) availability of advanced STEM courses [AEM+14, CML16, DGL+14], (2) IT/STEM-oriented learning (e.g. GPS, GIS, robotics programming) [DHL+14], (3) curriculum reform agendas and programs [FMT15, GMB +14, NLS16, Rob15] and (4) conceptualizing of STEM education [NLS16]. The other issues largely relate to technology. The choice of *appropriate technological tools* is important too (1) in creating adequate technological infrastructures to support collaboration [AEM+14], (2) for monitoring and programming easiness [HBM+15], (3) using the fully configurable user interface [HBM+15] and (4) making improvements in STEM learning using robotics [Hol14, KKY+15].

Finally, a large body of reviewed papers focuses on the selection of *suitable pedagogical methods, activities and resources*. Those issues include (1) providing learners' research, problem solving, critical computational thinking and collaborative learning skills [AEM+14, DGL+14, DHL+14, Ear15, KKY+15] and (2) making and tinkering activities [DG16], including robotics activities [KKY+15]. The others include (3) implementing consequential, side-by-side [DG16], inquiry-based [KKY +15 DG16, DHL+14, GMB+14, HBM+15], design-based [DHL+14], game-based [Ear15], project-based [GHV15] learning and (4) using sociocultural approaches to the design of learning environments [DG16].

2.2.2 The Role of CS in STEM-Oriented Education

The following extract from [Gan15], perhaps, is the best to characterize the role of CS in STEM education.

> *Computer Science is the leading science of the 21st century. It is used like mathematics in all sciences. It has to become part of general knowledge in education. Informatics Europe and ACM Europe convincingly state that computer science in the school must consist of two parts:*
>
> 1. *Learn to make good use of IT and its devices. This is called Digital Literacy, often also ICT. These skills are short living knowledge, they change with technology.*

2. *Learn the fundamentals of computer science, which are essential to understand our digital world. This is called Informatics. It is long living knowledge, which lasts forever and does not change with technology.*

The papers [DGL+14, DHL+14] also emphasize the role of CS in STEM-oriented education. According to the papers, CS within the context of STEM means the advanced use of ICT and its devices to perform data processing in different domains (e.g. biology, physics and chemistry).

In the context of STEM-oriented education, the development of computational thinking and problem-solving skills [JD16] is one of the most important targets. The concepts and approaches taken from CS, such as structured task decomposition, abstractions and pattern generalizations, iterative and parallel thinking, conditional logic, debugging and systematic error detection, etc., are directly influencing the development of computational thinking. Yet another source [Štu15] summarizes the challenges to teach CS fundamentals such as usage of adequate learning models; teaching context and learning personalization; learners' motivation improvement; cognitive problems related to high-level abstractions, theoretical knowledge and practice; content adaptation to learner's context; etc. The listed statements suggest that CS education requires to be changed and is an important part of STEM-oriented education.

2.2.3   The Role of Smart Devices and Educational Robotics in STEM-Driven CS Education

The paper [Ben12] provides a systematic review by exploring the educational potential of robotics in schools. The paper introduces three groups of the essential problems: (a) using robots as educational tools, (b) testing of effectiveness of robots and (c) providing future perspectives of use of robotics. The paper also concludes that robotics improve learning achievements in STEM-related areas such as construction, mechatronics and programming. The other works [Egu14, Egu14a] highlight the importance of educational robotics for promoting twenty-first-century core skills in creativity and innovation, critical thinking, problem solving, communication and collaboration, technological literacy and personal and social responsibility. The papers [AD14, SH16, Egu16] provide discussions on how educational robotics help to develop computational thinking skills. The following papers evaluate educational robotics as the most effective supporting tools and learning methods in CS education [FM02, AMA+07, Egu15, FPA+08, KKK+07, ZGK13]. The next portion of works focuses on robot-based learning environments to support modern learning methods and on the involvement of students in knowledge construction processes [GB11, GL11, BSM12, CCO+15, Egu15]. The following works [FM02, KJ09, WKK+07, KME+14, MK14, Hig14, SPA07] distinguish CS topics that relate to the use of robot-based learning environments.

2.2.4   The Role of Context in Analysis and Design of Educational Systems

Firstly, we state the following observation. *Any entity, any process, any design* and *any system* we want to study have two essential parts: the *base part* and *its context*. The context typically enables us to extract the additional knowledge to understand better the base system. One can get such a vision by studying the related literature from different domains (see [BR12, LK10] to name a few). Our topic is not the exclusion from this general rule. Therefore, we included the context-related analysis in our review.

In general, there are many attributes to characterize the context. There is also a variety of factors influencing its understanding (e.g. content representation forms, cognitive aspects, structure and model of LO, etc.). Furthermore, a diversity of related terms characterizes the context-related problem in learning: *adaptive learning, personalized learning* [BVV+10, MKS10], *adaptable LO, personalized LO* [BCW+08], *adaptive granularity* [MJ10], *adaptive learning scenarios* [BS08], *adaptive learning path* [BSS+12], etc.

As this research field is indeed very broad and, in fact, relates to multiple aspects and domains, we restrict ourselves presenting the review with our vision and our approach in mind only. First, we focus on context issues as the most influential factor in designing systems. Next, we analyse the adaptability problem from the *external* (i.e. the environment) and *internal* (i.e. the content model) views.

We start from definitions and interpretations of the term *context,* as it is understood in general and in the e-Learning literature. Context-related issues have been intensively researched, especially in the computer-human interaction and technology-enhanced learning. According to Zimmermann et al. [ZLO07], in the area of CS, there are a number of definitions of the term *context* and *context awareness*. A vast majority of earlier definitions can be categorized into two groups: definition by synonyms (e.g. application's environmental context or situation context) and definition by example (e.g. enumeration context elements like location, identity, time, temperature, noise as well as the beliefs and intentions of the human).

Dey [Dey01] defines context as *"any information that can be used to characterize the situation of an entity"*. In the other paper, Dey et al. extend the previous definition by stating, *"an entity is a person, place, or object that is considered relevant to the interaction between a user and an application, including the user and applications themselves"*. This can be viewed as an application-centric definition, which clearly states that the context is always bound to an entity and that information that describes the situation of an entity is context. The paper [LCW+09] defines the learning context as "information to identify the state of the item, i.e. learner's location, learning activities, the used tools and LOs". Dourish [Dou04] emphasizes a dual origin of the context: technical- and social-based aspects. From a social viewpoint, the author argues that context is not something that describes a setting or situation, but rather a feature of interaction. From a technical viewpoint, researchers try to define context in a more specific way as an *operational term* [VMO+12, Win01,

ZLO07], i.e. by enumerating categories of the term. The main contribution of the paper [ZLO07] is the introduction of a context definition that comprises three canonical parts: a definition per se in general terms, a formal definition describing the appearance of context and an operational definition characterizing the use of context and its dynamic behaviour. The paper [HSK09] presents a literature review of the context-aware systems from 2000 to 2007 and a classification framework on the topic using a keyword index and article title search. Dey defines the context-aware system as follows: *"A system is context-aware if it uses context to provide relevant information and/or services to the user, where relevancy depends on the user's task"*.

The paper [VMO+12] provides extensive analysis of context definitions with regard to designing recommendation systems to support technology-enhanced learning (TEL). The latter aims to design, develop and test sociotechnical innovations that will support and enhance learning practices of both individuals and organizations. With respect to our aims, one important result of this paper is the framework that summarizes the known so far definitions of the term context and presents how these definitions relate to each other.

The feature-based models are the core of a great body of research in and modelling, especially as applied to PLE. The feature commonality-variability modelling is at the focus, where context plays also a significant role [LK10]. One important aspect of variability modelling is also the use of ontology and context to model the base domain features. Ontology enables to extract and represent variability dependencies and interaction [LKS+07]. The paper [LK10], e.g. uses the context to configure and select features for the product family of embedded software. Sometimes context modelling is treated as a service. The paper [TLL10] proposes the context-based ontology whose property is to reason and describe the rules in e-Learning using Protégé software. The paper [JGK+07] presents an ontological framework aimed at the explicit representation of context-specific metadata derived from the actual usage of learning objects and learning designs.

The paper [BBH+10] provides an extensive study on context modelling along with reasoning techniques. Here, the authors discuss the requirements, a variety of context information types and their relationships and situations as related to abstractions of the context information facts, histories and uncertainty of the context information. This discussion also provides a comparison of the current context modelling and reasoning techniques and a lesson learned from this comparison. Based on the existing context-aware e-Learning systems, the paper [DBC+10] presents a model and taxonomy of context parameters from the learner's situation.

We reformulate the following finding of this short analysis below.

1. Context is a multidimensional category that, in general, may include the following features: *special time*, *physical conditions*, *computing*, *resource*, *user*, *activity* and *social*.
2. As many of these features are overlapping (see [VMO+12]), it is reasonable to combine some of them in a concrete situation such as teaching with the use of SLOs. Thus, we will focus on three context dimensions: computing/resource, user

(learner/teacher)/social and activity/task/content. Comparing these dimensions with pedagogical reusability as proposed in [PS04], we are able to connect a learning situation with the three context categories we will use later respectively: *pedagogical context, technological context* and *content context.*

In summary, one of the biggest challenges in STEM-driven CS education is the implementation the most effective learning methods, resources and tools to achieve learning goals. Though there are many possible solutions, the use of educational robotics in schools should be the focus in this regard. Though the provided analysis covers multiple topics and a variety of approaches, there is still a big gap between the current technological capabilities and needs for the improvement of CS education on the STEM paradigm at school. This is especially true in terms of integrating the advanced technology with STEM pedagogy aiming at achieving a higher efficiency through systematization, integration and automation. We hope that our approach is able to bring the relevant contribution in this respect.

2.3   A General Description of Our Approach

This description gives a general understanding of our approach. The description includes two parts: (1) a conceptual model of STEM-driven CS education and (2) a framework presenting more details on the model. The conceptual model deals with the pedagogical approach (learning-by-doing) and the scenarios and focuses on the STEM-driven knowledge introduced through activities of the scenarios. The framework introduces STEM-driven components, their interactions and attribute-based vision of two basic components, i.e. STEM pedagogy and STEM-related content.

2.3.1   A Conceptual Model of STEM-Driven CS Education

In our approach, educational robotics is a primary concept that leads to the development of the STEM-driven CS curriculum to educate students at the secondary school level. Figure 2.1 presents the conceptual model to understand our approach. As we stated in Sect. 2.2, educational robots are extremely useful instruments to provide interdisciplinary knowledge regarding all STEM components. Here, therefore, we accept the educational robot (ER) as a physical learning object (PLO) [BDŠ13] to provide STEM-driven learning and achieve education objectives. By notions S, T, E, M within the circles, we mean the adequate pieces of knowledge obtained using the ER as PLO. The darken area is to be thought as the integrated STEM knowledge.

The main pedagogical approach we use within the introduced model is *learning-by-doing.* A motivated involvement of students in this process is a primary concern. We split the process into two phases treated as scenarios here: (1) *activities of a*

Fig. 2.1 A conceptual
model of STEM-driven CS
education at school (© with
kind permission from IJEE
[ŠBB+17])

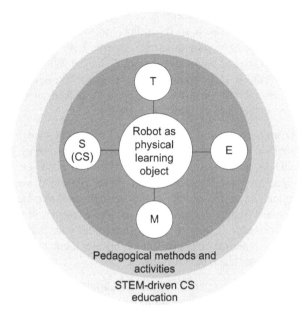

preparatory work to construct and test the robot itself and (2) the robot's use in full
functionality (in the *mode use-as-is*) to solve real-world tasks (subtasks) or their
prototypes. Scenario 1 includes a set of mini-tasks such as researching the characteristics of the robot's components (motors, sensors). As solving of mini-tasks is a
short-time process (students may enjoy immediately by the achieved result) and the
sequence of solving mini-task is logically dependent (i.e. the next mini-task requires
the previous knowledge of the previous mini-tasks), these factors highly self-
motivate students in the involvement into the process. The next motivating factor
is the possibility of the student to make an independent decision (teacher acts as a
mentor). A successful pass through Scenario 1 (i.e. a student sees a working thing
and its usefulness in practice) is also a motivating factor for Scenario 2, i.e. modelling
of robot's functionality. We also motivate students by introducing the real-world
tasks that robots are able to solve, or by showing a film or visual slides on how this is
happening in reality. The analysis of the robot as PLO in Scenario 1 as well as in
Scenario 2 leads to the following pieces of knowledge obtained in the process
"learning-by-doing".

Engineering knowledge (E). Robots may function using the only *motors* to realize
such tasks as the *straight-line movement* and *rotary motion*. Both are indeed subtasks
of more complex tasks such as carrying objects in manufacturing by the robot from
location A to location B, etc. However, sensors enable to extend the robot's
functionality and capabilities largely. There are different kinds of sensors used in
robots (ultrasonic, light, touch, colour, sound, infrared, etc.) [KLM15]. The list of
tasks that require the use of sensors is much wider (obstacle detection, line following, light following, service activities using touch and sound sensor, etc.). Note that
all these are prototypes of real-world tasks. In general, it is possible to interpret

sensors as either engineering or technology products. As our main focus in using Scenario 2 is taken to the robot control program (RCP) development to teach fundamentals of programming, students have to study characteristics of different types of sensors before developing RCPs. So, in this way, students are able to obtain knowledge in engineering. Next, a construction of educational robots from scratch, i.e. assembling the robot from parts, is indeed an engineering activity. Students provide this activity working in groups.

Technology-Related Knowledge (T) This knowledge comes through analysing robot's components such as mentioned before (motors; LED, light-emitting diodes; LCD, liquid crystal display; etc.). The robot itself, i.e. the kinds of robots such as Lego, Arduino, Raspberry Pi or others [KLM15], can be viewed as products of engineering or technology. Software tools used in e-Learning and those used in our approach (they will appear later) are also examples of the technology. As both kinds of knowledge (engineering and technology) are highly underpinned among themselves, sometimes it is difficult to consider them as separate items. Often, therefore, we consider them in combination.

Science Knowledge (S) A typical example of gaining scientific knowledge in using robots as PLOs is the scientific *inquiry method*. Say, we have two types of sensors: colour sensor and light sensor. As they are programmable units, it is possible to change colour sensor functionality capabilities, i.e. by changing the intensity of light, we are able to achieve the behaviour of the colour sensor similar to the light sensor through means of soft programming. The reason of using colour sensors in the role of light sensors may be pure practical: the number of available colour sensors is insufficient in the classroom to demonstrate a particular task for all students. In this case, students are encountering with physical laws of light combined with scientific experimentation. Furthermore, an analysis of sensor properties and capabilities takes another portion of scientific knowledge. We are able to see those capabilities explicitly through sensor testing experiments. For example, the ultrasonic sensor is able to recognize obstacles being in the vertical position much better in comparison to those obstacles that are in a shifted position. However, to know the limits of shifting, we need to provide a scientific experiment.

Knowledge in Mathematics (M) This knowledge appears in multiple cases (problem statement, analysis and representation of experimental results, task modelling, etc.). To illustrate that, we present the following examples. In formulating the robot's movement task, we have dependencies (distance/speed). This is a functional relationship in the mathematical sense, i.e. $s = f(v)$ [BSM12]. To ensure a stable construction of the robot, we need to perform its mathematical modelling. Furthermore, each task requires some calculations specific to a particular task. For example, the *ornament-drawing* task to be performed by the robot needs calculation to ensure a required shape of ornaments. Another example is Boolean algebra concepts in a traffic light problem statement. Note also that in most cases there is an integrated knowledge as we discuss below.

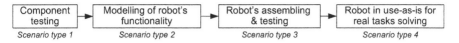

Fig. 2.2 A possible sequence in using types of scenarios

Integrated STEM Knowledge   So far, we have discussed pieces of knowledge for each STEM component separately due to methodological reasons, though perhaps in the case of using robots, there is no such a type of knowledge at all. Instead, there is the integrated knowledge. For example, this knowledge arrives through modelling and constructing the robot itself from components, investigating characteristics of components and testing capabilities of components as separate activities. However, a large body of integrated knowledge arrives through the full cycle of analysis, which covers modelling, constructing and testing, including the development of RCPs for the robot testing needs. Note also that the testing phase gives some fragments of RCPs. It is possible to use them in describing a real-task prototype to ensure STEM-based CS education. This, in fact, is the use of a previous knowledge in learning also contributing to the integration.

Possible Scenarios to Obtain the STEM Knowledge   This section is about the way we are able to extract and deliver the STEM knowledge to learners. In Fig. 2.2, we introduce an extended vision of possible scenarios. Here, we also indicate on the possible sequence of using the scenarios. The basis in defining the sequence is "from simpler to more complex", meaning that we examine constituents first and then the whole system. Though the suggested sequence is logical, it is not obligatory. We are able to miss some scenarios in the process, depending on the situation. For example, we are able to exclude or not the modelling of robot's functionality. The decision depends on the teacher's intention or external factors such as availability of robot's components, when the process takes place. Modelling enables to play robot's functionality without having physical components at hand. In general, modelling by using the available software is a powerful instrument in teaching and gaining a specific knowledge (e.g. on how we apply mathematics in practice). Modelling therefore may stand for Scenario 1 in the other case.

After introducing architectural issues and having robot's units at hand, it is possible to start the process from Scenario 1 as Fig. 2.2 indicates. Scenario 1 is about activities to learn more about the separate components (e.g. motors, sensors) of the architecture. Therefore, Scenario 1 is a logically grounded way to initiate the learning process. In order for the process to be successful during each scenario, the teacher should manage it adequately. The teacher's role is to formulate teaching objectives and tasks for each scenario as they relate to CS and STEM education, and what is most important is to motivate students so that they would be inspired for *self-motivation* in STEM learning. This is extremely important in terms of student-centred learning. We will return to this later.

Now let us focus on remaining scenarios and the whole sequence. Scenario 2, when applied, gives knowledge on the robot's functionality and results in preparation of the guide on how to perform the assembling tasks of the robot. We used this guide for activities of Scenario 3. The essential activity of Scenario 3 is testing. Though, after executing Scenario 1, the separate components have been tested and their working characteristics were identified, that does not mean that the whole robot's functionality is ensured. Therefore, we need to provide testing of the robot's correct functionality. This, for example, is possible by dealing with specific tasks. Before introducing Scenario 4, it is reasonable to consider and discuss with students the whole list of tasks (in the sense of curriculum and calendar plan possibilities) the educational robots may perform. One can consider this action as an additional scenario. Scenario 4 is about the use of the educational robot in the mode "use-as-is". In this case, we are able to exploit the full capabilities of the learning approach. That means that we apply:

- The integrative aspects of PLO
- The predefined list of tasks to be solved by the robot as PLO
- A variety of control program variants for each task to ensure flexibility in experimentation, to ensure achieving teaching objectives in both STEM and CS aspects

Note that we have introduced and discussed the scenario types aiming to show the way on how we intend to introduce STEM-driven knowledge only. We put aside the process of designing and fully implementing the scenario types. We return to this problem later in Chap. 11.

In the next subsection, we present more details regarding our conceptual model.

2.4   A Framework to Implement the Proposed Conceptual Model

The conceptual model brings the basic idea on CS STEM-driven education and motivates the paradigm only. Below therefore we present a framework that explains the way we need to pass to achieve the implementation phase that we discuss in Sect. 2.5. We have adopted the framework (see Fig. 2.3) from the more general one described in [Štu15]. The adopted version comprises a set of components, the hidden processes within components and two-sided external processes among components. The set of components includes *pedagogy-driven activities, technology-driven processes, knowledge transfer channels with the actors* involved, a set of *tools* used (including robots), STEM-oriented *teaching/learning content* and the *pedagogical/ learning outcome*. In fact, Fig. 2.3 specifies the whole problem domain, though very abstractly, which we call STEM e-Learning domain (further domain). To understand the domain, we need to look into the inside of each component, to discover their properties and their internal and external interaction. This can be done systematically using, for example, SWE approaches such as FODA [KCH+90] or other domain analysis methods.

Fig. 2.3 A framework to implement STEM-driven conceptual model of the CS curriculum (© with kind permission from IJEE [ŠBB +17])

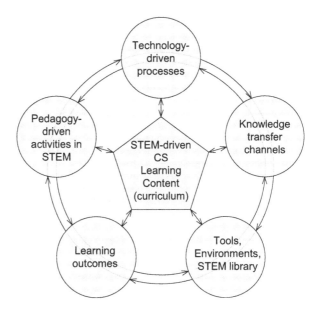

This framework, of course, is still general enough. Nevertheless, it highlights two important issues: an extremely high *heterogeneity* within the domain and *diversity of the interplay* among components when they are oriented for using in the STEM-based paradigm. Indeed the pedagogy-driven activities induce, for example, the interplay among e-Learning, STEM pedagogy and educational theories. The technology-driven processes, on the other hand, indicate on how we are able to transform and process the information induced by those components using educational tools (computers, robots and other devices, educational software tools) in order to achieve the pre-specified STEM objectives. The tools are for ensuring the functionality and efficiency of the whole system. The knowledge transfer channels connect the main actors (students and teachers) at different ends of the channels. The latter is the core of the education process as a pure social activity.

The STEM-oriented teaching/learning *content* (we treat that as a set of real-world tasks in the conceptual model) plays an exclusive role. From the viewpoint of functionality, content stands for *database* to enriching other components with the *information* that enables to start the processes, to initiate and support the functioning of the components and the whole system. Here, we use the term database as a generic concept. In our case, when the database is implemented, it becomes the STEM library, containing within the structured content being represented in different forms (LO, RCP instances or smart generative LOs that represent a set of related RCP instances). As a result, content stands for an intermediate link to connect and integrate the different nature domains – social and technological. Finally, in a social sense, the pedagogical (teaching/learning) outcome needs to be thought of as a measure to reason about on how the component interplay was relevant to prescribed

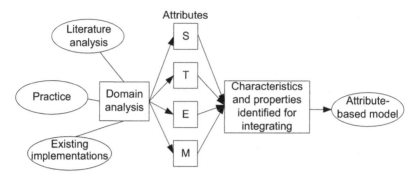

Fig. 2.4 A vision for integrating STEM-driven attributes (© with kind permission from IJEE [ŠBB+17])

objectives, what difficulties could be identified within components and what improvements could be done in the future.

In this context, there are some observations important to state as follows:

1. The interplay among components specifies the functionality of a learning/teaching process. We can model this functionality through component attributes. Though those attributes differ in semantics, when specified for modelling purposes, we are able to evaluate them using the adequate measures specific to each component and, then, to *express uniformly* (we will show that later in Chap. 4).
2. We need to harmonize the interplay between components with respect to the prescribed learning and teaching objectives. From the pure technological perspective, the harmonization should be correct, meaning that the interaction model is correct and we take into account the prespecified constraints.
3. It is possible to enlarge the *space* for modelling functionality (the interplay between components) significantly if we take into account the possible values of different attributes for each component. As it is possible to express those values uniformly, we are able to integrate and specify that as a single content-based specification.
4. Using this framework and providing analysis, it is possible to extract main attributes related to S, T, E, M aspects so that it would be possible to integrate them and represent as an attribute-based model (Fig. 2.4).

Here, by the term *domain*, we mean items related to STEM education, i.e. a set of objects (such as teaching materials, including literature sources), approaches, *processes* and standards defined by the terminology taken from the STEM-driven CS curriculum. Note that Fig. 2.4 outlines our domain at a higher level of abstraction only partially. Later, in Sect. 2.5, we define our domain more precisely with the focus on STEM processes and their contexts. By the term *domain analysis*, we mean activities, typically performed by the teacher or course designer, such as reading of teaching materials, extracting and representing the relevant information explicitly and using the previous knowledge and cognitive processes with or without the use of systematic domain analysis approaches (such as FODA [CH06, Bat05]).

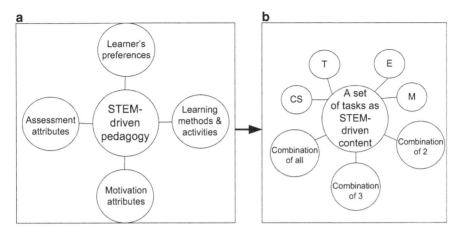

Fig. 2.5 STEM-driven integrative attribute-based aspects of pedagogy (**a**) and content (**b**) (© with kind permission from IJEE [ŠBB+17])

By the *attribute-based model*, we mean the integrated characteristics (i.e. attributes, properties and their relationships) obtained within the domain objects and represented explicitly by texts, tables, pictures, etc. More formally, in terms of the feature-based notion [Bat05], those characteristics are also known as *features* and their *variants*. In Fig. 2.5a, we present an attribute-based model that includes attributes of two main components, i.e. the STEM-driven pedagogy and STEM-oriented content. Table 2.1 provides variants of the STEM-driven pedagogy attributes. Note that these attributes related to the motivation, learning methods and activities specifically extended to be relevant for the STEM paradigm, while the remaining attributes (assessment and learner's preferences) are generic.

Here (see Fig. 2.5b), by *the STEM-driven content*, we mean the STEM library components, i.e. smart GLOs (further SLOs) and component-based LOs (CB LOs, i.e. tutorials, quizzes, models, etc.). Note that SLO is organized so that it contains within the GLO for generating RCPs and CB LO as a parameter of the SLO (that will be explained in more detail in Chap. 11). Now we are able to describe the way of how we implemented the proposed model. The next two sections are about that. In Sect. 2.5, we present a process-based vision to implement the model.

2.5   Basis for Implementing Our Approach: A Process-Based Vision

The central task of the STEM paradigm is on how to integrate aspects of different disciplines into a coherent system so that it would be possible to provide the so-called integrated STEM education [KK16]. The aim of this section therefore is

Table 2.1 STEM-driven pedagogy attributes (© with kind permission from IJEE [ŠBB+17])

Learner's preferences	Methods and activities	Motivation attributes	Assessment attributes
Learner's level: *beginner, intermediate, advanced*	Learning-by-doing methods: *consequential, side-by-side, inquiry-based, design-based, game-based, project-based, problem-based*	Technological devices, teacher as mentor, active learning, after-school STEM-related activities, short-time mini-task solving	Bloom's taxonomy-based model by levels: knowledge, comprehension, application, analysis, synthesis, evaluation
Learning style: *audial, visual, kinaesthetic*	Activities: *making and tinkering, robotics-related*		SOLO taxonomy-based model: *surface learning:* pre-structural, uni-structural, multi-structural; *deep learning:* relational, extended abstract
Learning pace: *slow, medium, fast*			Concepts' map model
Learning preference: *conceptual, example-oriented, case study, simulation, demonstration*			
Learning objective: *research, survey, quick reference, basic introduction, project, assessment* and *seminar*			

to highlight those aspects of our model on which basis we are able to achieve an overall integration and implement it in practice to provide CS teaching on the STEM paradigm. The core property of our approach is that we are able to recognize and extract the social, pedagogical, content and technology aspects related to STEM and represent them uniformly by features and their variants. Note that this property is universal and does not depend on the educational paradigm used. We have exploited this property, for example, in designing smart LOs [Štu15]. This property results in explicit representation of essential features. This, in fact, means that we are able to create the formal model that integrates the prescribed domain aspects through the features and their relationships and constraints. One can learn more about feature models either from the original sources taken from SWE literature (we recommend the one [CH06]) or from [Štu15] (here feature models are directly connected to the e-Learning domain).

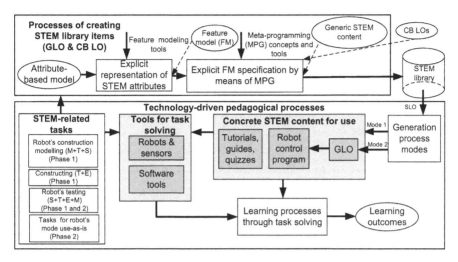

Fig. 2.6 A process-based view of the STEM-driven model at the implementation level (© with kind permission from IJEE [ŠBB+17])

The model we discuss in this chapter differs from those we considered in our previous research [Štu15] by the following aspects:

1. The STEM-oriented feature model contains a wider spectrum of features.
2. The variants of features correspond to specific attributes related to STEM components; therefore, the model itself becomes more complex and more specific in terms of features and their variants, relationships and constraints.
3. The STEM model focuses on smart generative learning objects (SLO) that essentially differ from the ones described in [Štu15]. The difference is not only in an extended semantics but also in a hierarchical structure, meaning that at the top there are pedagogy-oriented parameters and at the bottom content-based parameters (i.e. they are separated explicitly).
4. Smart GLOs (SLOs) in the STEM model are defined as the learning resource as follows:

$$SLOs = GLOs + CB\ LOs. \qquad (2.1)$$

Here, GLO (i.e. generative LO) is a generic specification represented by a family of the related RCPs for a given real task, which are coded by means of meta-programming; CB LO is a digital entity (text fragments, movies, models, guides, quizzes, tutorials) to be used and reused either for a single task or multiple tasks.

5. The STEM model has an explicit relation to the learning resources of distinct forms, if not to say more – they are deeply integrated in our model (see Fig. 2.6). There are hardware resources (robot as a PLO) and software-oriented resources (including SLOs and SW tools: either of general use or domain specific, such as modelling tools, robot-programming environments).

In Fig. 2.6, we outline our approach as a process-based vision that is relevant to the STEM paradigm and reveals on how we have implemented it. Here, we grouped the processes into two large groups: (1) processes of creating STEM library items and (2) technology-driven pedagogical processes. The first group includes two transformations: (a) the domain attribute-based model into the feature model and (b) the feature model into the meta-programming-based SLO specification [ŠBB +16]. This specification enables the two-level generation process represented as Mode 1 and Mode 2:

$$\overset{\text{Mode 1}}{\text{SLO} \Rightarrow} \text{GLOs} + \text{CB LOs}; \overset{\text{Mode 2}}{\text{GLO} \Rightarrow} \text{RCP}. \tag{2.2}$$

Why do we use the STEM-based RCP not as a single control program but as a generative one (GLO)? It is so because RCPs, specified as GLO, have many advantages. GLO is a predefined family of the RCP instances. They may cover a variety of use cases in designing individual learning paths. It is possible to derive a particular instance from the GLO specification automatically on demand. Therefore, we have a great flexibility in time saving and efficiency in use (either in the testing phase or in the learning process phase in which we are able to fulfil CS education objectives in the full range). We present more details regarding the implementation in our case studies later (in Chaps. 11 and 13).

In the next section, we continue our discussion on STEM educational processes, however, from the other perspective. We aim to introduce them as a domain with an extended context.

2.6   STEM-Driven Learning Processes as a Problem Domain

So far, we have presented our domain under consideration from the external viewer perspective. We have outlined it in Fig. 2.6 as fully implemented processes. Here, we want to remind readers that by "our domain" we mean "STEM-driven CS education at the secondary school using smart devices" or shortly "CS STEM education". Throughout the book, the educational or learning processes related to the defined domain are themes for research with the focus on enhancing functionality and efficiency through automation. In general, domain automation, even partial, is a complex task. There is a long way to achieve this objective. Therefore, in this section our aim is to start a gradual move towards achieving this objective. The primary task is the definition of the domain and its scope. We apply the principle taken from the FODA [CH06, Bat05, KCH+90] to define the scope of a domain. The principle states that there are three items to deal with in defining a domain under consideration. They are the *context* as a super-domain, the *subdomains* within the domain and *boundaries* restricting subdomains from its context. We present this vision, as applied to our domain abstractly in Fig. 2.7. Here, by Science, Technology,

Fig. 2.7 A domain of CS
STEM education and its
context

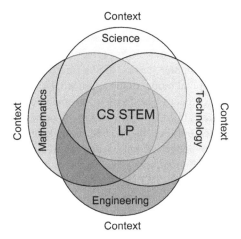

Engineering and Mathematics, we mean the adequate knowledge (see Sect. 2.3) that learners are able to obtain through dealing with the CS-related tasks and solving those using robots within the educational environment.

We outline our domain in more detail, with the focus on STEM process context, later in Chap. 5. This model defines STEM learning processes (LPs) as a base domain and its contexts as a part of the super-domain. Here, by a *base domain*, we mean the internal part of Fig. 2.7, where we have outlined processes very abstractly. Here, the notion CS STEM LPs stands for the base domain. The remaining constituent of our domain is context. It is a super-domain with respect to the base domain. In general, researchers define context in a variety of ways and use it in a variety of situations (see Sect. 2.2). Based on findings of Sect. 2.2, we have identified three constituents of context (pedagogical, technological and content). In the model of Fig. 2.7, we have the STEM pedagogical context (PC), the STEM technological context (TC) and the STEM content context (CC).

We have already defined all those context constituents, though without using the term context. To some extent, we have outlined the internal structure of the STEM PC in Fig. 2.5a and Table 2.1. We have presented the internal structure of the STEM CC (again, to some extent) in Fig. 2.5b. The STEM TC relates to technological tools (including hardware and software) we use within the educational environment. We discuss that later in Chap. 12 the above-stated constituents are highly influential on the base domain, the STEM learning processes. At this understanding level, we are able to show the dependency and interaction among the context constituents and the base domain only abstractly (by providing the adequate square intersections, see Fig. 2.7). Therefore, this model gives a surface knowledge on the domain. In fact, the model defines the scope of our domain, which we treat as *a problem domain* for the thorough and deeper investigation. To do that systematically, we need to introduce and formulate the methodological and theoretical backgrounds (we will discuss that in Chaps. 4 and 5).

2.7   Summary, Discussion and Overall Evaluation

In this chapter, we have presented a vision on how it is possible to introduce STEM into computer science (CS) education at school. By introducing the following: (i) a conceptual model of the approach, (ii) a framework to implement the model in large, (iii) a process-based vision for implementing the approach in small and (iv) context-aware STEM-driven learning processes as our problem domain. The conceptual model outlines the STEM knowledge pieces (i.e. S-knowledge, T-knowledge, E-knowledge, M-knowledge and I-knowledge, i.e. integrated knowledge) along with different types of scenarios to obtain the knowledge. The proposed framework describes six STEM-driven components in large (i.e. pedagogy-driven activities, technology-driven processes, knowledge transfer channels, tools and resources, learning content and learning outcomes). The process-based vision of our approach includes two parts. The first covers the *design processes* to design the support for STEM, i.e. the needed resources (content, scenarios, STEM library, etc.). The second includes the *use processes*, i.e. the learning itself. Finally, we introduce the context-aware STEM-driven educational processes as our *problem domain* for the further investigation. Therefore, the vision gives a general understanding of our approach. Its aim is to prepare a reader for considering a concrete theme or component of our approach we discuss in the subsequent chapters.

At the centre of our approach is the robot-based educational environment and STEM-driven resources as a part of this environment, though we presented those as by-products in this chapter. The resources include items that integrate the CS-oriented content (an essential part of it is the robot control programs in a generic format) along with pedagogical approaches adapted for STEM. We have represented this integration in a specific form called smart generative learning object. This format is an essential modification of smart learning objects (SLOs) described in [Štu15] in two aspects: (1) we have enriched semantics by introducing STEM features for both the content and pedagogy and (2) we have changed the internal structure of SLO by separating pedagogical parameters from content parameters and representing them at different levels aiming at achieving a higher flexibility. We have presented our vision from the perspective of an external viewer, i.e. we have discussed a process-based model (as a derivative product from the conceptual model) and outlined its possible implementation.

Our approach has multiple aspects that we consider as a novelty. (1) It focuses on the wide-scale analysis as a context to build the robot-based environment for STEM-driven CS education at school, though those aspects were revealed only fragmentally. (2) It covers the full life cycle processes ranging from constructing/testing of the robot itself to the development and use of robot control programs for the CS education. (3) The STEM knowledge is explicitly integrated within the processes and content and therefore can be easily extracted to present for learning. (4) When implemented, our approach exploits the advanced technologies such as feature-based modelling and meta-programming, enabling to introduce systemization and generalization and to achieve a higher extent of reuse through automation, though we have not yet disclosed those aspects here.

Indeed, educational robotics and STEM are two sides of the same coin. However, in order to achieve a full integration in creating the coherent STEM-driven educational environment, one needs to go a long way. Firstly, we need to clearly understand what separate constituents (i.e. robot, STEM content for CS and STEM pedagogy) are, dealing with them from the much broader perspective. It is not enough to use the robot in the mode *use-as-is*. There is to be created the possibility to pass by students the full life cycle of the robot functionality (from researching its components and units to modelling, constructing, testing and solving prototypes of the real-world tasks). On the other hand, the STEM content is to be well-defined (in terms of objectives and topics) before being transformed and integrated into the environment. The content designer and/or teacher is responsible for that. The relevant topics are to be associated with STEM features explicitly to make easier the integration and used later. All those activities require a great deal of analysis. In our model, we have considered that as a context or as a by-product only. Therefore, we have generalized the methodological issues of that part through the concept of the STEM library and its entities smart generative learning objects (SLOs) in our model.

The remaining part of the model relates to technology-driven pedagogical processes that appear in the real educational setting. They include a series of activities such as task solving, outcome evaluating on-the-fly, task modifying and repeating its solving. The model was implemented and used first without introducing the STEM paradigm explicitly. Later STEM features were integrated and exploited in the real setting to provide CS education. As the STEM pedagogy (i.e. pedagogical approaches relevant to STEM) is seamlessly integrated with STEM content, the teacher is able to reveal the possibilities of this paradigm to students in multiple contexts. Students are able to select and use the content so that it would be possible to respond to predefined objectives (i.e. one representation of the content more reflects the CS knowledge, such as algorithms, while the other better suits to provide the engineering knowledge, such as constructing the robot). The flexibility of choice is embodied into the menu-driven generative scenarios and contents to be discussed later. Therefore, learners are able to create different learning paths predefined by those technological capabilities, pedagogical models used (project-based, problem-based, inquiry-based, game-based, etc.) and individual preferences.

Therefore, the basic attribute of the proposed conceptual model for integration STEM into CS education is its multidimensionality. The model covers the full life cycle educational processes along with their context. As we could not be able to present some processes and the context in a full range here, this may cause some difficulties for those readers who are less acquainted with reuse-driven approaches. We hope that the further reading will diminish the lack of this knowledge.

2.8 Conclusion

As the educational robots are programmable entities having both the mechanical and computational capabilities, they fit well to provide STEM-driven education in CS, though the introduction of that in reality requires many efforts, resources and adequate approaches. The proposed framework covers both a vision and process-based model that outlines on how it is possible to implement the approach in practice and provide the adequate evaluation. The essence of our approach is the *seamless integration* of the essential attributes of the STEM-driven and CS-oriented content with the STEM pedagogy features. We argue that the use of meta-programming as the implementation technology enables to achieve this integration though the predesigned smart generative learning objects. Though our focus was mainly on CS education, we argue that our approach is partially applicable to other school courses, such as physics and mathematics. We hope also that our approach is applicable for college and university education, especially in engineering education.

References

[AD14]   Atmatzidou S, Demetriadis S (2014) How to support students' computational thinking skills in educational robotics activities. In: Proceeding of 4th international workshop teaching robotics, teaching with robotics & 5th international conference robotics in education Padova (Italy)

[ADG+15]   Ardies J, De Maeyer S, Gijbels D, van Keulen H (2015) Students attitudes towards technology. Int J Technol Des Educ 25(1):43–65

[AEM+14]   Arshavsky N, Edmunds J, Mooney K, Thrift B, Wynn L, Center S. E. R. V. E, ... Janda L (2014) Race to the top STEM affinity network

[AMA+07]   Alimisis D, Moro M, Arlegui J, Pina A, Frangou S, Papanikolaou K (2007) Robotics & constructivism in education: The TERECoP project. In: EuroLogo, vol 40, pp 19–24

[Bat05]   Batory D (2005) Feature models, grammars, and propositional formulas. In: International conference on software product lines. Springer, Berlin, pp 7–20

[BBH+10]   Bettini C, Brdiczka O, Henricksen K, Indulska J, Nicklas D, Ranganathan A, Riboni D (2010) A survey of context modelling and reasoning techniques. Pervasive Mob Comput 6(2):161–180

[BCW+08]   Brady A, Conlan O, Wade V, Dagger D (2008) Supporting users in creating pedagogically sound personalised learning objects. In: Nejdl W et al (eds) Adaptive hypermedia 2008, LNCS 5149. Springer, Heidelberg, pp 52–61

[BDŠ13]   Burbaitė R, Damaševičius R, Štuikys V (2013) Using robots as learning objects for teaching computer science. In: X world conference on computers in education. pp 101–110

[Ben12]   Benitti FBV (2012) Exploring the educational potential of robotics in schools: a systematic review. Comput Educ 58(3):978–988

[BR12]   Boyle T, Ravenscroft A (2012) Context and deep learning design. Comput Educ 59 (4):1224–1233

[BS08]   Boticario JG, Santos OC (2008) A standards-based modelling approach for dynamic generation of adaptive learning scenarios. J Univ Comput Sci 14(17):2859–2876

[BSM12]   Burbaite R, Stuikys V, Marcinkevicius R (2012) The LEGO NXT robot-based e-learn-
            ing environment to teach computer science topics. Elektronika Elektrotechnika 18
            (9):113–116
[BSS+12]   Bargel BA, Schröck J, Szentes D, Roller W (2012) Using learning maps for visuali-
            zation of adaptive learning path components. Int J Comput Inform Syst Ind Manag
            Appl 4(1):228–235
[BVV+10]   Butoianu V, Vidal P, Verbert K, Duval E, Broisin J (2010) User context and person-
            alized learning: a federation of contextualized attention metadata. J Univ Comput Sci
            16(16):2252–2271
[CCO+15]   Catlin D, Csizmadia AP, OMeara JG, Younie S (2015) Using educational robotics
            research to transform the classroom. In: RiE 2015: 6th international conference on
            robotics in education
[CH06]   Czarnecki K, Helsen S (2006) Feature-based survey of model transformation
            approaches. IBM Syst J 45(3):621–645
[CML16]   Chachashvili-Bolotin S, Milner-Bolotin M, Lissitsa S (2016) Examination of factors
            predicting secondary students' interest in tertiary STEM education. Int J Sci Educ 38
            (3):366–390
[DBC+10]   Das M, Bhaskar M, Chithralekha T, Sivasathya S (2010) Context aware e-learning
            system with dynamically composable learning objects. Int J Comput Sci Eng 2
            (4):1245–1253
[Dey01]   Dey AK (2001) Understanding and using context. Pers Ubiquit Comput 5(1):4–7
[DG16]   DiGiacomo DK, Gutiérrez KD (2016) Relational equity as a design tool within making
            and tinkering activities. Mind Cult Act 23(2):141–153
[DGL+14]   Dutta-Moscato J, Gopalakrishnan V, Lotze MT, Becich MJ (2014) Creating a pipeline
            of talent for informatics: STEM initiative for high school students in computer science,
            biology, and biomedical informatics. J Pathol Inform 5(1):12
[DHL+14]   Duran M, Höft M, Lawson DB, Medjahed B, Orady EA (2014) Urban high school
            students' IT/STEM learning: findings from a collaborative inquiry-and design-based
            afterschool program. J Sci Educ Technol 23(1):116–137
[Dou04]   Dourish P (2004) What we talk about when we talk about context. Pers Ubiquit
            Comput 8:19–30, Feb. 2004
[Ear15]   Earp J (2015) Game making for learning: a systematic review of the research literature.
            In: Proceedings of 8th international conference of education, research and innovation
            (ICERI2015). pp 6426–6435
[EE14]   Esmaeili M, Eydgahi A (2014) The relationship of active learning based courses and
            student motivation for pursuing STEM classes. In: Proceedings of the ASEE 2014
            zone1 conference, Bridgeport, CT, USA
[Egu14]   Eguchi A (2014) Robotics as a learning tool for educational transformation. In:
            Proceeding of 4th international workshop teaching robotics, teaching with robotics &
            5th international conference robotics in education Padova (Italy)
[Egu14a]   Eguchi A (2014) Educational robotics for promoting 21st century skills. J Autom Mob
            Robot Intell Syst 8(1):5–11
[Egu15]   Eguchi A (2015) Educational robotics as a learning tool for promoting rich environ-
            ments for active learning (REALs). Handbook of research on educational technology
            integration and active learning. IGI Global, Hershey, pp 19–47
[Egu16]   Eguchi (2016) Computational thinking with educational robotics. In: Proceedings of
            the society for information technology & teacher education international conference
[FM02]   Fagin BS, Merkle L (2002) Quantitative analysis of the effects of robots on introduc-
            tory Computer Science education. J Educ Resour Comput (JERIC) 2(4):2
[FMT15]   Freeman B, Marginson S, Tytler R (2015) Widening and deepening the STEM effect.
            The age of STEM: educational policy and practice across the world in science,
            technology, engineering and mathematics. Routledge, New York, pp 1–21
[FPA+08]   Frangou S, Papanikolaou K, Aravecchia L, Montel L, Ionita S, Arlegui J, ... Monfalcon
            S (2008) Representative examples of implementing educational robotics in school

based on the constructivist approach. In: SIMPAR workshop on teaching with robotics: didactic approaches and experiences, Venice, Italy

[Gan15] Gander W (2015) Informatics–new basic subject. Bull EATCS 2(116)

[GB11] Grabowski LM, Brazier P (2011) Robots, recruitment, and retention: Broadening participation through CS0. In: Frontiers in education conference (FIE), 2011. IEEE, pp F4H-1

[GHV15] Gallagher C, Huang K, Van Matre J (2015) STEM learning opportunities providing equity (SLOPE): an investing in innovation (i3) grant. Final evaluation report. WestEd, San Francisco

[GL11] Gerndt R, Lüssem J (2011) Mixed-reality robotics-a coherent teaching framework. In: Proceedings of 2nd international conference on robotics in education (RiE). p 193–200

[GMB+14] Gamse BC, Martinez A, Bozzi L, Didriksen H (2014) Defining a research agenda for STEM corps: working white paper. Abt Associates, Cambridge, MA

[HBM+15] Hloupis G, Bimpikas V, Stavrakas I, Moutzouris K, Stergiopoulos C, Triantis D (2015) Developing open source dataloggers for inquiry learning

[Hig14] Highfield K (2014) Stepping into STEM with young children: simple robotics and programming as catalysts for early learning. Technology and digital media in the early years: tools for teaching and learning. Routledge, New York, p 150

[Hol14] Holmquist S (2014) A multi-case study of student interactions with educational robots and impact on Science, Technology, Engineering, and Math (STEM) learning and attitudes

[HSK09] Hong JY, Suh EH, Kim SJ (2009) Context-aware systems: a literature review and classification. Expert Syst Appl 36(4):8509–8522

[JD16] Jenson J, Droumeva M (2016) Exploring media literacy and computational thinking: a game maker curriculum study. Electron J e-Learning 14(2):111–121

[JGK+07] Jovanović J, Gašević D, Knight C, Richards G (2007) Ontologies for effective use of context in e-learning settings. Educ Technol Soc 10(3):47–59

[KCH+90] Kang KC, Cohen SG, Hess JA, Novak WE, Peterson AS (1990) Feature-oriented domain analysis (FODA) feasibility study (No. CMU/SEI-90-TR-21). Carnegie-Mellon Univ, Software Engineering Inst, Pittsburgh

[KJ09] Kim SH, Jeon JW (2009) Introduction for freshmen to embedded systems using LEGO Mindstorms. IEEE Trans Educ 52(1):99–108

[KK16] Kelley TR, Knowles JG (2016) A conceptual framework for integrated STEM education. Int J STEM Educ 3(1):1–11

[KKY+15] Kim C, Kim D, Yuan J, Hill RB, Doshi P, Thai CN (2015) Robotics to promote elementary education pre-service teachers' STEM engagement, learning, and teaching. Comput Educ 91:14–31

[KKK+07] Kurebayashi S, Kanemune S, Kamada T, Kuno Y (2007) The effect of learning programming with autonomous robots for elementary school students. In: 11th European logo conference. p 46

[KLM15] Karim ME, Lemaignan S, Mondada F (2015) A review: can robots reshape K-12 STEM education? In: Advanced robotics and its social impacts (ARSO), 2015 I.E. international workshop on. IEEE, p 1–8

[KME+14] Kay JS, Moss JG, Engelman S, McKlin T (2014) Sneaking in through the back door: introducing K-12 teachers to robot programming. In: Proceedings of the 45th ACM technical symposium on computer science education. ACM, pp 499–504

[LCW+09] Liu L, Chen H, Wang H, Zhao C (2009) Construction of a student model in contextually aware pervasive learning. In: Pervasive computing (JCPC), 2009 Joint conferences on PC. IEEE, pp 511–514

[LK10] Lee K, Kang KC (2010) Usage context as key driver for feature selection. In: Bosch J, Lee J (eds) SPLC, LNCS, vol 6287. Springer, Berlin, pp 32–46

[LKS+07] Lee SB, Kim JW, Song CY, Baik DK (2007) An approach to analyzing commonality and variability of features using ontology in a software product line engineering. In: Software engineering research, management & applications, SERA 2007. 5th ACIS international conference on. IEEE, pp 727–734

[MBS15]   Mentzer N, Becker K, Sutton M (2015) Engineering design thinking: high school students' performance and knowledge. J Eng Educ 104(4):417–432

[MJ10]   Man H, Jin Q (2010) Putting adaptive granularity and rich context into learning objects. In: Information technology based higher education and training (ITHET), 2010 9th international conference on. pp 140–145

[MK14]   Misirli A, Komis V (2014) Robotics and programming concepts in early childhood education: a conceptual framework for designing educational scenarios. In: Research on e-Learning and ICT in education. Springer, New York. pp 99–118

[MKS10]   Mbendera AJ, Kanjo Ch, Sun L (2010) Towards development of personalized knowledge construction model for e-LeaRrning. In: 2nd intern conf. on mobile, hybrid, and On-Line learning. IEEE, pp 29–35

[NLS16]   Nelson TH, Lesseig K, Slavit D (2016) Making sense of "STEM education" in K-12 context. Paper presented at the 2016 NARST international conference Baltimore, MD

[PS04]   Pitkanen SH, Silander P (2004) Criteria for pedagogical reusability of learning objects enabling adaptation and individualised learning processes. In: Proceedings of IEEE international conference advanced learning technologies. pp 246–250

[Rob15]   Robertson C (2015) Restructuring high school science curriculum: a program evaluation

[SGW16]   Sochacka NW, Guyotte K, Walther J (2016) Learning together: a collaborative autoethnographic exploration of STEAM (STEM+ the arts) education. J Eng Educ 105(1):15–42

[SH16]   Sullivan FR, Heffernan J (2016) Robotic construction kits as computational manipulatives for learning in the STEM disciplines. J Res Technol Educ 48(2):105–128

[SPA07]   Sklar E, Parsons S, Azhar MQ (2007) Robotics across the curriculum. In: AAAI spring symposium: semantic scientific knowledge integration. pp 142–147

[SRS+09] Southwest Regional STEM Network (2009) Southwest Pennsylvania STEM network long range plan (2009–2018): plan summary. Southwest Regional STEM Network, Pittsburgh, p 15

[ŠBB+17] Štuikys V, Burbaitė R, Blažauskas T, Barisas D, Binkis M (2017) Model for introducing STEM into high school computer science education. Int J Eng Educ 33 (5):1684–1698

[ŠBB+16] Štuikys V, Burbaitė R, Bespalova K, Ziberkas G (2016) Model-driven processes and tools to design robot-based generative learning objects for computer science education. Sci Comput Program 129:48–71

[Štu15]   Štuikys V (2015) Smart learning objects for smart education in computer science. Springer, New York

[TLL10]   Tong MW, Liu QT, Liu XN (2010) A service context model based on ontology for content adaptation in E-learning. In: Frontiers in education conference (FIE), pp. S1D-1, the following terminological issues IEEE

[VMO+12] Verbert K, Manouselis N, Ochoa X, Wolpers M, Drachsler H, Bosnic I, Duval E (2012) Context-aware recommender systems for learning: a survey and future challenges. In: Learning technologies, IEEE transactions on. pp 318–335

[Win01]   Winograd T (2001) Architectures for context. Hum-Comput Interact 16(2):401–419

[WKK+07] Weingarten JD, Koditschek DE, Komsuoglu H, Massey C (2007) Robotics as the delivery vehicle: a contexualized, social, self-paced, engineering education for life-long learners

[ZGK13]   Zalewski J, Gonzalez F, Kenny R (2013) Creating research opportunities with robotics across the undergraduate STEM curricula. Age 24:1

[ZLO07]   Zimmermann A, Lorenz A, Oppermann R (2007) An operational definition of context, proc. sixth int. and interdisciplinary conf. modeling and using Context (CONTEXT '07). Springer, Heidelberg, pp 558–571

Chapter 3
Smart Devices and Educational Robotics as Technology for STEM Knowledge

Abstract This chapter deals with integrative aspects of STEM in CS education from the technological perspective. Here, we focus on the available platforms of smart devices, mainly educational robots, and discuss the way on how educational robotics serves for delivery of the interdisciplinary knowledge. In addition, we discuss architectural aspects of educational robots and introduce a generic architecture to build a technological part of the smart educational environments to teach CS.

3.1 Introduction

Today industry supplies many high-tech facilities for general use and educational purposes. Among those are smart devices. Typically, by smart devices we mean those that have some autonomy to perform various actions. In general, this category of devices includes smart phones, cameras and a variety of sensors to integrate them into other smart devices, such as smart educational robots, microcontrollers, Internet-of-Things technologies, etc.

Among smart devices, robots play an extremely significant role in education due to their "smart functionality". Indeed, robotics in education is an exciting approach entailing the possibility to demonstrate various tasks and situations taken from the real world. Educational robots are indeed smart and therefore are so widely used in the field. The robot is able to perform a mechanical job without or with little human interference. On the other hand, it contains within units to perform computations and control tasks to support mechanical actions. Therefore, it is possible to treat the robot as a dedicated computer with memory and processor, the main units of a conventional computer. For a long time in education, computers have been in use in the mode *use-as-is* (except perhaps specific electronics courses). Similarly, in many cases, we use educational robots in that mode. However, typically robots have a modular structure enabling teachers and students to assemble the whole architecture from the available parts. This activity, in fact, means the use of the pedagogical approach known in the literature under a generic term *learning-by-doing*, though there are other terms such as a *constructivist* approach. Based on this activity, it is possible to extend highly the space for introducing the interdisciplinary STEM

© Springer International Publishing AG, part of Springer Nature 2018
V. Štuikys, R. Burbaitė, *Smart STEM-Driven Computer Science Education*,
https://doi.org/10.1007/978-3-319-78485-4_3

knowledge. Therefore, both modes fit well to implement the STEM paradigm. In addition, we are able to achieve objectives of computer science (CS) education.

The aim of this chapter is to reveal the possibility to deal with integrative aspects of both CS and STEM deeper than we did that in Chap. 2, i.e. we consider the topic from the technological perspective. Here, we focus on the available platforms of smart devices, mainly educational robots, and discuss the way on how educational robotics serves for the delivery of the interdisciplinary knowledge. In addition, we discuss architectural aspects of smart educational robots and introduce a generic architecture to build smart educational environments to teach CS.

The remaining part of this chapter includes the related work (Sect. 3.2), introducing robotics into STEM-driven CS education (Sect. 3.3), educational robot generic architecture (Sect. 3.4), conceptual model of the STEM-driven environment (Sect. 3.5) and discussion and conclusion (Sect. 3.6).

3.2 Related Work

We start considering the related work by defining smart devices. They may play two roles, i.e. (1) as self-organized independent components and (2) as constituents of larger compounds such as robots, Internet-of-Things, etc. Typically, smart devices are those that have some autonomy to perform actions. They often have sensors and/or actuators to support communication with other devices to perform a variety of actions. The smart device paradigm originates from the RFID (radio frequency identifiers) and sensor world, where one adds information to a static sensor to enhance its functionality [SGH+15]. Nowadays the interconnected smart devices and other intelligent objects are components of the Internet-of-Things (IoT). The latter is a metaphor that envisions the connection of existing objects to ensure the universality of communication processes, to integrate any kind of digital data and content and to provide the unique identification of real or virtual objects that form architectures as a communicative glue among these components [SG08]. Therefore, the capabilities of smart devices include (1) communication, (2) sensing and actuating, (3) reasoning and learning, (4) identity and kind and (5) memory and status tracking [SGH+15]. The paper [HJL16] extends the characteristics and capabilities of smart devices as digitalized entities, enabling the constant connection to a network and including device concepts that embrace ubiquitous computing and artificial judgment. The paper [LRP+11] expands the concept of smart device by introducing key features of "smart object" using the so-called "I-S-A-D-N" specification. In this specification, "I" stands for *identity* and the storage of any other relevant data. The symbol "S" stands for *sensing* its physical condition and its situated environment. The notion "A" stands for *actuation* of internal or external devices. The notion "D" stands for *decision-making* and participation in controlling other devices or systems. Finally, "N" stands for *networking* to reach and receive information through a wired or wireless network. The papers [CP16, ZL16, UPB+16] describe smart devices in IoT applications in the context of smart computer science and engineering education.

Fig. 3.1 Educational robotic platforms: (**a**) iRobot Create® 2 [http://www.irobot.com]; (**b**) MarXbot [http://mobots.epfl.ch]; (**c**) Mindstorms NXT/EV3 [https://www.lego.com]; (**d**) MakeBlock [http://www.makeblock.com]; (**e**) Arduino Robot [https://store.arduino.cc]; (**f**) e-puck [http://www.gctronic.com]

There are two basic terms (robots and robotics). Typically, we define robot as a machine designed to execute one or more tasks automatically with the adequate speed and precision. There are as many different types of robots as there are tasks for them to perform. Typically, we define *robotics* as a broad field of engineering that involves the conception, design, manufacture and operation of robots. This field, in fact, overlaps with multiple disciplines such as electronics, computer science, artificial intelligence, mechatronics, nanotechnology and bioengineering [http:// whatis.techtarget.com/definition/robotics]. Educational robots belong to the specific category of smart devices dedicated to learning. They are cheap and simple in comparison to those used in industry. One may expect the following requirements, sorted by relevance, for robots used for educational purposes [APC+15]:

- *Cost* – robots should be as cheap as possible to overcome budget limitations and evaluate multi-robot applications (e.g. swarm robotics).
- *Energy autonomy* – robots should have a long battery life since they may have to operate long enough during development and experimentation.
- *Communication* – robots need to support wireless communication to increase the range of applications (e.g. multi-robot systems and networked robotics).
- *Sensory system* – robots should be equipped with some form of sensing capability to allow interaction between them and with their environment.
- *Processing* – robots need to be able to process information about other robots and the environment (e.g. sensing data) (Fig. 3.1).

Though they have a quite different external view, their internal structure is not much different. Therefore, for the further analysis, it is convenient to have a typical internal structure that we call a generic architecture.

According to [COM+16], robotics impacts STEM education in multiple aspects. Firstly, it is not only a tool for just enhancing education. It means much more. It revolutionizes K-12 STEM education. It has a direct impact on both formal and informal education. It enables to prepare and train a competitive workforce for the twenty-first century. Secondly, with regard to social aspects, social robots can boost the confidence and self-esteem of children from all socio-economic backgrounds, even in those families that may not appreciate the importance of STEM education or education of any kind. From the pedagogical perspective, robotics can make STEM courses more alive since students can build robots by themselves, to program robots, and therefore can learn directly from them. From the CS perspective, educational robotics fits well for contextualizing computing education because of the possibility to develop computational thinking and programming skills of learners.

With regard to those skills, the paper [RG–PJ+16] emphasizes the role of robotics learning environment on project-based learning because it creates a natural framework for multidisciplinary projects where technology and ICT meet art and humanities. This paper indicates also on a few problems for educators and instructors. They should have the necessary skill sets to overcome technical and conceptual problems related to hardware in use. In addition, teachers should familiarize themselves with the programming environment and other tools they are going to expose in a classroom.

The papers [KLM15, MRF+16] present detailed surveys of different technical characteristics of brick-based toolkits of educational robots. The paper [Pla13] introduces ontology for robot programming domain. This paper, in essence, brings a methodology to consider the interdisciplinary education based on using robots, though indirectly. The proposed ontology consists of nine sub-ontologies. (1) Core sub-ontology defines a robot and its environment. (2) Algorithms sub-ontology covers a set of algorithms used by the robot. (3) Actions sub-ontology defines the actions that the robot performs. (4) Communication sub-ontology defines types for the robot communication. (5) Sensors sub-ontology covers all sensors that could be connected to the robot. (6) Missions sub-ontology describes the tasks performed by the robot. (7) Location sub-ontology defines spatial properties of the robot as "physical thing". (8) Time sub-ontology presents temporal properties of the robot. (9) Grapheme sub-ontology defines categories of the graphical data representation.

The paper [Ben12] emphasizes that most researchers work in the field of educational robotics and deal with problems such as (a) the use of robotics as an educational tool, (b) empirical testing of the effectiveness of robots and (c) defining future perspectives of the use of the robots. A great deal of applications is "descriptive in nature, based on reports of teachers achieving positive outcomes with individual initiatives" [Ben12]. The paper also summarizes the educational potential of robotics in schools and concludes as follows: (a) "most of the studies found are concentrated in areas related to robotics" per se (i.e. robot construction, mechatronics, robot programming); (b) a predominance of the use of Lego robots is observed (90%); (c) robotics increases achievements in STEM concept areas. The paper [AK17] suggests using robots as educational tools that influence students' interests in STEM. The papers [AD16, J–JA17] show that robotics supports development of skills of computational thinking. Kasempsap [Kas17] presents an overview of robotics including its importance in the modern education. The paper [KS16] evaluates the impact of robotics on students' technical and social skills and scientific attitude.

On the other hand, we can treat the STEM-driven approach and its principles as a part of smart education that focuses on smart devices and intelligent technologies to ensure more effective and flexible learning [ZYR16]. Parker et al. [PSB+15] introduce an expanded framework that covers four aspects of technology implementation in STEM classrooms. That includes (1) the type of technology used, (2) the degree of alignment to STEM practices, (3) the use of learner-centered pedagogical approaches and (4) the degree of relevance to real-world contexts. These researchers identified three groups of the technology applications:

1. STEM workplace technology applications such as computer modelling and simulations, computer programming, engineering design and robotics. These technologies are common in STEM fields, but not common in classrooms.
2. Ubiquitous technology applications commonly used in STEM and other work-places and contexts include numerical data analysis, information presenting, web-based information retrieval and word processing.
3. Instructional technology applications designed specifically for assessing and instructing purposes.

3.3 Introducing Robotics in STEM-Driven CS Education

What is the way to introduce robotics in STEM-driven CS education problem? In our view, robot programming ontology is highly helpful in this context. We have adapted this ontology from [Pla13]. It contains series of sub-ontologies such as those outlined in Table 3.1. We define the role of each sub-ontology and its relevance to STEM education to teach CS. Sub-ontologies cover the most essential aspects to discover and integrate the interdisciplinary STEM knowledge. We split this knowledge into a set of separate components (S, T, E, M) as we have identified them in Chap. 2. Different sub-ontologies may define the same type of knowledge, though it represents the other aspects. For example, *core* and *communication* sub-ontologies are relevant for introducing the "pure" T-knowledge, while others (such as *actions* and *missions*) relate to the integrative knowledge.

Table 3.1 Robot programming ontology adapted to our STEM vision

Sub-ontology	Role definition	Relevance to STEM
Core	Defines robot and its environment	T-knowledge
Algorithms	Covers a set of algorithms used by the robot	S (CS)-programming knowledge
Actions	Defines the actions that the robot performs	S (CS)-programming knowledge
		E-T-knowledge
Communication	Defines the capabilities of robot communication	T-knowledge
Sensors	Covers all sensors that could be connected to the robot	E-T-knowledge
Missions	Describes the tasks performed by robots	S(CS, physics)-T-E-M
Location	Defines spatial properties of the robot as "physical thing" or "physical LO"	S(CS, physics)-T-E-M

Table 3.1, in fact, presents possibilities, but not real actions to introduce integrated knowledge. The real knowledge comes through practice in using robots. Our practice includes the following assumptions and attributes.

The initial concepts relate to providing CS (programming) knowledge. We introduce the integrative STEM knowledge gradually in the step-by-step manner. From the perspective of robot usage modes, we use a top-down approach, i.e. beginners use the robot in the mode use-as-is with the focus on programming aspects with a surface interdisciplinary knowledge.

From the pedagogical perspective, this approach ensures a higher level of motivation and engagement in learning. In addition, our experience and practice confirmed the initial assumption that students become motivated to raise and solve problems by themselves. This, in fact, is about the cognitive transformation in terms of the level of the gained knowledge. This is the way to move from the surface interdisciplinary knowledge to the "deeper" knowledge.

In Table 3.2, we connect the student knowledge level, STEM knowledge and pedagogical approaches with the robot usage mode and robot platforms.

Aiming at extending the scope of STEM knowledge, we use several robot platforms. In most cases, for the beginners, it is enough to use one or two platforms taken from the list (e.g. Lego Mindstorms, Makeblock, Arduino Robot, Raspberry Pi). We explain the need of introducing different platforms by the following reasons. Lego Mindstorms is the user-friendly platform. It supports different programming languages such as RobotC, Java and the Lego graphical programming language. Therefore, it is the most popular platform used in education. It fits well for CS and other STEM-related subjects (physics, engineering) too. However, this platform suffers from some functional limitation such as a variety of components (motors, sensors) and limitation of stability when robot is constructed. On the other hand, sensibility of sensors is higher, within the Makeblock platform, and therefore the construction is more stable.

The discriminating feature of the Arduino Robot is that there is a richer list of sensors, the possibility to add new components (sensors, LEDs, Buttons, etc.). However, its mechanical construction lacks of flexibility to introduce changes in the construction.

The above-mentioned platforms are *kits*. They fit better for the beginners and for learners of the intermediate level. In our view, for education of advanced learners, the *open platform suite* is the best. By open platforms, we mean the sets of different actuators (motors), sensors, microcontrollers (microprocessors) and mechanical parts. What components to include into the open platform, that depends on the task or a set of tasks. This approach, however, requires additional efforts and skills in electronics, in modelling and in constructing. Therefore, this brings a broader and deeper STEM knowledge. As a result, we prefer to use a variety of kits and open platforms.

Note that, in our approach, students starting robot programming already understand the basic concepts of programming, though the other vision is also possible.

Table 3.2 Robot usage practice in relation to the student knowledge level

#	Student knowledge level	Robot usage mode	Robot platforms	STEM knowledge delivered	Pedagogical methods
1	Beginner	Use-as-is, robot as physical LO	Mindstorms	S-programming	Problem-based
			Arduino Robot	T-component physical interfacing	Inquiry-based
			Makeblock	M-calculation of optimal component parameter values based on real experiment	
2	Intermediate	Constructing the robot from available parts (components) using the only one platform	Mindstorms	S-programming, physics	Problem-based
			Arduino Robot	T-component physical interfacing	Inquiry-based
		Mode 1: adding new components to the predesigned structure		E-constructing	Design-based
		Mode 2: constructing from scratch using guides	Makeblock	M-calculation of optimal component parameter values based on real experiment	
3	Advanced	Robot construction/ functionality modelling using multiple platforms	Mindstorms Arduino Robot Makeblock	S-programming, physics	Problem-based
			Raspberry Pi	T-component physical interfacing and modelling	Inquiry-based
				E-modelling and constructing	Design-based
				M-modelling and calculation of optimal component parameter values based on real experiment	Project-based

For example, it is possible to introduce programming concepts using the domain-specific languages (i.e. RobotC, ArduinoC) at the very beginning. In our view, the first case is more effective due to the separation and integration of concepts. On the other hand, there is a great similarity among syntax of different languages (both for domain-specific languages and of general programming languages).

3.4   Educational Robot Generic Architecture

Figure 3.2 shows a *generic architecture* of the educational robot. It is a result of generalizing three platforms: the Lego Intelligent Brick, Arduino Uno and Raspberry Pi. The generic architecture includes four basic units: *inputs, outputs, processing* and *communication*. Each unit consists of a set of components. For example, the *inputs* consist of sensors, buttons and joysticks and may have other components. The set of components within this unit serves for delivering initial information (signals) to initiate the working state of the other units. This information comes from the robot's environment either automatically as signals of sensors or semiautomatically by manual pushing on the control buttons. The outputs consist of a set of motors for ensuring robot's motions and components such as LCD and LEDs to visualize the results of the robot's action after solving a particular task. Note that typically the robot's motion should vary (with regard to the direction, speed, etc.) during the process of solving even the same task. Therefore, to ensure those capabilities, there is the need of having a set of motors.

The *processing unit*, depending on the platform used, may have specific names such as Lego Intelligent Brick, Arduino Uno or Raspberry Pi. Finally, the *communication* unit ensures the physical connections and logical links among the inputs, outputs and processing units.

Therefore, the robot's architecture defines the robot's structure. It is the first item needed to understand the robot's functionality. Students are able not only to view the architecture, i.e. how it looks in the picture, but also to have its components on the table for a more thorough examination. In that part, students use the robot as a physical learning object (PLO) and are able to examine the functionality of separate components and the whole architecture, for example, after constructing it from units and components. The main objective for the teacher is to apply the best way in obtaining STEM-based knowledge by students.

Fig. 3.2 Generic architecture of an educational robot

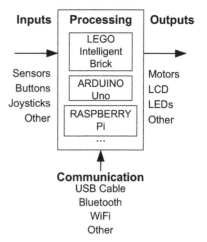

The second item a student needs to learn is a robot control program (RCP). Similarly, here we also have two processes: the RCP development and use (compare both processes with the PLO construction and use). Those processes, similar to analysis of the PLO, are very rich in the possibility to provide the STEM-based knowledge. In developing RCPs, the typical requirement is modifiability, adaptability and reusability. Furthermore, the currently available design methodologies and tools enable to automatize the processes. This is the addition source and extra possibility of the STEM-based knowledge.

Typically, as different tasks require different robot's actions, each RCP is task specific, though RCPs of different tasks may have common parts. RCPs, after integrating them into the robot' architecture (more precisely into the flash memory of the processing unit), predefine the whole functionality of a robot-based educational environment. On the other hand, there is a long way to achieve the status of a correct functioning of the educational environment. This is a concern of both the teacher and students. Pursuing this goal, teacher and students need to move together (of course, with regard to prescribed responsibilities) through multiple activities identified as possible scenarios (see also Fig. 2.2 in Chap. 2). The result of these activities is the creation of the robot-based educational environment. The latter is the basis of the smart educational environment. In the next section, we present a model of such an environment.

3.5 Conceptual Model of STEM-Driven Environment

In this section, we introduce a conceptual model of the smart educational environment. This model is a prototype of the real environment we discuss in detail in Chap. 12. The model gives a simplified picture of the real environment and therefore serves as a means to achieve the prescribed aim of this chapter. The robot-based environment is a key component of the classroom workplace.

The model (see Fig. 3.3) consists of four interrelated components. The STEM-driven workplace contains within two components, i.e. user's PC and robot-based

Fig. 3.3 Conceptual model of smart educational environment for STEM-driven CS education

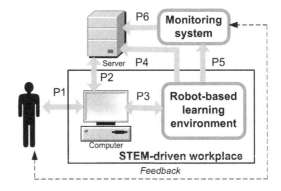

learning environment. The user's PC stands for interfacing with and managing of educational resources and serves as a tool to support learning activities. The role of the robot-based environment is to implement real-world tasks. In fact, the internal structure of the robot's environment represents the architecture of the system derived from the generic architecture (see Fig. 3.2), i.e. we use any indicated platform depending on the context. The external part of the model includes also two components, i.e. server and monitoring system. The latter stands for ensuring a feedback flexibly. In addition, its role is to transfer the selected data to the server. The role of the server is multi-facet. For example, it contains the knowledge base and the needed tools. We present the functionality of the model through processes P1–P6. Their roles are clear from the context. Note that we extend this model to the real smart educational environment we discuss in Chap. 12.

3.6 Discussion and Conclusion

In this chapter, we have discussed some technological aspects of educational robotics to support STEM-driven CS education. By introducing this topic, we have had the aim to extend the topics of the previous chapter and to show the way for introducing the STEM-related knowledge into CS (i.e. computer programming) education. We have adapted the known robot programming ontology to deliver the STEM-driven knowledge. In particular, we have chosen seven sub-ontologies (core, algorithms, actions, communication, sensors, missions and location) by identifying their role and the possibility to support in delivering the adequate knowledge. In addition, we have made the connection of this STEM-driven knowledge with possible robot platforms and student knowledge levels (beginner, intermediate, advanced). In doing so, we have analysed the most popular educational robot-based platforms and, on this basis, introduced a generic architecture. The latter serves for deriving the concrete architecture for the use in the real educational setting. The key aspect of this analysis is the proposed conceptual model we use later in the development of the smart STEM-driven educational environment.

References

[AD16]   Atmatzidou S, Demetriadis S (2016) Advancing students' computational thinking skills through educational robotics: a study on age and gender relevant differences. Robot Auton Syst 75:661–670
[AK17]   Afari E, Khine MS (2017) Robotics as an educational tool: impact of Lego Mindstorms. Int J Inf Educ Technol 7(6):437–442
[APC+15]   Araújo A, Portugal D, Couceiro MS, Rocha RP (2015) Integrating Arduino-based educational mobile robots in ROS. J Intell Robot Syst 77(2):281–298
[Ben12]   Benitti FBV (2012) Exploring the educational potential of robotics in schools: a systematic review. Comput Educ 58(3):978–988

[COM+16] Christensen HI, Okamura A, Mataric M, Kumar V, Hager G, Choset H (2016) Next generation robotics. arXiv preprint arXiv:1606.09205

[CP16] Charlton P, Poslad S (2016) A sharable wearable maker community IoT application. In: Intelligent Environments (IE), 2016 12th international conference on. IEEE, pp 16–23

[HJL16] Hong SO, Jung EJ, Lee SY (2016) Development of the A-STEAM type technological models with creative and characteristic contents for infants based on smart devices. Indian J Sci Technol 9(44):1–5

[J-JA17] Jaipal-Jamani K, Angeli C (2017) Effect of robotics on elementary preservice teachers' self-efficacy, science learning, and computational thinking. J Sci Educ Technol 26 (2):175–192

[Kas17] Kasemsap K (2017) Robotics: theory and applications. In: Cybersecurity breaches and issues surrounding online threat protection. IGI Global, Hershey, PA, pp 311–345

[KLM15] Karim ME, Lemaignan S, Mondada F (2015) A review: can robots reshape K-12 STEM education? In: Advanced Robotics and its Social Impacts (ARSO), 2015 I.E. International Workshop on. IEEE, pp 1–8

[KS16] Kandlhofer M, Steinbauer G (2016) Evaluating the impact of educational robotics on pupils' technical-and social-skills and science related attitudes. Robot Auton Syst 75:679–685

[LRP+11] López TS, Ranasinghe DC, Patkai B, McFarlane D (2011) Taxonomy, technology and applications of smart objects. Inf Syst Front 13(2):281–300

[MRF+16] Merino PP, Ruiz ES, Fernandez GC, Gil MC (2016) A wireless robotic educational platform approach. In: Remote Engineering and Virtual Instrumentation (REV), 2016 13th international conference on. IEEE, pp 145–152

[Pla13] Plauska I (2013) Ontology for robot programming domain. In: XV International PhD Workshop OWD

[PSB+15] Parker CE, Stylinski CD, Bonney CR, Schillaci R, McAuliffe C (2015) Examining the quality of technology implementation in STEM classrooms: demonstration of an evaluative framework. J Res Technol Educ 47(2):105–121

[RG-PJ+16] Rees A, García-Peñalvo FJ, Jormanainen I, Tuul M, Reimann D (2016) An overview of the most relevant literature on coding and computational thinking with emphasis on the relevant issues for teachers. TACCLE3 Consortium, Belgium

[SG08] Salzmann C, Gillet D (2008) From online experiments to smart devices. Int J Online Eng (iJOE) 4(LA-ARTICLE-2008-049):50–54

[SGH+15] Salzmann C, Govaerts S, Halimi W, Gillet D (2015) The smart device specification for remote labs. In: Remote engineering and virtual instrumentation (rev), 2015 12th international conference on. IEEE, pp 199–208

[UPB+16] Uskov V, Pandey A, Bakken JP, Margapuri VS (2016) Smart engineering education: the ontology of Internet-of-Things applications. In: Global Engineering Education Conference (EDUCON), 2016 IEEE. IEEE, pp 476–481

[ZL16] Zhong X, Liang Y (2016) Raspberry Pi: an effective vehicle in teaching the internet of things in computer science and engineering. Electronics 5(3):56

[ZYR16] Zhu ZT, Yu MH, Riezebos P (2016) A research framework of smart education. Smart Learn Environ 3(1):4

Part II
Methodological and Theoretical Background of Approaches to Implement the Proposed Vision

Part II consists of two chapters, i.e. Chaps. 4 and 5. Note that we aim at preserving the sequential numbering of chapters within each part of the book. This part introduces readers with two topics. We call them as methodological and theoretical backgrounds. They are essential for the in-depth understanding of our approach. As our approach to STEM education is reuse-driven, the backgrounds are from the same shelf too. Therefore, the first topic (discussed in Chap. 4) is about a systematic analysis of a domain under consideration with the focus on the *learning variability issues*. We argue that those issues predefine the success of introducing automation through component-based and generative reuse. Therefore, we discuss those issues as a *separate theme* separated from feature-based modelling, though in the other context, e.g. in SW engineering research, one needs to consider both together. We analyze variability as a separate theme from two perspectives, i.e. software engineering and e-Learning. We do that because of the following reasons. Firstly, variability is the methodological background for introducing automation with regard to the book's objectives. Secondly, the level of understanding the role of variability and its interpretation within both communities is different. Thirdly, variability in education is specific due to high heterogeneity of the domain. Therefore, we speak about *STEM learning variability* as a composite of variable aspects of different subdomains. In our view, learning variability deserves a far better recognition and exploration in the field of educational research as a separate theme. We introduce the STEM *learning variability model* resulting from the analysis and feature-based modelling. The STEM learning variability model covers integrative aspects or features discovered from heterogeneous subdomains (STEM pedagogy; sociology in a narrow sense, typically meaning learners behavior and profiles; technology, meaning robotics, software, tools; teaching content, meaning CS curricula). Note that Chap. 4 describes the role and representation aspects of the learning variability model only. The real variability models will appear in the adequate context in other chapters. The second topic we discuss in Chap. 5 covers two themes: (1) basics of feature-based modelling and (2) generative technology, i.e. basics of heterogeneous meta-programming. The first serves for the development of high-level specifications, i.e. for representing learning variability model(s), as well as for performing various transformations on those models. The second serves for the implementation of these models as executable lower-level specifications, meaning domain-specific program generators (aka meta-programs or meta-meta-programs). By these, we mean smart STEM-driven *content generators*, *STEM-driven scenarios generators*, and *generators to support maintainability of STEM-driven Personal Generative Libraries*. Note that in Chap. 5 we consider themes (1) and (2) *in separation* without showing actions of transforming feature-based variability models into meta-programming-based executable specifications. These are themes of subsequent chapters.

Chapter 4
A Methodological Background for STEM-Driven Reuse-Enhanced CS Education

Abstract In this chapter, we present a thorough analysis of variability-related research from two perspectives, i.e. software engineering and educational domains. On this basis, we introduce the concept of STEM learning variability in CS and its model. The STEM variability model enables to describe a high diversity and heterogeneity of the STEM-driven CS education domain semiformally. The model therefore stands for the methodological and conceptual background in achieving the goals of automation in our approach. We propose two approaches to deal with the variability issues. The first approach combines the context and base part variability at the early stage of the domain analysis. It treats variability as a common feature model. The second approach separates the context variability from the variability of the base functionality. It considers separate modelling of those variabilities. At the next design stage of this approach, we combine both variability models to form the common domain model. Aiming at easing the acceptance of learning variability by the educational community, we also introduce the motivating sample of feature diagrams to explain the capabilities of the feature-based notion to represent the STEM learning variability in adequate chapters.

4.1 Introduction

In this chapter, we present a methodological background of STEM-driven CS education. This background has its roots in the so-called *variability-related* research widely exploited in other domains, such as software engineering (SWE) [CBK13, GWT+14]. We do that because the *learning variability* stands for a methodological and conceptual basis in our STEM-driven approach. At the very beginning, the reader should accept the term *learning variability* as the property of high diversity and heterogeneity of the STEM domain. Later we define this term more specifically, i.e. we connect this property with the capabilities of automation. By automation, we mean automated design of the content to produce STEM-driven generic specifications, automated generation of the concrete content on demand from the generic

© Springer International Publishing AG, part of Springer Nature 2018   71
V. Štuikys, R. Burbaitė, *Smart STEM-Driven Computer Science Education*,
https://doi.org/10.1007/978-3-319-78485-4_4

specifications and the transformation of the generic specifications to support capabilities for adaptation and reuse. We discuss those issues in subsequent chapters. Here, we explore variability and learning variability in relation to the STEM-driven approach.

Note that typically there are two cases of using *variability*: as *a word* in everyday vocabulary and as *a term* in scientific works. In general, variability indicates on the property (visible or hidden) of items of the same category with multiple variants or values, and those values may vary or change over time. In SWE, for example, one understands variability as the ability of a software system or component of being changed to fit a specific context of use [BC05]. Variability is a fundamental concept. It formulates the design intent; it determines the roadmap for the development of techniques, tools and main instruments in the so-called software product line (SPL) approach (also known as a program family).

According to [GBS01], variability guides the definition of a product line, minimizing the cost of creating and evolving software products that compose a product family. Variability exposes the differences between the products with techniques based on the software reuse paradigm. Therefore, variability enables us to adapt the system's structure, behaviour or even underlying processes. As a term, however, variability has indeed an interdisciplinary nature and plays an extremely significant role in many fields such as psychology (e.g. cognition modes and models) [Sie94], biology (e.g. genetic variability of species) [LG93], mathematics (e.g. functions, variables, etc.), to name a few. However, different sciences may provide slightly different interpretations and variability measures. What are reasons of that popularity?

There are many reasons to explain that. The first is that the word expresses the essential property of an item, such as *categorization*, inherent to many domains ("there is nothing more basic than categorization to our thought, perception, action and speech" [Lak87]). The second reason is a relation to the other important terms such as *complexity*. Though both terms are not synonymous, there is an assumption that changes in variability are also influential to complexity. The complexity issues are extremely important in the context of the technological revolution and the need for interdisciplinary studies (e.g. in STEM). However, this is a separate topic not considered in this chapter. The next reason is the impact of variability on reuse, customization and adaptability of artefacts in designing and maintaining various systems, including educational systems. Finally, the term also has a broad social context, such as diversity of human behaviour, for example, in learning. The following extract illustrates that:

> *Specific learning causes changes – transitions from one state to another. Yet, the diversity of personal experience and representations implies different conditions at the outset for each person. In addition, modifications resulting from learning vary according to learning motivations, interactions and strategies. This is why the impact of instruction differs from one person to another and why we speak of variability.* [CER07]

In SWE, the variability-related research is extremely wide with a long history (more than 25 years). As this research is also highly influential to the e-Learning domain, especially in terms of creating educational tools and software, it is important to deal with on how it is possible to introduce the concept for studying it systematically in our approach.

The aim of this chapter is twofold. Firstly, we aim at analysing variability in general with the focus on two domains (SWE and education, i.e. e-Learning) in order to discover artefacts for the further exploration. Secondly, we aim at developing a framework for better understanding the *learning variability* and, relying on that, to create *the STEM variability model* as a methodological basis to implement our concepts and our vision to CS education using the STEM paradigm. The content within is organized similarly as in other chapters, and we start from analysis of the related work.

4.2 Related Work

Here, we analyse two domains: (a) software engineering (SWE) and (b) e-Learning. Our aim is to analyse how the researchers and practitioners understood and used the *variability-related* concepts across those domains.

4.2.1 Variability Research in SWE

In SWE, there is a variety of the related methodologies dealing with the variability issues in analysing, designing and maintaining systems. Due to the wideness of the topic, we restrict ourselves by discussing four methodologies here: software product lines (SPL) [PBL05], scope-commonality-variability (SCV) analysis [CHW98], component-based development (CBD) [KHC05] and systematic review, i.e. analysis of the literature on variability according to [GWT+14]. In the analysis, we focus mainly on the following aspects: definitions, variability taxonomies and dimensions, main mechanisms for variability representation and specification in designing systems. What is important to note is that a large portion of analysed works has the same conceptual and methodological basis – the understanding of a *domain* through analysis of its *feature variability*. Therefore, very often, it is possible to capture and represent the *commonality-variability* aspects within a domain abstractly using the *feature* notation. This notation was introduced by Kang et al. in their seminal work on feature-oriented domain analysis (FODA) [KCH+90] yet in 1990. Until now, this notation has prevailed in SWE research with multiple innovations and extensions introduced. Despite of this, however, there is no uniform definition of the term. On the contrary, now there are more than ten slightly different definitions of the term [AK09, BLR+15]. We present some of them below that are relevant to our context. A feature is "a logical unit of behaviour specified by a set of functional and non-functional requirements [AK09]" or "a distinguishable characteristic of a concept (system, component, etc.) that is relevant to some stakeholder of the concept" [CE00]. The paper [BLR+15] provides an investigation on a qualitative study of features in industrial SPLs and concludes: "One of the most important characteristics of a feature is that it needs to represent a *distinct and well-understood aspect* of the system".

A feature reflects the stakeholders' requirements. It is an increment in the product functionality and offers a configuration option [PBL05]. Given this definition for a feature, SPL engineering relies on the essential concepts of commonality and variability of features among products. This diversity is important from the methodological viewpoint. It tells us about the universality and commonality of the approaches in which the term stands for a conceptual basis. Therefore, a wide stream of research considers feature variability in the context of designing software product lines (SPL) or SPL engineering (SPLE). By SPL, it means a family of the related application programs that are built from the same set of reusable components. SWE Institute, for example, provides the following definition: "A software product line (SPL) is a set of software-intensive systems that share a common, managed set of features satisfying the specific needs of a particular market segment or mission and that are developed from a common set of core assets in a prescribed way". In this case, it is the main task to analyse and obtain variable features within "a common set of core assets". It is possible to plan and manage variability at different levels, ranging from the requirement elicitation and representing architectural design to coding with different feature characteristics such as quality. In this respect, variability refers to the ability of a system (artefact, asset, component, etc.) to be configured, customized, extended or changed for use and reuse in a specific context [BC05]. As it is with the term feature, variability also has a multiple interpretation and definitions. Variability identification and specification have been extensively studied in the context of domain analysis [AK09]. In that context, *commonality and variability* analysis aims at identifying common and varying attributes among systems that belong to the domain under consideration. The process results in creating the so-called *feature model*.

A feature model represents the information of all possible products of an SPL in terms of features and relationships among them. Feature models are a special type of the information model widely used in SPLE. A feature model represents a hierarchically arranged set of features. The set includes (i) relationships between a parent (or compound) feature and its child features (or sub-features) and (ii) cross-tree (or cross-hierarchy) constraints that are typically *inclusion* or *exclusion* statements. Their form is "*if feature F is included, then features A and B must also be included (or excluded)*" [BSR10]. Typically, we represent feature models by feature diagrams that have a tree structure, with features forming nodes of the tree (see also Sect. 4.3.2). Important attributes usually represented in a feature diagram are the relationship between features and variation points, the relationship among features and the feature binding time.

The scope-commonality-variability (SCV) methodology [CHW98], for example, uses the theory of sets for variability modelling and definition. The approach defines *commonality* as an assumption held uniformly across a given set of objects (S). Very often, such assumptions are attributes having the same values of S. In contrast to this, the approach defines *variability* as an assumption that is true for only some elements, or as an attribute with different values for at least two elements of *S*. Here, *the scope* is to be thought of as an extent to which commonality-variability pertains. The current understanding of variability issues is concerned with dynamic approaches to feature-based variability modelling [BQ15, CBK13] in the context of software development with the focus on automatic program generation [DMB16, JGS93]. As the variability issues are so important, there is an urgent need to conceptualize and generalize that. In this regard, the paper [KHC05] presents a formal view on variability in the context of component-based design (CBD). That includes precise definitions of variability-related terms, a classification of variability types. The authors argue that, on this basis, it is possible not only to provide the domain analysis but also to carry out the component customization more effectively and precisely. The paper makes a distinction among conventional variability and component-based variability.

Further, we focus on the extended variability terms and properties.

Variability Types: Functional Variability and Non-functional Variability. Typically, feature variability can be defined as the variation in the functional characteristics of a system or component. For example, a SW component can specify a variety of mathematical calculations such as *pi* value, *square root* of a number, etc. needed for other parts of the software. It is possible to evaluate the functional variability by the number of methods, attributes and subcomponents used within a component. Additionally, the interfaces of a component play a role of the functional variability for integration. On the other hand, when we focus on the integration aspects, it is more relevant to use the term *structural variability*. The latter is about the diversity in the structure of a system or component. Furthermore, the other non-functional characteristics such as performance, reliability, portability and security can also vary. In this case, we speak about *non-functional variability*. Typically, it is defined as the ability of a component to provide different levels of non-functional choices when conditions within the environment are changed. For example, the paper [MSR +16] considers the performance variability in the context of a mobile network base station product line with capacity variability. Though the modelling and management of structural variability remain at the focus, there is also *behaviour variability* based on using behavioural models in designing systems. They include used cases, activity models, state machines, etc. Therefore, by behaviour variability, it is meant the variation of the system's behaviour [CBT+14]. Note that behaviour variability is very close to functional variability. There is a subtle difference between these variability types. Behavioural variability is the functionality with *a time dimension* expressed explicitly (such as *the delay* in hardware circuits [GDD+13]) or implicitly (such as production processes [APM+14]).

Static and Dynamic Variability. Variability, to some extent, can be predefined and foreseen in advance. If one can accept that the variability space remains unchanged in its scope over time, we can speak about the static variability. The assumption on non-changeability may be true if we are able to introduce not only visible variation within the analysed domain but also foresee the possible variation that may occur in the future. However, most systems or domains evolve over time, and the prediction of their changeability is rarely being precise. The changes may be accidental and have a dynamic nature. The variability of the dynamic nature is dynamic variability. This kind of variability is researched in the so-called software dynamic product lines [CBT+14].

Base System Variability vs. *Context Variability.* In dealing with systems, it is a common practice to consider the base functionality or structure of a system and its context. In many cases, such as in the context-aware systems, context is highly influential to the base functionality. Therefore, it is convenient to exclude two types of variability: *base variability* and *context variability.* This distinction is due to two visions in modelling of systems. The first considers together both types of variability, while the second provides a separate modelling of the base functionality and its context. With the complexity growth of systems, the expansion of domains in which context awareness is a main concern, the second vision has a trend to dominate.

Variability Dimensions. The report [Wey14] and the paper [GWT+14] present two clusters of variability dimensions based on a systematic literature review: (1) variability types and (2) mechanisms on how does variability takes place or is brought about. The first includes:

* *Requirement types* (such as functional and quality)
* *Representation* (such as feature models, rules/conditions, variant labels/annotations profiles and change scenarios)
* *Artefact* (scenario, business process, architecture, component, code fragment, variable)
* *Orthogonality* (separated domain, integrated domain).

The second includes:

* *Trigger or source* (stakeholder, business process, system, environment)
* *Realization technique* (reorganization, selection, value assignment, code generation)
* *Time of binding* (software construction/evolution, runtime)
* *Automation* (manual, semiautomatic, automatic)

Variability Expression Levels. Typically, there are two basic levels for expressing variability: atomic, when we express variability through variants, variation points and relationships and systemic when we express variability through possible system configurations. More formally, in the treelike specification, a variation point is the parent, while variants of this variation point are children. In other words, variation point represents alternatives for the variant selection.

Variability Scope, Degree and Measures. Software variability, in fact, covers all life-cycle phases from requirements elicitation to system deployment and runtime [Wey14]. Therefore, in each phase, when the focus is the analysis and representation, it is possible to introduce a new variation point, to add variants and to introduce dependencies. Additionally, a specific variant can be bound to the variation point, and an already bound variant can be replaced with another variant. As, typically, we specify variability by features, it is possible to measure a degree of variability by the following feature-based characteristics: common feature count, feature type count, number of variation points and variants.

Variability Management. The paper [CBN09] introduces terms such as configuration, change, commonality and instantiation to define the context of software variability. Authors also introduce the notion "variability management" as the act of managing dependencies among different variabilities and supporting their instantiations. According to [GBS01], the variability management is the process composed of such activities as:

- *Variability identification* (i.e. identifying the product differences and their location within the PL artefacts)
- *Variability delimitation* (that defines the binding time and multiplicity)
- *Variability implementation* (i.e. the selection of implementation mechanisms)
- *Variant management* (i.e. controls of the variants and variation points)

4.2.2   Variability in Learning

In e-Learning, discussions on the variability are even broader and more diverse. It is so, because this domain is highly heterogeneous and consists of at least three subdomains: pedagogy-related (including social subdomain), technology-related and content-related. Very often, however, researchers use the term variability in a general sense without the explicit definition, or they use other terms as synonymous (e.g. *diversity*). Here, a very popular approach is to define the variability by enumerating a fixed list of possible *variants*, such as cognition levels or categories in taxonomies (Bloom's, Solo), levels of student previous knowledge and abilities (*high*, *good*, *intermediate*), etc. Another important issue is that social-oriented variability is highly specific and relates to psychological aspects, such as cognitive abilities. One part of the social variability is easily identifiable (such as age, diversity in social groups, etc.). The other part is hidden, such as cognitive abilities.

The study [BNA15], for example, examines the learners' self-efficacy variability during learning. The aim is to determine how that relates to their problem-solving performance and behaviour. The other paper [PJK13] proposes a model of problem-solving times to include variability of students' performance and students' learning during a sequence of problem-solving tasks. The paper [NSG08] considers the variability of learning strategies in perception of learning environments by students and on this basis discusses differences in variability of learning between the restricted and variable clusters to explain the impact of learning environment perceptions. Chapter 10 of the book [GB08] emphasizes the importance and difficulties in understanding the variability issues in learning statistics courses. There are two aspects in understanding variability: informal (such as data variation, e.g. differences in data values) and formal measures (such as range, interquartile and standard deviation). While students can learn how to compute these formal measures, they rarely understand what they represent and how they relate to other statistical concepts.

The project UDL (Universal Design for Learning) [UDL16] is "a framework for curriculum design that minimizes barriers and maximizes learning for all students by taking *diversity into account*". In a wider context, the project UDL deals with the following variability aspects in learning:

- Multiple means of representing information (i.e. technology and content)
- Multiple means of action and expression to allow students to approach tasks in different ways (i.e. social aspects and content)
- Multiple means of engagement to keep students interested and motivated (i.e. pedagogy and social aspects)

The paper [HPN+13] maps out the syntax and functional similarity of the submissions in order to explore the variation in solutions given by the huge number of students in teaching machine learning within the MOOC (Massive Open Online Courses) paradigm.

4.2.2.1   Feature-Based Variability in Learning

For a long time, researchers were seeking to introduce approaches borrowed from software engineering in designing educational software. An evident example is the effort to introduce and apply model-driven approaches into e-Learning. The earlier works are [DD06 and DZF+07]. One can find a more extensive study on that topic in [Štu15]. According to [Dam09, ŠDB+08], there are at least three reasons why feature models (FMs also FDs-feature diagrams) are beneficial for the LO domain [Dam09].

1. *Methodological.* In the development of learning objects (LOs), there is the need for specification of requirements and provided services at a higher level of abstraction. Because FMs are graphical languages, which are domain-independent and independent of the implementation technology of LOs, the language stands for a tool for specifying and modelling. In contrast to the UML notation, the syntax and semantics of FDs are simpler and easier to learn by different stakeholders (course designers, course experts, teachers and learners, etc.). On the other hand, FDs are useful to promote reusability and interoperability in analysis, sharing and distributing of knowledge related to LOs. In addition, FDs can contribute to the formation of the formal theory of LOs.

2. *Ontology-based knowledge representation.* LO is a breakdown of a teaching content into small chunks that we are able to reuse in various learning environments [Wil00]. When reused, it is possible to combine such knowledge chunks of the content in various ways leading to a composition of complex relationships that one can interpret as domain ontology. In the e-Learning domain as well as in various other domains (e.g. computer science, information science, artificial intelligence), an ontology is usually understood as a data model that represents a set of concepts within a domain and the relationships between those concepts.

For example, OMG [OMG03] defines ontology as "common terms and concepts (meaning) used to describe and represent an area of knowledge". Specifically, an ontology-based model is a form of knowledge representation about the world or some part of it. It is used to reason about the objects within that domain. As a feature can be treated as a chunk of knowledge to be learnt using LOs, FDs contribute to the explicit structuring of learning content (chunks of knowledge) at the different level of abstraction. FDs allow expressing the representation of relationships between basic knowledge chunks (features) explicitly, thus they relate to the representation of knowledge and may contribute to better understanding and perception. Knowledge of the LO is usually represented using some knowledge-based approach, such as ontology trees of LOs [BN04]. Domain ontologies, where domain knowledge is represented as ontology trees, have some syntactic and conceptual resemblance with feature hierarchies represented using FDs. However, FDs have weaker capabilities to express various relationships in representing knowledge [CKK06]. Therefore, FDs currently can be used for representation of lightweight ontologies only.

3. *Variability management.* LOs are complex entities entailing many different aspects with a great deal of variants. FDs allow expressing and grasping the common and variable features of LOs explicitly. Variability is especially important for the representation and development of the generative LOs [DŠ08, BLC04]. FDs also can be used for modelling LO product lines [PS06].

A large body of recent studies relates to using the SPL approach and feature-based models. The paper [GBR+14] analyses the issues in the development and use of learning management systems and suggests the use of SPL for the development of e-Learning applications. The approach allows overcoming the limitations of LMS systems and, on the other side, enables to provide institutions with e-Learning applications that fit their own requirements. The paper also presents different steps of the development process of an e-Learning product line, focusing on domain engineering. The process results in creating a set of core assets such as (1) the domain requirements documented by the feature model; (2) the reference architecture models, including variability presented by OVM model; and (3) the software components for reuse.

The paper [CN13] summarizes experiences of mining a SPL from nine existing e-Learning systems developed at nine different locations by nine different teams following nine varied development processes over a decade. The goal of this family is to address 287 million adult illiterates in India spread across 22 Indian languages. This presents a unique and challenging situation as SPL arises from a societal context rather than a business context as in traditional SPL. The work [LB15] presents an SPL derivation process based on model-driven architecture (MDA) concepts. The main idea is to represent each step of application engineering in the SPL with a model of MDA starting from requirement engineering until the product, i.e. e-Learning system implementation.

The paper [LPC+15] explores an approach that supports reuse and customization following product line engineering principles and tools. The approach uses product line-based document engineering tools to create the so-called learning object authoring tool (LOAT), which supports the development of learning materials following the Cisco's Reusable Information Object strategy. The paper also describes the principles behind LOAT, outlines its design, and gives clues about how it may be used by instructors to create learning objects in their own disciplines. The paper [EGJ+11] applies variability modelling techniques based on using feature models for representing and validating students' knowledge. The paper [BGP14] describes how to develop product line family for applications called e-Learning Web Minor that aims at extracting knowledge from the activity data stored on e-Learning platforms given in the form of rules and patterns. The paper [GBR+14] analyses social aspects, such as customer satisfaction through e-Learning software product line. One can learn variability aspects in the context of MOOC from the sources [HPN+13].

4.2.2.2   Social Variability, Inclusive Teaching and STEM

According to [RJL+06], inclusive teaching represents "a set of principles, goals, and practices grounded in research, experience, and commitments to social justice". Inclusive teaching strategies, as defined by the Center for Teaching Excellence (Cornell University, USA), refer to "any number of teaching approaches that address the needs of students with a variety of backgrounds, learning styles, and abilities. These strategies contribute to an overall inclusive learning environment, in which students feel equally valued". Therefore, it is about the *social variability* in large. This source determines the following benefits of inclusive teaching:

- It is possible to "connect with and engage with a variety of students".
- There is a possibility for "spark moments" or issues that arise when controversial material is discussed.
- Students connect with course materials that are relevant to them.
- Students feel comfortable in the classroom environment to voice their ideas/thoughts/questions.
- Students are more likely to experience success in their courses through activities that support their learning styles, abilities and backgrounds.

  The instruction on how you can teach inclusively follows:

- How might your own cultural-bound assumptions influence your interactions with students?
- How might the backgrounds and experiences of your students influence their motivation, engagement and learning in your classroom?
- How can you modify course materials, activities, assignments and/or exams to be more accessible to all students in your class?

Within the given set of principles, goals and practices, the inclusive teaching is a subset, which might be also identified as *effective teaching practices*. Because effective teaching fits within this broader framework of inclusive teaching, there

Table 4.1 A framework for inclusive teaching in STEM disciplines [RJL+06]

No	Dimension	Its content and meaning
1.	Problem definition	Clearly identify goals, rationales, starting conditions, appropriate design and principles of implementation to achieve optimal learning outcomes
2.	Redundant systems	Recognize that an effective system is designed to monitor and respond to feedback, adapt to changing conditions and provide alternate strategies when systems do not function or other obstacles are encountered
3.	Expert practice	Establish that your design and approach to teaching support effective learning of course content for all students
4.	External constraints	Anticipate and minimize or compensate in ways in which educational processes and outcomes are influenced by environmental factors and other external constraints
5.	Comprehensiveness	Maintain thoroughness and rigour of what is taught, grounded in actual (rather than idealized) conditions

will not be a conflict between the two, and in fact, it may be difficult to distinguish one from the other simply by looking at a sample of teaching practices [RJL +06]. Inclusive teaching adds to effective teaching a framework for understanding why teaching is effective, which in turn helps solve problems, extends effective practices to other contexts and facilitates adapting to change. This paper also presents a framework for inclusive teaching in STEM disciplines. It consists of five interrelated dimensions outlined in Table 4.1.

A learning variability model, as defined conceptually in [BBD+14] (see also its extended version in [Štu15]), represents attributes (or features) with multiple values of the following aspects of learning: pedagogy-related, social-related, content-related, technology-related and the interaction of the above-mentioned kinds of variability. In fact, learning variability describes the educational knowledge abstractly by the adequate attributes and their values.

4.3 Explicit Representation of Variability: A Motivating Example

The foremost aim of learning is to obtain knowledge and gain competence in some domain. Technologically, we define knowledge as a set of data (items, facts, processes, etc.) and their relationships. The relationship among data is the most crucial part in our efforts to understanding what we need to learn. The understanding goes through analysis. The latter has a variety of forms (observing, reading, drawing, reflecting, etc.). All these require of the adequate representation. There is a variety of forms for representing objects (pictures, graphs, texts, formulae, video, sounds, etc.).

Fig. 4.1 Triangle and its parameters

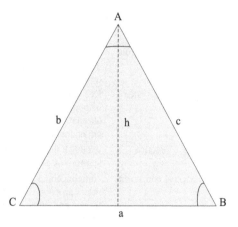

The explicit representation and diversity of its forms, used separately or in combination, may significantly enhance the human's (especially children) ability in understanding. We refer to the explicit representation as a model of real-world items one needs to learn.

The aim is to introduce the notation for the explicit representation of learning variability in such a form that it would be possible to perform various manipulations and transformation easily. Here, we focus on a formalism of the *feature diagrams* to represent the model. Therefore, we introduce a motivating example to explain the variability issues and formalism we use later. We use the concepts and visions taken from the software domain (see Sect. 4.2.1) and adapted them to learning (see also Sect. 4.2.2). Say, we need to transfer knowledge in geometry for secondary school students in a more general way. We consider the following theme "Properties of triangles". The aim of the teacher is to explain and deal with the topic asking students to answer the following questions:

- What is commonality within triangles?
- What is variability within the domain of triangles?
- What is its scope?
- How relationships among objects of this domain should be obtained and represented?

Commonality lies in the definition of the object "triangle" (see Fig. 4.1): "It is a planar closed figure with three straight sides and three angles". The statements ("Any triangle has an area that can be precisely calculated" and "triangle has a type") are commonality, while the statements ("there are different formulae to calculate the area" and "there are different types of triangles") are variability. Altogether, commonality and variability of the type and area define *the scope* of the domain one needs to learn. The statement ("Formulae to calculate the area may depend on the triangle type and what parameters are known") is the relationship expressed abstractly.

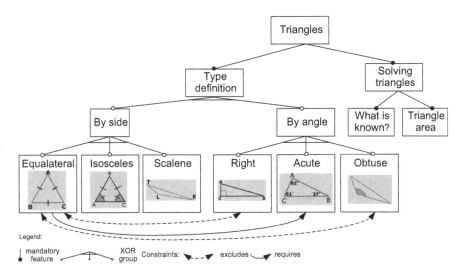

Fig. 4.2 Feature model representing the domain "triangles"

We introduce the feature-based notation to deal with the task abstractly. In Fig. 4.2, we present the feature model of the task. The model is represented by a treelike graph with constraints (*requires* and *excludes*). Features are enclosed within boxes. The root feature (*triangles*) represents the whole domain. The next level features (*type definition* and *solving triangles*) define the scope of the domain. Both are *mandatory features* denoted by black circles in Fig. 4.2. It is possible to define the feature *triangle type* in two ways, either as the feature *by the side* or as the feature *by angle*. Both are *optional features* denoted by white circles in Fig. 4.2. Those features are treated as *variation points* because they, at the next level, contain variants adequately (*equilateral, isosceles* and *scalene* for the left variation point and *right, acute* and *obtuse* for the right variation point). Variants are grouped features and represent the *xor*-group, i.e. the only one variant can be selected at a time. There are two types of relationships among features within the model: the *parent-child* relationship represented by the tree itself and the constraint relationship represented by the constraints *requires* and *excludes* (for the graphical notion, see a legend in Fig. 4.2, where white circles denote optional or alternative features).

Taking into account data of Table 4.2, this is a *concrete feature model* because, using it, it is possible to calculate the area in the concrete case. For methodological purposes, taking into account teaching context, the calculation is subdivided into two categories (treated as simple and complex). The feature *solving triangles* has two mandatory features (*What is known?* and *Area*) that are left undefined in this context and are seen as *abstract features* here. In Fig. 4.3, we extend these abstract features by introducing *concrete* variants for each abstract feature.

This model is for representing the content-oriented teaching aspects in mathematics in a generic way. The commonality-variability as well as the scope are integrated together to represent the domain. However, we are able to enlarge the

Table 4.2 Data and formulae to calculate area

#	What is known?	Area calculating formulae
1.	Base and height of a triangle	$S_1 = 0.5ah$
2.	Three sides of a triangle	$p = \frac{a+b+c}{2}$
		$S_2 = \sqrt{p(p-a)(p-b)(p-c)}$
3.	Two sides and the included angle	$S_3 = \frac{ab}{2}\sin(C)$
4.	Two sides and one angle that is not the included angle	$S_4 = \frac{bc}{2}\sin\left(180° - \arcsin(\sin(B)) - \arcsin\left(\frac{c\cdot\sin(B)}{b}\right)\right)$
5.	Two angles of a triangle and one side, which is the side adjacent to the two given angles	$S_5 = \frac{a^2 \sin(B)\sin(C)}{2\sin(B+C)}$
6.	Two angles of a triangle and one side, which *is not* the side adjacent to the two given angles	$S_6 = \frac{a^2 \sin(B)\sin(A+B)}{2\sin(A)}$
7.	Three angles	It is impossible to calculate the area

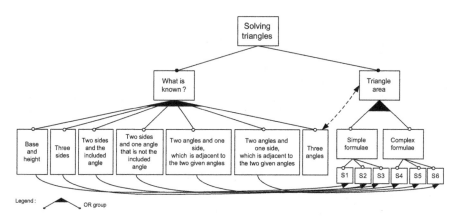

Fig. 4.3 Feature model extending the feature *solving triangles* to its concrete values

scope of the domain aiming to applying it for CS topics. For example, we are able to add CS features such as programming language, OS to develop computer programs for different cases to cover various algorithms and data structures. It is possible even to develop a generic program (meta-program) that generates a concrete target program for calculating area in a particular case. However, here we put aside those aspects and focus on the essence of the model itself. It is a motivating model. It brings the main terminology to understand the basic concepts inherent to explicit feature models.

It is a static feature model with the predefined scope. It is possible to make an association of the domain variability model with the learning variability model. The first provides the artefacts or content for learners to understand and learn. The second is the cognitive process affected by multiple attributes such as on how the content is presented, on how the learning aim is understood by the learner (motivation aspects), the abilities, student teaching/learning model, previous knowledge, the support (technological facilities, teacher's), physical and social environment, the feedback, etc. We argue that we are able to represent all attributes using the feature model notation.

4.3.1 Capabilities of Feature Diagrams in Learning Object Domain

First, we evaluate the capabilities of FDs as a modelling language for the LO domain, and then we outline limitations of using FDs in LOs domain and describe how these limitations can be reduced or overcome. We evaluate FDs as a tool for specification, representation and structuring of learning content in the e-Learning domain based on a set of general requirements formulated by Koper and Es [KE04]:

1. *Formalization*. FDs can be seen as a tool for formalization of LOs, though the syntax and semantics of FDs have not become standard, yet. There are efforts to describe generic semantics of FDs formally [SHT+07].
2. *Pedagogical flexibility*. FDs allow modelling LOs based on different pedagogical theories.
3. *Explicit expression of meaning*. FDs allow explicitly specifying commonalities and variabilities of LOs.
4. *Completeness*. FDs are a complete specification system that can be used to describe all types of LOs, the relationships between different LOs and the pedagogical activities related to LOs development and usage.
5. *Reproducibility*. The LO specification described using FDs can be used to reproduce learning content.
6. *Personalization*. FDs allow describing personalization aspects with LO as a part of variability management.
7. *Media neutrality*. FDs are independent of LO-publishing formats such as web or e-books.
8. *Interoperability and sustainability*. FDs as a description method are independent upon the implementation technology of LOs.
9. *Compatibility*. FDs do not contradict of using the existing LO standards such as LOM or SCORM.
10. *Reusability*. FDs promote the reusability of LOs.
11. *Life cycle*. FDs can be used throughout the entire life cycle of LOs.

4.3.2   Limitations of Feature Diagrams in Learning Object Domain

The limitations and restrictions of FDs are as follows:

1. *Non-standard notation.* Although FD has been known since the 1990s, when the FODA approach has appeared, its syntax and semantics are still being extended [Bat05, SHT+07]. FDs are evolving towards domain ontologies [CKK06].
2. *Immaturity.* There is a lack of maturity and experience of using FDs (except the PL development in software engineering), and the e-Learning community is not yet familiar with FDs at a large scale.
3. *Lack or immaturity of the tool support.*
4. *Lack of expressiveness.* FDs may lack of expressiveness, e.g. to describe domain ontology more comprehensibly or to describe heavyweight domain ontologies. In this case, FDs can be combined with more powerful methods for knowledge representation such as fuzzy logic [RP03] and ontologies.

4.4   A Framework to Implement Learning Variability in STEM Paradigm

As stated previously, various subjects use the term *variability* to express fundamental properties and concepts in a particular field of study. With respect to the introduced STEM-based components, typically the attributes of S, T, E and M components represent the content-related variability. By introducing STEM-based features, we also may introduce to some extent the other variability attributes. Therefore, we can speak about the STEM-based variability space, the abstract knowledge pool. The main issue is how we could be able to extract, to understand and to represent this integrated knowledge. We argue that this can be done by analysis and modelling of the domain.

Since education on the STEM paradigm relates to interdisciplinary aspects and variability has the interdisciplinary nature too, it becomes highly important to have a framework for better understanding of the term itself. The framework, as we hope, should explain not only the richness of possible interpretations of the term but also the essence of the methodology we describe in detail later. The framework identifies the following issues: objectives, scope, activities, main mechanism applied, consequences and expected results. We present the framework in a generic way as a sequence of interrelated questions: *why-what-how* (see Table 4.3). Each question within may contain multiple values and answers. They are concerned to three domains: SWE and e-Learning as it was identified by the literature review in this chapter and STEM-learning as it was defined in Chap. 1.

Why-related questions motivate the need to consider variability as a core concept in creating systems of any kind. They are about objectives, common activities used

Table 4.3 A framework to understand variability across different domains and STEM

Top attributes \domains	SWE	e-Learning	STEM-based CS education
Why-based attributes: they define objectives for dealing with variability	Reuse of SW artefacts	Reuse, systematization	The same as in e-Learning
	Adaptation of artefacts; more effective way in designing systems; automation	Adaptation, personalization for better cognition	Interdisciplinary learning
			Fundamental knowledge in CS, educational robotics
	others	Possibility for automatic generation and adaptation	Possibility for automatic generation and adaptation
What-based attributes: they define items to which variability pertains	Artefacts within life cycle	Taxonomies	CS curriculum
	Architectures	Environments	Robot-based environments
	Components	Learning content	STEM-related content
	Processes	Learning methods, activities and processes	Specificity of STEM learning methods, activities and processes
	Others	Social-based	Motivation and gender-based
How-based attributes: they define the way for achieving implementation	Domain analysis (DA) Modelling by SWE approaches	Learning DA, learning modelling, ontologies, taxonomies, etc.	STEM-driven CS education DA, feature-based modelling of STEM scenarios, STEM context, STEM-driven resources
	General-purpose models and methods such as model-driven transformation approaches and tools	Domain-specific models, domain-specific methods and tools	Applying model-driven transformation approaches, including meta-programming

to achieve the objectives. *What*-related questions describe domains, subdomains and items thereof to which the variability aspects are to be applied, investigated and implemented. *How*-related attributes specify the way, the means and approaches we use for implementing the proposed approach.

The *How*-aspects range from the simple to sophisticated ones:

- Through the analysis of defining terms (variability, diversity, variation points, variants, configuration, etc.), variability definitions taken from SWE and e-Learning in order, one could be able to identify their relevance in defining the term *STEM learning variability*.
- Through the analysis of variability-related research in relevant domains (SWE, e-Learning, including STEM).

- Through the implicit and explicit context modelling related to the pedagogy and STEM education.
- Through constructing and analysing the explicit feature-based variability models for the components (scenarios, smart learning objects, etc.) of the defined domain (i.e. STEM-driven CS education).
- Through applying model and program transformation approaches to build generative specifications for the components.

We define the *learning variability* as a set of *inherent structural properties* of the learning subdomains (such as pedagogy, content, technology, etc.) that an external observer is able *to identify* those properties through variants and their relationships. Learning variability model is a way of an external explicit representation of the learning variability, i.e. a set of component variants and their relationships. The STEM-driven learning variability is a set of inherent structural properties of STEM components that are identifiable through variants of those properties and their relationships. The STEM-driven learning model is a way for explicit expressing of this kind of learning variability.

4.5   Motivation of STEM-Driven Research Topics

1. It is a primary task to understand the need to focus more on holistic and systematic approaches in dealing with variability aspects in e-Learning in general and in STEM-learning in particular. Those we have borrowed from more matured domains such as SWE and CS. However, adaptation and customization of the approaches are a separate task for the e-Learning community due to a specific context and requirements.
2. Those research topics in this community might be focused on the concept *learning variability*. Though we have introduced this term in our previous research [Štu15] largely and intuitively and have exploited practically for a particular goal (for designing generative smart learning objects), so far the concept is still vaguely understood, and its potential is yet not exploited adequately. To our vision, the learning variability can be applied in multiple cases, starting from requirements statement for a variety of activities (requirements for creating tests, assessment scenarios, feedback scenarios, etc.) and ending with building educational software tools. The most crucial aspects in that are different types of *interaction variability*. That is rooted in the heterogeneity of the learning domain in the whole. Therefore, systematic approaches for management and handling learning variability are needed.
3. The approaches should be based on a clear objective statement and depending on objectives may cover a part or even the whole life cycle of e-Learning activities.

4. Here, we treat the following tasks as general ones:

Task 1: Definition of STEM-driven CS education using smart devices as *a problem domain* and the identification of its scope, requirements and the development of a framework to deal with STEM-driven learning variability aspects.

Task 2: Definition and use of the model-driven transformation approaches (e.g. for STEM variability modelling and educational resources design) as *a solution domain* to implement the problem domain *components* with the focus on reuse, adaptability and automation.

Task 3: Development of a set of components (we identify that as our approach) that support STEM-driven CS education, i.e. resources that include learning scenarios, learning content, supporting tools, educational environment and integration of those components within the environment.

Task 4: Introduction of the components into the real learning practice and investigation of the approach by providing an extensive research, i.e. exploring, assessing a variety of processes within the environment, obtaining bottlenecks, suggesting recommendations for a wider community, formulating new problems, etc.

Therefore, the educational processes related to the defined domain are themes for research. The main objective in researching the domain is automation through the introduction of technology-enhanced approaches as fully as possible to add more functionality and make educational processes more effective.

4.6   Two Approaches of Dealing with Variability in STEM

We have identified our problem domain as STEM learning processes. Variability resides within domain items and appears through multiple aspects. Learning processes integrate all kinds of variability (pedagogical, social, content and technological) within the domain. From the perspective of modelling, it is convenient to exclude within the domain its *base part* and its *context*. With regard to STEM learning processes, there are *content design processes* and *content use processes*. Both have the context. It might be different or the same. Context plays an extremely significant role. With regard to the teaching content, pedagogy and social aspects stand for the context, as well as technology. If we accept the content as the base domain, then pedagogy and technology, we are able to treat as context. Both the content and context have variability. There might be two approaches in dealing with and managing variability for STEM. The first approach combines both kinds of variability's (context and base part) at the early stage of the domain analysis. It treats variability expressed within as a common feature model. The second approach separates the context variability from the variability of the base functionality. It

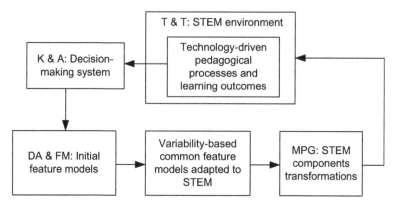

Fig. 4.4 Framework 1: To adapt base functionality to a certain context

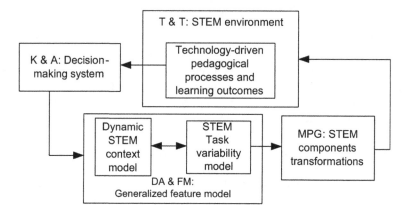

Fig. 4.5 Framework 2: A combined modelling of base functionality and context

considers separate modelling of those variabilities. At the next design stage, both variability models are combined to form the common domain model.

In Fig. 4.4, we outline a framework for considering the first approach in the full use cycle of our approach. This approach treats the feature models as static entities predefined in advance through modelling. In Fig. 4.5, we outline another framework. Here, the context model is a separate item. In addition, it is dynamic and composed of collaborative features that will exchange data and control information at runtime. Here, the abbreviations mean K&A, knowledge and agent-based approaches; T&T, technology and tools; DA, domain analysis; FM, feature model; and MPG, meta-programming.

4.7 Summary, Evaluation and Extended Discussion

The concept variability plays a significant role in many fields and disciplines. It is so because the term captures and reflects the fundamental properties that are inherent to those fields. We are able in some way to capture, to express, to represent, to measure and to manipulate by the items within a particular field to which variability is a central concept, and as such, to be researched and applied. Therefore, it is not surprising that the term has indeed the interdisciplinary nature. Researches and practitioners widely exploit it in different contexts. As each context has specificity, this exploration differs substantially. This diversity goes also from the fact that variability is applicable to a variety of *items* within a particular field. Those items have concrete names such as *artefacts, processes and requirements* (terms common for many fields), *architectural designs, software components and software code* (items taken from SWE or CS) or *learning objects, learning paths and cognition levels* as defined, e.g. by Blooms taxonomy (items taken from e-Learning).

More generally, when we apply the variability analysis to multiple items within a particular field, the more relevant term is *domain variability*. In SWE, for example, by a *domain* one means the area of human activities that bear a common terminology, the relevant data and processes. In CS, for example, there is a two-sided interpretation of the term domain, i.e. as a *problem domain* and as a *solution domain*. In Chap. 2 (see Sect. 2.7), we have defined our problem domain and have extended its interpretation in this chapter. Though we have not used the solution domain in our analysis directly, it may be seen as a context to what was discussed before. Typically, by a solution domain, we mean a set of approaches (methods, models, algorithms, etc.) used to solve tasks taken from the problem domain. Therefore, the term variability can be applied to both the problem domain and the solution domain, though to a varying degree.

So far, we have summarized one important aspect of our previous analysis: we have explicitly stated and enlisted the items, or more generally, domains to which the variability-related research we apply. In a more general sense, domains also outline the extent (also known as scope) and the context for that research. Though the provided analysis is by no means comprehensive in both aspects (we mean research on variability in SWE and in e-Learning as areas taken for the restricted analysis), we are able to summarize the following main findings.

1. Researchers recognize the importance of dealing with the variability aspects equally in both domains (SWE and e-Learning, including STEM-driven learning). However, the means, the extent, the efforts in doing so and findings are quite different. First, the way of understanding the role of the topic differs because of the different maturity level. If SWE focuses on explicit modelling and representation of the domain variability at least two decades, in e-Learning in most cases, this understanding is implicit, though the term has been introduced in this domain far earlier. Very often, in e-Learning, variability is called by the other terms such as diversity and variety or simply by enumerating possible variants among similar items (e.g. in defining pedagogical models, learning styles). If researchers in

SWE are moving towards systematization in this research branch, there is a lack of the systemic vision in e-Learning, though the impact of variability, e.g. on reusability issues in learning is also recognized and understood.

2. As SWE can be considered, to some extent, as a solution domain for e-Learning (we mean technological capabilities), it is an undeniable fact that well-proven ideas and approaches are moving across relevant fields. A typical example is the SPL approach that was customized to e-Learning. We have shown in our analysis that there are multiple works that use this approach in e-Learning; however, very often, variability aspects are implicit there, not being presented explicitly through feature models. A great body of variability research in both domains is concerned with using feature-based modelling. That is so because the notation of feature models is intuitive and has both graphical and analytic representation, including the well-grounded formalism, i.e. the first-order logic. Furthermore, it is supported by multiple tools. In addition, what is most import for learning is that the notation has a conceptual resemblance to the other widespread formalism in e-Learning such as ontology and knowledge representation.

3. Variability within feature models can be evaluated by variation points, variants and the relationships and constraints among thereof. The extent (degree) of variability can be easily measured by obtaining the number of valid configurations. Formally, by a configuration of a feature model, it is meant the subtree that covers all variation points and the only one variant selected for each variation point in the feature model represented by the tree. A valid configuration takes into account possible constraints among variation points and variants. This measure is quite different from those used in other domains such as variability measures in statistics. As feature models specify a relationship among features in two forms (as a parent-child dependency and as constraints of the type *requires* and *excludes* among adequate variation points and variants), this relationship can be treated as a way to represent knowledge. In this regard, feature models have a conceptual resemblance with ontology-based models. Those models are widely exploited in e-Learning. Therefore, both domains (SWE and e-Learning) may benefit each other not only on the concept SPL (that is already evident fact now) but also using ontology-oriented approaches.

4. The e-Learning domain is highly heterogeneous. The STEM domain has, in fact, the extended heterogeneity (see Chap. 2). Technology advances and internal driving forces of e-Learning and STEM are factors that directly impact on expanding heterogeneity. Therefore, the heterogeneity of STEM is the primary point from which we need to start researching variability. There is a variety of variability levels and forms. It already appears at defining strategy (e.g. inquiry learning for STEM, introducing STEM as a separate interdisciplinary course or as a selected discipline). It appears when deciding in which course (e.g. mathematics, physics, biology, CS, etc.) to introduce STEM teaching.

When all these are resolved, the variability appears practically within all components that define the structure of STEM (pedagogy, technology, content, etc.). With respect to STEM and e-Learning in general, an important ingredient is the social variability. It is perhaps one of the most crucial parts of the whole variability problem. It is so because there is not only an easily identifiable part of variability (such as learner's age, social groups, etc.). There is a hidden part also. This part has two aspects. One is pure psychological or cognitive, such as student's behaviour and motivation, or on how the learners accept information and understand it. The second is that variability we may detect in a real situation by providing experiments in real time. For example, students' performance in considering learning tasks, acquiring knowledge about the educational environment, etc. may be detected in this way, though the accuracy is limited. For the "external" resolving of difficulties in cognitive variability, researchers have proposed multiple approaches (see Table 2.1 in Chap. 2).

5. There are different forms and possibilities to obtain and deal with variability in a domain. There is *anticipated* and *planned* variability. Very often, we refer to this kind of variability as *static variability*. For a long time in SWE, static variability was the focus in modelling research using feature-based models. As there are also dynamic aspects, especially in context variability and unpredictability of changes, one can observe the evident shift from *static variability modelling* to *dynamic feature-based variability modelling*. The latter does not deny the previous knowledge in static variability. In contrary, researchers introduce dynamic aspects by extending approaches based on static variability. In this regard, *context awareness* and its role to the dynamic variability becomes an important issue. So far, all these are in SWE only, but not in e-Learning.

6. What is common in researching variability aspects within different domains is that those aspects can be understood thoroughly only going through explicit analysis and modelling (meaning the use of well-defined approaches). It is so, because only the explicitly represented models are able to open a way that leads to the *complete or partial automation* using the capabilities of modern technology, the main trend for a variety of domains in a long-term perspective. This motivates the large community in e-Learning to borrow SWE and CS approaches and customize and apply them in learning.

A methodological basis of such a customization could be the idea based on the *learning variability* concept. By learning variability in large, we mean variability aspects to be applied to each subdomain of the highly heterogeneous STEM-driven education in CS. It is not an easy task to obtain and represent variability aspects or features in a separate subdomain (pedagogy, technology, content, etc.). The task becomes far more complicated when we apply the concept to the whole domain. Therefore, we need to focus on systematic approaches to deal with learning variability.

As many other researches (cited in our analysis or not), we are proponents of a more systematic use of those approaches in learning. In this respect, there is a long list of problems that needs the increased attention and efforts of researchers. Below we formulate the most crucial problems from the perspective of our previous research. Some of them are a subject of research to be discussed in the other chapters.

(a) Identification of the interaction among semantically different kinds of variabilities (social, pedagogical, technological, content)
(b) Modelling of dynamic variability such as context
(c) Correctness checking of variability-based feature models

4.8 Conclusion

1. Though the provided analysis is by no means comprehensive, we have collected enough information to develop a framework for understanding variability-related issues in conceptualizing and developing the STEM paradigm.
2. In software engineering, variability forms a separate research branch covering multiple fields (ranging from requirement statement to software automated coding). The content to which variability is applied is software artefacts. As software, in fact, is not only a technological solution but also a social-technological compound, the variability dimensions have a great potential for extensions. It is possible to bring knowledge on variability from software engineering to e-Learning.
3. Learning variability is a new concept that defines diversity aspects within e-Learning, which in essence is a highly heterogeneous domain. The STEM paradigm, when it is considered along with robotics, extends variability aspects in all dimensions:

    (i) Methodology (e.g. through the use of richer and more diverse scenarios)
    (ii) Pedagogy (e.g. through a set of conventional learning methods enriched by new ones such as inquiry-based)
    (iii) Learner's preferences (e.g. example-oriented, simulation, demonstration of real-world situations and tasks)
    (iv) Technology (e.g. a variety of robot use modes, variety of software tools, etc.)

4. Computer science themes and topics, due to their interdisciplinary nature, are easily adaptable to the vision and needs of STEM. This entails additional variability aspects. For example, it is possible to treat some robot-oriented algorithms as a carrier of knowledge in mathematics, in science and technology, depending on the learning objectives and the mode of delivery.
5. Based on a good practice taken from SWE, based on our previous research on smart LO and smart teaching in CS and already existing findings of other researchers in the field, it is possible to state that:

(i) Learning variability, despite of its heterogeneity aspects and different semantics, enables to uniformly express essential properties within e-Learning domain, using feature models; *feature* is indeed a universal concept to capture those properties.

(ii) We are able to measure a degree of learning variability through variation points and variants (in the simplest case) and valid configuration of feature models.

(iii) Despite of the simplicity and attractiveness of the concept, learning variability modelling also contains many restrictions and difficulties such as variability interaction, dynamism and variability model correctness. Those problems should be considered along with the adequate theoretical background.

6. Learning variability, when we represent it explicitly by feature models, is the key for introducing the automation in developing and using the STEM-driven content. Learning variability is a conceptual background of the methodology we use in achieving goals of automation in designing the STEM content and in adapting it to the diverse contexts of use.

7. To be valuable and practical, this methodological background needs the adequate theoretical background. We discuss that in the next chapter.

References

[AK09]   Apel S, Kästner C (2009) An overview of feature-oriented software development. J Object Technol 8(5):49–84

[APM+14] Alférez GH, Pelechano V, Mazo R, Salinesi C, Diaz D (2014) Dynamic adaptation of service compositions with variability models. J Syst Softw 91:24–47

[Bat05]   Batory D (2005) Feature models, grammars, and propositional formulas. In: International conference on software product lines, Springer, Berlin, pp 7–20

[BBD+14] Burbaite R, Bespalova K, Damasevicius R, Stuikys V (2014) Context aware generative learning objects for teaching computer science. Int J Eng Educ 30(4):929–936

[BC05]   Bachmann F, Clements PC (2005) Variability in software product lines, Technical report CMU/SEI

[BGP14]   Barreiro PS, García-Saiz D, Pantaleón MEZ (2014) Building families of software products for e-learning platforms: a case study. IEEE Rev Iberoam Tecnologias Aprendizaje 9(2):64–71

[BLC04]   Boyle T, Leeder D, Chase H (2004) To boldly GLO – towards the next generation of learning objects, World conference on eLearning in corporate. Government, Healthcare and Higher Education, Washington, DC, USA

[BLR+15] Berger T, Lettner D, Rubin J, Grünbacher P, Silva A, Becker M, Chechik M, Czarnecki K (2015) What is a feature? A qualitative study of features in industrial software product lines. SPLC 2015, July 20–24, 2015, Nashville

[BN04]   Brace J, Nejdl W (2004) Ontologies and metadata for elearning. In: Staab S, Studer R (eds) Towards an ontological support for eLearning courses, LNCS 3292. Springer, London, pp 555–574

[BNA15]   Bernacki ML, Nokes-Malach TJ, Aleven V (2015) Examining self-efficacy during learning: variability and relations to behaviour, performance, and learning. Metacognition Learn 10(1):99–117

[BQ15]   Baresi L, Quinton C (2015) Dynamically evolving the structural variability of dynamic
            software product lines. In: 10th International symposium on software engineering for
            adaptive and self-managing systems, May 2015, Florence, p 7
[BSR10]   Benavides D, Segura S, Ruiz-Cortes A (2010, 2010) Automated analysis of feature
            models 20 years later: a literature review. J Inf Syst 35(6)
[CBK13]   Capilla R, Bosch J, Kang KC (2013) Systems and software variability management.
            Concepts tools and experiences. Springer, Berlin
[CBN09]   Chen L, Babar MA, Nour A (2009) Variability management in software product lines:
            a systematic review. SPLC, San Francisco
[CBT+14]   Capilla R, Bosch J, Trinidad P, Ruiz-Cortés A, Hinchey M (2014) An overview of
            dynamic software product line architectures and techniques: observations from
            research and industry. J Syst Softw 91:3–23
[CE00]   Czarnecki K, Eisenecker UW (2000) Generative programming: methods, tools, and
            applications. ACM Press/Addison-Wesley Publishing Co, New York
[CER07]   Centre for Educational Research and Innovation (2007) Understanding the brain: the
            birth of a learning science. Organization for Economic Co-operation and Development,
            Paris
[CHW98]   Coplien J, Hoffman D, Weiss D (1998) Commonality and variability in software
            engineering. IEEE Softw 15:37–45
[CKK06]   Czarnecki K, Kim CHP, Kalleberg KT (2006) Feature models are views on ontologies.
            In: Proc. of 10th Int. software product line conference, SPLC'06, Baltimore, pp 41–51
[CN13]   Chimalakonda S, Nori KV (2013) What makes it hard to apply software product lines
            to educational technologies? In: Product line approaches in software engineering
            (PLEASE), 2013 4th International Workshop on (pp. 17–20). IEEE
[Dam09]   Damaševičius R (2009) Specification of learning content using feature diagrams. In:
            Information systems development. Springer, US, pp 821–829
[DD06]   Dodero JM, Díez D (2006) Model-driven instructional engineering to generate adapt-
            able learning materials. In: Advanced learning technologies, 2006. Sixth international
            conference on, IEEE, pp 1188–1189
[DMB16]   Deepika HV, Mangala NN, Babu SC (2016) Automatic program generation for
            heterogeneous architectures. In Advances in computing, communications and infor-
            matics (ICACCI), 2016 International conference on, IEEE, pp 102–109
[DŠ08]   Damaševičius R, Štuikys V (2008) On the technological aspects of generative learning
            object development. In: Mittermeir RT, Syslo MM (Eds), Proc. of 3rd International
            conference on informatics in secondary schools evolution and perspectives ISSEP
            2008, 1–4 July, 2008, Torun, Poland. LNCS vol. 5090, Springer, London, pp 337–348
[DZF+07]   Dodero J, Zarraonandía T, Fernández C, Díez D (2007) Generative adaptation reuse of
            competence development programmes. J Interact Media Educ 2007(1)
[EGJ+11]   Elfaki AO, Johar MGM, Aik KLT, Fong SL, Bachok R (2011) Towards representation
            and validation of knowledge in students' learning pathway using variability modeling
            technique. arXiv preprint arXiv:1110.2859
[GB08]   Garfield JB, Ben-Zvi D (2008) Learning to reason about variability. In: Garfield JB,
            Ben-Zvi D (eds) Developing students' statistical reasoning: connecting research and
            teaching practice. Springer Netherlands, pp 201–214
[GBR+14]   Guendouz A, Bennouar D, Ramdani A, Hamza Mazeri H (2014) Customer satisfaction
            through E-learning software product line. ICIW 2014: the ninth international confer-
            ence on internet and web applications and services

[GBS01]   van Gurp J, Bosch J, Svahnberg M (2001) On the notion of variability in software product lines. In: The working IEEE/IFIP conference on software architecture (WICSA), Amsterdam, pp 45–54

[GDD+13]   Gupta P, Agarwal Y, Dolecek L, Dutt N, Gupta RK, Kumar R et al (2013) Underdesigned and opportunistic computing in presence of hardware variability. IEEE Trans Comput Aided Des Integr Circ Syst 32(1):8–23

[GWT+14]   Galster M, Weyns D, Tofan D, Michalik B, Avgeriou P (2014) Variability in software systems—a systematic literature review. IEEE Trans Softw Eng 40(3):282–306

[HPN+13]   Huang J, Piech C, Nguyen A, Guibas L (2013) Syntactic and functional variability of a million code submissions in a machine learning MOOC. In: AIED 2013 workshops proceedings, p 25

[JGS93]   Jones ND, Gomard CK, Sestoft P (1993) Partial evaluation and automatic program generation. Peter Sestoft

[KCH+90]   Kang KC, Cohen SG, Hess JA, Novak WE, Peterson AS (1990) Feature-oriented domain analysis (FODA) feasibility study (No. CMU/SEI-90-TR-21). Carnegie-Mellon University Pittsburgh Pa Software Engineering Institution

[KE04]   Koper R, van Es R (2004) Modelling units of learning from a pedagogical perspective. In: McGreal R (ed) Online education using learning objects. Routledge, New York

[KHC05]   Kim SD, Her JS, Ho Chang SH (2005) A theoretical foundation of variability in component-based development. Inf Softw Technol 47:663–673

[Lak87]   Lakoff G (1987) Women, fire, and dangerous things: what categories reveal about the mind. University of Chicago Press, Chicago

[LB15]   Lahiani N, Bennouar D (2015) A model driven approach to derive e-learning applications in software product line. In: Proceedings of the international conference on intelligent information processing, security and advanced communication, ACM, p 78

[LG93]   Lloyd, Gould SJ (1993) Species selection on variability. Proc Natl Acad Sci Evol USA 90:595–599

[LPC+15]   Labib AE, Penadés MC, Canós JH, Gómez, A (2015) Enforcing reuse and customization in the development of learning objects: a product line approach. In: Proceedings of the 30th annual ACM symposium on applied computing, ACM, pp 261–263

[MSR+16]   Mylläriemi V, Savolainen J, Raatikainen M, Männistö T (2016) Performance variability in software product lines: proposing theories from a case study. Empir Softw Eng 21(4):1623–1669

[NSG08]   Nijhuis J, Segers M, Gijselaers W (2008) The extent of variability in learning strategies and students' perceptions of the learning environment. Learn Instr 18:121–134

[OMG03]   OMG (Object Management Group) (2003) Ontology definition meta model

[PBL05]   Pohl K, Böckle G, van der Linden FJ (2005) Software product line engineering: foundations, principles and techniques. Springer, New York/Secaucus

[PJK13]   Pelanek R, Jarusek P, Klusacek M (2013) Modeling students' learning and variability of performance in problem solving. In: Educational data mining 2013

[PS06]   Pankratius V, Stucky W (2006) A strategy for content reusability with product lines derived from experience. In: Inverardi P, Jazayeri M (eds) Online education, software engineering education in the modern age: challenges and possibilities, LNCS 4309. Springer, London, pp 128–146

[RJL+06]   Reddick L, Jacobson W, Linse A, Yong D (2006) A framework for inclusive teaching in STEM disciplines. In: Ouellett M (ed) Teaching inclusively: diversity and faculty development. New Forums Press, Stillwater

[RP03]   Robak S, Pieczynski A (2003) Employing fuzzy logic in feature diagrams to model variability in software product-lines. In: Proc. of the 10th IEEE international conference and workshop on the engineering of computer-based systems (ECBS'03), pp 305–311

[ŠDB+08] Štuikys V, Damaševičius R, Brauklytė I, Limanauskienė V (2008) Exploration of
          learning object ontologies using feature diagrams. In: Proceedings of world conference
          on educational multimedia, hypermedia & telecommunications, ED-MEDIA 8, pp
          2144–2154
[SHT+07] Schobbens P-Y, Heymans P, Trigaux J-C, Bontemps Y (2007) Generic semantics of
          feature diagrams. Comput Netw Int J Comput Telecommun Netw 51(2):456–479
[Sie94]   Siegler RS (1994) Cognitive variability: a key to understanding cognitive develop-
          ment, current directions in psychological science, 3, 1, Cambridge University Press:
          New York
[Štu15]   Štuikys V (2015) Smart learning objects for smart education in computer science.
          Springer, New York
[UDL16]   Universal Design for Learning (2016) Framework for addressing learner variability
          network objectives. http://www.udlnet-project.eu (2013–2016)
[Wey14]   Weyns D (2014) Variability: from software product lines to self-adaptive systems. In:
          SPLC workshops, p 12
[Wil00]   Wiley DA (2000) Learning object design and sequencing theory. PhD thesis, Depart-
          ment of Instructional Psychology and Technology, Brigham Young University, Provo

Chapter 5
Theoretical Background to Implement STEM-Driven Approaches

Abstract In this chapter, we first motivate the needs of automation, focusing on three dimensions, i.e. the growth of diversity, complexity and software content in designing educational systems. Next, knowing this context, we introduce the theoretical basis to implement the automation in STEM-driven CS education. This basis includes two parts. The first is about feature-based analysis, modelling and feature model transformations typically applied to the problem domain. All these we borrowed from software engineering. The second part includes the basics of heterogeneous meta-programming techniques. We extend those techniques by introducing new types of heterogeneous meta-programs that represent our efforts to move from the component-level meta-programming to the system-level to design such systems as the generative scenario creator for STEM. However, this approach requires a more extensive research, though we implemented and tested the approach practically. A more thorough analysis of the system-level meta-programming is beyond the scope of this book.

5.1 Introduction

This chapter presents the theoretical background independently upon the topics we consider in this book. Throughout the book, we are discussing the STEM paradigm from the automation perspective. In other words, we seek to discover and apply the reuse-enhanced transformation-based approaches, where they are appropriate and applicable for STEM aiming at making STEM processes more innovative and effective. In fact, those approaches are about automation. Therefore, the theoretical part has direct links to automation through modelling and generative reuse approaches. On the other hand, the vision of automation in computer science (CS) is as such. CS deals with the problem solving, or more generally the development of systems by means of tools, as the process of mapping the *problem domain* onto the *solution domain*. The mapping follows with regard to the prescribed requirements and constraints. In our case, *at the primary stage*, the STEM-related artefacts and requirements represent the problem domain. At the next stage, when we focus *on STEM-driven processes* (we derive them from the results of the primary

© Springer International Publishing AG, part of Springer Nature 2018
V. Štuikys, R. Burbaitė, *Smart STEM-Driven Computer Science Education*,
https://doi.org/10.1007/978-3-319-78485-4_5

stage), those processes represent a narrowed and more concrete problem domain. In different contexts, we apply multiple solutions. With regard to possibilities of automation, meta-programming approaches stand for the solution domain. To make the mapping feasible, both domains are to be represented as precisely as possible. The abstract or even a formal representation of the domains is the core of the background.

We represent the problem domain (i.e. its artefacts, models, relationships and constraints) using the feature-based notation. We extract artefacts and their relationships through feature-based modelling. Therefore, the theoretical background has two parts. The first is about the feature-based analysis and modelling. The second part considers meta-programming-based transformation approaches. Note that the mapping of the problem domain model or models onto the solution domain model is also high-level programming (i.e. meta-programming). We motivate this choice later. Here, more important is to stress the following aspects. We have already discussed those issues in our previous research (see books [ŠD13, Štu15]). As in recent years there is an evident shift from the static to dynamic feature-based modelling, we found the dynamic feature models being more relevant to the STEM domain. Therefore, in contrast to the above-mentioned books, this chapter also introduces dynamic feature models. With regard to meta-programming approaches, here we introduce two new types of structural heterogeneous meta-programs. They enable to build not only the single *generative component* but also a *system* composed of a set of generative components. The *generative scenarios* to build an educational scenario for a concrete context of use (including STEM) are just the example of such a system. Therefore, this research extends the applicability of this kind of meta-programming.

Note also that the first part has no new fundamental concepts but rather new capabilities in the application and treatment of those fundamentals. However, the second part has a few novel attributes, such as two new meta-program types identified further as *Type 3* and *Type 4*. The next two sections motivate the background. Section 5.2 gives our vision. Section 5.3 extends our vision by providing the analysis of the related work.

5.2   Motivation and Methodology of Describing the Background

Why we need the automation, or why we need to extend the level of automation, for the STEM education? Perhaps for some readers, the first part of the question may look trivial. Especially for those who are involved in designing educational software. The second part of this question is for designers, but it is still trivial. To avoid the misunderstanding, we explain our intention: this question is for the novice end-users (students or teachers) as well as for STEM policymakers who are not so much aware about current trends on system building and automation issues. For designers, the question should be as follows: what is the best way to achieve a higher degree of automation in designing various systems, including educational software for STEM?

The efforts of researchers and designers to raise the level of automation result from the ever-increasing capabilities of technology advances. On the other hand, with the technology expanses, the user's needs grow adequately, including the educational sector. For a long time, because of the technological revolution, one can notice the evident signs of the extremely rapid growth of capabilities of application systems, including educational systems, in three dimensions: *diversity*, *complexity* and *software content*. With regard to educational systems, the diversity aspects range from the PC stand-alone, Internet-based or mobile-based systems to the MOOC and STEM-oriented systems. The complexity grows adequately because of the user's needs, technology capabilities and the *evolutionary trends* within the educational domain per se where the systems are applied. The *software content* within educational hardware facilities (PC, remote educational laboratories, smart devices, including phones, robots, etc.) increases too due to the interruptible advances in technological characteristics such the memory size, working frequency, decreasing amount of energy consumption, etc.

Now let us focus on our domain under consideration, i.e. CS education using STEM and robots. All the above-mentioned factors are the context to understand the external sources affecting our domain. How can we manage the complexity issues within this domain? The basic idea is to hide the technological complexity from the users (teachers and students) as much as possible. The educational tools stand for that purpose. Therefore, the designer's responsibility is to develop the educational tools in such a way that it would be possible to manage the issues and, on the other hand, to respond to the needs of users in terms of simplicity of use, applicability and efficiency. To achieve this, typically the designer relies on the well-defined design methodologies. Here, by the well-defined methodology, we mean its theoretical background and good practice. In Chap. 4, we have introduced such a methodology borrowed from software engineering and adapted in our context. The *learning variability* in general and the *STEM variability* in particular stand for the methodological background to develop the methodology.

In designing educational tools on this basis, the designer needs to manage the variability issues in three dimensions: (1) *understanding* the domain and *extracting* the needed artefacts through analysis, (2) *representing* the variability at a higher level of abstraction *by* the *adequate model* or *models* and (3) *transforming* the models into executable specifications by means of adequate tools. Both, the executable specifications that implement STEM variability and tools that support the specifications' run, enable to achieve the adequate level of automation and efficacy in use. Therefore, in this chapter, we focus on two topics: (i) feature-based modelling as applied to our application domain and (ii) meta-programming as a solution domain. The third important topic of the background, i.e. principles of mapping the application domain on the solution domain to achieve the goals of automation, we postpone until Chap. 7. The extended motivation of our approach follows partially from the analysis of the related work (Sect. 5.3) and our previous research.

What methodology we use in presenting those topics? Our aim is to respond to the flavour of readers, having a different background on the topics. Therefore, we describe the topics at two levels: the users and designers (researchers). We assume that the formal definition of the topics is for researchers, though that should be useful for designers too.

5.3   Related Work

We categorize the related work into two streams: (A) feature-based modelling with the focus on static and dynamic variability modelling and (B) meta-programming-based approaches as a basis of the solution domain. Note that we have already analysed the related work on feature modelling in Chap. 4. If in Chap. 4 the focus was variability aspects, here we focus more on feature model syntax, semantics and formalism.

Stream A   There is indeed a very broad research on feature-based modelling if one looks from the perspective of the SWE domain. Therefore, we need to restrict the analysis before moving to the educational domain. Here, we are able to discuss, to our vision, the only most essential concepts on feature-based modelling taken from the SWE. The historians dealing with the evolution of education research should confirm the following observation: for a long time, there was and still remains a trend in e-Learning, aiming to adapt the most robust approaches earlier developed (and used with a very successful approval) in other domains, such CS and SWE. Feature-based modelling is one of those examples, though that is still not so much evident. So far, it does not widely used and not yet fully recognized as a useful instrument in this domain. There are a few reasons for that. Firstly, there is a lack of the awareness of the power of this approach. Secondly, there are relevant approaches in the educational domain, such as ontology-based approaches (conceptually, they have much in common with the feature-based notation (see, e.g. [CKK06]) with a much longer experience. Why, therefore, one should become a supporter of using feature-based approaches in education? The next short review, to some extent, explains that:

Observation 1. Researchers define the concept *feature* as a very broad entity. There are at least ten slightly different definitions as follows [AK09].

1. Feature is "a prominent or distinctive user-visible aspect, quality, or characteristic of a software system or systems" [KCH+90].
2. Feature is "a distinctively identifiable functional abstraction that must be implemented, tested, delivered, and maintained" [KKL+98].
3. Feature is "a distinguishable characteristic of a concept (e.g. system, component and so on) that is relevant to some stakeholder of the concept" [CE00].
4. Feature is "a logical unit of behaviour specified by a set of functional and non-functional requirements" [Bos00].

5. Feature is "a product characteristic from the user or customer views, which essentially consists of a cohesive set of individual requirements" [CZZ+05].
6. Feature is "a product characteristic that is used in distinguishing programs within a family of related programs" [BSR04].
7. Feature is "a triplet, $f = (R; W; S)$, where R represents the requirements the feature satisfies, W the assumptions the feature takes about its environment and S its specification" [CHS08].
8. Feature is "an optional or incremental unit of functionality" [Zav03].
9. Feature is "an increment of program functionality" [Bat05].
10. Feature is "a structure that extends and modifies the structure of a given program in order to satisfy a stakeholder's requirement, to implement and encapsulate a design decision, and to offer a configuration option" [ALM +08].

The abundance of definitions, in fact, means that the concept is applicable in a variety of different contexts of use. Why the educational context should be ignored, having in mind the relationships among SWE, CS and educational software of general use?

Observation 2. What are or might be the most attractive attributes of feature-based approaches for the educational community and STEM? The list (by no means exhaustive) is as follows:

(i) Intuitiveness and easiness to grasp and understand the semantics of feature models [BSR10].
(ii) Feature-based languages have both graphical and textual representations; therefore, they are human readable, as well as machine readable [ACL+13, CBH11].
(iii) The well-defined background (the first-order logic) enables to build robust tools not only to create the feature models [ACL+13, MBC09] but also to satisfy their correctness [MBC09].
(iv) Feature models fit well to represent different objects and entities (see, e.g. *Definitions 3, 10* above) due to the uniformity and universality of the concept feature and, on the other hand, due to heterogeneity of educational domain; the latter may include specification educational resources, educational approaches, educational technology, etc.
(v) Feature models enable to represent the CS concepts, the technological concepts, the engineering concepts and the mathematical concepts at a higher level of abstraction; therefore, they support an abstract thinking and fit well to deliver STEM ideas for learners.

Observation 3. In SWE, there are well-founded assumptions that the capacity in automation relies on the domain variability representation [PBD05] and the use of the adequate technology and methodology. The feature-based notion, as no other one of this sort, fits well to represent the variability. This statement follows, for example, from the analysis of the recent systematic review paper on variability

[SBA+16]. If one wants to raise the degree of automation in the education domain, there is no more reliable way to do that as focusing on learning variability or, in our case, on the STEM variability.

Observation 4. The following research papers already consider feature-based approaches as relevant ones to the educational domain. Researchers within the e-Learning community already recognize the role and the need of applying *the feature-based domain analysis and modelling* approaches. For instance, Dodero et al. [DZF+07] introduce an instructional engineering generative method to create and adapt competence development programs (CDPs). Though SWE approaches were introduced in e-Learning far earlier, the above-mentioned authors and their colleagues have pioneered to combine generative methods along with the use of feature models [DD06]. The paper [DŠ08] considers the use of feature diagrams (FDs, a.k.a. feature models) as tools to specify generative LOs first, and then, to implement them using meta-programming techniques. The paper [ŠDB+08] analyses the possibility of using FDs to specify ontology as a type of knowledge for e-Learning. The paper [DS09] discusses the use of FDs as applied to the sequencing problem. The paper [BS11] analyses the LO research in the large using the feature-based models. The paper [DDA12] uses the models for specifying architecture in creating of e-Learning systems. For the other proposals, see [CNC12].

The paper [DT16] presents a model for assessing e-Learning courses through the application of quantitative methods based on feature-oriented domain analysis and feature models. The approach gives an opportunity to assess (1) the variation degree of electronic courses specified in university standards through invariant feature diagrams, which can be modified for the specific purpose, and (2) the quality and design of e-Learning platforms. The paper [CN13] presents an experience of mining a software product line (SPL) from existing e-Learning systems developed in different locations by different teams over a decade. It also discusses the key challenges of applying SPL to e-Learning systems: societal context, dealing non-technical stakeholders, cross-organizational SPL, global SPL, process diversity and version management along with domain specific challenges. The paper [EJA+11] introduces the variability technique to represent the knowledge in an e-Learning system using feature models. This representation provides different learning pathways, which supports the students' diversity.

Observation 5. Though feature-based modelling approaches exist for nearly three decades, in recent years, one can observe the intensifying efforts in this research area. The paper [LSW15] proposes an approach to discover and to explain contradictions in attributed feature models efficiently in order to assist the developer with the correction of mistakes. The paper uses extended feature models with the attributes and arithmetic constraints, translates them into a constraint satisfaction problem and explores those for contradictions. When a contradiction is found, the constraints are searching for a set of contradicting relations by the QuickXplain algorithm.

The paper [ACF+09] investigates the systematic use of feature models for modelling the context and the software variants, together with their interrelations, as a way to configure the adaptive system with respect to a particular context. A case study in the domain of video surveillance systems is used to illustrate the approach.

Over the last two decades, SPLs have been used successfully in industry for building families of systems of related products, maximizing reuse and exploiting their variable and configurable options.

In a changing world, modern software demands more and more adaptive features, many of them performed dynamically, and the requirements on the software architecture to support adaptation capabilities of systems are increasing in importance. Today, many embedded system families and application domains such as ecosystems, service-based applications and self-adaptive systems demand runtime capabilities for flexible adaptation, reconfiguration and post-deployment activities. However, as traditional architectures of SPL fail to provide mechanisms for runtime adaptation and behaviour of products, there is a shift towards designing more dynamic software architectures and building more adaptable software able to handle autonomous decision-making, according to varying conditions. Recent development approaches such as Dynamic Software Product Lines (DSPLs) attempt to face the challenges of the dynamic conditions of such systems, but the state of these solution architectures is still immature [CBT+14]. This research work provides an overview of the state of the art and current techniques that attempt to face the many challenges of runtime variability mechanisms in the context of DSPLs. In addition, this paper provides an integrated view of the challenges and solutions that are necessary to support runtime variability mechanisms in DSPL models and software architectures.

Stream B This stream of works is about meta-programming. Typically, by meta-programming, we mean high-level programming in which the language constructs manipulate not on data but on a program or its fragments (types, expressions, etc.) as data. The program that specifies the manipulations we represent either in the same language (case 1) or in the other language (case 2). Therefore, we have two kinds of meta-programming: homogeneous (case 1) and heterogeneous (case 2). It is a very old programming technology having its roots in pre-processing systems or even earlier systems [ŠD13]. We know three taxonomies to define basic meta-programming concepts: Sheard's [She01], Pasalic's [Pas04] and the one given in [ŠD13]. For example, Sheard's taxonomy excludes the following aspects: (i) kinds of meta-programs (generator, analyser), (ii) separation of languages (homogeneous, heterogeneous), (iii) use time (compile, runtime) and (iv) separation of static and dynamic coding (manual, automatic). The second taxonomy is similar to the first but considers additionally the type of meta-languages (Open, Close). The third taxonomy focuses on two classes of concepts (structural and process-based).

Meta-programming is also about the implementing domain-specific languages (DSLs) [NLS+16]. Though meta-programming approaches are researched practically from the dawn of computing, they are still under focus by many research communities, especially in theoretical computer science. For example, at the *International Summer School on Meta-programming* (8–12 August 2016, Robinson College, Cambridge, UK), the following topics were discussed (www.cl.cam.ac.uk/events/metaprog2016):

(i) *Stage programming*, enabling the execution of a staged program to be spread over several phases, with each stage using the available data to generate specialized code

(ii) *Generic programming* aiming at improving code flexibility, allowing to give a single definition of a function that operates in a predictable way on many different types

The other venue, i.e. the International Conference on Generative Programming: Concepts & Experience (GPCE 2017, 23–24 October, Vancouver, Canada), focuses on researching techniques that use program generation, domain-specific languages and component deployment to increase programmer productivity, improve software quality and shorten the time to market of software products. The call for papers states [GAS17]:

> Generative and component approaches and domain-specific abstractions are revolutionizing software development just as automation and componentization revolutionized manufacturing. Raising the level of abstraction in software specification has been a fundamental goal of the computing community for several decades.

In fact, generative programming is about meta-programming. Note that there are many approaches, with slightly different names, that conceptually we are able to treat as meta-programming. They include *multistage programming* [Dam05, DHA +13, ŠBB+16a, ŠBB14, She01, Tah99], i.e. the development of programs in several different stages, *parameterized programming* [Gog96], *generative programming* [CE00], *generic programming* [DS98, MS89], and *reflection-oriented programming* [Rid99], program *specialization* or *partial evaluation* [Ira03, JGS93, MLC02, Štu15]. Furthermore, meta-programming techniques closely relate to novel software development technologies such as *aspect-oriented programming* [KLM+97].

Meta-programming was also known and used for a long time in *formal logic programming* [Pas04, Tem95]. However, now the scope of the application of the meta-programming techniques is much wider. These include the domains such as programming language implementation [BDG+95], including parser and compiler generation [LMB92, Ter97], application and software generators [Bat98], product lines [Bat98], generic component design [Bec00], program transformation [ŠD02, LH01], program evaluation and specialization [JGS93], generative reuse [Big98], software maintenance, evolution and configuration [CE00a], middleware applications [CS02], XML-based web applications and web component deployment [LN02]. The other applications include recursion, reflection [MJD96], including introspection and intercession [CE00], meta-classes [KRB91], meta-object protocols [Chi95], anticipatory optimization [Big98], mixin-based programming [Pet96], design patterns [Din03], scripting languages [Ous98] and domain-specific languages (DSLs), soft IP (intellectual property component) design and design of generative learning objects [ŠD13, Štu15] and mark-up languages.

One can learn more on the evolutionary aspects of meta-programming from [ŠD13]. The following definitions give the primary understanding of this field.

Therefore, meta-programming is "creating application programs by writing programs that produce programs" [Lev86]. Sheard [She01] emphasizes the role of meta-programming in program generation explicitly. He states that "Meta-programs manipulate object-programs". A meta-program is a program, which "may construct object-programs, combine object-program fragments into larger object-programs, observe the structure and other properties of object-programs". Rideau gives a similar definition: "Meta-programming, the art of programming programs that read, transform, or write other programs" [Rid99]. The Bartlett's definition is: "Meta-programming is writing programs that themselves write code" [Bar05]. Veldhuizen expends the view to meta-programming by stating that meta-programming is "the study of generalizations in software and a meta-language is the one, in which we express those generalizations" [Vel06].

Therefore, the diversity of viewpoints on meta-programming can be summarized as exploring high-level abstractions, processes such as meta-analysis, languages, tools such as compilers or programming techniques. In this book, we consider and apply the so-called structural heterogeneous meta-programming (see Sect. 5.5).

5.4   Background of Feature-Based Modelling

In Chap. 1, we have discussed the challenges to educate CS topics at school and the importance of STEM for the twenty-first century. In Chap. 2, we have formulated a vision on how to introduce STEM into CS courses at school. We have also formulated requirements to do that as effectively as possible through introducing the concept of automation, where it is appropriate. The realization of this concept is impossible without a systemization and researching of the relevant tasks. We have already started our journey towards achieving these objectives by introducing STEM-learning processes as a problem domain (see Sects. 2.4 and 2.5 in Chap. 2).

5.4.1   A Vision for Researching STEM-Driven CS Education

In this section, we introduce both the problem and solution domains for researching the tasks at large. We need *a deeper understanding* of the research context. We identify further *research domains*, namely, the *problem domain* (Fig. 5.1a) and the *solution domain* (Fig. 5.1b). In addition, each domain has its own context. Both tightly relate to each other. Typically, we specify this relation yet before the realization, at the phase of the requirements statement. More specifically, for the problem domain, we identify two interrelated parts, i.e. the *base problem domain* within the STEM paradigm and *context*.

Here, by the base problem domain, we mean STEM-driven processes to teach CS topics at school. We do not provide details on those processes here (they were already described, of course, to some extent, from the perspective of an external viewer; see Fig. 2.6 in Chap. 2). We remind readers that we categorize the processes into two large categories: (i) *design-based* and (ii) *use or learning-oriented* ones.

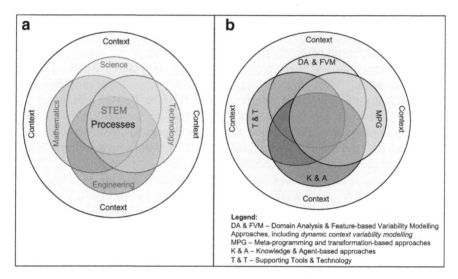

Fig. 5.1 STEM as a problem domain (**a**) CS and SWE and CS methods, approaches as a solution domain (**b**)

Aiming at achieving the prespecified objectives, we need to plan and specify the design processes in advance as precisely as possible. To which extent we are able to do that, to the same or similar degree, it would be possible to improve the STEM learning in terms of innovations through the automation concept.

The *solution domain* is a set of the CS-oriented approaches and methods we use for implementing the processes, having in mind objectives for automation. They include (i) problem domain analysis and feature-based variability modelling (DA & FVM), (ii) meta-programming (MPG) approaches, (iii) knowledge and agent-based (K&A) and (iv) supporting tools and technology (T&T). In this chapter, we focus mainly on the two, i.e. DA & FVM and MPG. As both have an extremely wide context, we outline a vision of the context interaction abstractly in Fig. 5.2. Later we will provide more details on that.

For the analysis of STEM domain, we use two DA methods, i.e. FODA [KCH +90] and SCV analysis [CHW98]. We apply three basic FODA principles: (1) identification of domain boundaries and context, (2) modelling of the context by features and (3) modelling of subdomains within the boundaries of features. We also use the SCV analysis to identify the domain variability in the large. We describe the basics of feature modelling in the next section.

5.4.2   Basics of Feature Modelling

Feature diagrams (FDs) are a graphical language used for representing and modelling variability at a higher level of abstraction. Traditionally, designers use them in

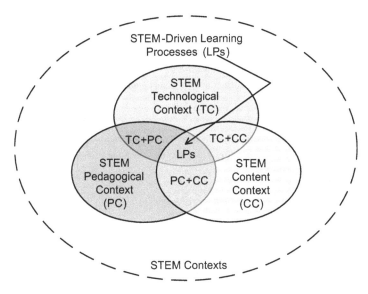

Fig. 5.2 A framework of defining STEM contexts

the early design stages, such as formulation of requirements for the design of software product lines. Now, however, in terms of variability modelling [GWT +14], their use practically covers the entire life cycle of software artefacts. As there are a slightly different notions and interpretations of elements of FDs, it is possible to consider FDs as a set of graphical languages (though FDs have also a textual representation [ACL+13]). We refer to an FD representing some domain as its feature model. Below, we present basic definitions of the syntax and semantics of the conceptualized FDs.

From the perspective of software engineering, it is commonly accepted that a domain can be analysed and modelled at a higher level of abstraction using feature-based approaches. Informally, the feature is a prominent characteristic of a *system*, *entity* or *concept* in a domain to capture its essential structural or functional aspects (see Sect. 5.3 for known definitions of the term *feature* taken from [AK09]). The fact of the diversity of definitions is very important per se. It actually defines the scope of feature modelling possibilities to interpret the feature concept as the user wants. This is yet another motivation of the benefits of using feature models in the e-Learning domain.

Feature modelling is the activity of modelling the common and the variable properties of concepts and their interdependencies in a domain and organizing them into a coherent model referred to as a feature model [CE00]. The intention of a feature model is to represent and model a domain or its subdomains using the feature concept. Specifically, this activity can be seen as a part of the domain analysis process, for example, as it is described by FODA [KCH+90]. The advantage of feature models is the provision of an abstract, implementation independent, concise and explicit representation of the variability present in the software [HHU08].

Table 5.1 Extended feature diagram notation based on GPFT [CE00]

Basic feature model concepts	Definition	Graphical notation
Mandatory (AND relationship)	**If** *feature-A* **then** *feature-B* **If** *feature-A* **then** *feature-C* and *feature-D*	
Optional	**If** *feature-A* **then** *feature-B* or none *feature* **If** feature-A **then** *feature-C* or *D* or none feature	
Alternative (OR decomposition)	**If** *feature-A* **then** *any of features* (B, C, D)	
Alternative (XOR decomposition)	**If** *feature-A* **then** (B **xor** C)	
Constraint <*mutex*> or <*excludes*>	Feature K *excludes* feature F and vice versa	
Constraint <*requires*>	Feature K *requires* feature F	
Annotated feature	Feature F with annotation A	
Collaborative (context) features	Feature A sends a message to feature B	
Value transfer from generic to concrete features	Selected value of feature A is transferred to the feature B at the lower level of abstraction	

A feature model represents the common and variable features of concept instances (sub-features) and the dependencies and relationships between the variable features. The model delivers the intention (usually implicitly) of a concept, whereas the set of instances it describes is referred to as an extension, which narrows the meaning and scope of the concept. This extension is often referred to as a hierarchy of features with variability [CKK06]. The primary purpose of a hierarchy is to represent a potentially large number of features into multiple levels of increasing detail. Variability defines what the allowed combinations of features are. To organize a hierarchy as an allowed combination of features, the identification of feature types is essential. *Feature types* are the inherent part of the feature model.

There are three basic types of features: *mandatory*, *optional* and *alternative* (see Table 5.1). Mandatory features allow us to express common aspects of the concept (usually they are referred to as *commonality* [CHW98]), whereas optional and alternative features allow us to express *variability*. All basic features may appear either as a *solitary* feature or *in groups*. If all mandatory features in the group are derivatives from the same parent in the parent-child relationship, we can speak about the AND relationship among those features (see also Table 5.1). An optional feature is the one which may be included or not if its parent is included in the feature model. Alternative features, when they appear in groups as derivatives from the same parent, may have the following relationships: OR, XOR, etc. The XOR-relationship also can be treated as a constraint (typically called *excludes*) if the relationship is identified for features derived from different parents.

5.4.3   Formal Definition of Features and Constraints

It is possible to express features not only graphically but also formally, using the notation of the propositional logic [Bat05, CHE05, TBK09]. Let P be the parent feature and the set $\{C_1, ..., C_n\}$ are children features of P. Then we can specify the feature relationships as follows (see also Table 5.1):

$(P \Rightarrow \wedge_{i \in M} C_i) \wedge (\vee_{1 \leq i \leq n} C_i \Rightarrow P); M \subseteq \{1, ..., n\}$ (AND - relationship)

$(P \Leftrightarrow \vee_{1 \leq i \leq n} C_i) \wedge_{i < j}(\neg C_i \vee \neg C_j)$ (XOR − relationship)

$P \Leftrightarrow \vee_{1 \leq i \leq n} C_i$ (OR − relationship)

$\neg K \vee \neg F$ (Constraint < *mutex*>)

$\neg K \vee F$ (Constraint < *Require*>)

We have presented the basic features and their formal relationships. More advanced subtypes of alternative features are grouped constraints, attributes, cloning and additional constraints [CKK06]. Though the feature-based representation is attractive from various viewpoints, however, there is also some inconsistency of the graphical notation. The existing discrepancies in representing and interpreting graphical elements of feature models are mostly due to the lack of standardization and inconsistency of the available tools. Figure 5.3 introduces a meta-model that summarizes the basic concepts along with their relationships.

This meta-model is helpful in getting the overall knowledge about the notion of feature-based languages. It is also useful for deriving model instances in constructing concrete feature models.

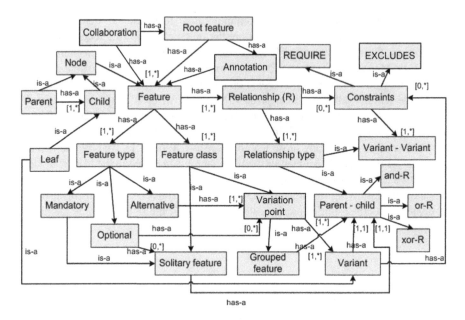

Fig. 5.3 Meta-model of the feature diagram to represent a domain

5.4.4 Static and Dynamic Feature Models

There are two kinds of the feature variability models, i.e. *static variability* and *dynamic variability*. Often researchers call the first *structural* or compile time variability. The second is also called runtime or binding time variability. In traditional feature model definitions, when discovered through analysis and modelling, features remain unchanged during the entire life cycle. Those features are static. A *static feature model* is the model that once defined remains unchanged throughout a product's lifecycle [LLW16]. With the arrival of Dynamic Software Product Lines (DSPL), the need for managing the variability at post-deployment time arises. This approach focuses on changes in the state of the features and more advanced mechanisms capable of modifying the structural variability at runtime (e.g. adding a variant) and promoting open variability models which are easier to evolve [CBT +14, HWS+09]. Bosch and Capilla [BC12] indicate on three possible ways for introducing dynamicity in system model evolution: (1) Variation points become increasingly dynamic and changing while the system is operating. (2) The set of variants for a variation point can be extended after a system is deployed at the customer site and ultimately while the system is operating. (3) Systems increasingly select the variants as they seek to maintain or achieve certain metrics as part of their operation, often referred to as self-behaviour.

Dynamic variability refers to open variability models that can be easily extended, reconfigured and evolved. The reasons for that may be multiple: (i) activate/deactivate features at post-deployment time, (ii) modify the structural variability dynamically and (iii) provide valid and perhaps optimal solutions of the variability model by checking the constraints between features online. Today, therefore, many critical and complex systems demand collaborative capabilities where different functional modules of the system need to share and exchange data to manage complex scenarios, sometimes critical for the system's normal operational mode. In this regard, the paper [CHD15] introduces five collaborative scenarios:

(i) *Exchange and share data*, i.e. when different functional modules need to exchange critical information or a centralized control system needs real-time data from the different functional and operational modules

(ii) *Activate and deactivate functions*, i.e. when features must be activated and deactivated according to different context conditions

(iii) *Add a new functionality*, e.g. when a new critical functional module must be incorporated into the system at runtime and the features supporting that functionality need to be recognized and exchange data with other features or system modules

(iv) *Update software*, e.g. when critical systems like robots may need an update of their software to, for example, change the navigation strategy in coordination with other robots that need to know the situational awareness of the rest of the robots

(v) *Coordinated missions*, when systems like drones may need to carry out a mission for which real-time data must be exchanged and updated at runtime

All these scenarios indicate that runtime changes affecting a system's features, and many times context information, are critical for systems collaborating with each other or functional modules that necessitate on-demand information exchange dynamically.

Typically, dynamicity comes through context changes. The term *context* is very broad as the following definitions state:

(i) "Any information that can be used to characterize a situation of entities (i.e. person, place or object)" [DAS01]

(ii) "The set of the external parameters that can influence the behaviour of the application by defining new views on its data and its available services" [CLC05]

(iii) "A dynamic construct as viewed over a period of time, episodes of use, social interaction, internal goals and local influences" [Gre01]

Therefore, its role is significant for many systems that range from critical to noncritical systems like educational systems. In general, it is possible to obtain the contextual information in three ways:

- *Explicitly*, i.e. by directly approaching relevant people and other sources of contextual information and explicitly gathering this information by asking questions.
- *Implicitly* from the data or the environment. The source of the implicit contextual information is accessed directly, and the data is extracted from it.
- *Inferring* the context using statistical or data mining methods [AT11].

Connected context computing – smart devices will collect data, relay the information or context to each other and process the information collaboratively [Che12].

5.4.5 Mechanisms to Support Dynamicity for STEM

In general, a large body of feature models we have developed and applied for specifying our tasks and processes are static models. However, when we try to apply and adapt those models to a concrete situation and context, the dynamicity may appear. This happens at both the design processes (we mean the design of the content and scenarios) and learning processes. For example, in designing STEM teaching content, there is the need to take into account the pedagogical context which is very broad, i.e. it has a high degree of variability (see Fig. 5.4). It is possible, largely, to foresee this variability in advance through analysis. The model developed on this basis, in fact, is static. Though the pedagogical context is stable enough, nevertheless the dynamicity may appear in two cases. The first is due to limitations of analysis, i.e. some important pedagogical aspects may be missed, for example, because STEM evolves rapidly. The second is because of the feedback information received. For instance, after implementation, it may become clear that we need to introduce new values in some context features or modify the previously defined values.

The other factor affecting dynamicity is the modelling mode. For STEM, we apply a separate feature modelling for the context and base domain, i.e. STEM-driven processes. In this case, some context features may send messages to the features from the base domain. Typically, those features are *collaborative features*. Note that collaborative features are due to the contribution of Capilla et al. [CHD15]. Collaborative features support dynamicity. In our previous work [BBD +14, ŠBB+16, ŠBB+16a and Štu15], in solving the content adaptation problem, we have introduced the context-awareness modelling, using the *feature priorities* to manage the context variability. The priority-based mechanism, in fact, enables the dynamicity aspects to consider statically. We also apply this mechanism for STEM. We return to this topic with more extensive analysis in Chap. 7. The feature annotation (see Table 5.1) has also an influence on dynamicity, though not directly.

Finally, however, the most evident dynamicity appears when we use robots as agents with a smart sensor system to deal with specific STEM-related tasks. We will consider these aspects in more detail in subsequent chapters. Now we introduce two feature models. One represents the STEM context (Fig. 5.4). The other represents the STEM processes (Fig. 5.5). Both, in fact, are abstract feature models, i.e. not providing concrete feature values (except *pedagogical* context; see Fig. 5.4). Furthermore, for simplicity and readability reasons, we present constraints as separate entities for the context model (Fig. 5.4).

As both models are abstract (excluding the feature "Pedagogical" see Fig. 5.4), to make them practical for implementing, we need to extend features by providing their concrete values (introducing atomic features). However, this is a subject of other chapters.

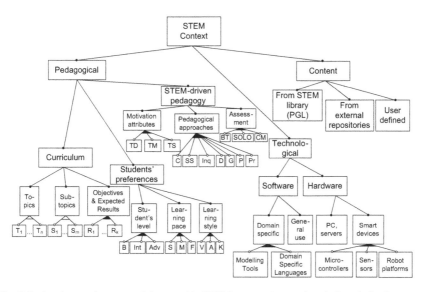

Fig. 5.4 An abstract feature model to specify STEM context (constraints 1–7 are below)

Constraints <*requires*> include:

1. Pedagogical *requires* technological
2. Pedagogical *requires* content
3. Technological *requires* content
4. Objectives and expected results *requires* subtopic
5. Objectives and expected results *requires* topic
6. Topic *requires* subtopic
7. Objectives and expected results *requires* pedagogical approaches.

Legend:

$T_1...T_n$ set of topics, $S_1...S_m$ set of subtopics, $R_1...R_k$ set of objectives and expected results, *B* beginner, *Int* intermediate, *Adv* advanced, *S* slow, *M* medium, *F* fast, *V* visual, *A* audial, *K* kinesthetic, *TD* technological devices, *TM* teacher as mentor, *TS* task solving, *C* consequential, *SS* side-by-side, *Inq* inquiry-based, *D* design-based, *G* game-based, *P* project-based, *Pr* problem-based, *BT* Bloom's taxonomy, *SOLO* SOLO taxonomy, *CM* concept map

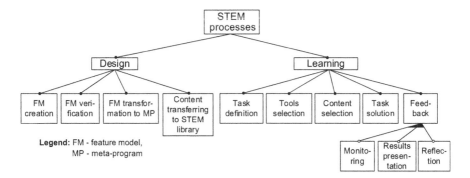

Fig. 5.5 An abstract feature model to represent the base domain, i.e. STEM processes

5.5　Meta-programming as Solution Domain

Introduction to Heterogeneous Meta-programming A great deal of the *learning content* we refer to throughout the book is the so-called generative learning objects (GLOs) or smart learning objects (SLOs), i.e. GLOs with enhanced *generative* capabilities. From the pure technological perspective, a GLO/SLO is in fact a *meta-program*. Programming and meta-programming is a main theme among other topics CS deals with. Sometimes we understood teaching in CS as teaching in computer programming. Meta-programming is a branch of computer programming disciplines (and other automatic equipment such as robots). Therefore, readers, the CS teachers and educational software designers in the first place should receive a concise knowledge on meta-programming. One can learn more on meta-programming from [ŠD13]. The following definitions give the primary understanding of this field. To make reading independent, we need to repeat some definitions from Sect. 5.3 Stream B).

As it was stated in Sect. 5.3, meta-programming is "creating application programs by writing programs that produce programs" [Lev86]. Sheard [She01] emphasizes the role of meta-programming in program generation explicitly. He states that "Meta-programs manipulate object-programs". Meta-program is the program, which "may construct object-programs, combine object-program fragments into larger object-programs, observe the structure and other properties of object-programs". Rideau gives a similar definition: "Meta-programming, the art of programming programs that read, transform, or write other programs" [Rid99]. The Bartlett's definition is: "Meta-programming is writing programs that themselves write code" [Bar05]. Veldhuizen expends the view to meta-programming by stating that meta-programming is "the study of generalizations in software and a meta-language is the one, in which we express those generalizations" [Vel06].

　　Therefore, meta-program is the program, which generates or manipulates a program code. Otherwise, meta-program is a generator of the other program (in terms of a GLO, it is a target content generator, i.e. robot's control program generator in our context). In the context of our approach, by the term meta-programming, we mean the structured heterogeneous meta-programming [ŠD13]. The term "structured" has its roots in earlier works of E.W. Dijkstra (1969) on structured programming. The main idea of this paradigm is the use of the only three control structures (i.e. *sequence, selection, repetition*), of course, in a variety of combinations within a program. Such a structure enables to eliminate the use of *go to* statements and, in this way, to improve the understandability and testability of a program. In a concrete programming language, those structures may have a few types (e.g. for *sequence*, **read, write, call,** =:; for *selection*, **if, case**; for repetition, **for, while**). In terms of functional programming, one can treat those structures as *functions*.

　　The term "heterogeneous" means that we need to use at least two languages (meta-language and target language) for writing meta-programs. The target language (often we refer to it as an *object* or *domain* language) stands for expressing the base domain functionality presented by an object program. The meta-language stands for generalization of a target program. The main mechanism for doing that is the *external parameterization*. Semantically, external parameters and their values represent the *variability of a domain* we aim to automate. Typically, when we write a meta-program, we specify parameters and possibly their values in the *interface* of the meta-program. We specify the implementation of the meta-program in its functional part called *meta-body*. The latter, we describe using meta-language functions in the structured programming mode. The arguments of the functions are *external parameters, target language fragments, other functions* and *combination thereof*. Therefore, meta-program (interface and meta-body) is the specification to implement the domain variability. In terms of SPL, a meta-program specifies a family of related *target program instances*.

In practice, any general-purpose programming language (e.g. C, C#, C++, Java, Pascal, PHP, etc.) can be used in the role of the meta-language. Typically, in writing meta-programs, it is enough to use the only subset of the language to manipulate a target program or its parts. We use PHP in the role of the meta-language in all our case studies and examples. Furthermore, it is our programming language to develop other educational software. For advanced students, when they act as codesigners of GLOs, PHP is also a learning content one needs to learn. With respect to the target language, the situation is quite different. The context predefines the use of that language. For example, we use RobotC, ArduinoC, Python and Java, to specify GLOs/SLOs. It is also a tool (or LO) to be learned by students in the computer programming course. In other cases (e.g. for representing the scenarios functionality and generative procedures to maintain the STEM library), we use HTML and MySQL as target languages. Therefore, those are the multi-language specifications.

What Are Benefits of Meta-programming in General and for CS Learning?
The aim of this sub-section is to motivate the benefits of meta-programming in a wider context. Note that by meta-programming, we mean the structural heterogeneous meta-programming in all our discussions throughout the book. As the meta-program is a program generator (in fact, the meta-language processor or compiler for which the meta-program is an input data), the automatic program creation is a value per se. Such a statement, to some extent, motivates the need of meta-programming in general as a specific kind of programming, enabling to achieve a higher productivity and reusability in developing systems. A domain program generator, in fact, supports both kinds of reuse, i.e. generative reuse and component-based reuse [FK05, LS00]. Though there are many driving forces stimulating a higher productivity through reuse in software design, we emphasize two dominating factors: (a) the *complexity* of systems we need to design and (b) the *growth of software content* within modern systems (mobile phones, computer, robots, etc., including educational software). For a long time, in fact from the very beginning of computing, designers and programmers were struggling with the complexity problem. How serious the problem is, we can conceive from the observation given by Ozzie, the Chief Software Architect of Microsoft in 2006–2010 [LM06]:

> *Complexity kills. It sucks the life out of developers, it makes products difficult to plan, build and test, it introduces security challenges, and it causes end-user and administrator frustration.*

Complexity is the intrinsic attribute of systems and of design processes through which we create systems. Having complexity measures, it is possible to reason about the system's structure, understanding system behaviour, comparing and evaluating systems or foreseeing their evolution. The designer's main objective in developing a system or its components is to hide this complexity from the end-user. Typically, it is possible to achieve that by using the well-proven design principles such as separation of concepts (also decomposition) and information hiding. Those are due to the Parnas's earlier work [Par72]. He presents the information hiding and decomposition criterion as follows: *"Every module . . . is characterized by its knowledge of a design decision which it hides from all others. Its interface or definition was chosen to reveal as little as possible about its inner workings."* In contrast to the Parnas modules, the meta-program structure implements *the multiple separation of concepts* and *information hiding* [ŠD13].

The meta-program hides the complexity in designing educational software and generative content in the following way. Firstly, there are two separate parts within a structure of a meta-program: *interface* and *meta-body*. The graphical interface delivers the information (i.e. parameters, their values, context data or other instructions; altogether are metadata for generation) for the end-user (i.e. learner or teacher) to manage the specification in his/her natural language. The user may have a little knowledge or no knowledge at all about the meta-language or on how it specifies the meta-program's functionality. Secondly, meta-language functions stand for modules (in terms of Parnas's) to specify the functionality of the meta-body. They represent a separate design decision hidden from the others. The designer's responsibility is to make the second part, i.e. meta-body working correctly. The meta-body implements the overall functionality and hides its complexity from the user.

Therefore, meta-programming enables to deal with and manage the complexity issues from the perspective of the end-user. From the designer's perspective, however, there are two points to state. Firstly, meta-programming also enables to manage the complexity in case when the designer and programmer are different persons. In this case, the designer is released from the burden in writing code manually and is able to focus more on system integration tasks. From the programmer's viewpoint, however, the complexity problem remains, and it may vary considerably. This mainly depends on the scope of the domain task variability. Note that there are different measures to evaluate the degree of the meta-program complexity [ŠD13].

What are or might be the role of meta-programming for CS education? In general, all the above-stated are valid for the educational software design in large; however, CS education has to not only deliver the fundamental knowledge in the field but also respond to existing trends in computing. Now researchers and practitioners commonly recognize that with the continuous technological advances and the growth of complexity, we need to move to a higher level of abstraction in representing and dealing with computing problems. That means the acceptance and realization of approaches based on the use of model-driven transformations as much as possible. In essence, meta-programming in large is just the approach suitable to deliver that knowledge.

Types of Meta-programs and Examples of Their Specifications   In the context of this meta-programming paradigm, there are a few types of meta-programs. We investigate them in our research and apply for CS education implicitly or explicitly. Further, we identify them as *Type 1*, *Type 2*, *Type 3* and *Type 4*.

Type 1: Meta-program as *a single program generator* (or generative component such as GLO/SLO)
Type 2: Meta-meta-program as a *single multistage generator*
Type 3: Meta-meta-program as *a single meta-generator*
Type 4: Meta-meta-program as a *system composed of generators and meta-generators*

Note that *Type 1* is the simplest form of representing the structure of the meta-program (we mean the structural heterogeneous one). *Type 2* is a derivative item from the *Type 1*. For example, this type enables to automate the *content adaptation* to the use context [ŠBB+16a]. One can get more information on those types from [Štu15]. Here, we extend the list of meta-program types by introducing two *new types* (*Type 3*, *Type 4*). The need for that has arose in dealing with the problem to construct a *generative scenario for STEM* (we will discuss that in Chap. 11). Now we have a set of meta-program types. Therefore, we need to introduce some scheme to characterize the introduced types more systematically. We present it from the user's viewpoint. The scheme includes the following attributes: **purpose, structure, properties, usage and restrictions.** We outline those in more detail below.

5.5.1   Meta-program of Type 1

Purpose is to ensure a *component-level generative reuse*; in other words, the aim is to specify *the predefined static variability* of a domain component and make it executable by means of meta-programming to produce one instance on demand at a time.

Structure contains two interrelated parts: (i) *interface* to provide parameter values as metadata for generation (it also may include a contextual information) and (ii) *meta-body* to implement the entire functionality and hide it from the end-user.

Properties include:

1. *Interactive* selection of parameter values by the end-user on demand.
2. The selection mode is "one value for each parameter".
3. *One-stage* processing.
4. One instance produced by the meta-language processor at a time.
5. The possible number N of derivable instances depends on the number of parameters and the number of valid parameter values; in case of independent (not interacting) parameters, it is equal to $N=|P_1|\times|P_2|\times.. \times|P_n|$ ($|P_i|$ – the number of values of parameter i).
6. Data transfer mode within meta-program is *"parameter-function relationship"* (see also Fig. 5.6 data transfer from (a)-(b) to (c)).

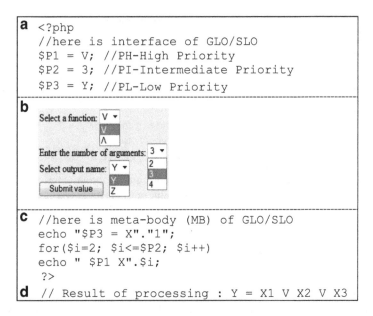

a
```php
<?php
//here is interface of GLO/SLO
$P1 = V; //PH-High Priority
$P2 = 3; //PI-Intermediate Priority
$P3 = Y; //PL-Low Priority
```

b
Select a function: V ▾
Enter the number of arguments: 3 ▾
Select output name: Y ▾
Submit value

c
```php
//here is meta-body (MB) of GLO/SLO
echo "$P3 = X"."1";
for($i=2; $i<=$P2; $i++)
echo " $P1 X".$i;
?>
```

d
```
// Result of processing : Y = X1 V X2 V X3
```

Fig. 5.6 PHP meta-program to specify the Boolean equation generator: (**a**) textual interface; (**b**) graphical interface; (**c**) meta-body; (**d**) generated instance

Usage covers single program generators (e.g. GLO/SLO within the STEM library or as a separate item outside the library) to produce a *target instance* on demand automatically predefined by the selected parameter values.

Restrictions are a lack of flexibility, a manual selection of parameter values from the predefined list, the only one value at a time, restricted capabilities to introduce new values.

Firstly, we define the concept "interacting parameters", and then we illustrate some of those characteristics by a simple motivating example.

Definition. Two parameters, P_i and P_j, *interact or are dependent* if for the parameter values $v_{ik} \in P_i$ and $v_{jl} \in P_j$ ($i \neq j$) at least one or both conditions (5.1) and (5.2) hold:

$$\textbf{exist } k \text{ and } l \text{ such that } \left(v_{ik} \text{ excludes } v_{jl} \right) = \textbf{\textit{true}} \tag{5.1}$$

or

$$\textbf{exist } k \text{ and } l \text{ such that } \left(v_{ik} \text{ requires } v_{jl} \right) = \textbf{\textit{true}}. \tag{5.2}$$

Otherwise, parameters P_i and P_j are *independent* or *not interacting*, i.e.
for all k and l [$(v_{ik}$ requires $v_{jl})$ or $(v_{ik}$ excludes $v_{jl})$] $= \textbf{\textit{false}}$.

Say, we want to have a generator that generates a homogeneous logic equation of the type: Y = X1 V X2 V X3. We want to implement the following variability through parameterization: the logic function type (parameter P1) is taken from the set $\{\vee, \wedge\}$, the number of arguments (parameter P2) is taken from the set $\{2, 3, 4\}$, and the left side function's name (parameter P3) is taken from the set $\{Y, Z\}$. In Fig. 5.6, we implement the meta-program of *Type 1*, using PHP as a meta-language. The text string to represent the equation is a target language. Note that parameters P1, P2 and P3 are independent. We specify the context information by comments given in the interface.

Note that we present the implementation of the interface in a simplified form. Typically, its complexity overpasses the implementation complexity of the meta-body in the following sense. The implementation of the interface *guides* the implementation of the meta-body. Therefore, it is reasonable to automate the interface development. The possible number of instances to produce automatically from this specification is equal to $|P1| \times |P2| \times |P3| = 2 \times 3 \times 2 = 12$.

5.5.2   *Meta-program of Type 2*

Purpose is to ensure **an automated** adaptability at the *component level.* In other words, *the intent is* to rearrange the internal structure of *Type 1* into the multistage format using *deactivation-activation of meta-language constructs (mechanism 1).* The adaptation problem arises when there are a large number of parameters (e.g. 7 and more) and multiple contexts of use. **Structure is** multistage, i.e. the structure at each stage contains own interface and own meta-body as it is shown in Fig. 5.7.

Properties include (1) *Type 2* is *derivative* from *Type 1* by rearranging the given parameter space of *Type 1* into a multistage one according to prespecified rules (e.g. at least one parameter at any stage, interacting parameters should appear on the same stage, rearrangement is context-dependent, etc.). (2) The mechanism *of deactivation-activation of meta-language constructs (mechanism 1)* is the basis to

Fig. 5.7 Internal structure of meta-program of *Type 2* (i.e. *meta-meta-program*)

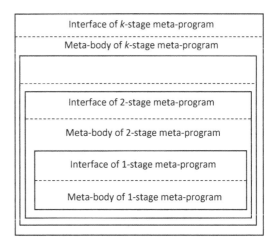

implement multi-staging. The symbol "\" written before a PHP construct such as a function f (e.g. \$f$) *deactivates* it, i.e. the compiler interprets the construct "\$f$" as a string but not as a function. After the one-stage processing, this construct becomes active. The number of deactivating symbols depends on the stage order and on the PHP specificity, i.e. the symbol "\" has yet another role, i.e. to denote the end of the line. (3) The parameter value selection is *context-dependent, interactive* and *multi-stage*. (4) The selection mode is "one value for each parameter at each stage". (5) *Multistage processing*, each next processing narrows the parameter space responding to the adaptation needs. (6) At each stage, the processor generates the only one meta-program (having a narrowed parameter space). For stage $k > 1$, the item is an adapted meta-program with a narrowed functionality. For stage $k = 1$, after processing, the item is a target program adapted to the user's needs. (7) Data transfer mode within meta-program is *"parameter-function relationship"*.

Usage is the generation of other generators for automated adaptation to the context of use (adaptable to the teacher's or student context). For more detail, see Chap. 8.

Restrictions include (i) a lack of readability and understandability and (ii) manual writing of such specifications that is possible only for a small number of stages (practically 2 or 3). We need to have a refactoring tool to transform original (correct) meta-program into its multistage format (for such an experimental tool, see [BBŠ13]).

We illustrate all that by the same motivating example. In Fig. 5.8, we present a two-stage meta-program derived from the one of the *Type 1*. The context, i.e. *fuzzy variables* (PH, PI, PL; see the interface specification in Fig. 5.6), serves for defining on how we intend to allocate parameters to stages.

The model of *Type 2* supports the automated content adaptation to the context of use (e.g. teacher or learner's, see Chap. 8*).*

```
<?php
//here is Interface of stage 2
$P1 = V;
$P2 = 3;
//here is the MB of stage 2, including its interface
echo "<?\n";
echo "\$P3 = Y;\n";
echo "echo \" \$P3 = X\".\"1\";\n";
echo "for(\$i=2;\$i<=$P2;\$i++)\n";
echo "echo \" $P1 X\".\$i;\n";
echo "?>\n";
?>
//Result after two-stage processing
// Y = X1 V X2 V X3
```

Fig. 5.8 Two-stage meta-program

5.5.3 Meta-program of Type 3

Purpose is *component-level reuse for integration*. In other words, the intent is to specify *the dynamic variability* of a domain component and make it executable.

Structure is the two-stage specification implemented *by external files* (*mechanism 2*), in contrast to mechanism 1; see properties of *Type 2*.

Properties include (1) *interactive or automatic* parameter value selection, (2) selection mode which is "*any* number of parameter values for each parameter is possible" (cp. with *Type 1 and Type 2*) and (3) the above-stated selection mode that requires resolving the parameter interaction problem. The interaction model should be specified in advance at the statement of requirements. (4) At each stage, a set of items is generated. For stage 2, items are meta-programs (generators). For stage 1, items are target programs derived from each generator produced at stage 2. (5) Data transfer modes are as follows: TM1, values transfer through the *parameter-function relationship*; TM2, *file-based* values transfer; and TM3, *file link-based* value transfer. For formal definition, see Sect. 5.7.

Usage is the generation of other generator for its integration into a larger system (e.g. into the generative STEM scenario).

Restrictions or difficulties include (i) interaction among parameters is more complicated; (ii) therefore, the implementation is more complex, i.e. we need to pay a higher price for the extended functionality, though this is the concern of a designer, but not the user.

We illustrate that with the same motivating example (see Fig. 5.9) and the same implementation language.

Note that this example implements the meta-level, using the file-based mechanism (previously identified as mechanism 2) and the simplest mode for selecting parameter values (i.e. the only one value at a time for each parameter). If we want to apply the multiple value selection at a time, we need to resolve the parameter interaction problem. We illustrate the interaction model under the following requirements. We want to produce (1) two equations of the same length at a time: (2) the equation Y contains the operator "or"; (3) the equation Z contains the operator "and".

Selection of parameter values is P1= $\{\lor, \land\}$, P2 = 3 and P3=$\{Y, Z\}$.

The interaction model includes the following constraints: (a) Y *requires* "$\lor$", (b) Z *requires* "$\land$", (c) Y *excludes* "$\land$", and (d) Z *excludes* "$\lor$".

Generated items, i.e. a set of instances after two-stage processing are:

$$Y = X1 \lor X2 \lor X3$$
$$Z = X1 \land X2 \land X3.$$

a
```
<?
    // Interface of meta-generator
    $P1 = V;
    $P2 = 3;
    // Meta-body of meta-generator
    $file = "stage1.php";
    $fd = fopen($file, "w");
    // Generator creation
    fwrite($fd, "<?"."\n");
    fwrite($fd, '$P3'." = ".'"Y"'.";"."\n");
    fwrite($fd, "echo ".'"$P3 = X"'."."."."."."."1"'."."."."."."\n");
    $T="";
    for ($i = 2; $i <= $P2; $i++)
    $T = $T." $P1 X".$i;)
    fwrite($fd, "echo ".'$T'.";"."\n");
    fwrite($fd, "?>"."\n");
    fclose($fd);
    // Initiation of the created generator
    include "stage1.php";
?>
```

Created generator with automatic initialization

b
```
<?
    // Interface of generator
    $P3 = "Y";
    // Meta-body
    echo "$P3 = X"."1";
    echo $T;
?>
```
c Y = X1 V X2 V X3

Fig. 5.9 Meta-meta-program and (**a**) meta-program derived from the first (**b**) and generated instance (**c**)

5.5.4   Meta-program of Type 4

Purpose or intent is to ensure the *system-level reuse for designer and user*. In other words, the intent is to specify *the static and dynamic variability* of a set of domain components and make the system executable, thus to enable (1) a higher productivity for the designer and (2) *bringing more functionality for the user*.

Structure is an aggregation of meta-program of *Type 1* and *Type 3* through a set of composition mechanisms to transfer data from one component to another.

Properties are: (1) The need to write a *precise* requirement file for a given task extracted from its feature model. (2) The development of the meta-generator of *Type 3*, to produce parameters annotations automatically by the generators, is manual created once for all tasks. (3) The number of these generators is equal to the number of parameters (see the box 4 in Fig. 5.10). (4) There are yet three meta-generators of Type 3 to produce graphical interfaces: G_1 (for selecting the values in the mode "one value for each parameter'), G_2 (for selecting any number of values for each

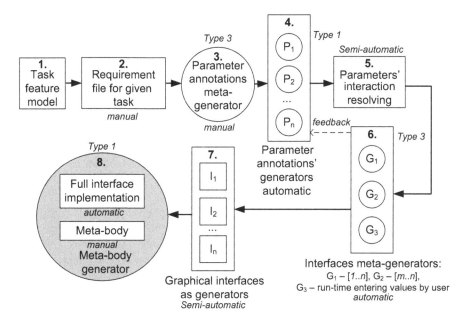

Fig. 5.10 Model specifying the functionality of the meta-program of type 4

parameter') and G_3 (for entering values by the user at run time for a given parameter). (5) Those meta-generators result in creating *n* generators (*n* is the number of parameters) to form a meta-program for the system or component fully automatically (see box 8 in Fig. 5.10) (see also). (6) The basis to aggregate generators and meta-generators into a system is the Chap. 10 external data transfer; these are the three transfer modes: TM, values transfer through the *parameter-function relationship*; TM2, *file-based* values transfer; and TM3, *file link-based* values transfer. The latter indicates not the file itself through which to transfer the data but the link to the other file, which serves for that transferring.

Usage is the generative STEM scenario to be considered in detail in the chapter generation of other generator for its integration into a larger system. In addition, it can be used for creating the component generator able to produce a set of instances at a time.

Restrictions are: (i) the need of a *feedback* among boxes 6 and 4 (see Fig. 5.10 to check the parameter interaction in case of using the generator G3); (ii) the approach requires a higher skill and experience of using meta-programming-based approaches by the designer. (iii) With the growth of the selected parameter values by one try (boxes 5–6), the complexity of representing the graphical user interface increases significantly due to the parameter interaction problem, when a more than one value is selected. (iv) Currently, we use the meta-generator G_2 only in case of not interacting parameters.

With regard to this model, there are still two unanswered questions: (1) *where* and (2) *how* it is possible to introduce the elements of languages during the meta-

Table 5.2 Which languages are used and where?

Box #	Meta-language	Target languages
3	PHP	HTML
4	PHP	HTML
5	PHP	HTML
6	PHP	HTML
7	PHP	HTML
8	PHP	Depends on the task
		For GLO/SLO – RobotC, ArduinoC, Python
		For STEM library and scenario: HTML and MySQL

program constructing process? Table 5.2, in essence, gives the answer to the questions (see also Fig. 5.10). The adequate fragments of the meta-language, i.e. PHP, participate in all next constructing phases, starting from the box 3. There are two sorts of target languages: one for data *representation* (HTML) and another for *describing* the *domain functionality*. The representation language appears in phases (from 3 to 8), while the domain languages appear in the final phase to specify the meta-body interactively. Which target (domain) language or languages to use that depend on the task.

Note that this type of meta-program requires a more extensive research that is beyond the scope of this book.

5.6   Data Transfer Modes Formal Definition

Definition 5.1 Data transfer within meta-program through the *parameter-function relationship* (shortly TM1) is defined as $f(p)$, where f is a function of the meta-language and $p \subset P$ (*P*- full set of parameters, p is a subset of *P*).

Definition 5.2 Data transfer TM2 is defined as a *file-based* values; transfer mode from $File_j$ to $File_i$ is the sequence of functions: $File_i$ [*Open* ($File_j$) → *Read* (*Data*) → $F(Data)$]; F is a set of functions within the $File_i$.

Definition 5.3 Data transfer TM3 is defined as *file link-based* values; transfer from $File_i$ to $File_j$ is the sequence of functions: $File_i$ [*Link* ($File_j$)].

5.7   Summary, Evaluation and Conclusion

With regard to the aims of the book, we have defined two domains (problem and solution) for our research and introduced formalism to represent them for a more extensive exploration. Therefore, this chapter has two independent parts. The first is about the feature-based language given in the form of feature diagrams. Sometimes researchers interpret the use of feature-diagrams as feature-based programming. The second is about meta-programming (more precisely structured heterogeneous meta-programming) as a solution domain to achieve aims of automation in designing STEM-driven processes.

Feature diagram is the notation to specify the variability-based models in defining the problem domain as well as the solution domain. Here, by variability models, we mean the STEM-driven learning variability that we have discussed in Chap. 4. We have adapted feature-based notation from software engineering. We have motivated (through an extensive analysis of the relevant works taken from software engineering and e-Learning) the benefits of using this notation for e-Learning in general and for STEM in particular. We need, however, to state that so far, those benefits are yet not recognized and exploited in e-Learning as extensively as could be. We have also borrowed the ideas of dynamic feature models and suggested to apply them to model the context of our problem domain, i.e. STEM-driven processes (design and learning). We have presented the basics of static feature models and elements to specify dynamicity in the context change. Those elements are feature annotation, priorities and collaborative features. They enable to model context changes. We have presented abstract feature models to illustrate the high-level specification of our domain. We assume that the basic formalism along with illustrative examples is sufficient for understanding the topics and concepts we discuss in the subsequent chapters.

With regard to the second part, we have defined basic features of *structured heterogeneous meta-programming*. They include, firstly, the use of a conventional programming language as meta-language in the mode of *structured programming*, the old approach introduced by Wirth. The meta-language is for specifying of prespecified modifications (in fact, learning variability). The meta-language specifies (and its processor or compiler) performs not data processing (as it is the case in standard programming) but the processing of a target language program or its parts. Therefore, this kind of meta-programming uses at least two different languages (meta- and target). We use PHP as a meta-language and a set of target languages (RobotC, ArduinoC, Python, HTML and MySQL) depending on the task. Secondly, this kind of meta-programming allows expressing generalization, i.e. managing variabilities at the *compile time* through the external parameters. Therefore, the *external parameterization* is the main mechanism to implement heterogeneous meta-programming. In fact, the parameters and their values specify the domain variability (in our case STEM learning variability) at the higher level of abstraction, and in this way to perform managing of the processes, we seek to automate.

We have introduced four types (*Type 1*, *Type 2*, *Type 3* and *Type 4*) of meta-programs with motivating examples (except *Type 4* due to complexity) to show the capabilities of each. We have introduced those types aiming to move from the *component-level* meta-programming to system-level meta-programming (*Type 3* and *Type 4*). We have introduced the following scheme to describe and evaluate the capabilities: *purpose, structure, properties, usage and restrictions*. *Type 1* represents the simplest form of a target program generator. *Type 2* is a derivative meta-program that we are able to derive from the *Type 1*, using the refactoring tool [Štu15]. *Type 2* implements the idea of compile time stage-based meta-programming. Each stage specifies context parameters for possible adaptation of the content to the context of use (e.g. teacher or student). To implement the compile time staging, we use *deactivation-activation mechanism* that is supported by the metalanguage we use. *Type 2* specifies the capabilities for meta-meta-programming, i.e. enables to create meta-generators that produce other program generators. *Type 3* is also specifies meta-meta-programs and differs from the *Type 2* by the use of another mechanism (the use of external file). *Type 4* serves for building not only a single generative component (program generators) semiautomatically. The main intention is to create the *generative system*, such as the STEM-driven scenario generator, containing a set of components (including generative ones). We have explored *Type 1* and 2 extensively in our previous research [Štu15]. *Type 3* and *Type 4* are new exemplars of heterogeneous meta-programs. Though we have realized those types in practice, they need for a more extensive researching yet.

References

[ACF+09] Acher M, Collet P, Fleurey F, Lahire P, Moisan S, Rigault JP (2009) Modeling context and dynamic adaptations with feature models. In: 4th International Workshop Models@run.time at Models 2009 (MRT'09), p 10

[ACL+13] Acher M, Collet P, Lahire P, France RB (2013) FAMILIAR: a domain-specific language for large scale management of feature models. Sci Comput Program 78 (6):657–681

[AK09]   Apelm S, Kastner C (2009) An overview of feature-oriented software development. J Object Technol 8(5):49–84

[ALM+08] Apel S, Lengauer C, Möller B, Kästner C (2008) An algebra for features and feature composition. In: International Conference on Algebraic Methodology and Software Technology, Springer, Berlin, pp 36–50

[AT11]   Adomavicius G, Tuzhilin A (2011) Context-aware recommender systems. In: Recommender systems handbook, Springer US, pp 217–253

[Bar05]   Bartlett J (2005) The art of metaprogramming. IBM Developer Works, Oct 2005. http://www-128.ibm.com/developerworks/linux/library/l-metaprog1.html? ca=dgrlnxw06MetaCoding

[Bat05]   Batory D (2005) Feature models, grammars, and propositional formulas. Springer, Berlin, pp 7–20

[Bat98]   Batory J (1998) Product-line architectures. Invited presentation, smalltalk and Java in industry and practical training. Erfurt, pp 1–12

[BBD+14] Burbaite R, Bespalova K, Damasevicius R, Stuikys V (2014) Context aware generative learning objects for teaching computer science. Int J Eng Educ 30(4):929–936

[BBŠ13]   Bespalova K, Burbaite R, Štuikys V (2013) MP-ReTool tools. http://proin.ktu.lt/ metaprogram/ MP-ReTool/

[BC12]   Bosch J, Capilla R (2012) From static to dynamic and extensible variability in software-intensive embedded system families. Computer: 1

[BDG+95] Batory D, Dasari S, Geraci B, Singhal V, Sirkin M, Thomas J (1995) Achieving reuse with software system generators. IEEE Softw: 89–94

[Bec00]   Beck K (2000) Extreme programming explained. Addison-Wesley, Reading

[Big98]   Biggerstaff TJ (1998) A perspective of generative reuse. Ann Softw Eng 5:169–226

[Bos00]   Bosch J (2000) Design and use of software architectures, adopting and evolving a product-line approach. Addison-Wesley, New York

[BS11]   Burbaite R, Stuikys V (2011) Analysis of learning object research using feature-based models. In: Information technologies' 2011, proceedings of the 17th international conference on information and software technologies. Lithuania, pp 201–208

[BSR04]   Batory D, Sarvela JN, Rauschmayer A (2004) Scaling step-wise refinement. IEEE Trans Softw Eng 30(6):355–371

[BSR10]   Benavides D, Segura S, Ruiz-Cortés A (2010) Automated analysis of feature models 20 years later: a literature review. Inf Syst 35(6):615–636

[CBH11]   Classen A, Boucher Q, Heymans P (2011) A text-based approach to feature modelling: syntax and semantics of TVL. Sci Comput Program 76(12):1130–1143

[CBT+14]   Capilla R, Bosch J, Trinidad P, Ruiz-Cortés A, Hinchey M (2014) An overview of dynamic software product line architectures and techniques: observations from research and industry. J Syst Softw 91:3–23

[CE00]   Czarnecki K, Eisenecker U (2000) Generative programming: methods, tools and applications. Addison-Wesley, Boston

[CE00a]   Czarnecki K, Eisenecker U (2000) Separating the configuration aspect to support architecture evolution. In: Proceedings of 14th European conference on object-oriented programming (ECOOP'2000), international workshop on aspects and dimensions of concerns, Cannes, France, 11–12 June 2000

[CHD15]   Capilla R, Hinchey M, Díaz FJ (2015) Collaborative context features for critical systems. In: Proceedings of the Ninth International Workshop on Variability Modelling of Software-intensive Systems, ACM, p 43

[CHE05]   Czarnecki K, Helsen S, Eisenecker U (2005) Staged configuration through specialization and multilevel configuration of feature models. Softw Process Improv Pract 10 (2):143–169

[Che12]   Chen YK (2012) Challenges and opportunities of internet of things. In: Design Automation Conference (ASP-DAC), 2012 17th Asia and South Pacific, IEEE, pp 383–388

[Chi95]   Chiba S (1995) A metaobject protocol for CCC. ACM SIGPLAN Not 30(10):285–299

[CHS08]   Classen A, Heymans P, Schobbens PY (2008) What's in a feature: a requirements engineering perspective. In: International Conference on Fundamental Approaches to Software Engineering, Springer, Berlin, pp 16–30

[CHW98]   Coplien J, Hoffman D, Weiss D (1998) Commonality and variability in software engineering. IEEE Softw 15:37–45

[CKK06]   Czarnecki K, Kim CHP, Kalleberg KT (2006) Feature models are views on ontologies. In: Proceedings of the 10th International on Software Product Line Conference, 2006, 41–51

[CLC05]   Chaari T, Laforest F, Celentano A (2005) Service-oriented context-aware application design. In: First International Workshop on Managing Context Information in Mobile and Pervasive Environments

[CN13]   Chimalakonda S, Nori KV (2013) What makes it hard to apply software product lines to educational technologies? In: Product Line Approaches in Software Engineering (PLEASE), 2013 4th International Workshop on, IEEE, pp 17–20

[CNC12]   Castro J, Nazar JM, Campos F (2012) EasyT: apoiando a construção de objetos de aprendizagem para uma linha de produtos de software. Conferencias LACLO 3(1)

[CS02]   Cross JK, Schmidt DC (2002) Metaprogramming techniques for distributed real time and embedded systems. In: Proceedings of 7th IEEE international workshop on object-oriented real-time dependable systems, San Diego, 7–9 Jan 2002, pp 3–10

[CZZ+05]   Chen K, Zhang W, Zhao H, Mei H (2005) An approach to constructing feature models based on requirements clustering. In: Requirements Engineering, 2005. Proceedings. 13th IEEE International Conference on, IEEE, pp 31–40

[Dam05]   Damaševičius R (2005) Transformational design processes based on higher CS level abstractions in hardware and embedded system design. Doctoral dissertation, Kaunas University of Technology

[DAS01]   Dey AK, Abowd GD, Salber D (2001) A conceptual framework and a toolkit for supporting the rapid prototyping of context-aware applications. Hum-Comput Interact 16(2):97–166

[DD06]   Dodero JM, Díez D (2006) Model-driven instructional engineering to generate adaptable learning materials. In: Advanced Learning Technologies, 2006. Sixth International Conference on, IEEE, pp 1188–1189

[DDA12]   Díez D, Díaz P, Aedo I (2012) The ComBLA method: the application of domain analysis to the development of e-learning systems. J Res Pract Inf Technol 44(3):331

[DHA+13]   DeVito Z, Hegarty J, Aiken A, Hanrahan P, Vitek J (2013) Terra: a multi-stage language for high-performance computing. In: ACM SIGPLAN notices, vol 48, no 6, ACM, pp 105–116

[Din03]   von Dincklage D (2003) Making patterns explicit with metaprogramming. In: Proceedings of 2nd international conference on generative programming and component engineering, GPCE 2003, Erfurt, Germany. LNCS, vol 2830. Springer, New York, pp 287–306

[DŠ08]   Damaševičius R, Štuikys V (2008) Development of generative learning objects using feature diagrams and generative techniques. Informat Educ-Int J 7(2):277–288

[DS09]   Damasevicius R, Stuikys V (2009) Specification and generation of learning object sequences for E-learning using sequence feature diagrams and metaprogramming techniques. In: Advanced Learning Technologies, 2009. ICALT 2009. Ninth IEEE International Conference on, IEEE, pp 572–576

[DS98]   Dehnert JC, Stepanov AA (1998) Fundamentals of generic programming, report of the Dagstuhl seminar on generic programming, Schloss Dagstuhl, Germany. LNCS 1766:1–11

[DT16]   Damyanov I, Tsankov N (2016) Variation degree in e-learning courses: assessment through feature models. Bulg J Sci Educ 25(2):2016

[DZF+07]   Dodero J, Zarraonandía T, Fernández C, Díez D (2007) Generative adaptation reuse of competence development programmes. J Interact Media Educ 2007(1)

[EJA+11]   Elfaki AO, Johar MGM, Aik KLT, Fong SL, Bachok R (2011) Towards representation and validation of knowledge in students' learning pathway using variability modeling technique. Int J Comput Sci Issues 8(3):30–35

[FK05]   Frakes WB, Kang K (2005) Software reuse research: status and future. IEEE Trans Softw Eng 31(7):529–536

[GAS17]   Gokhale A, Asai K, Schultz UP (2017) Special issue on the 2015 International Conference on Generative Programming: Concepts & Experiences (GPCE)

[Gog96]   Goguen JA (1996) Parameterized programming and software architecture. In: Proceedings of 4 th international conference on software reuse, ICSR-4, Orlando, 23–26 April 1996, pp 2–11

[Gre01]   Greenberg S (2001) Context as a dynamic construct. Hum-Comput Interact 16 (2):257–268

[GWT+14]   Galster M, Weyns D, Tofan D, Michalik B, Avgeriou P (2014) Variability in software systems—a systematic literature review. IEEE Trans Softw Eng 40(3):282–306

[HHU08]   Hubaux A, Heymans P, Unphon H (2008) Separating variability concerns in a product line re-engineering project. In: EA-AOSD '08, Brussels, Belgium, March 31, 2008

[HWS+09]   Helleboogh A, Weyns D, Schmid K, Holvoet T, Schelfthout K, Van Betsbrugge W (2009) Adding variants on-the-fly: modeling meta-variability in dynamic software product lines. In: Proceedings of the Third International Workshop on Dynamic Software Product Lines (DSPL@ SPLC 2009), Carnegie Mellon University, pp 18–27

[Ira03]   Iranzo PJ (2003) Thesis: partial evaluation of lazy functional logic programs. AI Commun 16(2):121–123

[JGS93]   Jones ND, Gomard CK, Sestoft P (1993) Partial evaluation and automatic program generation. Peter Sestoft, New York

[KCH+90] Kang K, Cohen S, Hess J, Novak W, Peterson S (1990) Feature-oriented domain analysis (FODA) feasibility study. TR CMU/SEI-90-TR-21, Software Engineering Institute, Carnegie Mellon University, November 1990

[KKL+98] Kang KC, Kim S, Lee J, Kim K, Shin E, Huh M (1998) FORM: a feature-oriented reuse method with domain-specific reference architectures. Ann Softw Eng 5(1):143

[KLM+97] Kiczales G, Lamping J, Mendhekar A, Maeda C, Videira Lopes C, Loingtier J-M, Irwin J (1997) Aspect-oriented programming. In: Proceedings of the European conference on object-oriented programming (ECOOP'1997). LNCS, vol 1241. Springer, New York, pp 220–242

[KRB91]   Kiczales G, Jdes R, Bobrow DG (1991) The art of the metaobject protocol. MIT Press, Cambridge, MA

[Lev86]   Levy LS (1986) A metaprogramming method and its economic justification. IEEE Trans Softw Eng 12(2):272–277

[LH01]   Ludwig A, Heuzerouth D (2001) Metaprogramming in the large. In: Butler G, Jarzabek S (eds) Generative and component-based software engineering, LNCS, vol 2177. Springer, Berlin, pp 178–187

[LLW16]   Liu X, Li Y, Wang L (2016) Combining dynamic machining feature with function blocks for adaptive machining. IEEE Trans Autom Sci Eng 13(2):828–841

[LM06]   Lohr S, Markoff J (2006) Windows is so slow, but why? Sheer size is causing delays for Microsoft. New York Times

[LMB92]   Levine JR, Mason T, Brown D (1992) Lex and Yacc. O'Reilly and Associates, Sebastopol

[LN02]   Lowe W, Noga M (2002) Metaprogramming applied to web component deployment. Electron Notes Theor Comput Sci 65(4):106–116

[LS00]   Leavens GT, Sitaraman M (2000) Foundations of component-based systems. Cambridge University Press, Cambridge

[LSW15]   Lesta U, Schaefer I, Winkelmann T (2015) Detecting and explaining conflicts in attributed feature models. In: Atlee and Gnesi S (eds) FMSPLE 2015 EPTCS 182, 2015. pp 31–43, https://doi.org/10.4204/EPTCS.182.3

[MBC09]   Mendonca M, Branco M, Cowan D (2009) SPLOT: software product lines online tools. In: Proceedings of the 24th ACM SIGPLAN conference companion on object oriented programming systems languages and applications, ACM, pp 761–762

[MJD96]   Malenfant J, Jaques M, Demers F-N (1996) A tutorial on behavioral reflection and its implementation. In: Proceedings of the reflection 96 conference, April 1996, San Francisco, pp 1–20

[MLC02]   Le Meur AF, Lawall JL, Consel Ch (2002) Towards bridging the gap between programming languages and partial evaluation. PEPM '02, Jan. 14–15, 2002 Portland

[MS89]   Musser DR, Stepanov AA (1989) Generic programming. In: Proceedings of symbolic and algebraic computation, international symposium ISSAC'88, Rome, Italy, 4–8 July 1988. LNCS, vol 358. Springer, Berlin, pp 13–25

[NLS+16] Najd S, Lindley S, Svenningsson J, Wadler P (2016) Everything old is new again: quoted domain-specific languages. In: Proceedings of the 2016 ACM SIGPLAN Workshop on Partial Evaluation and Program Manipulation, ACM, pp 25–36

[Ous98]   Ousterhout JK (1998) Scripting: higher level programming for the 21st century. IEEE Comput 31(3):23–30

[Par72]   Parnas DL (1972) On the criteria to be used in decomposing systems into modules. Commun ACM 15(12):1053–1058

[Pas04]   Pasalic E (2004) The role of type equality in meta-programming. PhD thesis, Oregon Health and Sciences University, OGI School of Science and Engineering

[PBD05]   Pohl K, Böckle G, van Der Linden FJ (2005) Software product line engineering: foundations, principles and techniques. Springer Science & Business Media, Berlin

[Pet96]　　Pettorosi A (1996) Future directions in program transformation. ACM Comput Surv 28 (4):171–174

[Rid99]　　Rideau F (1999) Metaprogramming and free availability of sources. In: Proceedings of Autour du Libre Conference, Bretagne

[SBA+16]　da Silva LM, Bezerra CI, Andrade RM, Monteiro JMS (2016) Requirements engineering and variability management in DSPLs domain engineering: a systematic literature review. ICEIS 2016:544

[ŠBB+16]　Štuikys V, Burbaitė R, Bespalova K, Ziberkas G (2016) Model-driven processes and tools to design robot-based generative learning objects for computer science education. Sci Comput Program 129:48–71

[ŠBB+16a]　Štuikys V, Burbaite R, Bespalova K, Drasute V, Ziberkas G, Venckauskas A (2016) Stage-based generative learning object model to support automatic content generation and adaptation. In: Computer Software and Applications Conference (COMPSAC), 2016 I.E. 40th Annual, vol 1. IEEE, pp 712–721

[ŠBB14]　　Štuikys V, Bespalova K, Burbaitė R (2014) Refactoring of heterogeneous meta-program into k-stage meta-program. Inf Technol Control 43(1):14–27

[ŠD02]　　Štuikys V, Damaševičius R (2002) Taxonomy of the program transformation processes. Inf Technol Control 1(22):39–52

[ŠD13]　　Štuikys V, Damaševičius R (2013) Meta-programming and model-driven meta-program development: principles, processes and techniques, vol 5,. Springer

[ŠDB+08]　Štuikys V, Damaševičius R, Brauklytė I, Limanauskienė V (2008) Exploration of learning object ontologies using feature diagrams. In: Proc. of World Conference on Educational Multimedia, Hypermedia & Telecommunications (ED-MEDIA, vol 8, pp 2144–2154

[She01]　　Sheard T (2001) Accomplishments and research challenges in meta-programming. In: Proceedings of 2nd international workshop on semantics, application, and implementation of program generation (SAIG'2001), Florence, Italy. LNCS, vol 2196. Springer, Heidelberg, pp 2–44

[Štu15]　　Štuikys V (2015) Smart learning objects for smart education in computer science. Springer, New York

[Tah99]　　Taha W (1999) Multi-stage programming: its theory and applications. PhD thesis, Oregon Graduate Institute of Science and Technology

[TBK09]　Thum T, Batory D, Kastner C (2009) Reasoning about edits to feature models. In Software Engineering, 2009. ICSE 2009. IEEE 31st International Conference on, IEEE, pp 254–264

[Tem95]　Templ J (1995) Metaprogramming in Oberon. Ph.D. dissertation, ETH Zurich

[Ter97]　　Terry PD (1997) Compilers and compiler generators: an introduction with CCC. International Thomson Computer Press, London

[Vel06]　　Veldhuizen TL (2006) Tradeoffs in metaprogramming. In Proceedings of ACMSIGPLAN workshop on partial evaluation and semantics-based program manipulation, Charleston, 2006, pp 150–159

[Zav03]　　Zave P (2003) An experiment in feature engineering. In: Programming methodology, Springer, New York, pp 353–377

Part III
Design, Re-design, and Use of Smart Content for STEM-Driven CS Education

Part III includes four chapters. It starts with Chap. 6 and ends with Chap. 9. The aim of this part is to show the way on how to design, re-design, and use the so-called *smart content* for STEM-driven CS education. Typically, by smart content, we mean generative learning content (also known in the research literature as generative learning object, shortly GLO), with enhanced functionality. The term "generative" carries the meaning and the GLO possibility to generate the other content as an instance, i.e. Learning Object (LO) for the concrete context of use. This property is the base to introduce the automation through generative reuse and generators. However, there are different possibilities to enforce this main property. Part III is just about those possibilities. In Chap. 6, we provide the extended discussion on how one should understand the term smart content. In this regard, we introduce the evolution curve of GLO/SLO and the adequate framework. The framework deals with smart content from different perspectives that include learner's, teacher's, designer's, and researcher's visions. In Chap. 7, we discuss model-driven design and re-design of smart content for STEM. This discussion includes two conceptual models and two approaches to design SLOs. We present these approaches at the top level along with the theoretical background to perform the adequate transformations that we consciously missed in Part II. In Chap. 8, we consider the extension of GLO/SLO "smartness" or functionality by introducing the stage-based model. The aim is to solve the *content adaptation problem* using the *stage-based* (meaning *automated*) generation process. The basic assumption is that we are able (for example, using the adequate tool, or sometimes manually) to *refactor* the structure of the initial correct GLO/SLO specification into the stage-based specification without the loss of functionality of the first. This model uses the context information and special mechanism for deactivating of constructs within the specification in defining stages. In this regard, we introduce a background, discuss properties, context-awareness and staging relationship, adaptation scenario, present a case study, and analyze capabilities of the model. In Chap. 9, we extend smartness of GLO/SLO by merging two technologies, i.e. generative and agent-based. In other words, we consider GLO/SLO as a weak software agent. In the context of GLO/SLO use, the software agent enables to define values of *technological parameter more precisely*.

Chapter 6
Understanding of Smart Content for STEM-Driven CS Education

Abstract By this chapter, we start considering a thorough analysis of the first component of our approach, i.e. smart content to support STEM-driven CS education. We define the smart content as a compound of generative learning objects (GLOs), i.e. robot control programs implemented as meta-programs to generate program instances on demand, and component-based learning objects, i.e. quizzes, movies, instructions and other supporting material. We call GLOs smart (SLO) if their structure implements enhanced capabilities for reuse, adaptation or enforced functionality using agent-based technology. GLOs/SLOs are dynamic entities. They have evolved over 7–8 years in the context of our research. For better understanding of GLOs/SLOs, we present an evolution curve and framework of those entities. Using the evolution curve, we have identified three models, i.e. *initial M0*, *intermediate M1* and *current M2*, to define the growth of GLOs/SLOs functionality. The model *M0* is the simplest. The model *M1* specifies more functions but without the explicit use of STEM features. The model *M2* implements explicit STEM attributes with enhanced functionality. The framework defines the understanding of these entities, using the following visions: learners, teachers, designers and researchers.

6.1 Introduction

In this chapter, we firstly discuss the evolution of meta-programming-based GLOs concept, its transcending limits and arrival of a new concept, i.e. smart learning object (SLO) for STEM. Now one can find the use of the term "smart" very often in the scientific literature on STEM and CS education. However, researchers try to assign a different meaning to this term, depending on the context. On this account, for example, Brusilovsky and his colleagues [BEK+14] state: "Computer science educators are increasingly using interactive learning content to enrich and enhance the pedagogy of their courses. A plethora of such learning content, specifically designed for computer science education, such as visualization, simulation and web-based environments for learning programming, are now available for various courses. We call such content **smart** learning content". In the book [Štu15], we have defined SLO as a meta-programming-based GLO with extended generative

© Springer International Publishing AG, part of Springer Nature 2018
V. Štuikys, R. Burbaitė, *Smart STEM-Driven Computer Science Education*,
https://doi.org/10.1007/978-3-319-78485-4_6

capabilities, e.g. for automated adaptation and context awareness. In this book, we treat SLO also as meta-programming-based GLO with enlarged *new* functional capabilities for STEM. Those SLOs have also structural changes caused by new functional capabilities such as additional integrated learning materials (guides, movies, etc.) called component-based learning objects (CB LOs).

Though the number of proponents who use the generative content grows (see, e.g. [Chi16]), in essence, the understanding what this kind of the content is still vague. Therefore, the aim of this chapter is to introduce a framework enabling a better understanding of those items, i.e. generative technology-based SLOs for STEM. The central point of this framework is the use of the multidimensional vision. We have borrowed the latter from the Minsky's theory of frames to represent knowledge [Min75]. Next, we do not try to define the item by presenting some definition, but rather our intention is to build *meta-models* for each vision. Therefore, we introduce the learner's, teacher's and technological designer's visions. We represent a meta-model by a set of attributes and their relationships inherent to a particular vision. Additionally, we introduce the researcher's vision. It summarizes the remaining visions and considers the evolution of the SLO concept from the researching perspective that focuses on the enlargement of functional capabilities.

The structure of this chapter includes the related work (Sect. 6.2), GLO/SLO evolution curve (Sect. 6.3), a framework to analyse and understand SLO (Sect. 6.4), analysis of SLO from the researcher's perspective (Sect. 6.5) and the overall summary and discussion (Sect. 6.6). The framework describes the learner's, the teacher's and the designer's visions through the introduced adequate meta-models.

6.2   Related Work

Technology advances have opened new ways to represent the educational content for CS courses such as programming. A variety of program representation forms to enhance the pedagogy exits now. Among others, they include visualization, simulation, gamification, etc. Typically, such content is interactive, i.e. educators and learners use it interactively. The adequate tools through the automated process enable this interactive mode. Brusilovsky and his colleagues [BEK+14] call the *CS interactive learning content* smart. As interactivity is impossible without automation, the generative learning object (GLO) is also a smart content in this regard. Taking into account this vision as the core, we are able to extend the definition of smart CS content as follows. Any enrichment of the CS learning content, by adding advanced features such as visualization [BEK+14], gamification [HKS16], genericity [Štu15], STEM features [ŠBB+17], automated adaptation [SBB+16], etc., enables us to enhance smartness of the content. It is so, because the interactivity and the adequate level of automation stand for the basis to introduce those features.

As interactivity features in educational systems are separate topics, we restrict ourselves by reviewing only the research on *generative learning objects* here (note that the term generative also tells about interactivity and automation, though indirectly).

Now it is possible to exclude at least three streams of papers researching generative learning objects (GLOs). The first represents works of Boyle, Morales, and Leeder et al. [BLC04, Boy03, MLB05]. The second stream represents our papers and work of Han and Kramer [HK09]. The third stream represents works of Chirila and his colleagues [CCS15, Chi15, Chi16, Chi16a, CRR16].

The concept GLO represents an innovative approach in technology-enhanced learning. The GLO model is due to the contribution of Boyle, Morales et al. [BLC04, MLB05]. They characterize GLOs as "the next generation learning objects". The Centre for Excellence in the design, development and use of LOs in the UK (shortly, RLO-CETL) defines GLO as "an *articulated* and *executable* learning design that produces a class of learning objects" [BLA+08]. Therefore, this concept means much more than the conventional LO. With the introduction of GLOs, the extremely large LO research community has received an evident signal to move from the *component-based reuse model* to the *generative reuse model*. The articulation in [Boy06] is understood (1) as human-understandable explicit or implicit decisions involved in design for learning, and (2) these decisions can be executed by computer software to produce LOs based on the design. In practice, i.e. when the GLO authoring tool GLO Maker [GLO17] is used, the pedagogical designs are represented explicitly as the *plug-in patterns*. The tool is used to create specific LOs based on the chosen pattern. Each of these LOs created in this way can be repurposed by the local users, with the help of the same tool, to adapt the resources to their needs and preferences. Then all the LOs so created (or adapted) run as stand-alone web-based LOs. This approach has been borrowed from the systemic grammar [BR12]; however, it can be also viewed as the template-based approach in the sense of use. In terms of software reuse, the template-based approach is treated as the earliest and, therefore, the simplest generative technology [Sam97].

The concept uses software engineering principles like modularity, cohesion, decoupling and composition [Boy03]. According to this paper, LO is cohesive, decoupled and pedagogically rich content. One can repurpose it for different use cases. Another paper [JB07] represents GLOs as design patterns implemented as reusable templates. This GLOs principle is borrowed from the object-oriented programming paradigm where the object model is described at the meta-level through the class concept and afterward at run-time is instantiated into a concrete object. Thus, the reuse focused not on the content but on the design.

The paper [ŠD07] (second stream) presents a knowledge-based GLO model composed out of the knowledge-based interface and a knowledge-based body. The body contains a rich structure: declarative part, a procedural part, a contextual part and a managerial part. The content is based on commonality-variability analysis for creating the model. The authors present an object for the learning of homogeneous

Boolean functions where the parameter variability scope determines the scope of the whole LO domain. The paper [ŠD08] describes the GLO model through the variability dimension of the LO domain. The result of the domain analysis is expressed with the help of feature diagrams (FDs). The FD representation expresses the intention of a concept using mandatory, optional and alternative features. It is considered as a generic high-level model for the GLO.

The work [ŠB09] defines GLOs' aggregation as internal sequencing of generative contents. [DS09] presents how LO sequences can be generated from models expressed with feature diagrams using meta-programming techniques. The paper [ŠBD13] presents an application of GLO models in disciplines of computer science using Lego robots. The GLO model includes several modules responsible with the robot manipulation, according to its learning objective. Another paper [BBD+14] introduces context-aware GLOs for computer science topics where a new GLO dimension is found, namely, the one of teaching context which may have variants. The paper [HK09] proposes the learning object model similar to the GLO. It uses the idea of configurable samples managed by pedagogical parameterization.

The paper [Chi16] of stream three presents the main principles in the implementation of experimental GLO assessment modules created for different computer science disciplines like (1) data structures and algorithms (DSA), (2) fundamentals of programming languages (FPL), (3) compiling techniques (CT) and (4) operating systems (OS). The works [CCS15, Chi15] present generative techniques for LOs based on random numbers applied to primary and middle school arithmetic disciplines. The other papers [Chi16b, CRR16] introduce the GLO models related to CS disciplines and gamification in CS education.

In summary, the concept of GLOs formulates the vision for enhancing reuse through higher productivity and flexibility in creating and using the educational content. Proponents of the approach use different technologies to implement the concept. In our view, heterogeneous meta-programming [ŠD13] is one of the most powerful technology due to the possibility to represent and manage the learning variability explicitly though external parameterization.

6.3 GLO/SLO Evolution Curve

Inspired by the works of Boyle, Morales et al. [BLC04, MLB05], we have introduced the other sort of generative learning objects (GLOs), i.e. meta-programming-based ones in 2007–2008 [DŠ08, ŠD07, ŠD08]. However, this research was pure academic. At that time, we have focused on methodological issues and not yet used GLOs in the real setting at school. In Fig. 6.1, we present the table-like *evolution curve* that illustrates the functionality growth of GLOs during the years 2011–2017.

We have started using GLOs to teach CS at school in 2011. In this early stage, GLOs were simple enough with the explicit content variability and implicit pedagogy. During the years 2013–2015, we have introduced essential improvements, i.e. we have incorporated pedagogical aspects as explicit attributes into the internal

# of school students involved	2011-2012 – 44 2012-2013 – 67	2013-2014 – 75 2014-2015 – 80 2015-2016 – 68	2016-2017 – 86
Tasks	Robot calibration Ornaments design	Plus Line follower Light follower Traffic light Scrolling text on LCD	Plus Obstacle identification Colour recognition Help system Objects transferring and others
Robot platforms	LEGO Mindstorms (NXT)	Plus LEGO Mindstorms (EV3) ARDUINO-based	Plus MakeBlock RASPBERRY PI-based
Mode for STEM support	No	Integration CS + Technology	Integration Science (CS + Physics) + Technology + Engineering + Mathematics
Focus on subjects	Computer Science	Computer Science + Technological Aspects	CS + Physics + Technology + Mathematics
Functionality & structure of learning variability	Technological Content explicit, pedagogy implicit	Explicit integration of Pedagogy, Technology and Content	Pedagogy Technology, Content based on explicit separation of concepts
Learning resources	GLO	Context-aware SB GLO, Stage-based LO, Smart Learning Objects (SLOs)	Personal generative library (PGL) of SLOs, Agent-based GLO, Smart Generative scenarios
Methodological aspects	Initial model (*Model 0*)	*Model 1*	*Model 2*
	2011-2012 (Initial)	**2013-2015 (Middle)**	**2015-...(Current)**

Fig. 6.1 Evolution of meta-programming-based GLOs/SLOs approaches (from 2011 to 2017)

structure along with the content variability. We have introduced context-awareness and stage-based (SB) GLOs aiming at enhancing the adaptability to the context of use. In addition, we have developed tools to design GLOs and tools for refactoring the initial GLO into the stage-based format. Having in mind new features and extended capabilities, we have renamed GLOs and called them smart learning objects (SLOs). We have validated all these efforts not only in the real setting at school, but also we have generalized these concepts and results presented in the book [Štu15] (for practice and implementation, see Chaps. 12 and 13 [ŠB15a, ŠB15b]).

Now let us return to Fig. 6.1. The evolution curve shows the growth of functional characteristics (see vertical axis) over the years 2011–2017. We have identified three evolution periods: *Initial*, *Middle* and *Current*. The latter has started in the middle of 2015, covered the period of the book writing and is lasting since now. For the initial understanding, we have included only the most general characteristics that might be interesting to a reader. Later we provide more specific characteristics interpreted as attributes of GLOs/SLOs. One can see how each characteristic has evolved during those periods. Note that during the years 2013–2015, we have focused on using GLO/SLO as a means for CS education using robots, though implicit STEM aspects have been within the internal structure of GLO/SLO too. We have introduced the STEM-driven concept in CS education explicitly, starting from the middle of 2015. This paradigm change resulted in the need of making a revision of the GLO/SLO internal structure.

So far, we have used the double abbreviation "GLO/SLO" without an explicit explanation. It may cause some confusion for the reader. Therefore, we need once again to explain why we are doing that. First, we need to return to the "smart" term itself. Note that now researchers use this term very often; however, in a concrete context, the meaning of the term may vary. For example, the paper [BEK+14] calls the *smart learning content* that was "specifically designed for computer science education, such as visualization, simulation, and web-based environments for learning programming". Note that our CS educational content is also about *visualization* (due to real tasks solving by robots). It is about *simulation* too (due to the need to check the correct functionality of the robot and its functional components). It is about the *web-based environments* for teaching programming as well (due to the use of server with the personal generative library containing SLOs and other tools). In this regard, therefore, the meaning of the term *smart* is identical to [BEK+14]. However, in our case, the term *smart* means much more – the additional functional capabilities for the automated adaptation, context awareness, and relationship to agent-based approaches and of course the capabilities to provide STEM knowledge.

Therefore, STEM-driven CS education at school, using the meta-programming-based GLO concept, has a predefined pre-history. This education paradigm was born because of the previous extensive research efforts. They have evolved gradually from years to years. This process is continuing until now, bringing new ideas for improvement and innovations. Because of the enlarged number of explicit attributes or features (i.e. S, T, E, M content and STEM pedagogy features), it was reasonable to move pedagogy-related features into the scenario specification as a separate component. We identify those structural changes as the move from *Model 0* (shortly M0) to *Model 1* and *Model 2* (shortly *M1* and *M2*).

6.4   A Framework to Define and Understand SLOs

By reading the previous section, one should conclude that SLOs are real objects; they have a predefined history of use and are beneficial for learning, though the latter lacks of evidence yet (that we disclose later). On the other hand, one can admit the technological complexity of the items discussed. Therefore, we need to have an adequate framework for deeper understanding of those items. What is the best approach to overall analysis and understanding of complex objects or issues in terms of knowledge gaining? In our view, the *multidimensional vision* is helpful for that. Our framework just uses this vision. We have borrowed it from the Minsky's theory of frames to represent knowledge [Min75]. More specifically, we represent our framework at a few levels: *stakeholder visions, main attributes* to define the visions, the possible *values of the attributes* and their *interaction* or relationships. Therefore, we introduce the following stakeholder's visions: *learner, teacher, technology designer and researcher.* The latter, we call also methodological vision. At the top level, meaning stakeholder visions, we define the roles and responsibilities of stakeholders with regard to SLOs. The teacher and learner are end-users of SLOs and their roles are evident. However, the roles of the remaining stakeholders require a more extensive explanation.

We accept that the CS teacher is also a *learning content designer*, whose responsibility is to define learning scenarios, learning content fragments and provide sequencing of those fragments to form the whole course (in our case with regard to CS and STEM education). By the technological designer, we mean the designer whose responsibility is to implement SLO starting from the initial requirements for the development of the entire SLO specification. The latter, in fact, is a tool enabling to derive a concrete content from the executable SLO specification automatically on demand, regarding the use context. By the researcher, we mean the one whose responsibility is firstly to analyse STEM-oriented CS education research and to extract the relevant knowledge (e.g. such as CS and STEM frameworks [YMV +15]) for transferring to SLO designers. Next, the researcher is responsible for the selection of relevant methods used by designers. However, the most important issue is the anticipation of the consequences in using SLO, analysis of the possible contribution of the SLO concept for solving new scientific problems that are important, perhaps are difficult and influential for future research. We do not exclude the possibility of combining different roles to perform them by the same actor, for example, by the smart CS teacher. In fact, in our case, the second author was acting over this period as the CS teacher, as the content designer and as the technological designer fully and as the researcher partially.

At the next level, we categorize the attributes for each vision into two main categories: *structural attributes* and *process-based* ones. There are multiple structural attributes or values; however, their importance for each vision may differ. The same is with the process-based attributes. The other important component in understanding SLO is the interaction or relationships among attribute values. It appears within a concrete vision as well as different visions. At the final level of the framework, we express interaction among attributes by the following relationships ("is-a", "has-a", "requires" and multiplicity properties [*..*], where "*" stands for 0, 1, any). Therefore, different visions bring a different level or perspective in understanding of SLO. We provide more details on those visions in the next sub-sections.

6.4.1   Learner's Vision

We start the analysis of the learner's vision from the observation of Brusilovsky et al. [BEK+14]. They state that "some form of interactivity is a central aspect in all

SLCs" (i.e. smart learning contents). "Content that is presented to learners without any interaction is not smart learning content". The authors also introduce the term *level of smartness of learning content*. They characterize it as continuum "from pre-specified input/generic output to free-form input/customized output". They provide the following example: "A fully computational tool with free-form input, customized output is certainly smart, e.g. an automatic essay evaluation system which gives tailored feedback on various aspects of a submitted essay". In other words, their vision is pure process-based: it requires a tool; the latter requires the adequate input in order to produce the customized outcome automatically. Our meta-programming-based GLO is also a tool that generates the other LO with the help of a meta-language processor. In this sense, even the GLO is a smart content. However, we want a higher degree of smartness.

In our case, it is not enough to consider the process-based attributes. Additionally, we need to focus on structural aspects and their relationships. It is so, because structural attributes directly relate to the formation of input to fuel the processes. Therefore, we characterize the smart CS educational content, i.e. SLO for STEM by multiple attributes and their interaction. We categorize them into two categories: structural and process-based ones. To present the learner's structural vision on SLO, we need to return to Fig. 5.4 (see Chap. 5). We are able to define the student's structural attributes as a meta-model presented in Fig. 6.2. We have derived it from Fig. 5.4 (in fact, it represents a common vision). There are two basic structural units: SLO interface and SLO meta-body (see Fig. 6.2). The latter specifies the implementation, i.e. the overall functionality of the specification. It is invisible for the learner. The learner operates with the interface only. Its attributes are parameters. The values of parameters prespecify the variability space of the learning content for the given task. The learner needs to select parameter values in order to generate the relevant SLO instance, i.e. a robot control program to solve the real-world task. Therefore, the learner also needs to focus on processes-based attributes. Note that we have omitted *pedagogical-social* parameters here, assuming that they will appear ether in the

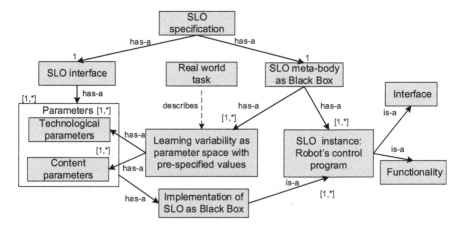

Fig. 6.2 Learner's structural vision on SLO as a part of meta-model

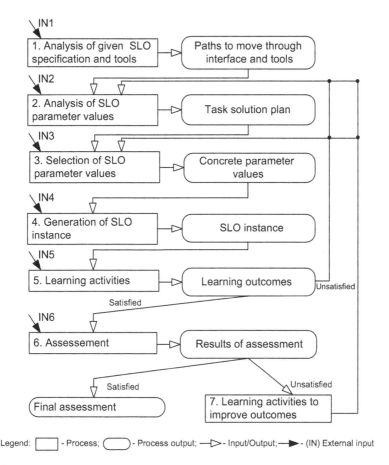

Fig. 6.3 Process-based vision to understand SLO specification by the learner

teacher's meta-model (see Fig. 6.4, in fact, this vision represents SLO of *Model 0/ Model 1*), or in the STEM scenario (SLO of *Model 2*).

In Fig. 6.3, we present the remaining part of the meta-model, i.e. process-based attributes and their interaction enabling to understand the SLO specification by the learner. This meta-model describes the interaction between the learner (operating through the interface) and the tools that support the SLO specification. We have identified the sequence of attributes as processes enumerated from one to seven (see rectangular boxes in Fig. 6.3). The external input (INi) and the internal inputs initiate the adequate process. The latter creates the adequate output to transfer it as input to the next process.

Below we explain the meaning of the external inputs INi.

The input IN1 includes a real-world task given by the teacher as a SLO specification as well as required software tools such as browser, meta-language compiler (processor). The input IN2 includes SW of general use such as spreadsheets, text editors, etc. The input IN3 represents the browser, meta-language compiler (processor). The input IN4 is the same as IN3, i.e. represents the browser, meta-language compiler (processor). The input IN5 includes SW of general use, target language (e.g. RobotC) environment and robot itself. The input IN6 includes assessment criteria given by the teacher.

Finally, we present the interaction learner tools using structural and process-based attributes. *Process 1* covers the interaction among the learner, SLO interface and SLO meta-body (i.e. SLO implementation as black box). *Process 2*, in fact, is a reflection on what the learner has learned so far. *Process 3* covers the learner's interaction with the SLO interface. *Process 4* describes the interaction between the learner and meta-body, though it is invisible for the learner. Finally, *Process 5* describes the learner's interaction with SLO instance, i.e. the generated control program.

6.4.2   Teacher's Vision

We apply the same scheme for describing this vision. The teacher's structural vision includes more details (see Fig. 6.4) as compared to the student's vision. For example, the teacher's concern is to deliver the initial SLO specification for the learner. The metadata for search serves for that. Additionally, the teacher's vision on learning variability and SLO meta-body includes more aspects. For example, the teacher has to have enough knowledge on the implementation of the SLO meta-body in order to make some improvements or changes, because the specification tends to evolve over time. Furthermore, the teacher has to have a much deeper and wider understanding of learning variability space, parameters sequencing, and dependencies between parameter values.

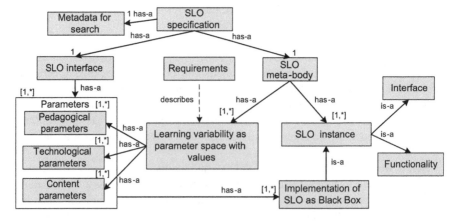

Fig. 6.4 Teacher's structural vision on SLO (Model 1) as a part of meta-model

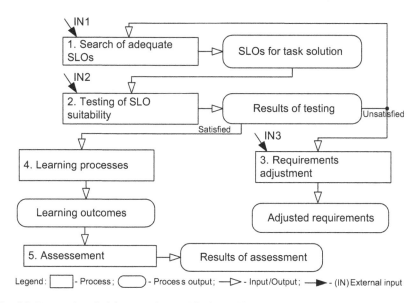

Fig. 6.5 Process-based vision to understand SLO specification by the teacher

The teacher's process-based vision is specific and differs highly from that of the student's (see Fig. 6.5). If the student operates with a concrete SLO specification, the teacher's role is to identify a set of SLOs from the external source (such as personal generative library – PGL), because the same task may have a few specifications (Process 1). Next, the teacher should provide testing for suitability of SLO for the student (Process 2).

The meaning of inputs is as follows. IN1 stands for topic and objectives, SLO location (PGL, repository) and software of general use. IN2 represents browser and meta-language compiler (processor). IN3 stands for feedback information given by the designer, such as a requirement model for correction (if any). Interactions include the following issues. Process 1 describes the teacher's interaction with metadata for search. Process 2 covers interactions with SLO meta-body, SLO interface and learning variability and implementation. Process 3 covers the interaction with the requirements and learning variability. Process 4 covers the interaction with the SLO instance and learner's actions. Finally, Process 5 concerns with the assessment of the learning outcomes and student's knowledge.

6.4.3   Designer's Vision

The designer's vision additionally includes attributes related to the development of the SLO specification. The top-level development requires modelling and design tools (see Fig. 6.6). The bottom level requires those attributes that relate to coding,

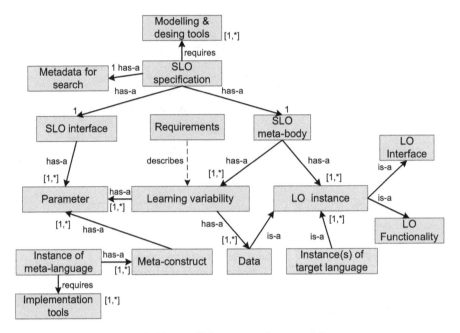

Fig. 6.6 Designer's structural vision on SLO as a part of meta-model

i.e. the meta-language, its compiler or processor and target language. The remaining attributes are the same as discussed in the previous sub-sections. However, the process-based vision is highly specific in this case.

In Fig. 6.7, we outline design-related processes, again using the same scheme. As we focus on model-driven design, the output always is the model with adequate properties. In order to achieve the model state with the suitable properties, the designer should go through processes to enable model verification, transformation and adjustment. We provide the extensive study on those issues in the next chapter. Here, at this understanding level, we explain the semantics of inputs. The input IN1 represents TPACK/CPACK data [YMV+15] for concrete topic from the teacher's perspective in order it would be possible to create initial model. The input IN2 is software for the model verification. The input IN3 is software for model creation and verification. The input IN4 represents software for the model verification. The input IN5 stands for the meta-language, its processor and target language. The input IN6 is the target language processor. We omit the interactions among the processes, because it is clear from the context.

1. Process 1 interacts with the requirements and learning variability, modelling and design tools and SLO specification.
2. Process 2 interacts with SLO specification.
3. Process 3 interacts with SLO specification.

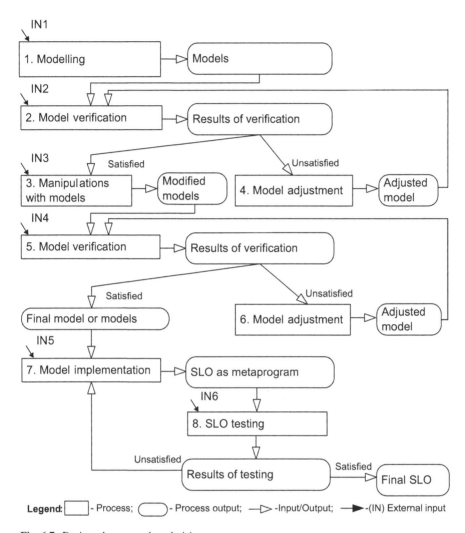

Fig. 6.7 Designer's process-based vision

4. Process 4 interacts with requirements and learning variability, modelling and design tools and SLO specification.
5. Process 5 interacts with SLO specification.
6. Process 6 interacts with requirements and learning variability, modelling and design tools and SLO specification.
7. Process 7 interacts with implementation tools, instance of ML, ML constructs and learning variability and instance(s) of target language.
8. Process 8 interacts with SLO instance.

6.5   SLO Evolution Vision: Researcher's Perspective

The researcher's view is much wider and deeper in multiple aspects, i.e. technological, methodological and theoretical. As automation is the focus in considering our smart LOs, the researcher's concern is the selection of the adequate generative technology and understanding of its capabilities in this regard. In our case, structured heterogeneous meta-programming [ŠD13] stands for the base technology. The researcher needs to understand the principles and capabilities of this technology well. They include the role of languages used, i.e. meta-language and target language or languages, external parameterization aspects, processing by the adequate tools, the creation or selection of the entire technological environment and integrative aspects within this environment. On the other hand, methodological aspects include the thorough understanding of the following issues: (i) the essence of the STEM paradigm, including STEM pedagogy; (ii) specificity of educational models, on how interdisciplinary knowledge should be introduced through solving of the real-world tasks, i.e. what the relevant scenarios should be used; (iii) the mechanism of integrating technological and methodological aspects, i.e. understanding of the role of STEM-driven learning variability to achieve the goals of automation. Perhaps the integrative aspects are of the highest importance. We, as researchers, categorize those aspects into two categories: *internal*, i.e. within the SLO specification itself, and *external*, i.e. within the entire supporting environment. The internal integration includes SLO *internal models* in terms of their evolution (*M0*, *M1* and *M2*) and the *parameter variability interaction* among pedagogical, social, technological and content features. The external integration includes the links of the SLO specification with STEM scenarios and STEM-oriented personal generative library (PGL) and the process-based functionality within the environment. The integration of technological and methodological aspects requires of correct implementation. The theoretical background ensures this correctness. The researcher's responsibility is to bring the theoretical background, to evaluate and to test it. As we are not able to approve all aspects using pure theoretical approaches, some experimental approval is also the researcher's concern.

We present the evolution of internal structural SLO models below.

The structure (Fig. 6.8) consists of two parts, i.e. interface and meta-body. The interface is a set of parameters and their relationships (typically, they are hidden). The meta-body specifies the implementation through parameter-function relationships that define *the pre-programmed content of learning variability*. Parameters represent the top-level learning variability expressed by pedagogical and social, technological and content attributes with their possible values. Syntactically, the interface delivers all parameters uniformly, though semantically they play different roles. One can identify those roles in two ways. The simplest way is an arrangement of parameter types (i.e. pedagogical parameters appear firstly, content parameters appear lastly as it was realized in *M0*). The other possibility is a prioritization by introducing explicit priorities as a context information, i.e. weights HP (high priority

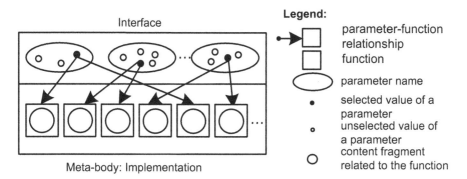

Fig. 6.8 Initial structural model *M0* (*M1*) from researcher's perspective

for pedagogy and social aspects), IP (intermediate priority, e.g. for technology) and LP (low priority for pure content) [SBB+16, ŠBB+17]. In model *M1*, we have realized both possibilities. This context awareness appears in the interface as a comment for the user as well as for interpretation by a computer.

So far, from the researcher's perspective, we have missed one important aspect or research question. It is about the relationship of introduced models *M0* (*M1*) with the learning scenario. One may be able to ask to which extent and how the models reflect or relate to the learning scenario, i.e. activities and actions needed to provide by the teacher and learner in the real teaching setting. It is an important question, because we need to exploit the possibilities of the learning variability in practice as fully as possible in order to bring the expected efficiency of learning process using this approach. In model *M0*, the learner guides the process by selecting the parameter values. It is only a small part of the scenario. The teacher predefines instructions to form the remaining part of the learning scenario. The scenario therefore is static and implicit, i.e. there is a minimal amount of the scenario-related information within the specification itself. In model *M1* (see Fig. 6.9), parameters are distributed among stages according to the context information (i.e. priority weights). Staging splits the whole variability space into pieces called stages, thus narrowing the possibility of choice in selecting parameter values for adaptation. This is additional action and it enriches the scenario, though it is still static and lack of explicit representation of the scenario.

Staging enables an automated (interactive) content adaptation to the user context. Typically, the top stage represents the content related to the teacher's context. The intermediate stage represents the learner's social content (level, activities, etc.) for choice. The third stage represents the pure technological content (related to robots and programming). From the automation viewpoint, the multi-stage SLO is a meta-generator, i.e. the k-stage SLO generates (k-1)-stage SLO already adapted to the user needs and so on. As the multi-stage SLO is, in fact, multi-stage meta-program, its structure represents the hierarchically imbedded specification containing at each stage its interface and meta-body (see Fig. 6.10). Note that we repeat this model (see Fig. 5.7) because of the reading of this chapter independently from the others.

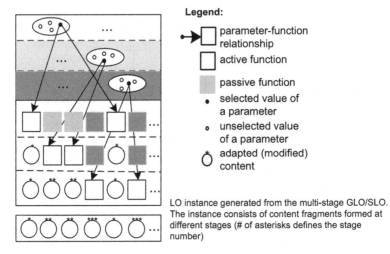

Fig. 6.9 Stage-based structural model *M1* (staging enhance smartness) from researcher's perspective (© with kind permission from the Baltic J. Modern Comp. [ŠBB+17])

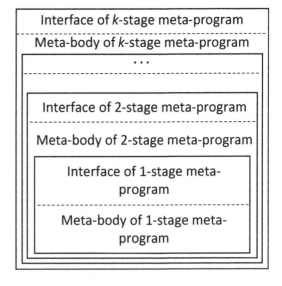

Fig. 6.10 Structural model of the *k*-stage meta-program, i.e. SLO *Model 1*

Staging, however, is not the only property that characterizes the meta-programming-based SLO. Syntactically, we are able to express uniformly through parameters any feature related to the content, for example, links to other objects important for learning (e.g. movies, guides) that reside in the library. Furthermore, we are able to re-arrange the sequence of parameters within the interface so that it

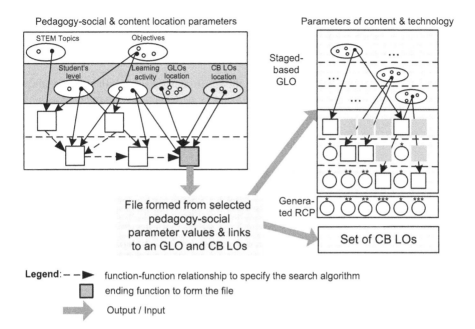

Fig. 6.11 The structure of SLO defined by the Approach 2 (using model *M2*)

would be possible to recognize by the user the roles of parameters specifying STEM learning variability and invoke the adequate actions, e.g. related to the learning scenarios. Typically, the rearrangement requires of introducing some hierarchy within the interface. The rearrangement of course requires also structural changes within the meta-body. The model *M2* of SLO was designed just taking into account those capabilities. The model *M2* implements a deep separation of concepts through the hierarchical structure (see Fig. 6.11). The top-level part specifies the pedagogy-social aspects as well as the content's location. We have implemented this part as a two-level meta-program. Note that it differs from the stage-based structure (the latter exploits the deactivation-activation of meta-functions, while the first no). Therefore, in Fig. 6.11 (see the top part), meta-language functions are represented as white boxes (meaning that they are active to perform needed operations).

By introducing the model *M2*, we seek (i) to enhance capabilities of SLO by integrating additional learning materials for the learner and (ii) to ensure a higher flexibility and higher-level of aggregation of the learning content. The model *M2* integrates within the model *M1* (i.e. GLO) and others LOs called component-based (CB) LOs (see Fig. 6.11). One can interpret the latter as a part of the learning scenario. Therefore, we can write the following formulae to express the structure of SLO defined by the model *M2*:

$$SLO = GLO + CB\ LOs.$$

For example, CB LOs may represent movies, guides, quizzes or other additional material, representing in fact a fragment of the learning scenario. The GLO itself may be multi-staged (i.e. model *M1*; see Fig. 6.9) or not (i.e. one-staged as model *M0*; see Fig. 6.9).

*Note that here we have summarized the researcher's vision without presenting details. We have already presented them in previous Chapters. The reader can find more of those aspects also in Chap. 7.

6.6   Summary, Evaluation and Conclusion

We have discussed how one, with a different background and having different intention and aims, is able to understand the smart learning object (SLO) for CS education. Firstly, we have presented the evolution of this concept by describing the most general characteristics that have been evolving over a decade or so. The intention of the evolutionary curve was to convince the reader that the STEM-based SLO is not only the scientific concept but also its real implementation based on the accumulated experience and practice in the real educational setting. Looking from the current perspective (we mean the year 2017 of writing the book), we were able to identify three periods of SLO evolution: *initial, intermediate* and *current.* We have identified that as the evolution of models: from the initial model *M0*, through the intermediate model *M1*, to reach the current model *M2*, respectively. This sequence of models indicates on the growth of functional capabilities over the indicated period.

Those capabilities include characteristics of the learning resources as GLOs, aspects of functionality, the mode of smartness in terms of STEM disciplines covered, robot platforms used, tasks considered and the number of students involved in each academic year. The evolution of meta-programming-based GLOs from the model *M0* to model *M2* has resulted in creating the learning resource that is indeed smart in terms of functionality and of course in complexity. For better understanding of such a complex structure, we have proposed a framework that provides the multidimensional multi-perspective view to this structure. We have adopted Minsky's multi-perspective vision in developing the framework. More specifically, we have introduced the learner's, the teacher's and the designer's visions that include structural and process-based attributes presented with the varying details so that to reflect the relevant interests of each stakeholder. We have also included the researcher's vision that we hope provides the deeper knowledge for understanding the internal structure of SLOs.

In summary, smart learning objects as defined by the model *M1* have the following properties. They are meta-programming-based generators to produce the required instance on demand through selecting the adequate parameter values. The parameters and their values predefine the space of the predefined learning variability. Current SLOs represent the explicitly stated STEM-driven learning variability. Therefore, the level of "smartness" of those SLOs (model *M2*) is much higher in all main characteristics. The meta-programming techniques enable to express all learning variability aspects (i.e. pedagogy, technology, content and scenario) uniformly through parameterization. This opens the way of flexible manipulation within the SLO structure aiming to achieve additional benefits such as context awareness, transformation and automated adaptation.

In terms of high technology, SLO is a heterogeneous meta-program, i.e. a generator of domain-specific programs (meaning, robot-oriented ones). In terms of educational applications, SLO is the executable high-level specification that implements the STEM-driven CS-oriented learning variability. We have shown that SLO has a great potential to evolve in terms of enlarging functionality. Therefore, we were able to discuss and disclose the only basic functional properties of SLO here. The more advanced properties, such as context awareness and automated adaptation, automated selection of parameter values by software agents, the integration of SLO with learning scenarios and the capabilities of SLO to manage not only single robot but also a swarm of robots are topics that require a separate discussion and investigation. The smart content is a backbone of smart learning within the smart CS educational environment. The series of subsequent chapters, starting from Chap. 7, is about that.

References

[BBD+14] Burbaite R, Bespalova K, Damasevicius R, Stuikys V (2014) Context aware generative learning objects for teaching computer science. Int J Eng Educ 30(4):929–936

[BEK+14] Brusilovsky P, Edwards S, Kumar A, Malmi L, Benotti L, Buck D, ... Urquiza J (2014) Increasing adoption of smart learning content for computer science education. In: Proceedings of the Working Group Reports of the 2014 on Innovation & Technology in Computer Science Education Conference, ACM, pp 31–57

[BLA+08] Boyle T, Ljubojevic D, Agombar M, Baur E (2008) The conceptual structure of generative learning objects (GLOs). In: Proceedings of World Conference on Educational Multimedia, Hypermedia and Telecommunications, pp 4570–4579

[BLC04] Boyle T Leeder D, Chase H (2004) To boldly GLO – towards the next generation of learning objects, world conference on eLearning in Corporate, Government, Healthcare and Higher Education, Washington USA, Nov. 2004

[Boy03] Boyle T (2003) Design principles for authoring dynamic, reusable learning objects. Aust J Educ Technol 19:46–58

[Boy06] Boyle T (2006) The design and development of second generation learning objects. In: World Conference on Educational Multimedia, Hypermedia and Telecommunications, 2006(1):2–12

[BR12] Boyle T, Ravenscroft A (2012) Context and deep learning design. Comput Educ 59 (4):1224–1233

[CCS15] Chirila CB, Ciocârlie H, Stoicu-Tivadar L (2015) Generative learning objects instantiated with random numbers based expressions. BRAIN Broad Rese Artif Intell Neurosci 6(1–2):70–83

[Chi15] Chirila CB (2015) A comparison of MCQ and AGLO generative learning object models. Ann Fac Eng Hunedoara 13(4):37

[Chi16]   Chirila CB (2016) Generative learning object assessment items for a set of computer science disciplines. In: Balas V, Jain LC, Kovačević B (eds) Soft computing applications. Advances in intelligent systems and computing, vol 356. Springer, Cham

[Chi16a]   Chirila CB (2016) Reuse models for generative E-learning content dedicated to computer science disciplines. In: Proceedings of 12th international scientific conference eLearning and software for education, Bucharest, Apr 21–22

[Chi16b]   Chirila CB (2016) Towards the gamification of auto-generative learning objects. In: First international conference on smart learning ecosystems and regional developments, Timisoara

[CRR16]   Chirila CB, Raes R, Roland A (2016) Towards a generic gamification of sorting algorithms. In: Electronics and telecommunications (ISETC), 2016 12th IEEE international symposium on. IEEE, pp 133–136

[DŠ08]   Damaševičius R, Štuikys V (2008) On the technological aspects of generative learning object development. In: Informatics education-supporting computational thinking: third international conference on informatics in secondary schools-evolution and perspectives, ISSEP 2008 Torun Poland, July 1–4, proceedings, vol 5090. Springer, pp 337–348

[DS09]   Damasevicius R, Stuikys V (2009) Specification and generation of learning object sequences for e-learning using sequence feature diagrams and metaprogramming techniques in advanced learning technologies, 2009. ICALT 2009. Ninth IEEE international conference, July, pp 572–576

[GLO17]   GLO Maker. Authoring tool for learning objects. Available: http://glomaker.software. informer.com/3.0/

[HK09]   Han P, Kramer BJ (2009) Generating interactive learning object from configurable samples. In: Proceedings of int. conf. on mobile, hybrid and on-line learning, IEEE, pp 1–6

[HKS16]   Huh JH, Kim HB, Seo K (2016) A design of smart-based education gamification platform using mobile devices for digital content. Int J Multimedia Ubiquit Eng 11 (12):101–114

[JB07]   Jones R, Boyle T (2007) Learning object patterns for programming. Interdiscip J Knowl Learn Objects 3(1):19–28

[Min75]   Minsky M (1975) A framework for representing knowledge. In: Winston P (ed) The psychology of computer vision. McGraw-Hill, New York

[MLB05]   Morales R, Leeder D, Boyle T (2005) A case in the design of generative learning objects (GLOs): applied statistical methods. In: World conference on educational multimedia, hypermedia and telecommunications, pp 2091–2097

[Sam97]   Sametinger J (1997) Software engineering with reusable components. Springer, New York

[ŠB09]   Štuikys V, Brauklytė I (2009) Aggregating of learning object units derived from a generative learning object. Inform Educ-An Int J 8(2):295–314

[ŠB15a]   Štuikys V, Burbaitė R (2015) Robot-based smart educational environments to teach CS: a case study. In: Smart learning objects for the smart education in computer science: theory, methodology and robot-based implementation, Springer, Cham, pp 265–285

[ŠB15b]   Štuikys V, Burbaitė R (2015) Smart education in CS: a case study. In: Smart learning objects for the smart education in computer science: theory, methodology and robot-based implementation, Springer, Cham, pp 287–310

[SBB+16]   Stuikys V, Burbaite R, Bespalova K, Drasute V, Ziberkas G, Venckauskas A (2016) Stage-based generative learning object model to support automatic content generation and adaptation. In: Computer software and applications conference (COMPSAC), 2016 I.E. 40th annual, vol 1, pp 712–721

[ŠBB+17] Štuikys V, Burbaitė R, Bespalova K, Blažauskas T, Barisas D (2017) Stage-based generative learning object model for automated content adaptation. Balt J Mod Comput 5(2):183–205

[ŠBD13] Štuikys V, Burbaitė R, Damaševičius R (2013) Teaching of computer science topics using meta-programming-based GLOs and LEGO robots. Inform Educ An Int J 12 (1):125–142

[ŠD07] Štuikys V, Damaševičius R (2007) Towards knowledge-based generative learning objects. Inf Technol Control 36(2):202–212

[ŠD08] Štuikys V, Damaševičius R (2008) Development of generative learning objects using feature diagrams and generative techniques. Inform Educ An Int J 7(2):277–288

[ŠD13] Štuikys V, Damaševičius R (2013) Meta-programming and model-driven meta-program development: principles, processes and techniques. Springer, London

[Štu15] Štuikys V (2015) Smart learning objects for the smart education in computer science: theory, methodology and robot-based implementation, Springer, Cham

[YMV+15] Yaşar O, Maliekal J, Veronesi P, Little L, Vattana S (2015) Computational pedagogical content knowledge (CPACK): integrating modeling and simulation technology into STEM teacher education. Res Highlights Technol Teach Educ 2015:79

Chapter 7
Model-Driven Design and Redesign of Smart STEM-Driven CS Content

Abstract This chapter deals with the design and redesign of the smart (generative) learning objects (GLOs/SLOs) as the smart content. We describe the model-driven framework to design CS-based SLOs with respect to their evolution curve and models *M1* and *M2* discussed in Chap. 6. In this regard, we outline two approaches, i.e. *Approach 1* that focuses on the use of the model *M1* and *Approach 2* that focuses on the model *M2*. To represent the design framework for both approaches, we use the multi-level Y-charts to specify the design as a multi-level model-driven transformation process. Typically, the left branch of the Y-chart represents the problem domain, the right branch represents the solution domain and the vertical branch represents the solution itself at the given level of transformation. We introduce a horizontal transformation to map attributes of the problem domain onto the adequate attributes of the solution domain. To make the horizontal transformation feasible, we define a vertical transformation on each left and right branches resulting on the decreasing level of abstraction to represent the models and sub-models so that it would be possible to apply the adequate transformation rules. At the top level, we represent models (sub-models) by features models. They serve to represent either problem domain or solution domain, depending on the transformation level. At the implementation level, we represent the solution domain by meta-programming concepts resulting in the development of GLO/SLO as the executable meta-program specification. We illustrate that by providing examples of models and their executable specifications. We evaluate Approach 1 and Approach 2 by comparing their basic characteristics.

7.1 Introduction

In Chap. 6, we have discussed the evolution of meta-programming-based GLOs/SLOs. We have introduced three periods (initial, intermediate and current along with three models *M0*, *M1* and *M2* for each period, respectively). We have analysed on how stakeholders, i.e. learners, teachers, designers and researchers, should understand GLOs/SLOs. We have also defined SLO as an evolutionary process of transforming GLO by adding new functionality and changing the structure. Now, on this basis and based on

© Springer International Publishing AG, part of Springer Nature 2018   157
V. Štuikys, R. Burbaitė, *Smart STEM-Driven Computer Science Education*,
https://doi.org/10.1007/978-3-319-78485-4_7

the methodological background (Chap. 4) and theoretical background (Chap. 5), it is much easier to explain the issues of designing SLOs as derivative items from GLOs (in the sense of evolution). This chapter is about that.

First, we need to explain some terms used in the title. By the model-driven design, we mean the design of the educational content so that the specification of the design is given by the adequate high-level model or models and then they are gradually transformed into the next level of representing (typically lower) until the implementation level (i.e. coding using meta-programming techniques). By redesign, we mean the process that starts not from scratch but using previously developed and used items (GLOs, SLOs). The aim of redesign is to add STEM features with minimum efforts. We make a clear distinction between the *design models* (they specify requirements for SLOs, using the feature modelling notion) and models *M0, M1* and *M2* presented in Chap. 6 (they give a general understanding of items, i.e. SLOs we need to design; we use the object-oriented notion and process-based vision in representing those models). Therefore, models *MO, M1* and *M2* are *design objects*, whereas the design models, largely, are a part of the *design processes*. In this chapter, we introduce two approaches. The *Approach 1* relates with the design of GLOs/SLOs that we identify by models *MO/M1*. The *Approach 2* relates to the design of SLOs that we identify by model *M2* (i.e. largely relevant to STEM). Partially, we have presented the *Approach 1* in [ŠBB+16]; however, we have substantially extended the content of this paper here. In this chapter, we describe the *Approach 2* for the first time.

The basic idea to design SLOs is common for both approaches. The idea relies on two top-level processes. The first includes our efforts to specify the *predefined learning variability space* for STEM-driven CS education *uniformly* at the higher-level of abstraction using feature-based modelling concepts [CL13, KCH+90, MBC09]. The second covers our efforts to express the features via parameters in creating meta-specifications based on feature model transformations and meta-programing [ŠD13, ŠBB+16, Štu15]. If we neglect the semantics, the SLO specification is indeed a domain-specific meta-program. We can also view the SLO specification as a *family* of the related LOs expressed in a target language and specifically woven by means of the meta-language. In case of using educational robots, the target language (equally teaching one) is robot-oriented, such as RobotC (http://www.robotc.net), Java (http://www.lejos.org). In this case, LOs are robot control programs. Those (after generation) are to be loaded into the robot's memory to model the teaching tasks physically in real time.

The structure of this chapter includes eight sections. In Sect. 7.2, we present the related work. In Sect. 7.3, we outline the essence of *Approach 1* and *Approach 2*. In Sect. 7.4, we provide the problem statement to design and redesign the STEM content. In Sect. 7.5, we describe the model-driven framework to design CS-based SLOs. In Sect. 7.6, we present a background of introduced approaches. In Sect. 7.7, we compare conceptual models (*Model 1* and *Model 2*). In Sect. 7.8, we summarize the discussion and provide overall evaluation and a conclusion.

7.2   Related Work

The related work focuses on modelling and model-driven approaches in designing educational content. For analysis of generative/smart learning objects, see Sect. 6.2 in Chap. 6. Modelling of the learning content and learning processes is at the focus of the modern e-Learning research. The paper [RM04] indicates, for example, on three main directions in this regard: (1) use of the formal specifications, (2) creation of the representative frameworks to model the educational material and (3) motivated choice of the abstraction level to ensure reusability of LOs. The paper [PLL+06] defines a learning design as *the result of a knowledge engineering process where knowledge and competencies, learning design and delivery models are constructed in an integrated framework.* To support modelling activities, the paper [LC06] proposes educational modelling languages (EMLs) and establishes the following result: (1) EMLs are involved in the last step of the instructional design phase (e.g. for specifying the underlying learning scenario). (2) They enable to structure the contents (i.e. LOs) and containers (educational scenario, learning unit) in order to support reuse, assembling, interoperability, etc. (3) EMLs have the XML-based mappings in order to be easily implemented and interpreted. (4) They do not always fit into specific learning situations because of their generic or independent approach in order to be fully compliant.

The paper [BDB+06] evaluates EMLs using the following criteria:

(1) *Stratification* (nominal: flat, layered). A layered language offers a set of tools or representations for describing entities of different types, such as people and roles, activities, or learning materials.

(2) *Formalization* (formal, informal). A formal language defines the stringent closed set of concepts and rules for composing the concepts in order to describe designs.

(3) *Elaboration* (conceptual, specification, implementation). Each particular design language is able to provide more or less detail of a specific artefact. The conceptual level allows for a general, aggregate view on the design, indicating its rationale and main elements; the specification level provides a means for a more comprehensive description, including all elements; the implementation level represents the highest level of detail achieving maximum precision.

(4) *Perspective* (single, multiple). While layered languages foresee the use of multiple representations of different entities, multiple perspective languages exploit different tools for representing more than one view on the same entities.

(5) *Notation System* (textual, visual).

The paper [CLA06] defines two main problems in using EMLs: (1) modelling of elements related to the units of learning (individuals, purposes, artefacts) and (2) modelling of relationships among elements (sequence of activities, tasks, purposes). The researchers recognize the importance of modelling using EML and higher-level models. In order to enforce modelling capabilities, there are efforts to apply software engineering methods in e-Learning. This paper also presents a separation of concern approach to EMLs proposing to structure these languages in a way different from the one proposed by the IMS *learning design* (LD) specification, currently considered as the standard EML. The authors argue that the LD specification is too complex to be applicable in the runtime applications to produce the EML-based educational materials.

The paper [RM04], for example, presents a framework with reference to the language PALO as a cognitive-based approach to EMLs. The language PALO, therefore, provides a layer of abstraction for the description of learning material, including the description of learning activities, structure and scheduling. The framework makes the use of the domain and pedagogical ontology as a reusable and maintainable way to represent and store the instructional content. The paper [PLL +06] presents a general graphical language and a knowledge editor to support the construction of learning designs compliant with the IMS-LD specification. The authors move up one step in the abstraction scale, showing that the process of constructing learning designs can itself be viewed as a unit of learning (or a "unit of design"): designers can be seen as learning by constructing learning designs, individually, in teams and with staff support.

The paper [LC06] discusses a teacher-centred approach for the specification of learning scenarios (design), as well as the comprehension of learning scenarios (reuse), by focusing on the application of theory and results from the model-driven engineering (MDE) and model-driven re-engineering domains. This approach is, in fact, the illustration on how SW engineering (SWE) approaches are beneficial to e-Learning. Indeed, the MDE [Sch06] and product line engineering (PLE) [Bos00] approaches prevail in designing SW systems. Both methodologies highlight the use of high-level models, model-driven processes and variability modelling. A great deal of papers in variability modelling is based on feature models. This research trend is due to the seminal work of Kang et al. [KCH+90] published in 1990 known as FODA (feature-oriented domain analysis). The feature is defined as an *externally visible distinguishable characteristic* of a system or domain, though Apel and Kastner [AK09] have extracted from the literature ten slightly different definitions of the term *feature* (see also Sect. 5.3). This fact indicates on the soundness and generality of feature-based approaches. One can learn more about the feature-oriented variability modelling from the following publications [CBK13, CHW98] to name a few (also see Sect. 4.2). Now the modelling approaches have a strong methodological and technological support. The samples we use in our research are the domain language FAMILIAR (*feature model script language for manipulation and automatic reasoning*) [CL13] and the tool SPLOT (*Software Product Lines Online Tools*) [MBC09].

Researchers within the e-Learning community already recognize the role and the need of applying *the feature-based domain analysis and modelling* approaches. For instance, the paper [DZF+07] introduces an instructional engineering generative method to create and adapt competence development programs (CDPs). Though SWE approaches were introduced in e-Learning far more earlier, the above-mentioned authors and their colleagues have pioneered to combine generative methods along with the use of feature models [DD06]. The paper [DŠ08] considers the use of feature diagrams (FDs, aka feature models) as tools to specify generative LOs first and then to implement them using meta-programming techniques. The paper [ŠDB+08] analyses the possibility of using FDs to specify ontology as a type of knowledge for e-Learning. The paper [DS09] discusses the use of FDs as applied to the sequencing problem. The paper [BS11] analyses the LO research in the large using the feature-based models. The paper [DDA12] uses the models for specifying architecture in creating of e-Learning systems. For the other proposals, see [CNC12].

There are two basic approaches for implementing SLOs as educational content, template-based (also pattern-based [JB07]) and based on using meta-programming [Štu15]. Now there are also other proponents of the latter approach (see Sect. 4.2, for details). In general, meta-programming is about the model and program transformation and generation. For example, Czarnecki and Helsen [CH06] indicate the following hierarchy of terms (*meta-programming – model transformation – program transformation*), where meta-programming is at the top and therefore encompasses the remaining terms. In the narrow sense, meta-program is a program generator. There are two kinds of meta-programming: homogeneous and heterogeneous [She01]. The first paradigm uses the generative capabilities of a single language, typically interpreted as a meta-language, while the second paradigm typically uses at least two *independent* languages: the target language (TL) for expressing the base domain functionality and the meta-language (ML) for expressing generative capabilities. Note that there is no single vision on the meta-programming paradigm. One can learn more on that, for instance, from the sources [CE00, ŠD13, She01]. See also Sect. 5.3 (Stream B, Chap. 5) and Sect. 6.2 (Chap. 6), for other research papers that deal with generative approaches in CS education.

7.3 Two Conceptual Models and Two Approaches to Design SLOs

In Fig. 6.1 (see Sect. 6.3 in Chap. 6), we have presented the table-like evolution curve of the meta-programming-based GLOs. In this curve, we have expressed the evolution through three models. The initial model, called *the Model 0*, is the simplest one. Using this model, we have designed the first generation of GLOs from scratch, i.e. without applying of a systematic approach. The remaining two models, i.e. *Model 1* and *Model 2*, are derivative. We have derived them from the initial; however, in doing so, we have enriched their capability and, of course, complexity. Therefore, the implementation of those models requires the use of systematic approaches. Further, we refer to the *Approach 1* and *Approach 2* as a systematic process to implement *Model 1* and *Model 2*, respectively. The functional capabilities implemented into SLO specifications during the years 2012–2015 are due to *Approach 1* (*Model 1*). Note also that with regard to the additional capabilities, we have renamed GLOs and called them smart LOs (SLOs). The capabilities implemented in SLO specifications after 2015 are due to *Approach* 2 (*Model 2*). The latter specifies the STEM aspects explicitly (see also Fig. 6.1). Firstly, we formulate requirements that are common to both models.

Common Requirements for Both Models. They include (1) incorporation of enhanced reusability aspects, (2) incorporation of broad explicit context to support context awareness and (3) the use of the same implementation technology. The first requirement includes the use of the product line concept borrowed from SWE, generative reuse, adaptation possibilities and automatic generation of instances and high-level models extracted through analysis and modelling. The enhanced reusability also means that the content is generic. The second requirement calls for the use of explicit context as widely as possible. By wide context, we mean combined pedagogical-social attributes that cover the multiple pedagogical models (inquiry-based, design-based, project-based, etc.,) and different social models (learner's level, learning style, learning pace, preferences, etc.,). Therefore, the context is also generic. The third requirement refers to the possibility of redesigning the previously developed SLOs using the *Model 2* and *Approach 2*.

Requirements to Support SLO Designs Using Model 1. This model should specify the generic content, the generic context and scenario uniformly in the same specification. Those attributes are explicit and define the interface of the specification. We express the interface through parameters uniformly. The user is able to distinguish the role of parameters from the context. The sequence of parameters is prioritized within the graphical interface. The pedagogical-social parameters have a higher priority with respect to technological and content parameters. The sequence of parameters forms a scenario. Therefore, each SLO has within own scenario. We represent *Model 1* at three levels, i.e. specification, design and implementation (coding). We represent the specification level using static feature models. We represent a design level using the meta-programming.

Requirements to Support SLO Designs Using Model 2. In *Model 2*, the scenario is a separate component and common for all SLOs. The scenario is generative. The user (teacher and partially students) derives the concrete scenario from the generative one. The scenario forms the call to the personal generative library (i.e. STEM library) for the needed GLO/SLO. Though *Model 1* and *Model 2* have some common structural aspects, the design processes differ.

7.4 Problem Statement for STEM Content Design and Redesign

At the very beginning, we present a simplified structural definition of the generative learning object also (SLO):

$$SLO = (STEM) \ CS \ learning \ variability \oplus meta\text{-}algorithm \qquad (7.1)$$

This definition represents *Model 2*. However, if one omits the phrase STEM, formula (7.1) represents *Model 1* as well. Note that we have defined the concept *CS learning variability* in Chap. 4. The symbol $\oplus$ (see 7.1) means the high-level integration of the respective items in writing the specifications. The word "meta-algorithm" means the generalized or higher-level algorithm. On the other hand, in terms of CS, we are able to interpret the STEM CS learning variability as *the learning-oriented data structure*. In fact, due to the variability aspects, it represents a family or a set of data. In other words, this data structure is generic, i.e. higher-level or "meta". Therefore, we can rewrite (7.1) as (7.2):

$$SLO = data \ meta\text{-}structure \oplus meta\text{-}algorithm \qquad (7.2)$$

Now we are able to compare this specification with the title (*Algorithms + Data Structure = Programs*) taken from the Wirth's famous book [Wir78]. This title expresses the essence of the CS content that educators taught in a variety of different contexts. In the book [ŠD13], we have applied this Wirth's vision to define the essence of meta-programming by stating:

Meta-program = program $\oplus$ meta-algorithm. Note that here *program* stands for *data structure.*

Therefore, we are able to conclude that, in terms of CS, the SLO specification is, in fact, the meta-program we represent the generic content for teaching and learning. This specification, if adequately represented, supports enhanced reuse in terms of automated generation and adaptation and brings new capabilities for educational practice such as a personal generative library (Chap. 10). Now we define the design problem.

By the design of the SLO, we mean the writing or coding of the SLO specification. As it is with a program or meta-program, we can do this in two different ways: *manually*, or using *appropriate tools* (if any). By manual coding, we mean the manual writing of the SLO specification with the aid of a PC and the use of some editor and meta-program processor. We use the latter for detecting of coding errors only, but not as a development tool. Such an approach does not require the use of models as mandatory attributes, though the explicit models that describe the input information are highly helpful. The input information in this case is (1) a concrete target language instance (or instances), (2) requirements for generalization of the instance (s) (one can also treat them as a set of changes or manipulations to express learning variability) and (3) a description of the selected meta-language. To design the code manually, the designer has to connect or map each requirement with the adequate meta-operations of the given meta-language.

We are able to view the sequence of those mappings as the development of the meta-algorithm. The use of tools in designing the SLO may be very helpful. The development of tools, especially those that relate to creating the intellectual property such as SLO, is hard. The development of tools is the topic of software engineering, though the CS community provides extensive research too. Currently there prevail the model-driven approaches and transformation tools to design the systems or system of systems (such as PLE approach [Bos00]). The latter requires the specification of the input design information as precisely and fully as possible. Therefore, the input information and the internal data within the tool should be represented as adequate models, such as feature models [CH06]. We have adapted the feature-based modelling approaches to analysis and representation of the CS education domain (see Chap. 5). The result of this activity is the creation of the *abstract feature models* for each subdomain (pedagogy, social, technology, teaching content). By the abstract feature model, we mean the one that is dedicated for the general use and, as a rule, lacks of concrete features for the concrete implementation. By the *concrete feature models*, we mean those with the predefined values of all features for implementing them. The latter are derivative models derived from the abstract models through the choice of adequate features, adding values of the concrete features and aggregating the features into a coherent model structure. In this chapter, we restrict ourselves with constructing the *concrete feature models* to specify the learning variability of the concrete SLOs. This is with the application domain, but it is not enough.

In designing SLO, STEM-driven CS learning variability (CLV for short) stands for *the problem domain*, and meta-programming (MPG for short) stands for *the solution domain*. Therefore, in order to apply the model-driven approach, we need to specify both domains uniformly using feature models. At the most abstract level, we formulate the task to design SLO as *mapping of CS education requirements onto meta-programming capabilities*. In general, in terms of feature models, we are able formulate the task as defined by Eq. (7.3):

$$\text{FM } (SLO\ Solution) = \text{FM } (CLV) \times \text{FM } (MPG) \tag{7.3}$$

Here, FM, feature model; '$\times$', mapping operations; and *CLV, STEM CS learning variability*. It also represents the problem domain, and MPG – *meta-programming* – also is the solution domain.

Therefore, in terms of CS, solution of a problem is the mapping of the problem domain requirements onto the solution domain. In other words, to solve a given problem, we need to express the given task concepts through solution domain concepts using some transformation (i.e. mapping) rules. For better understanding of the presented abstract statements, we consider two examples.

Example 1. Let we have the one-dimensional numerical array X (*100*). The student needs to develop an algorithm that describes the sum of positive numbers of the array and represents the algorithm graphically, using the notion of structured diagrams.

Example 2. Let we have a solution of the first task, i.e. a concrete structured diagram. Now the student needs to develop the program, say, in programming language C++ that solves the problem of Example 1.

With regard to Example 1, the array X (*100*) along with requirements (i.e. summation of positive numbers) represents the problem domain, and the elements of the structural diagrams (i.e. operation, alternative and loop) represent the solution domain, while the concrete diagram developed by the student is the solution itself. With regard to Example 2, the concrete diagram represents the problem domain, and some document describing the language C++ is the solution domain, while the developed program in C++ is the solution in this case.

With regard to formula (7.3), we present one important methodological observation. We are able to represent formulae of this sort graphically using the Y-chart. The chart has three branches: *left* (for representing problem domain items), *right* (for representing solution domain items) and *vertical* (for representing the solution itself). Note that Gajski and Kuhn introduced the Y-chart to represent electronic circuit designs [GK83]. We found this notion useful and convenient to specify our design framework.

7.5   Model-Driven Framework to Design CS-Based SLOs

The basis in creating SLOs is the expert's knowledge about the education as a problem domain. The TPACK framework [KM09], for example, summarizes that as the *intersection* of the technological knowledge, pedagogical knowledge and content knowledge within the overall educational *context*. This framework, in fact, is the conceptual model to understand any education domain. We use this framework too by introducing some adaptation (see Fig. 7.1). The adaptation includes two aspects. The first relates to our vision to STEM-driven CS education (see Fig. 7.1a). The

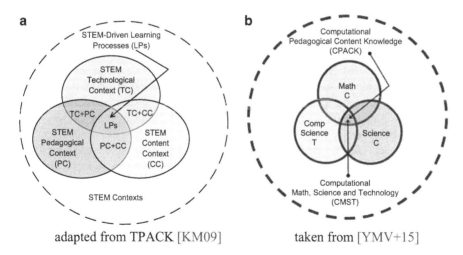

adapted from TPACK [KM09]   taken from [YMV+15]

Fig. 7.1 A framework of defining STEM contexts (**a**) and content (**b**) (**a** adapted from TPACK [KM09] and **b** taken from [YMV+15])

second extends the STEM and the content context (CC) and presents that as a computational pedagogical and content knowledge (CPACK) (see Fig. 7.1b). We have borrowed this concept from [YMV+15].

How do we need to understand this framework in designing SLO? Typically, the designer uses some well-proven principles to govern the design process. Two general principles such as *the separation of concerns and integration of concerns* are helpful. The first principle is well-known in SWE (CS) due to the early seminal work of Parnas [Par76]. Very often, one understands the second principle as an outcome for which the first principle we introduce. In other words, both are dual, and we apply them together as a means of *analysis* and *synthesis* in designing systems.

In practice, however, we apply those principles in two ways: *implicitly* or *explicitly*. When applied, the first case means, in fact, the use of ad hoc approaches. For example, the CS teacher is able to create SLO in an ad hoc manner, relying on his/her competence and knowledge only, i.e. applying the TPACK framework and knowledge about meta-programming implicitly. Here, however, we focus on the systematic approach in designing SLO and the authoring design tools. This approach relies on the use of the explicit separation of concerns. We apply the explicit separation of concerns at multiple levels: domains, domain meta-model, models, elements of models and processes.

At the domain level, we separate the problem domain (i.e. STEM-driven CS education) from the solution domain (i.e. structural heterogeneous meta-programming). At the process level, we separate modelling of the CS education domain from the SLO specification and design. At the model level, we separate meta-models from their models and the latter from their instances. Finally, at the model element level, it is possible to create transformation rules that, in fact, describe the integration of the previously separated concerns.

We present the model-driven design framework at three levels: *top*, *intermediate* and *low*. At each level, we use Y-charts to represent models of this level and their transformations adequately. We identify three kinds of transformations: *horizontal*, *vertical* and *combined* (see Fig. 7.2). The *horizontal transformation* results in mapping of some elements of the problem domain (left branch) onto the adequate elements of the solution domain (right branch). Here, by the element we mean a *part* of the adequate model. The *vertical transformation* specifies the actions for excluding the model elements. We need that for simplifying the transformation process itself. We apply this transformation for both kinds of models (problem domain and the solution domain, i.e. for left and right branches). However, for the solution domain branch, the vertical transformation includes much more activities, i.e. model specialization and validation using the adequate tools (we present them later). We refer to the *combined transformation* as a process that combines the horizontal and vertical transformations and yields the aggregated validated model for use in the next level.

Therefore, we have the sequence of Y-charts (Fig. 7.2). The sequence indicates on how the designer needs to move through the framework by gradually lowering the abstraction level and introducing more and more details in creating the final solution – the STEM-driven meta-programming-based SLO. In the next sections (7.5.1, 7.5.2, 7.5.3 and 7.5.4), we explain our framework in more details.

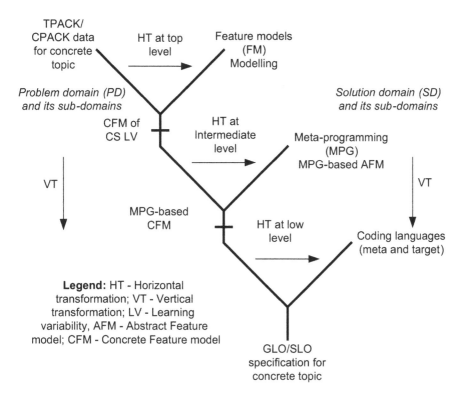

Fig. 7.2 Multi-level Y-based chart framework to represent the model-driven SLO design

7.5.1   Understanding of Context in Our Approaches

As stated before, any system or item has the base part and its context. The latter highly influences the base part. Therefore, in designing systems, the context plays an extremely important role. First, we look at this concept more generally and present some well-known definitions. We repeat them because of independent reading of this chapter. Dey [Dey01] defines context as *any information that can be used to characterize the situation of an entity*. In the other paper [DAS01], Dey et al. extend the previous definition by stating that context is *a person, place, or object that is considered relevant to the interaction between a user and an application, including the user and applications themselves*. This is an application-centric definition, which clearly states that the context is always bound to an entity, i.e. the base part and that information that describes the situation of an entity is context. The paper [LCW+09] defines the learning context as *information to identify the state of the item, i.e. learner's location, learning activities, the used tools and LOs*. Dourish [Dou04] emphasizes a dual origin of the context: *technical-* and *social-*based aspects. The paper [VMO+12] provides an extensive analysis of context definitions with regard to designing recommendation systems to support technology-enhanced learning (TEL). Based on those findings, we are able to conclude that context is a multi-dimensional category that, in general, may include the following features: *special-time, physical conditions, computing, resource, user, activity* and *social.*

As many of these features are overlapping (see [VMO+12]), it is reasonable to combine some of them in a concrete situation such as design and use of SLOs. Thus, in our case, we focus on three context dimensions: computing/resource, user (learner/teacher)/social and activity/task/content. Comparing these dimensions with pedagogical reusability [PS04], we are able to categorize the context as follows: *pedagogical context, technological context* and *content context.* By the *pedagogical context,* we mean STEM-driven educational models (e.g. inquiry-based, project-based, etc.) along with learner's social models (e.g. learner's preferences, previous knowledge, etc.). Depending on the situation, we are able to consider those models as separate items. By the *technological context,* we mean tools that support STEM-driven CS education activities. In case of STEM and robotics, this context is extremely wide. We categorize the technological context as of *general use-* and *task-related* (see darken boxes in Fig. 7.3).

By the *content context,* we mean the *semantics* the content contains, the *situation* of use (e.g. scenario to which the content pertains), the *place* where the content resides (e.g. personal generative library) and similar items.

From this short discussion, it is clear that the context is (1) highly heterogeneous; (2) its components play different roles. In order to capture and express those roles explicitly, for example, for ensuring a flexible managing, we need to have an adequate mechanism. In [ŠBB+17], we have proposed a context-aware model to define explicit priorities of separate context components. We represent the model as a set of *fuzzy variables* $\{HP, IP, LP\}$. The variables specify adequately *high priority* for pedagogical context, *intermediate priority* for technological context and *low priority* for content context. We integrate this model within the SLO specification. In fact, it is a part of the entire context model. It provides capabilities for context-aware adaptation of SLO specification. In Chap. 8, we return to this problem for a more

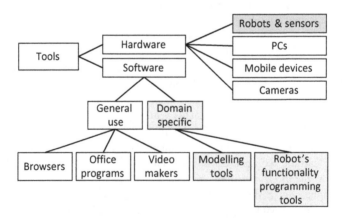

Fig. 7.3 Supporting tools as a technological context

extensive discussion. We summarize the discussion of this section with the following observation. To which degree we want to introduce contextual aspects into the SLO specification at the design phase, to the same or similar degree, and we will be able to exploit those aspects at the use, i.e. learning phase.

7.5.2   Model-Driven SLO Design at the Top Level

Firstly, we describe *Approach 1* (*Model 1*, see Sect. 7.3). It is convenient to demonstrate the explicit separation of concerns using the Y-chart (Fig. 7.3). The TPACK framework, as applied to STEM CS education, serves as the initial, i.e. *informal representation* of the problem domain. Another important aspect of the initial phase is the identification of the scope of the domain we aim to model. The scope depends on the aim of modelling. As our aim here is to extract the relevant information for building high-level models (meaning feature models, see also Chap. 5) and to specify STEM-oriented SLOs, the modelling scope is restricted, because a separate SLO does not cover the whole CS education domain. Typically, the scope of the content, for which we provide variability modelling, corresponds to *one task* or *one topic*.

We apply the analysis using multi-dimensional separation of concerns (MDSC) as Fig. 7.2 explains (see also [ŠBB+16]). Here, we separate the problem domain (meaning CS topic along with the related subdomains) from the solution domain (meaning feature-based modelling approach). The left branch of the Y-chart represents the constituents of the problem domain informally. The right branch represents the solution domain. Analysis of the domain, in fact, is the process of extracting the knowledge and then representing it formally through transformations. Typically, the initial knowledge resides in the published documents (papers, books, instructions, manuals of relevant systems, etc.), human's mind and the ability of the analyser to understand the problem domain. The TPACK framework (see Fig. 7.1a) stands for a roadmap indicating on what aspects the analyser needs to focus. For doing that, one can use either the ad hoc approach or some systematic approach. The first approach relies on the knowledge and competence of the analyser about the domain. The second approach relies on systematic domain analysis methods (such as FODA [Har02, KCH+90], FORM [AR07], SCV-analysis [CHW98]). Within the introduced MLSC framework, we have combined the basic ideas of both approaches. Then we need to transform the extracted knowledge into terms of the solution domain.

The transformation process is a part of the analysis and modelling. We apply the process for each subdomain separately. The process results in creating the adequate feature models. They represent the solution domain. Here, by modelling we mean the expression and the learning variability by feature relationships and constraints and extracting the important characteristics of the relationships. We use the FAMILIAR tool [ACL+13] to support the modelling process and obtain modelling characteristics because of the process. By verification, we mean the procedure that ensures the correctness of feature models with respect to their formal definition (we use the

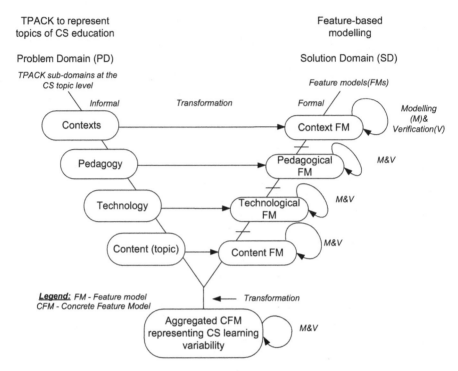

Fig. 7.4 Top-level SLO design framework represented using Y-chart (design according to *Model 1*)

SPLOT tool [MBC09] for this purpose). Note that after each modelling and verification step, there is the possibility to perform the specialization (denoted by the symbol '—' in Fig. 7.4; see the right branch), for example, for using the modelling outcomes in another context.

Secondly, we describe *Approach 2* (i.e. *Model 2*; see also Sect. 7.3). As we apply the same methodology, we restrict ourselves by presenting only the other way of using the methodology and a quite different result it yields. In *Approach 2*, we separate the STEM contexts, the STEM pedagogy (i.e. additional models such as inquiry approach) and the STEM technology from the STEM content explicitly. Here, by STEM contexts we mean the international context, i.e. various recommendations, frameworks, etc. This separation results in two separate Y-charts and two separated parts of the learning variability model (see Fig. 7.5). The bold Y-chart represents the highest level, i.e. the left branch indicates on initial (informal) constituents of STEM and the right branch indicates on formal (i.e. feature-based) representation of the same constituents. The vertical branch represents the aggregated concrete feature model to define STEM-driven CS education context. The remaining Y-chart specifies STEM content.

How do those feature models look like? In Fig. 7.6, we present the STEM context model. Note that it is the same as in Fig. 5.4 (see Chap. 5). We have made this

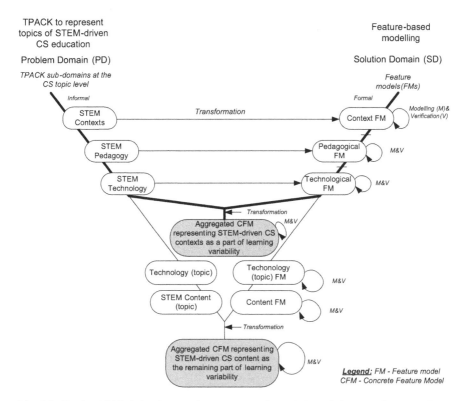

Fig. 7.5 Top-level SLO design framework represented using a Y-chart (design according to *Model 2*)

replication consciously for reading the chapters independently. Note also that this model is concrete to some extent (i.e. curriculum, student preferences, STEM pedagogy features have concrete values) and the remaining part is abstract (i.e. without concrete values). In Fig. 7.7, we present the STEM-driven content feature model in terms of tasks (see also Sect. 2.3 in Chap. 2).

What is the value of using the MDSC approach? First, it simplifies the modelling and verification. Second, it enables to apply the specialization of the created models. The result of modelling and verification is the aggregated concrete feature model (CFM) (see the vertical branch of the Y-chart (Fig. 7.2)) to represent the CS learning variability (LV) [ŠBD13]. Therefore, the solution domain, in fact, is an instrument to represent the extracted knowledge formally or semi-formally to enabling the further transformations in the model-driven design.

To explain the intermediate level with more details, we introduce motivating example taken from [ŠBB+16] with some modification. It represents the task "help system" managed by the robot to illustrate the problem domain. The functionality of the "help system" is simple: the robot should send a sound signal in case of emergency. That happens when somebody (that may be the other robot) presses

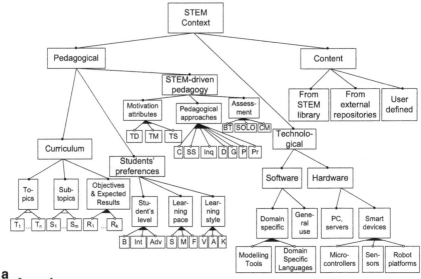

a

Legend:

$T_1...T_n$ – set of Topics; $S_1...S_m$ – set of Subtopics; $R_1...R_k$ – set of Objectives & Expected Results; B – Beginner; Int – Intermediate; Adv – Advanced; S – Slow; M – Medium; F – Fast; V – visual; A – Audial; K – Kinesthetic; TD – Technological Devices; TM – Teacher as Mentor; TS – Task solving; C – Consequential; SS – Side-by-Side; Inq – Inquiry-based; D – Design-based; G – Game-based; P –Project-based; Pr – problem-based; BT – Bloom's taxonomy; SOLO – SOLO taxonomy; CM – Concept Map.

b

Constraints *<requires>* include:

1. Pedagogical *requires* Technological; 2. Pedagogical *requires* Content; 3. Technological *requires* Content; 4. Objectives & Expected Results *requires* Subtopic; 5. Objectives & Expected Results *requires* Topic; 6. Topic *requires* Subtopic; 7. Objectives & Expected Results *requires* Pedagogical approaches.

Fig. 7.6 Feature model to specify STEM context variability (**a**) along with constraints (**b**)

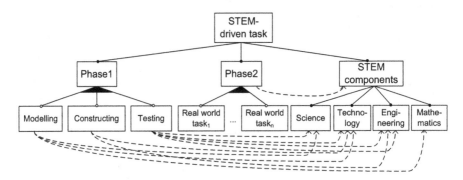

Fig. 7.7 Aggregated abstract feature model to represent content variability for STEM-driven CS education (dotted arrows indicate the constraint requires)

the touch sensor mounted on the robot's construct panel. The teaching task is to explain the essence of programming of the robot's touch sensors for the students. With regard to STEM, there are two teaching aspects: *engineering* and *programming*. From the engineering viewpoint, we can consider the task of controlling the real physical object, i.e. the sensor using the control program. From the programming viewpoint, the implemented task represents nested loops. The designer or teacher creates the problem domain model. The model have to describe the pedagogical, technological and content aspects (i.e. features and their relationships) as an integrated learning variability model in case of using *Approach 1* (*Model 1*). In case of using *Approach 2* (*Model 2*, it relates to the explicit STEM), the *generic* pedagogical aspects are within the scenario component. When initialized, the *concrete values* of those aspects are transferred from the scenario to the selected SLO. Here, we illustrate just the latter case, however, ignoring the concrete pedagogy aspects for simplicity.

7.5.3 SLO Design at the Intermediate Level

The aim is to decrease the abstraction level further. At this level, we use the same principles as before, but in the other way. Again, we do that by transforming the aggregated CFM models defined at the top level (i.e. learning variability models at the top level, see Figs. 7.4 and 7.5) into a more appropriate executable specification (i.e. language-based programming). However, the implementation of the variability models requires the use at least two programming languages at once. Therefore, meta-programming is just the case for implementing the model. Now the CS learning variability model (i.e. CFM) represents the problem domain (PD), and meta-programming (MPG) represents the solution domain (SD). In order to make the model transformation feasible, we need to represent each domain using the same formalism (notion). Therefore, we present both domains by feature models (see Chap. 5). Initially, we represent the SD by the abstract feature model (AFM) (i.e. some features values, or variants are not yet concrete). We explain this later.

At this level, we apply the vertical transformation uniformly for both domains (i.e. PD, SD). By vertical transformation, we mean the excluding of elements, i.e. the essential features of both feature models. In fact, the essential features are variation points to specify the transformation rules and on this basis to perform transformations. As there is a set of transformation rules, we apply them in some well-defined manner (Figs. 7.8, 7.9).

In Fig. 7.10, we present the concrete feature model for our task (see upper part of the left branch in Fig. 7.10). Note that three features (*SensorInput*, *SoundFile*, *SensorPosition*) are also *variation points*, each having the adequate *variants* or values. Also, note that *SensorInput* and *SensorPosition* are technological (context) features needed for the content specification, while *SoundFile* is the content feature. Once again, we need to return to the perception of the context in our case. The technological

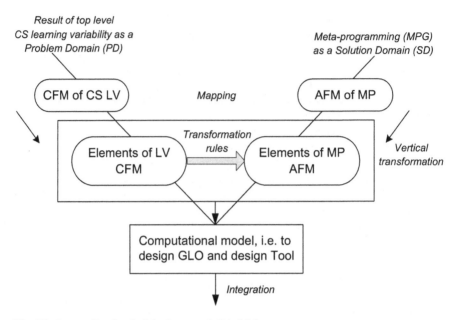

Fig. 7.8 Intermediate level of the framework (*Model 1*)

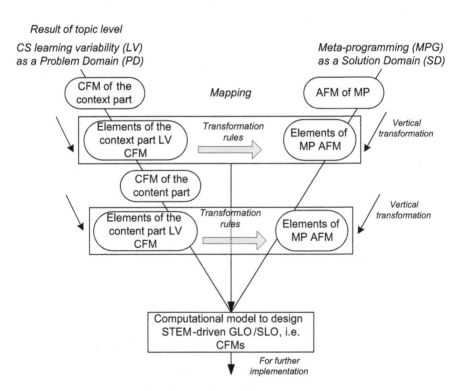

Fig. 7.9 Intermediate level of the framework (*Model 2*)

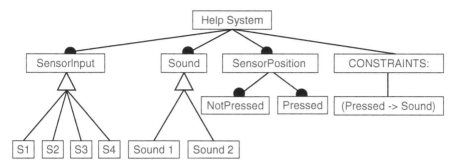

Fig. 7.10 "Help system" feature model in the format of SPLOT system (© with kind permission from Science of Computer Programming [ŠBB+16])

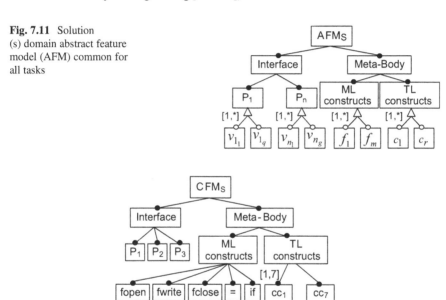

Fig. 7.11 Solution (s) domain abstract feature model (AFM) common for all tasks

Fig. 7.12 Solution (s) domain concrete feature model (CFMs) for "help system". $P_1 \equiv$ *SensorInput*; $P_2 \equiv$ *SensorPosition*; $P_3 \equiv$ *SoundFile*; *ML*, meta-language and its functions used (e.g. $f_1 = fopen,...$, $f_5 = if$); *TL*, target language and its constructs used: cc1 – while; cc2 – touch sensor; cc3 – play sound; cc4 – nxtDisplayCenteredTextLine; cc5 – sensor value; cc6 – sound variable; cc7 – **wait**1 Ms (© with kind permission from Science of Computer Programming [ŠBB+16])

context has two parts: the general part and the content part (see Sect. 7.5.1). The content part, in fact, is a physical LO (see Sect. 2.3.1, Chap. 2). The general part includes the context for design for modelling, results handling, etc. In Fig. 7.11, we present the abstract feature model (AFM$_s$) to represent the solution domain (see also the upper part of the right branch in Fig. 7.11). In Fig. 7.12, we present the model that represents the solution itself, i.e. the concrete feature model CFM$_s$ (see also a vertical branch in Fig. 7.9). Note that $P_1 \equiv$ *SensorInput*, $P_2 \equiv$ *SensorPosition* and $P_3 \equiv$ *SoundFile* (see

Legend in Fig. 7.12) illustrate the transformation rule for transforming the elements of the "help system" feature model to the model CFM$_s$.

7.5.4 SLO Design at the Low (Coding) Level

At this level, on the left branch, we have the concrete feature model *CFM$_S$* in terms of the solution domain. On the right branch, we need to have documents representing syntax of the meta-language and the target language (i.e. PHP and RobotC in our case). Then model *CFM$_S$* transformation into the executable specification consists of two parts (for interface and meta-body, see also Fig 7.12). We are able to accomplish the interface part transformation either manually or using the adequate tool [BBŠ13]. The meta-body coding is manual. Note that the model-driven approach makes the manual coding easier. In Fig. 7.13, we present a fragment of the interface specification in PHP. In Fig. 7.14, we present the meta-body implementation in PHP and RobotC.

In Fig. 7.15, we present the concrete LO instance derived from the SLO "help system".

Therefore, we have presented the model-driven SLO design framework. The framework includes three levels. At each level, we have had to accomplish the adequate transformations. However, in describing our framework, we have missed some details of those transformations. Transformations relate to inherent model properties and rules. Those form a part of the background we consider in the next section.

```
<?
//-------------------Meta-interface----------------------
 $SensorInput =$_POST['SensorInput'];
 $SensorPosition =$_POST['SensorPosition'];
 $Sound =$_POST['Sound'];
if (!isset($SensorInput) && !isset($SensorPosition) && !isset($Sound)) {
?>
<form method = "POST" action = "">
Select parameter SensorInput value:
<select name="SensorInput">
<option value="S1"> S1 </option>
<option value="S2"> S2 </option>
<option value="S3"> S3 </option>
<option value="S4"> S4 </option>
</select>
<br>
<input type = "submit" value ="Submit" name = "submit" style="height: 28px">
</form>
 ...
```

Fig. 7.13 A SLO interface fragment of "help system" (© with kind permission from Science of Computer Programming [ŠBB+16])

```
//---------------------Meta-body-------------------------
$myFile = "result.c";
 $fr = fopen($myFile, 'w');
 fwrite($fr, "#pragma config (Sensor,".$SensorInput.", touchSensor, sensorTouch) \n");
 fwrite($fr, "task main() \n");
 fwrite($fr, "{\n");
 fwrite($fr, "while (true) {\n");
 fwrite($fr, "while(SensorValue(touchSensor) == 0) \n");
 fwrite($fr, "nxtDisplayCenteredTextLine(4".', "OK"'."); \n");
 fwrite($fr, "while(SensorValue(touchSensor) == 1) {\n");
 if($Sound == "Sound1") $s ='soundBeepBeep';
 else if ($Sound == "Sound2")    $s = 'soundLowBuzz';
 fwrite($fr, "PlaySound (".$s.");\n");
 fwrite($fr,"wait1Msec(500); \n");
 fwrite($fr, "}\n");
 fwrite($fr, "}\n");
 fwrite($fr, "}\n");
 fclose($fr);
 echo" <br> <a href=\"result.c\">Program file</a></span></span></strong><br>";
 }?>
```

Fig. 7.14 SLO "help system" meta-body (© with kind permission from Science of Computer Programming [ŠBB+16])

```
#pragma config (Sensor,S3, touchSensor, sensorTouch)
 task main()
 {
     while (true) {
         while(SensorValue(touchSensor) == 0)
           nxtDisplayCenteredTextLine(4, "OK");
         while(SensorValue(touchSensor) == 1) {
           PlaySound (soundLowBuzz);
           wait1Msec(500);
         }
       }
 }
```

Fig. 7.15 CS LO instance, i.e. nested loops in RobotC derived from the SLO "help system" (© with kind permission from Science of Computer Programming [ŠBB+16])

7.6 Theoretical Background of the Approaches

Note that we have already presented the theoretical background in Chap. 5. However, this presentation, largely, was informal. This background extends the one introduced previously. Here, we focus on the formal representation of *our domains* and tasks (in fact, *Approach 1* and *Approach 2*). This background includes the *formal definition of feature models* and *their elements, transformation rules* to transform elements of the FM (PD) to adequate elements of the FM(SD) as well as *properties* (here PD, problem domain, and SD, solution domain). We present the basic definitions only (for the full list, see [ŠBB+16]).

Definition 1 Feature model is the compound defined by (7.4):

$$FM = \langle G, E_{mand}, \; E_{opt}, G_{xor}, G_{or}, REQ, EX \rangle \qquad (7.4)$$

Here, the graph $G = (F, E, r)$ is a rooted tree; F is a finite set of features; $E \subseteq F \times F$ is a finite set of edges; $r \in F$ is the root feature; $E_{mand} \subseteq E$ is a set of edges that define *mandatory features* with their parents; $E_{opt} \subseteq E$ is a set of edges that define *optional features* with their parents; the graphs $G_{xor} \subseteq P(F) \times F$ and $G_{or} \subseteq P(F) \times F$ define the *alternative and optional* feature groups with their common parent feature P; *REQ* and *EX* are finite sets of constraints *requires* and *excludes* (adapted from [ACL+13]).

The reader should connect these formal concepts with their informal, i.e. graphical representations given in Table 5.1 (see Chap. 5, Sect. 5.4.2).

Definition 2 Variation point is the parent feature whose children are grouped alternative or optional features. *Variant* is the value of the variation point (i.e. a child of the variation point) [Bat05].

Definition 3 Feature model is the *concrete model* if all variants are *concrete values* of its variation point; otherwise, the model is the *abstract model*.

Definition 4 Configuration of the feature model (also feature diagram) is a subtree of the feature diagram such that it covers all variation points and the only one variant of each variation point; *valid configuration* is the configuration that takes also into account the existing constraints [Bat05].

Definition 5 Feature model aggregation is the process of composing of a new model from the given ones that have not common parts [ACL+13].

Definition 6 A STEM CS learning variability model is the feature model that we express through the set of variation points and their variants and feature relationships; semantically features represent the pedagogical, social, technological and content aspects (i.e. feature values). In *Model 1 (Approach 1)*, all features belong to the same feature diagram. In *Model 2 (Approach 2)*, pedagogical-social features represent a separate feature diagram.

Definition 7 Generative (smart) learning object (further SLO) is the structured heterogeneous meta-program. The latter is the higher-level executable specification, which is coded using the meta-language L_M and the target (teaching) language L_T to specify and generate a set of teaching resources that are interpreted as LOs.

Definition 8 The SLO model M_{SLO} is a composition of the interface model M_I and the meta-body model M_{MB}. Formally, that is defined by Eq. (7.5):

$$M_{SLO} = M_I \otimes M_{MB} \qquad (7.5)$$

Here, the symbol $\otimes$ stands for a composition. If one conceives M_I and M_{MB} as files, then the composition is the concatenation of the files.

Definition 9 The interface model M_I is the graph $G\,(P,U)$. The latter is defined as follows:

(i) The set of vertexes P is the full set of the SLO parameter names, i.e. $P = \{P_1, P_2, \ldots, P_i, \ldots, P_n\}$; n – the number of parameters.

(ii) $P_i := V_i = \{v_{i1}, v_{i2}, \ldots, v_{iq}\} \in V$; V – the ordered set of all parameter values. The symbol "$:=$" means "is defined"; i_q – the number of values of the parameter P_i.

(iii) The set U is the set of edges of the graph. The edge $u_{ij} = 1$ exists if parameters P_i and P_j are interacting or dependent; otherwise $u_{ij} = 0$ (means that the edge does not exist between vertexes P_i and P_j).

Definition 10 Two parameters P_i and P_j $(P_i, P_j \subseteq P(i \neq j))$ are *dependent upon the choice of their values (i.e. interacting)* if there exists a pair of values $\left(v_{i_d}, v_{j_t}\right)$ $\left(v_{i_d} \in P_i, v_{j_t} \in P_j\right.$, where $d \in [1, i_q]$ and $t \in [1, j_m]$; q, m – the number of values adequately) such that the following condition holds:

$$\left(v_{i_d} \ requires \ v_{j_t}\right) \vee \left(v_{i_d} \ excludes \ v_{j_t}\right) = \textbf{true}.$$

Definition 11 Two parameters P_i and P_j $(P_i, P_j \subseteq P(i \neq j))$ are *independent upon the choice of their values (i.e. not interacting)* if for all pairs of the values $\left(v_{i_d}, v_{j_t}\right)$, the following condition holds:

$$\left(v_{i_d} \ requires \ v_{j_t}\right) \vee \left(v_{i_d} \ excludes \ v_{j_t}\right) = \textbf{false}.$$

Definition 12 The graph $G\,(P^W, U)$ is the interface model of the *context-aware* SLO, where W is the set of parameter weights to model (manage) the context of the parameter use.

This model is also the parameter interaction model, according to Definition 9, Definition 10 and Definition 11.

Definition 13 The *priority-based context model* is the ordered set W of fuzzy variables or constants: $W = \{w_1, w_2, \ldots, w_i, \ldots, w_n\}$; $w_i \in \{PH, PI, PL\}$ for all i. PH – high priority; PI – intermediate priority; PL – low priority; n- the number of parameters.

Definition 14 The meta-body model of the SLO is the ordered set of the functions $f_k(a)$ defined by (7.6):

$$M_{MB} = \{f_k(a)\} \tag{7.6}$$

f_k are constructs or functions of the meta-language L_M (i.e. $f_k(a) \in L_M$); a is the argument of a function; the argument can be either a parameter (or even the other function of L_M), a fragment of the target (teaching) language L_T or both.

Definition 15 SLO feature model is the result of mapping the problem domain model (i.e. CS learning variability model) onto the solution domain (i.e. heterogeneous meta-programming model). Formally, it is defined by Eq. (7.7):

$$FM_{SLO} = FM_{LV} \times FM_{MPG} \tag{7.7}$$

Here, LV – CS learning variability; MPG – heterogeneous meta-programming; *FM* – feature model; and the symbol "×" treat as mapping.

Definition 16 Feature model aggregation is the process of composing of a new model from the given ones that have not common parts [ACL+13].

Definition 17 Feature model specialization is the process of transforming the feature model *A* into the model *B* so that its configuration is a subset of configurations of the model *A* [ACL+13].

Property 1 The problem domain attributes as well as the context-based attributes and the solution domain attributes in the feature models are represented *uniformly* through features and the feature parent-child relationships and constraints.

Property 2 For the conceptual *Model 1*, the learning variability model FM_{LV} is the aggregated feature model that includes the entire context features.

Property 3 For the conceptual *Model 2*, the learning variability model FM_{LV} is the aggregated feature model too; however, the pedagogical context is not included (it is a part of the scenario model) to gain a higher flexibility due to STEM attributes.

Property 4 The model mapping (i.e. Eq. 7.7) is feasible if the learning variability model FM_{LV} is the concrete model (see Definition in Sect. 7.4). Therefore, before applying the transformation rules, the learning variability model has to be transformed into the concrete model.

Property 5 Mandatory features of the model FM_{LV} specify the *domain commonality*. Variation points and their variants of the model FM_{LV} along with the adequate constraints specify the *domain variability*.

7.7 Generic Transformation Rule

Before applying the transformation rules, the initial state of the models is as follows:
(1) Input models are (a) the learning variability model to represent the CS learning domain and (b) heterogeneous meta-programming model. (2) Both are represented as feature models. (3) The learning variability model FM_{LV} is the concrete aggregated model (denoted as CFM_{LV}), also containing within the context features. (4) Heterogeneous meta-programming model is yet the abstract feature model (denoted as AFM_{MPG} or as AFM_s for short).

The concrete model (denoted as CFM_s) is created because of using transformation rules within the given computational model to enable the conversion of both input models into the output model, i.e. the SLO feature model.

Here, we present the *generic rule* as a set of the base rules. The base rule defines the correspondence among some elements of the problem domain model and the adequate element of the solution domain model. Therefore, the set of base rules defines the valid correspondence among models of the problem and solution domains.

7.7.1 Generic Rule

All valid configurations, which are expressed through the *concrete feature model* (CFM_{LV}) representing the learning variability, are to be mapped onto the set of configurations of the solution domain *abstract feature model* (AFM_S), and then the latter is to be transformed into the *solution domain concrete feature model* (CFM_S) using a set of the base transformation rules (a)–(f). Finally, CFM_s is to be coded by the constructs of the selected meta-language and target language as it is specified by rules (g) and (h).

To understand the design framework in detail, one needs to follow our running example and Figs. 7.10, 7.11 and 7.12 along with the base rules:

(a) *Variation point* in the feature model CFM_{LV} (Fig. 7.10) corresponds to a *parameter name* in the feature model AFM_S (see Fig. 7.12).
(b) *Variants* of a variation point within the feature model CFM_{LV} correspond to the parameter values in the feature model AFM_S.
(c) The ordered set of variation points and variants defines the interface of the model AFM_S.
(d) The priority feature of the model CFM_{LV} defines the sequence of parameters within the interface in the model AFM_S (they are omitted in Fig. 7.10 for simplicity).
(e) Constraints of the model CFM_{LV} correspond to the parameter interaction (i.e. the graph G (P^W, U), in the model AFM_S (they are omitted in this model).
(f) A particular valid configuration of the model CFM_{LV}, when coded using the target language, corresponds to the target program instance; a variation point is treated as the placeholder to insert the adequate meta-function.
(g) When constructing the interface, parameters and parameter interaction constraints are coded, using the constructs of the meta-language according to the semantics of the interface model with the parameter interaction and priority context models in mind.
(h) When constructing the meta-body, placeholders within the target program instance (or instances) are substituted by the adequate meta-functions according to the semantics of the learning variability model. Coding of both interface and meta-body results in the introduction of the concrete semantics into the solution domain model, thus transforming the abstract model AFM_s into the concrete model CFM_s, which, when coded by the meta-language and target language, yields the executable SLO specification.

In summary, we compare conceptual models (see Table 7.1) with respect to key characteristics. They include common, design, implementation and usage aspects.

Table 7.1 A comparison of conceptual *Model 1* and *Model 2*

Approaches characteristics	Approach 1 (*Model 0/ Model 1*)	Approach 2 (*Model 2*)	Explanation
Conceptual model	GLO/SLO as related to overall processes for CS education, Fig. 12.1 [Štu15]	STEM-driven CS learning content (see Fig. 2.3, Chap. 2)	STEM concepts are implicit in *Approach 1*; they are explicit in *Approach 2*
Modelling aspects	Static feature modelling of CS education	Dynamic modelling of STEM-driven CS education with collaborative features	CS education is treated as the problem domain (PD) and structured meta-programming as the solution domain (SD)
Design aspects			
Context aspect implementation	In the same generic model for a given task	In different models (see Fig. 7.5)	Pedagogy + social+ technological are common for all tasks
Content aspects	Context-aware generic model for a given task	Generic *context- distributed* model for a given task	In *Model 2*, some context attribute values are transferred from higher level to content specification level; the remaining part of the context is incorporated in the content specification
Scenario aspects	Are defined through semantic priority model that identifies the sequence of context and content aspects	Generative scenario for STEM topics is a separate component (see Chap. 10)	By generative scenario, we mean a generalized structure to manage learning processes and content sequencing
Implementation aspects			
Problem domain (PD) model	Pure CS learning variability model	STEM-driven CS learning variability model	*Model 2* represents the extended PD
Solution domain (SD) model	Structural heterogeneous meta-programming (MPG)	Structural heterogeneous MPG with extended features	*Model 2* uses four types of generators, while *Model 1* two types
PD mapping onto SD	Adequate transformation rules	Adequate transformation rules	The same for both models
Testing	Experimental	Experimental	The same for both
Usage aspects			
Learning content	GLO/SLO as stand-alone unit	SLOs+CB LOs as the whole of learning content	In *Approach 2*, this structure is due to STEM scenario
Learning process management	By choosing parameter values within a single GLO/SLO	A detailed description of activities (instructional guide) along with adequate content	In *Approach 2*, the management covers the entire topic while in *Approach 1* that is a *part of* the *Approach 2* only

(continued)

Table 7.1 (continued)

Approaches characteristics	Approach 1 (*Model 0/ Model 1*)	Approach 2 (*Model 2*)	Explanation
Activities	Oriented to CS concepts explanation and visualization	Oriented to STEM-driven CS concepts, PLO dependencies of characteristics through inquiry-based learning, including modelling, constructing, etc.	In *Approach 2*, there are more types of activities
Knowledge delivery mode	Implicit STEM knowledge, weak (narrow)	Explicit STEM knowledge, strong (wide)	Explicit knowledge are due to the generative scenario
Tools and environments	Support different robotics platforms	Additionally support to IoT	See Table 3.1 in Sect. 3.3
Pedagogical outcomes	Robot control programs as CS content	Additionally, Robot's model, Robot's designing guide, testing results	In *Approach 2*, there is to a larger degree the interdisciplinary knowledge
Scope of tasks	See Sect. 6.3 in Chap. 6 (Fig. 6.1)	See Sect. 6.3 in Chap. 6 (Fig. 6.1)	*Approach 2* covers a far more real-world tasks oriented to STEM as compared to *Approach 1* (tasks oriented to programming)

7.8 Summary, Overall Evaluation and Conclusion

Previously, in Chap. 2, we have formulated our vision for integrating STEM into CS education at school through enhanced reuse and automation. In this chapter, we have discussed the issues on how to transform the vision into a *model-driven methodology* to design the educational content (note that this methodology is a *constituent part or component* of the whole approach we discuss throughout the book). To do so, we have borrowed concepts of the model-driven design from software engineering. Those concepts (i.e. CS learning variability, feature models, model transformations, etc.) stand for the methodological basis. We have already presented this methodology partially in [ŠBB+16, Štu15]. In this chapter, however, we have extended it essentially towards STEM specificity and requirements.

The presented methodology includes (i) formal statement of the content design task, (ii) creating and managing of feature models for both the problem domain and the solution domain, (iii) decomposing of the models into constituting parts and elements (i.e. sub-models), (iv) visualization and sequencing of models and sub-models to enable the task-solving processes through model transformations and (v) identification and specification of intermediate and final outcomes of the processes. We have defined the content design task as the mappings of the problem domain models (sub-models) onto the solution domain models (sub-models) with gradual decreasing the level of abstraction. The later requires two kinds of transformations, i.e. *vertical transformation* to exclude model parts resulting in decreasing the level of abstraction for both problem and solution domains and *horizontal transf*ormation resulting in expressing problem domain items through the concepts of the solution domain. Note that, depending on the abstraction level, feature models serve to represent either the problem domain or the solution domain. For example, at the top level of abstraction, we represent STEM learning domain by TPACK/CPACK data (i.e. informally) and the solution domain by feature models. At the middle level of abstraction, feature models stand for representing both domains (STEM learning variability as a problem domain and meta-programming as a solution domain).

We have presented our methodology using *multi-level Y-charts*. They fit well to visualize *multi-dimensional separation of concerns*, i.e. models (sub-models) and transformational processes (sub-processes). We treat this visualization as innovative aspects of our methodology. Indeed, the graphical representation enforces the cognitive level of model-driven transformation-based approach for novices (e.g. CS teachers). On the other hand, it explains well the theoretical reasoning of our approach. The formulated transformation rules define on how the elements of the problem domain model correspond to the adequate elements of the solution domain.

The core part of the methodology is two *conceptual models*. The first, i.e. *Model 1* (*Approach 1*), represents our previous research. The second, i.e. *Model 2* (*Approach 2*), represents new findings we describe in this book. When applied, our methodology produces the outcome, i.e. the educational content given as *smart learning objects* (SLOs). SLO represents a portion of learning content, meaning the adequate topic or theme. We specify each SLO, using meta-programming techniques, as a *generalized* robot control programs (meaning a set of *concrete* robot control programs to solve a real-world task during the educational process). Before solving the task, the user (i.e. teacher or student) needs to manage the designed SLO specification in order to derive from it the *needed instance* of the robot control program. The user defines the needed instance by selecting parameter values associated with his/her context. Then the process of deriving or generating instances is fully automatic. The meta-language processor performs this job.

What are the main distinguishing features and contribution of the methodology? The implementation of the model-driven vision has many benefits. Firstly, it enables to deal with the highly heterogeneous STEM-driven CS education as the uniformly integrated domain. Secondly, it allows a better understanding (by CS teachers, CS education researchers, etc.) of the role of the separate subdomains and their interaction. Thirdly, it brings the knowledge to educational tool designers on which basis it is possible to integrate the essential features of heterogeneous sub-systems. Finally, it enables to increase the level of generative reuse, thus introducing the automation capabilities in the social-oriented application, such as e-Learning. In addition, the methodology supports transferring of the well-proven knowledge (such as *design for reuse and design with reuse within the PLE design paradigm in SWE*), applying and extending it to the needs of CS education. Furthermore, the enhanced features of SLO specifications such as context awareness (here we have considered the simplest case only; more on that can be found in [Štu15]) open the way for adaptive learning. One can view the methodology as a new way in CS teacher preparation. In addition, the methodology is relevant to use for other CS courses because it is independent on using target languages. In the case of teaching, for instance, themes of data structures, instead of the target language RobotC, should be used the other language that is suitable to specifying those items. With regard to the other courses (not just related to CS), it should be stated the following. If it is possible to discover and represent the learning variability explicitly, the approach is applicable too.

What are the difficulties of the proposed methodology? The main difficulties of the methodology relate to its heterogeneity and complexity. Therefore, it requires far more efforts from CS teachers. Some CS teachers may feel an additional burden to learn robotics (before using the educational robots, one needs to carry out thorough modelling of real-world tasks in the context of robotics). There is an additional burden to learn the modelling and design tools and be aware with basic principles of writing meta-programs. This is because of the difficulty to combine the formal and abstract models to provide their transformation. However, this is not so much the lack of tools but rather the complexity of the task itself.

What are the perspectives for diminishing these difficulties? The important issue is the use of the same principle on which the methodology has been constructed (i.e. multi-level separation and integration of concerns). Such important topics as feature modelling, context awareness, aspects of robotics and meta-programming should be first studied separately. Then the integrative aspects of the methodology should be studied. From the user perspective, however, the best way to overcome indicated difficulties is the use of this methodology as a "component from the shelf". To achieve that, additional researching efforts are needed. They may include (a) creating the *feature model library* for saving and disseminating of the CS learning variability models, (b) the development of the *appropriate instructions* to facilitate the use of the tools for novices and (c) creating *procedures for disseminating items* of the robot-based STEM-driven SLO library and perhaps *creating the community* of the supporters and proponents of this approach.

References

[ACL+13] Acher M, Collet P, Lahire P, France RB (2013) Familiar: a domain-specific language for large scale management of feature models. Sci Comput Program 78:657–681
[AK09]   Apel S, Kästner C (2009) An overview of feature-oriented software development. J Object Technol (JOT) 8(5):49–48
[AR07]   Alana E, Rodríguez AI (2007) Domain engineering methodologies survey. GMV Innovating Solutions
[Bat05]   Batory D (2005) Feature models, grammars, and propositional formulas. Springer, Berlin, pp 7–20
[BBŠ13]   Bespalova K, Burbaite R, Štuikys (2013) MP-ReTool tools. http://proin.ktu.lt/metaprogram/MP-ReTool/

[BDB+06] Botturi L, Derntl M, Boot E, Figl K (2006) A classification framework for educational modeling languages in instructional design. In: 6th IEEE international conference on advanced learning technologies (ICALT 2006). Kerkrade, pp 1216–1220

[Bos00] Bosch J (2000) Design and use of software architectures: adopting and evolving a product-line approach. Pearson Education, New York

[BS11] Burbaite R, Stuikys V (2011) Analysis of learning object research using feature-based models. In: Information technologies' 2011: proceedings of the 17th international conference on information and software technologies, pp 201–208

[CBK13] Capilla R, Bosch J, Kang KC (eds) (2013) Systems and software variability management (concepts, tools and experiences). Springer, Heidelberg

[CE00] Czarnecki K, Eisenecker U (2000) Generative programming: methods, tools and applications. Addison-Wesley, Boston

[CH06] Czarnecki K, Helsen S (2006) Feature-based survey of model transformation approaches. IBM Syst J 45:621–645

[CHW98] Coplien J, Hoffman D, Weiss D (1998) Commonality and variability in software engineering. IEEE Softw 15(6):37–45

[CL13] Collet P, Lahire P (2013) Feature modelling and separation of concerns with FAMILIAR, CMA@RE. IEEE, Rio deJaneiro, pp 13–18

[CLA06] Caeiro-Rodríguez M, Llamas-Nistal M, Anido-Rifón L (2006) A separation of concerns approach to educational modeling languages. In: Frontiers in education conference, 36th Annual (9–14). IEEE

[CNC12] Castro J, Nazar JM, Campos F (2012) EasyT: Apoiando a Construção de Objetos de Aprendizagem para uma Linha de Produtos de Software. Conferencias LACLO 3(1)

[DAS01] Dey A, Abowd G, Salber D (2001) A conceptual framework and a toolkit for supporting the rapid prototyping of context-aware applications. Hum-Comput Interact 16:97–166

[DD06] Dodero JM, Díez D (2006) Model-driven instructional engineering to generate adaptable learning materials. In: Advanced learning technologies, 2006. Sixth international conference on IEEE, pp 1188–1189

[DDA12] Díez D, Díaz P, Aedo I (2012) The ComBLA method: the application of domain analysis to the development of e-learning systems. J Res Pract Inf Technol 44(3)

[Dey01] Dey AK (2001) Understanding and using context. Pers Ubiquit Comput 5(1):4–7

[Dou04] Dourish P (2004) What we talk about when we talk about context. Pers Ubiquit Comput 8:19–30. Feb. 2004

[DŠ08] Damaševičius R, Štuikys V (2008) Development of generative learning objects using feature diagrams and generative techniques. Inform Educ 7(2):277–288

[DS09] Damasevicius R, Stuikys V (2009) Specification and generation of learning object sequences for E-learning using sequence feature diagrams and metaprogramming techniques in advanced learning technologies, 2009. ICALT 2009. Ninth IEEE international conference, July, pp 572–576

[DZF+07] Dodero J, Zarraonandía T, Fernández C, Díez D (2007) Generative adaptation reuse of competence development programmes. J Interact Media Educ 2007(1)

[GK83] Gajski DD, Kuhn RH (1983) New VLSI tools. Computer 16(12):11–14

[Har02] Harsu M (2002) A survey on domain engineering. Tampere University of Technology, Tampere, pp 1–27

[JB07] Jones R, Boyle T (2007) Learning object patterns for programming. Interdiscip J Knowl Learn Objects 3(1):19–28

[KCH+90] Kang KC, Cohen SG, Hess JA, Novak WE, Peterson AS (1990) Feature-oriented domain analysis (FODA) feasibility study. In: DTIC Document

[KM09] Koehler M, Mishra P (2009) What is technological pedagogical content knowledge (TPACK)? Contemp Issues Technol Teach Educ 9(1):60–70

[LC06]   Laforcade P, Choquet C (2006) Next step for educational modeling languages: the model driven engineering and reengineering approach. In: Advanced learning technologies, 2006. Sixth international conference on IEEE, pp 745–747

[LCW+09]   Liu L, Chen H, Wang H, Zhao C (2009) Construction of a student model in contextually aware pervasive learning. In: Pervasive computing (JCPC), 2009 joint conferences on PC. IEEE, pp 511–514

[MBC09]   Mendonca M, Branco M, Cowan D (2009) SPLOT: software product lines online tools. In: Proceedings of the 24th ACM SIGPLAN conference companion on Object oriented programming systems languages and applications. ACM, p 761–762

[Par76]   Parnas DL (1976) On the design and development of program families. IEEE Trans Softw Eng 1:1–9

[PLL+06]   Paquette G, Léonard M, Lundgren-Cayrol K, Mihaila S, Gareau D (2006) Learning design based on graphical knowledge-modeling. J Educl Technol Soc 9:97–112

[PS04]   Pitkanen SH, Silander P (2004) Criteria for pedagogical reusability of learning objects enabling adaptation and individualised learning processes. In: Proceedings of IEEE international conference advanced learning technologies, pp 246–250

[RM04]   Rodríguez-Artacho M, Maillo MFV (2004) Modeling educational content: the cognitive approach of the PALO language. Educ Technol Soc 7(3):124–137

[ŠBB+16]   Štuikys V, Burbaitė R, Bespalova K, Ziberkas G (2016) Model-driven processes and tools to design robot-based generative learning objects for computer science education. Sci Comput Program 129:48–71

[ŠBB+17]   Štuikys V, Burbaitė R, Bespalova K, Blažauskas T, Barisas D (2017) Stage-based generative learning object model for automated content adaptation, Baltic J. Mod Comput 5(2):183–205

[ŠBD13]   Štuikys V, Burbaitė R, Damaševičius R (2013) Teaching of computer science topics using meta-programming-based SLOs and LEGO robots. Inf Educ- Int J 12:125–142

[Sch06]   Schmidt DC (2006) Guest editor's introduction: model-driven engineering. Computer 39(2006):0025–0031

[ŠD13]   Štuikys V, Damaševičius R (2013) Meta-programming and model-driven meta-program development: principles, processes and techniques. Springer, London

[ŠDB+08]   Štuikys V, Damaševičius R, Brauklytė I, Limanauskienė V (2008) Exploration of learning object ontologies using feature diagrams. In Proceedings of world conference on educational multimedia, hypermedia and telecommunications (Ed-MEDIA 2008). June 30–July 4, Vienna, Austria. AACE, Chesapeake, pp 2144–2154

[She01]   Sheard T (2001) Accomplishments and research challenges in meta-programming. In: Semantics, applications, and implementation of program generation, (Springer, 2001), pp 2–44

[Štu15]   Štuikys V (2015) Smart learning objects for the smart education in computer science: theory, methodology and robot-based implementation. Springer, Heidelberg

[VMO+12]   Verbert K, Manouselis N, Ochoa X, Wolpers M, Drachsler H, Bosnic I, Duval E (2012) Context-aware recommender systems for learning: a survey and future challenges. In: Learning technologies, IEEE Transactions on, pp 318–335

[Wir78]   Wirth N (1978) Algorithms + data structures = programs. Prentice Hall PTR, Upper Saddle River

[YMV+15]   Yaşar O, Maliekal J, Veronesi P, Little L, Vattana S (2015) Computational pedagogical content knowledge (CPACK): integrating modeling and simulation technology into STEM teacher education. Res Highlights Technol Teach Educ 2015:79

Chapter 8
Stage-Based Smart Learning Objects: Adaptation Perspective

Abstract In Chap. 8, we deal with a specific model of the smart content, i.e. the stage-based (SB) generative (smart) learning object (GLO/SLO) model. This model supports the automated adaptation of the educational content. We aim at showing how it is possible to integrate the STEM-driven CS education concepts into the SB GLO model. The model is a derivative from the initial GLO/SLO specification. Two dependent concepts, i.e. staging and context awareness, are basic to understand this model. The first means refactoring the structure of the original GLO specification into the stage-based structure without the loss of functionality. Semantically staging means the rearrangement of parameter space of an original GLO among stages so that it would be possible at the stage k $(k > 1)$ to produce a meta-meta-program with $(k–1)$ stages and finally at stage 1 to produce the target program. The user, making the context-dependent selection of parameter values at each stage, enables the system to narrow the parameter space according to his/her context and, in this way, to adapt gradually the generated content. We analyse a case study, the stage-based adaptation processes and learning scenarios. Finally, we discuss the capabilities of this methodology and present an overall evaluation with the focus on pedagogical aspects.

8.1 Introduction

This chapter is about the adaptation of the educational content, typically known in the literature as learning object (shortly LO or LOs). We remind the reader that, in terms of reuse, there are component-based LOs and generative LOs (GLOs). The concept of GLO is due to the contribution of Boyle, Morales et al. [BLC04, MLB05]. They characterize GLOs as "the next generation learning objects". The centre for excellence in the design, development and use of LOs in the UK (shortly, RLO-CETL) defines GLO as "an articulated and executable learning design that produces a class of learning objects" [BLA+08]. Their approach has been borrowed from the systemic grammar [BR12]; however, it can be also viewed as the template-based approach in terms of software generative reuse [Sam97].

To implement GLOs, we use the other generative technologies, such as programming languages, compilers and meta-programming-based approaches. In essence, they are more powerful in their capabilities of automation and adaptation. Therefore, they fit well to implement GLOs. Especially it is true with regard to CS education, because those technologies, in a wider context, are also the educational contents. More specifically, we use structured heterogeneous meta-programming techniques to implement GLOs. The external parameterization applied on the internal content stands for the base principle to understand the essence of this mechanism (for more details, see meta-program model of *Type 1* in Sect. 5.5).

To implement adaptation of GLOs, we use stage-based heterogeneous meta-programming [ŠD13] (see also meta-program model of *Type 2* in Sect. 5.5). This approach enables to specify various transformations of the original GLO aiming to achieve specific goals such as content adaptability for the learners' context. Even more, we are able to automate the adaptation process using this approach. A more extensive exploration of this technology in CS education enabled us to rename meta-programming-based GLOs and treat them as *smart LOs* (shortly SLO or SLOs) [Štu15]. We define SLOs as GLOs with extended capabilities for generative reuse, meaning also enhanced possibilities of automation, transformation and adaptation (later, in Chap. 9, we extend the smartness additionally by introducing agent-based GLOs).

The aim of this chapter is twofold. Firstly, we focus on a specific model, called *stage-based GLO model* (further SB GLO; note also that SB GLO and SLO are synonyms in our definition). Our aim is to show how this model supports automated adaptation of the educational content, i.e. GLO as meta-program. Secondly, we aim at showing how it is possible to integrate the STEM-driven CS education concepts into the SB GLO model. Note that this chapter is a generalization of results published in our papers [SBB+16, ŠBB+17]. We discuss the following tasks here:

Task 1. Exploration of the SB GLO/SLO model with the focus on automated adaptation of the CS educational content, when the STEM context is implicit.
Task 2. Explicit integration of STEM context into the SB model.

The remaining part contains the following sections. In Sect. 8.2, we analyse the related work. In Sect. 8.3, we motivate our research methodology. In Sect. 8.4, we categorize learning objects as entities of the STEM library. In Sect. 8.5, we outline a framework to present overall aspects of the methodology without details. In Sect. 8.6, we present a background of the approach through the definition of basic terms and statement of assumptions and properties. In Sect. 8.7, we introduce the concepts staging and context awareness. In Sect. 8.8, we analyse the integration of STEM concepts into stage-based model. In Sect. 8.9, we consider a case study that includes the robot-based implementation of the model in solving the educational tasks to teach CS. In Sect. 8.10, we analyse the stage-based adaptation processes and learning scenarios. In Sect. 8.11, we discuss the capabilities of the methodology and present an overall evaluation with the focus on pedagogical aspects. Finally, in Sect. 8.12, we conclude the main results.

8.2 Related Work

We categorize the related work into three groups: (A) context-related issues in technology-enhanced learning TEL (also e-Learning), because the adaptation problem is context-dependent; (B) approaches related to the model-driven stage-based development; and (C) adaptation in e-Learning.

8.2.1 Context-Related Issues in TEL

As there is no common understanding of the term context, multiple definitions and views have been proposed so far. Among those, Dey [Dey01] defines context as "any information that can be used to characterize the situation of an entity". By an entity, it is meant "a person, place, or object that is considered relevant to the interaction between a user and an application, including the user and applications themselves". The paper [VMO+12] gives an extensive analysis of definitions in relation to engineering of recommendation systems to support TEL. Dourish indicates that context has a technical and social origin [Dou04]. He argues that, from the social perspective, context is not something that describes a setting or situation but rather a *feature of interaction*. Researchers in TEL say that this user-centred emphasis on factors affecting an activity is precisely what makes this notion of context meaningful for learning. From a technical perspective, context is understood as an *operational term* [Win01]. In this regard, papers [Dey01, SAW94] define context by enumerating its categories as follows: *computing context* (such as network connectivity, etc.), *user context* (such as the user's profile, etc.), *physical context* (such as noise level, etc.), *time-related context* and *task-related context* [VMO+12]. The Zimmermann et al. [ZLO07] operational view includes the following context categories: *individuality*, *activity*, *location*, *time* and *relations*. Individuality is subdivided into four elements: *natural entity*, *human entity*, *artificial entity* and *group entity*. This definition is perhaps one of the most comprehensive context definitions to date.

In TEL, such enumerations have also been proposed as an attempt to define the learner or teacher context as an operational term. Many enumerations are defined for mobile learning. For example, Berri et al. [BBA06] distinguish between technical and learner context elements. The first category deals with the technical aspects of mobile devices, their operational environment and constraints. The second category defines the learner context elements (e.g. aims and objectives of the learner, prerequisites, etc.). It is also essential to capture *interactions* between the *environment*, the *user*, their *tasks* and other *users*. The paper [DA06] aims at defining a context ontology of teacher's personal annotation, in order to use it in a context-aware annotation tool "MemoNote". The paper defines the active and passive contexts in the tool (annotation ontologies selection, annotation memorization, pattern definition and selection) to develop the complete teacher's context annotation ontology using the classical method specified for Protégé.

The *content granularity* and *context information* are related. Both are important factors to the efficiency and reusability of learning objects (LOs). The context information, e.g. is necessary to facilitate the discovery and reuse of LOs stored in global repositories or local libraries. Typically, LOs are incorporated into repositories without the context information. Users have to do some extension of the LO descriptions to fit their special use. Therefore, the paper [MJ10] introduces a context-rich paradigm, the related service-driven tagging strategy and a context model of LOs. This model realizes the adaptive granularity of the content and LOs.

The paper [HP05] describes a four-tier reusability model for making reuse happen in practice within organizations. The items that affect the viability of object reuse are the properties of the object itself (e.g. structural reuse and contextual reuse) and the organization's preparedness to undertake LO reuse (operational reuse and strategic reuse). *Structural reusability* is thought of as a function of how the object has been engineered. By *contextual reusability*, *it* is meant the applicability of the object to new learning events that affects the potential audience size. *Operational reusability* has dependencies on organizational culture, personnel, procedures and technology. *Strategic reusability* is seen as a function of organizational strategy for systematic or opportunistic reuse.

8.2.2 The Term Stage and Relevant Methodologies

In the literature (typically, between SWE and CS fields explicitly and among e-Learning implicitly), the term stage is used in two roles: (1) *as a time dimension* to split some process into parts and (2) *as a design principle and the design process* itself. The process duration, however, may vary within wide boundaries. For example, the paper [BD08] identifies the physical, cognitive and psychosocial characteristics of learners that influence learning at various *stages of growth and development* and also discusses appropriate teaching strategies. Also in e-Learning, the term is used under other names such as *level*. Indeed Bloom's taxonomy [AKB01], e.g. identifies the cognitive levels (they can be interpreted as stages) in knowledge gaining by learners, though the time dimension is implicit. A similar example is the methodology [UV09] to assess the knowledge of the learning process through engagement levels that include the following levels (stages): *viewing*, *responding*, *changing*, *constructing* and *presenting*. In terms of role 1, the paper [RB00] deals with the *stage-based* software lifecycle model that includes the initial development, evolution, servicing, phaseout and close-down.

In role 2, *stage and staging* can be thought of as the *separation of concepts* (also, the term concern is used), the well-known design principle since 1970 [Dij70], in which Dijkstra has applied information hiding and separation techniques to describe structured programming. Note also that Greer, for example, considers separation of concepts "as a principle and a process" used in designing systems [Gre08]. We speak about that not only to explain the origin of introduced terms. We aim at highlighting the importance of the terms in TEL in general (in fact, the course designers and teachers use the terms, perhaps without the explicit naming). Therefore, the explicit use of the terms (stage and staging) can be found in the following contexts: stage programming in Taha works [Tah04, Tah99], stage-based meta-programming [ŠD13] and feature-based modelling. For example, the paper [CHE05] discusses *multistage configuration* of feature diagrams, and the paper [ECH+09] proposes the *multi-level staged configuration* of feature diagrams to facilitate configuration in SW product line engineering (PLE). The other paper [Kru13] considers a *multistage configuration tree* proposed in the context of feature-based modelling for the second-generation PLE. The latter supports the engineering, deployment and maintenance of product family trees. Feature selections and down selections are incrementally staged throughout the nodes in a product family tree.

8.2.3 Adaptation in e-Learning

The paper [BRH+15] discusses the design, implementation and preliminary evaluation of Adaptive Educational System for personalized course delivery, which integrates lecture videos, text, assessments and social learning into a mobile application. The system collects click stream-level behavioural measurements about each student as they interact with the material. These measurements can subsequently be used to update the student's user model, which can in turn be used to determine the content adaptation. The paper [AT11] proposes a module-based content adaptation approach for adapting composite e-Learning web pages composed by *Microsoft (MS) Producer* tools for delivering the contents onto mobile learners.

The paper [GAP+16] presents: (1) a Sharable Auto-Adaptive Learning Object (SALO) that includes learning content and describes its own behaviour supported by dynamic languages; (2) an example implementation of SALO for the delivery and assessment of a web development course using Moodle rubrics. As a result, the SALO can dynamically adapt their characteristics and behaviour in e-Learning platforms.

The paper [PG15] explores the adaptation based on learner context parameters, on the learning content (learning object) and the configuration of e-Learning environment. It also provides a detail review about the various levels of adaptation, learning object design and process for learning content design, learner context parameters and models/components of e-Learning, including the associations among the components to achieve the well-defined adaptation in e-Learning environment. The approach [DAC+16] uses an expert system to implement a set of rules, which classifies LO according to their teaching style and then automatically filters LO according to students' learning styles.

8.3 Motivation of the Approach

The reuse concepts, first being borrowed from more matured domains (such as HW and CS) and then adapted to e-Learning, dominate in TEL now. Similarly to other domains, TEL seeks for more effective solutions, especially in terms of seamless integration of pedagogical and technological approaches. In heterogeneous domains (TEL is just the case), context plays an extremely important role. There is a variety of contextual forms: the content-related, the technology-related, the social-related and the pedagogy-related ones [VMO+12]. Content adaptation is a specific form of reuse always dependent on the context. The adaptation process is highly related on how it is represented and delivered. The general methodological principle is as such: before delivering the whole content should be structured into parts to achieve the adequate granularity level and well-organized by sequencing (typical example is slides showing). In delivering the content (for audience, e.g. for students), the general pedagogical scenario can be outlined as follows: (1) defining objectives explicitly, (2) partitioning the whole content into parts, (3) starting explaining simpler parts first and then moving to items with more complexity and (4) choosing items for delivery (from possible variants, either simple or complex) so that the selected variant would be more relevant to a particular interest (it may be treated as context) to the audience.

What does the presented scenario in essence mean? In fact, the first motivates the whole activity. The second means the physical staging, though the other terms can be used such splitting, decomposing, partitioning, etc., but we prefer to use *staging* here. The third means both the staging and sequencing and an intent for adaptation. Finally, the fourth means a real action to support adaptation. Of course, to be viable, this scenario should be well-planned in advance. Therefore, the scenario describes the relationship chain: *staging-sequencing-adapting*. However, there is the fourth item, *context*, which is influential to the whole chain. The context may predefine the way on how the chain should be formed and used. As motivation and staging appear at the beginning, we can call the chain as *pedagogical staging* (for more detail, see Case Study in Sect. 8.7). In fact, the pedagogical staging motivates the need of using technological staging if one wants to achieve the aims of automated adaptation. One can learn more on technological staging from stage-based (SB) programming [Tah04, Tah99] and SB meta-programming [ŠD13].

Here, by technological staging, we mean the technological capabilities first to specify the content in *stages explicitly* and then to interpret the specification using the adequate tool. The tool brings automation. As we focus on automated adaptation, the following question arises. Where and how should each other meet the two concepts: pedagogical staging and technological staging? We argue here that the meeting point should be *a stage-based model*. The latter is derived from the initial MPG-based GLO.

Externally, both models have a similar structure as known two-level generic models (i.e. *metadata* and *content implementation*). The internal structure, however, is quite different in both parts. The use of the external parameterization technology based on preprogramming predefines the internal structure. Furthermore, the structure is derived from the initial parameterized GLO model using the refactoring tool. Typically the generic LO model has two levels: *meta-level* and *implementation level*. The meta-level serves for *delivering data to* the implementation level to support such processes as *search* and *generation*. The implementation level serves for the physical realization of the processes with the help of any computing environment (or technology). Therefore, the generic model has two parts: *metadata* plus *implementation* of the functionality.

The SB model GLO differs from the initial one by the following attributes: (1) internal structure is multistaged and derivative from the initial one; (2) the content generation is the multistaged process generating other GLOs having the context-related functionality until the LO is created; and (3) the generation process is governed by the context model semiautomatically or even automatically.

Why the SB model is needed? As the initial model GLO is designed for reuse with the extended reuse extent through enlarging the variability space, the adaptation of the model to the concrete context of use lacks of flexibility and requires intensive manual efforts. The SB GLO has two essential advantages: (1) separating the different context information (e.g. teacher's, student's, technological) through staging explicitly and (2) solving the adaptation problem semiautomatically or even automatically.

Why the SB model for STEM is needed? The stated above is valid for STEM too. Additionally, with the introduction of STEM-related features and reuse in mind, the STEM variability increases, and the complexity of contents grows. The SB model is valuable because of the possibility to manage this complexity.

8.4 Categories of Learning Objects to Support STEM

Here, we categorize the STEM-driven educational content, i.e. learning objects (LOs). In general, categorization is a subject of taxonomy. The latter is the science of classification according to a predetermined system. In e-Learning, there was a great deal of efforts to introduce taxonomies to identify various aspects of LOs through analysis of LO properties, structure, type and other attributes such as similarities and differences given by different sources. As the LO domain is highly heterogeneous, different taxonomies present different aspects. For example, Bloom's taxonomies (there is a long list of extensions of the base taxonomy) [Blo56] (see, e.g. [Kra02]) mainly focus on learning objectives and processes. Wiley's taxonomy [Wil00] focuses on LO types and characteristics. Redeker's taxonomy [Red03] aims *to conceptualize a didactical taxonomy* of LOs and provides a didactic metadata approach for the facilitation of reusable instructional navigation patterns. More specifically, he presents an educational taxonomy for LOs for the facilitation of generic sequencing strategies. The OSEL taxonomy [CAM+06] represents the joint product of Redeker's and Wiley's taxonomies. Rossano et al. [RJR+05] provide a meta-analysis and present a taxonomy for definitions and applications of LO as they were presented in the ICALT'05 papers. The taxonomy presented in [Štu15] comprises a more durable period and is oriented to extract not only definitions per se but also processes and activities applied to LOs (see Table 2.1, pp. 38–43 in [Štu15]).

In the context of STEM, we use a variety of LO types. With regard to the mode of their obtaining, we categorize them into categories A and B. The category A includes those items searched from the external LO repositories. The category B includes those designed by the designer or CS teacher. As there are two kinds of reuse (component-based and generative reuse [FK05]), from this perspective, we categorize LOs again into two groups: *component-based* (shortly CB LOs) and *generative ones* (shortly GLOs). In fact, from the implementation and use perspective, CB LOs are stand-alone instances, while GLOs are families of related instances to generate a particular instance or instances on demand.

Typically, from the functional role, CB LOs for STEM represent the following types:

   (i) Instructions (e.g. on how to construct an educational robot)
  (ii) Guidelines (e.g. on how to test the robot's correct behaviour)
 (iii) Guidelines to provide a scientific experiment as a part of STEM paradigm
  (iv) Films (e.g. to motivate the engagement in STEM learning)
   (v) A domain-specific software (e.g. for modelling robot's behaviour, languages to program robots)
  (vi) Descriptions of algorithms to solve the STEM-oriented robot's tasks
 (vii) Guidelines on how to develop robot control programs

Those types belong to category A, because we are able to obtain them from the external sources. However, there is also the internal source: we are able to extract or derive CB LOs from GLOs. We categorize GLOs (category B) as follows:

   (i) Original GLOs designed for CS education without the explicit focus on STEM
  (ii) Redesigned GLOs for CS with the specific focus on STEM
 (iii) Newly designed GLOs for STEM, meaning the introduction of new robot-oriented tasks
  (iv) Stage-based GLOs (SB GLOs/SLOs) as derivative entities derived from the GLO types (i)–(iii)

As we stated before, our objective is to discuss the STEM CS content adaptation problem using the SB GLO model. This approach is complex in its own rank. The complexity is due to multiple reasons: (i) heterogeneity of the domain itself, (ii) a high coupling of both the pedagogical-social and technological issues, (iii) the complexity of the context information to be considered in the process and (iv) technological issues to tackle tasks through automation, to name a few. We therefore introduce a framework aiming at better understanding of our approach.

8.5   A Framework and Tasks to Develop SB GLOs

We define the framework in a reuse-oriented manner. In essence, reuse among other issues is also concerned with the time dimension, though implicitly (say as a context). As a result, we consider the framework as a life cycle of our objects (GLOs). In this cycle, we outline the derivation process to derive SB GLO from its initial GLO specification. The life cycle includes four main processes (see Fig. 8.1): *design, refactoring, generation* and *use (learning)*. Each process contains within the adequate subprocesses. For example, the design covers the TEL domain modelling and the development of GLO specifications using the model transformation approaches (see Chap. 7). We treat the process as *design-for-reuse* (also meaning the potential for a wide-scale adaptation). The process results in creating the *local GLO library* to cover topics of the whole course (e.g. CS in our case). We consider the next process (refactoring) as *design-for-adaptation*. We treat the generation process as *design-with-adaptation*. The latter, in fact, fuels the learning process. The framework also outlines actors (their responsibilities and actions) and tools used within the life cycle model.

The model (i.e. SB) we discuss in this chapter falls within both processes (refactoring and learning). More specifically, refactoring is the process to transform the initial GLO (obtained as a product of the design process) into the representation of the SB model without the loss of the initial functionality. The *use* is about the teaching and learning process using the initial GLOs, SB GLOs and adapted LOs. The latter is an actual content students need to learn.

Now we are able to extend the framework and formulate the context to our tasks. First, we need to define the reuse extent. Typically, properties of the domain artefacts predefine the reuse potential. The TEL domain is highly heterogeneous and includes pedagogical, social, technological and content aspects, each containing multiple variants. STEM extends those aspects largely. Therefore, the learning variability space is indeed huge and expanding continuously (see also Sect. 4.2). To which

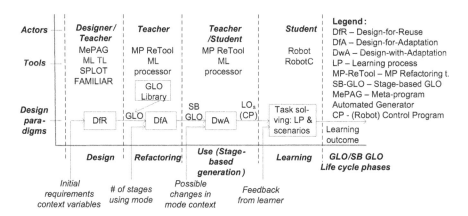

Fig. 8.1 A framework of the approach: GLO and SB GLO life cycle

extent we are able to recognize, extract and explicitly represent the knowledge within this variability space, in the same or similar extent we can automate the domain. This statement is the base of generative reuse [FK05]. It was well known in software reuse for a long time (e.g. since [Pri88] and now (to some extent) in e-Learning [Boy03, Pol06]).

The explicit learning variability model is the only one side of the problem. We need to have yet the relevant technology and methodology to implement the learning variability model (see Chaps. 5 and 7 for details). In fact, the implemented variability predefines the reuse scope and extent for adaptation. The preprogrammed GLO model, discussed in Sects. 5.5 and 7.5.3, has been just implemented on this conceptual basis. Parameters and their relationships are objects to express the variability aspects. If we take into account the implicit context (e.g. pedagogy-related parameters have a higher priority with respect to others), the model itself has the potential for adaptation. However, to make the adaptation more flexible, we need (1) to introduce the explicit context and (2) to rearrange the model structure by introducing the stage-based model. The explicit context is the prerequisite to manage the stage-based generation and automated adaptation.

We consider the adaptation task not from scratch but assuming that we already have a preprogrammed GLO specification as an input data for implementing automated adaptation. We also assume that the initial specification is syntactically and semantically correct and includes the explicit context. Furthermore, the specification implements a high degree of variability space, meaning its potential use by teachers and students within the same course.

8.6   A Background of the Approach

The background covers the assumptions, definitions of basic terms and properties that are concerned with both the initial GLO and SB GLO.

8.6.1   Basic Assumptions

Assumption 1 Explicit knowledge on educational aspects in large (meaning to support a high reuse extent) should be extracted through *analysis and variability modelling* (both are reuse-driven activities) to be performed in advance by the domain expert.

Assumption 2 The initial GLO model is correct, and the correctness is approved by modelling and experimental validation.

Assumption 3 The interface of the initial GLO (it can be thought also as metadata) additionally supplies comments on the context selection.

Assumption 4 The number of eligible stages is obtained by the tool [BBŠ13] and the number of needed stages – by the user (typically by teacher).

8.6.2   *Definition of Basic Terms*

First, we define the terms related to the parameterized GLO and then the stage-based GLO definitions as follows:

Definition 1 Parameter is the unified representation of some learning variability aspect, such as pedagogical, social, technological or content (see Assumption 1 and Property 1).

Definition 2 The parameter's value is the concrete value of the parameter (see Property 2).

Definition 3 Parameter's context is the value expressed through a *fuzzy variable* explicitly and allocated to the parameter. Fuzzy variable is a value taken either from the *short set of priorities* {HP, IP, LP} (where HP is high priority, IP intermediate priority and LP low priority) or from the extended set of priorities (see also Properties 3 and 4).

Definition 4 The interface of parameterized GLO is a set of the contextualized parameters along with their values (see also Assumption 3, Properties 5 and 6).

Definition 5 The function is the *(meta-)language construct* to define a possible manipulation (insertion, deletion, change, etc.) through the parameter-function relationship (see also Property 7).

Definition 6 Implementation of the GLO specification is the set of the predefined parameter-function relationships to specify the learning variability.

Definition 7 The initial GLO model is the specification containing two parts: interface (Definition 4) and GLO implementation (see Definition 6).

Definition 8 Generation is the process of the following actions: (a) a manual selecting of parameter values for each parameter and (b) executing the specification by the tool (i.e. processor of the meta-language in which the functions are described).

Definition 9 Adaptation is the process of the following actions: (a) context-related selection of parameter values for each parameter by the user (teacher or student) and (b) automatic executing the specification by the tool (i.e. processor of the language in which the functions are described) (see Assumption 2).

Definition 10 Stage is an abstraction to specify the *context-dependent part* of the whole process (e.g. generation or adaptation). The whole process is defined as multistage one.

Definition 11 Staging is the process to express the initial GLO model by stages without the loss of its functionality, using the adequate support, i.e. meta-language functions, and the adequate mechanism to *deactivate* them at each stage accordingly.

Definition 12 Stage-based (aka multistage) model is the model describing the way on how parameters and functions are allocated to stages without intersection (see Fig. 8.3).

Definition 13 Construct (i.e. parameter or function) is either in the *active* or *passive state*. The construct is said to be *active* if it, when executed by the processor, performs the prescribed action (have no symbol "\" to deny the state, e.g. $f(p)$). The construct is said to be *passive* if it cannot perform the prescribed action due to the denying symbol "\" written before the construct (e.g. $\backslash f(\backslash p)$), where the function f and its parameter p are passive) (see also Property 9).

Definition 14 The language processor performs the stage-based generation. It is the process of evaluating parameters at the top stage (say k stage) first. The evaluation results in (a) the change of the specification according to the values of the selected parameters, (b) the decrease of the number of stages by 1 (meaning also the decrease of *passiveness degree* at the remaining stages) and (c) the intermediate (narrowed) specification. Next, the process is repeated until the stage 1 is achieved (see also Properties 10 and 11).

Definition 15 Stage-based adaptation is the process of selecting the values of the context-driven parameters by the user at each stage gradually and then invoking the stage-based generation process.

Definition 16 Stage-based GLO specification is the derivative specification created using the adequate refactoring tool that transforms the initial specification into the stage-based one according to the model (Fig. 8.3) and using the staging strategy defined by Definitions 10, 11, 12 and 13 (see also Assumption 4, Properties 10 and 11).

8.6.3   Basic Properties

Property 1 Parameters are represented uniformly, but they differ in semantics, the latter being recognized from the context.

Property 2 Values of different parameter may interact (i.e. to be dependent). If that is the case, the interaction is expressed through constraints *requires* (e.g. **beginner** *requires* **simple content**) and *excludes* (e.g. **topic 1** *excludes* **topic 2**, i.e. can be used only one at a time). Otherwise, these parameters are not interacting, i.e. are independent.

Property 3 Typically, pedagogy-related parameters have the high priority (HP), and the content-related parameters have lower priority (LP). However, there might be more complex parameter-context relationships [Štu15], not considered here.

Property 4 Context can be preprogrammed and expressed through a set of fuzzy variables (such as HP/IP or IP/LP) to form the parameter-context relationship.

Property 5 As some parameters may interact, we need to consider the parameter groups. Therefore, the interaction may appear within a group, but not among groups. A group may also consist of a single independent parameter. The context information is defined not for a separate parameter (if it is a member of the group) but for the whole group.

Property 6 In general, the interface of GLO is a set of context-aware parameter groups. The interface predefines the *variability space* for possible adaptation.

Property 7 The argument of a function to implement the GLO functionality may be the parameter, the fragment of the content, the other function or a combination thereof.

Property 8 There are constraints to perform staging such as the one: the interacting parameters should appear at the same stage.

Property 9 The language processor performs the action of changing the construct state from passive to active by deleting the symbol "\" through the one pass of executing the specification. However, if the construct has multiple symbols "\" at some intermediate stage, it remains passive, but the "degree of its passiveness" is decreased by 1.

Property 10 If stages are numbered as $(k, k-1, \ldots, 1)$, where k is the number of the top stage, all constructs at the stage k are active, while the remaining are passive with the growing degree of "passiveness" at each subsequent stage.

Property 11 Staging decreases *readability of the* stage-based specification due to the use of multiple symbols "\" to deactivate the constructs. However, there exists the exact relationship between the stage number and the "degree of passiveness" at the given stage, expressed through the deactivating symbols [Štu15].

Based on this and other stated properties, it was possible to build the tool providing the automatic generation and adaptation. The tool [BBŠ13] fully hides the technological mechanism of staging (for more details, see Case Study, Sect. 8.9).

Definitions from 1 to 16 are concerned with the initial GLO model and its technological staging. Assumption 1 and Property 1 are concerned with the integration of pedagogical and technological staging. Figure 8.2 illustrates the initial GLO model in more detail. The graphical symbols (see Legend) explain the terms before being defined formally. Figure 8.3 illustrates the stage-based model. It is a derivative model derived from the initial based on the presented background. Again, the

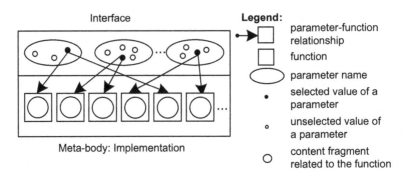

Fig. 8.2 Initial parameterized GLO model

Fig. 8.3 Stage-based GLO model (**a**) and the LO instance derived from the model (**b**) (© with kind permission from the Baltic J. Modern Comp. [ŠBB +17])

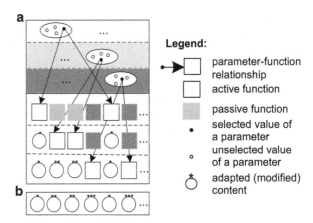

adequate formally defined terms are explained here by graphical symbols for better understanding (see Legend, in Fig. 8.3). Note that shading is an abstract representation of the stage's de-activation process. We apply both models in CS education using robots. From the given description, one might receive the impression that the approach is relevant to CS education only, though we try to use not so much specific CS terms, but rather the general terms, such as teaching content. The basic teaching content in CS is computer (robot) programs treated as *textual* LOs. However, they also may contain pictures, diagrams or movies within (those are to be either modifiable or non-modifiable). Therefore, the models might be applied to other kinds of LOs if the following condition holds: the explicit variability model is known for those contents.

8.7 Staging and Context Awareness

In general, learning attributes, i.e. parameters in terms of GLOs, fall into four categories (adapted from [KM09]): P, pedagogy-related (i.e. teaching goal, teaching model, etc.); S, social-oriented (e.g. student previous knowledge, abilities, etc.), T, technology-oriented (e.g. characteristics of educational robots when teaching is based on this technology); and C, content-related (e.g. algorithms to realize the CS teaching tasks using robots). As those categories differ in semantics and roles, an order (i.e. priority) of their interpretation is to be introduced, when LOs are designed and used. We can express their ordering by the relations

$$P \preceq= S \prec T \preceq= C \tag{8.1}$$

here the record $X \preceq= Y$ means that X has the same or higher priority with respect to Y (the relation $X \prec Y$ means a strong priority). In fact, this relation can be treated as context information. It is more convenient, however, to represent the context more directly through priorities taken from the set of fuzzy variables:

$$W = \{HP, IP, LP\} \quad \text{or} \quad W = \{HP \prec IP \prec LP\} \tag{8.2}$$
$$W = \{HP, IP_1, IP_2, LP\} \quad \text{or} \quad W = \{HP \prec IP_1 \prec IP_2 \prec LP\} \tag{8.3}$$

Here, fuzzy variables have the following meaning: HP, high priority; IP_1, intermediate priority first (higher); IP_2, intermediate priority second (lower); and LP, low priority. The set W, being defined through fuzzy variables, is treated as context. As some categories of parameters are indeed closely related or, in some other cases, they can be treated as the ones (e.g. teacher-based and student-based are indeed pedagogical or technology and content), we are able to consider typical cases in describing the parameter category-context relationships (see Fig. 8.4a–e are possible variants). However, there is another sort of relationship, i.e. parameter-parameter

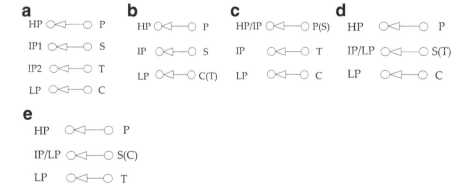

Fig. 8.4 Relationship between context (priorities) and parameter categories. Legend: *P, S, T, C* parameter categories; *P(S)* combined categories; ◁— relationship *Requires*; *HP, IP, LP* single priority; *IP/LP* multiple priorities

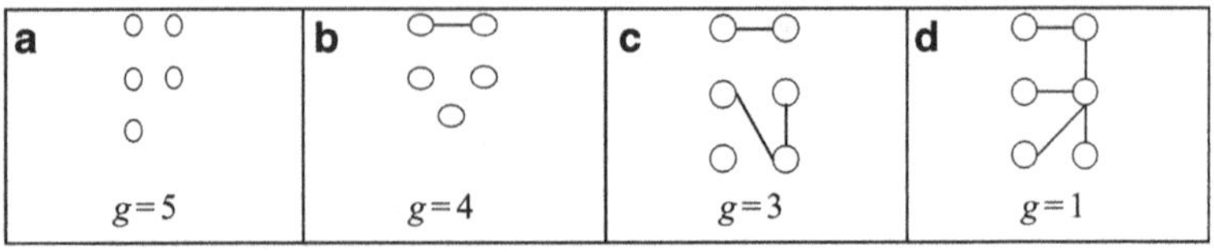

| **a** $\quad$ O O
 $\quad$ O O
 $\quad\quad$ O
 $\quad$ *g* = 5 | **b** $\quad$ O—O
 $\quad$ O $\;$ O
 $\quad\quad$ O
 $\quad$ *g* = 4 | **c** $\quad$ O—O
 $\quad$ O $\;$ O
 $\quad$ O $\;$ O
 $\quad$ *g* = 3 | **d** $\quad$ O—O
 $\quad$ O—O
 $\quad$ O $\;$ O
 $\quad$ *g* = 1 |

Fig. 8.5 Relationship among parameter groups (g # of groups). (**a**) $g = 5$. (**b**) $g = 4$. (**c**) $g = 3$. (**d**) $g = 1$

relationship (among different categories and/or among parameters of the same category). We call any kind of parameter relationship as parameter interaction or dependency (see Property 2). It is convenient to represent the parameter dependency groups by treelike graphs, where nodes represent parameters and branches represent interactions among the parameters. In Fig. 8.5, we present all possible variants of the parameter interactions abstractly, ignoring the categories of parameters. The variant (a) represents not interacting parameters ($g = 5$ defines the number of independent groups). The variant (d) represents a theoretically possible case when all parameters are interacting. However, the most practical variants are (b) and (c), where 4 and 3 not interacting parameter groups are given, respectively. The number g is important, because it also specifies the number of eligible stages. It is so because the dependent parameters should appear at the same stage when interpreted (otherwise the interpretation would be erroneous).

8.8   Integration of STEM Concepts into SB Model

So far in this chapter, we have discussed issues related to *Task 1*, i.e. what are the structure and functionality of the SB model and how this model supports automated adaptation technologically. In this discussion, we omitted the STEM context. Now we shortly address *Task 2*, i.e. the possible ways to integrate STEM context into the SB model. We need to remind reader that there are two general approaches of integration: intuitive (implicit) and specific (using explicit specifications that outline the use of STEM context directly). We use both in our methodology. With regard to implicit integration, it comes with a variety of technologies we use in our methodology; however, robotics is the main source of the STEM knowledge that we able to deliver implicitly or explicitly to teaching classes. The explicit specification of the STEM knowledge, however, is more powerful. As we consider it as a foremost objective of our methodology, we need to disclose those integrative aspects also within the SB model.

We are able to integrate STEM context explicitly, for example, by changing the model's structure. The structure of the SB model considered so far is monolithic, i.e. it includes the stage-based interface and stage-based meta-body as a single entity (see Fig. 8.3a). We have presented this structure more abstractly also in Fig. 8.7. Structural changes relate to the introduction of new parameters that have quite different semantics as compared to those in the monolithic structure. Typically, the values of parameters of the monolithic structure are within the specification itself. In case of the modified structure, the value of the parameters is the *Internet link* to external components taken either from external sources or from the personal generative library (PGL). Note that the latter is a constituent of our methodology. The change of parameter semantics results in changing the structure of SB model; it becomes aggregative encompassing the base structure and one or a few external entities. The external entity may be a component-based educational resource, monolithic GLO or even SB GLO (see Fig. 8.6).

The component-based (CB) LO, for example, may represent movie, instructional text, etc. (see Sect. 8.4). Those LOs can be dedicated to introducing STEM knowledge entirely. For instance, the movie is good in motivating students to gain STEM knowledge. In addition, it is possible to design GLOs specifically oriented for STEM by selecting the adequate task. The external component may be another SB GLO that focuses on the other adaptation aspects. Therefore, the aggregated model enables to deliver the STEM-driven CS knowledge and additionally deal with the problem of automated content adaptation to the learner's context. We show that in our case study.

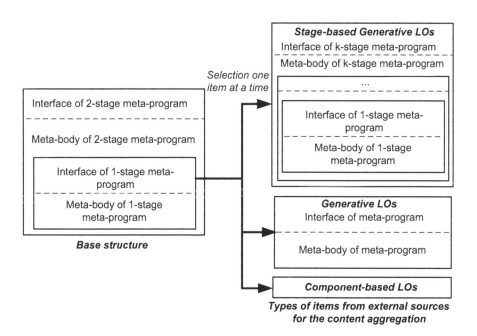

Fig. 8.6 Stage-based aggregated model

8.9   Case Study

The aim of the case study is to demonstrate the viability of the implementation of the SB GLO model in the real robot-based educational setting to provide the course "Programming Basics" for the tenth grade secondary school students. The preconditions for that are (a) the PGL with the initial GLOs already exists and it covers (partially or fully) the whole topics of the course and (b) the teacher first selects the initial GLO specification from the library, identifies the needed number of stages and using the adequate tool transforms the initial specification into the SB GLO. However, SB GLOs can be prepared in advanced and taken from the library (if the existing item fits the educational needs, e.g. the number of stages; otherwise the teacher creates the SB GLO anew using the refactoring tool [BBŠ13]). Note that the tool may be used in two modes: (a) automatic staging (the stages are formed using the context information {HP, IP, LP}) and (b) manual staging (the user is able to allocate parameters to stages interactively according to his/her vision).

Figure 8.7a outlines the abstract implementation vision of the GLO model for the task "Following the line with obstacles" by robot to learn the topic "Conditional statements and loops". For simplicity, we consider the two-stage GLO here (the context information is not shown). Figure 8.7b shows the top stage (I) user interface after selecting the adequate parameter values. Figure 8.8a shows the stage II parameters of the initial GLO and makes the selection from the menu. Note that the parameter *learning object* (its values) defines the content related to STEM aspects in CS education. The execution of this GLO generates the result (Fig. 8.8b) adapted to the *beginner*, i.e. the movie as an *expected result* that will be really achieved after learning (creating and executing the robot control program through *practice*). Therefore, the movie is LO for the *beginner*, being generated through the two-stage process.

Now let us go through the other adaptation path by selecting the parameter values. Assume that the student selected at the execution stage II: "Intermediate", "Practice" and "GLO Following the line with obstacles" (see Fig. 8.9a). Then the system opens

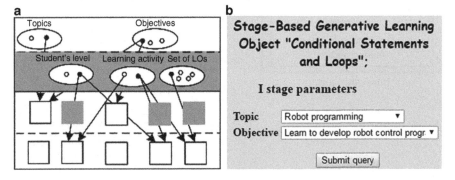

Fig. 8.7 Two-stage GLO model: (**a**) abstract implementation vision; (**b**) vision through the user interface (stage II is hidden)

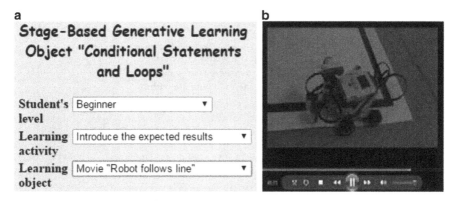

Fig. 8.8 Abstract vision after evaluation of the top stage (according to values of Fig. 8.7b) (**a**) user interface to evaluate the stage II; (**b**) movie, illustrating the expected result to motivate the learning task "Following line with obstacle" by robot (© with kind permission from the Baltic J. Modern Comp. [ŠBB+17])

the interface with the multiple menus (see Fig. 8.9b). Then student inserts own values according to the task as it is shown in Fig. 8.9b. The result of processing is the control program (CP) with conditional statements and loops in RobotC (its fragment is given in Fig. 8.9c). Then the generated CP is to be loaded into the robot's memory, and the student is able to monitor the execution of the CP and get not the "motivating movie", but the line following produced by the robot in real time. In addition, this result might be quite different from the "motivating movie" depending on the task.

The created SB GLOs have a hierarchical structure and represent an aggregated LO. Furthermore, this model, after processing, generates either CB LO (Fig. 8.8b) or GLO (Fig. 8.9b). In addition, this model enables to provide the integrated STEM knowledge, to some extent, in teaching other subjects, such as mathematics, physics and engineering. For example, the task "ornament drawing" is based on mathematical calculations of the trigonometric functions, the time-velocity dependency predefines the robot's movement (knowledge in physics), and students can also be involved in constructing the educational robots to gain the engineering skills.

8.10   Stage-Based Adaptation Processes and Scenarios

Before considering those issues, firstly we define terms *surface learning*, *deep learning* and *active learning*. According to Houghton [Hou04], surface learning is "accepting new facts and ideas uncritically and attempting to store them as isolated, unconnected items". And deep learning is "examining new facts and ideas critically, and tying them into existing cognitive structures and making numerous links between ideas". According to [Yan13], active learning is "a process whereby students engage in activities, such as reading, writing, discussion, or problem solving that promote analysis, synthesis, and evaluation of class content". Note

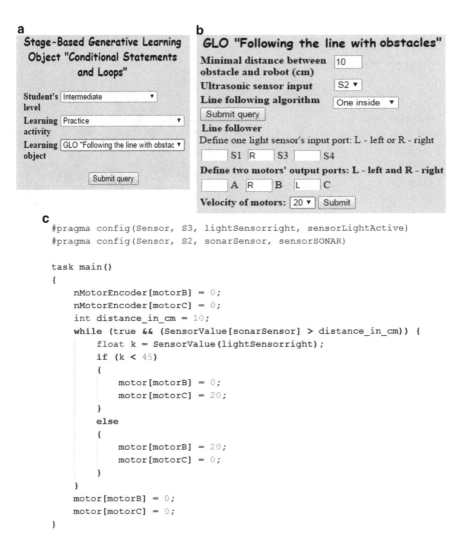

a

Stage-Based Generative Learning Object "Conditional Statements and Loops"

Student's level | Intermediate ▼

Learning activity | Practice ▼

Learning object | GLO "Following the line with obstac ▼

Submit query

b

GLO "Following the line with obstacles"

Minimal distance between obstacle and robot (cm) | 10

Ultrasonic sensor input | S2 ▼

Line following algorithm | One inside ▼

Submit query

Line follower

Define one light sensor's input port: L - left or R - right

[ ] S1 [R] S3 [ ] S4

Define two motors' output ports: L - left and R - right

[ ] A [R] B [L] C

Velocity of motors: 20 ▼ Submit

c

```
#pragma config(Sensor, S3, lightSensorright, sensorLightActive)
#pragma config(Sensor, S2, sonarSensor, sensorSONAR)

task main()
{
    nMotorEncoder[motorB] = 0;
    nMotorEncoder[motorC] = 0;
    int distance_in_cm = 10;
    while (true && (SensorValue[sonarSensor] > distance_in_cm)) {
        float k = SensorValue(lightSensorright);
        if (k < 45)
        {
            motor[motorB] = 0;
            motor[motorC] = 20;
        }
        else
        {
            motor[motorB] = 20;
            motor[motorC] = 0;
        }
    }
    motor[motorB] = 0;
    motor[motorC] = 0;
}
```

Fig. 8.9 Selection made at the execution of stage II (**a**); interface and menu induced by the value "Following the line with obstacles" (**b**); a fragment of the robot control program (**c**) (© with kind permission from the Baltic J. Modern Comp. [ŠBB+17])

that educational robots promote active learning because there is the possibility to combining active learning methods.

Now we are able to present the stage-based adaptation process in learning in more detail. In Fig. 8.10, we outline the approach schematically as a multiple process with different sorts of adaptation scenarios and feedbacks. The top part relates to the teacher's context while the other to the student's context. Here, we show the stage-based specification abstractly through stage numbers (top stage k is for the teacher). There are three kinds of adaptation scenarios: (i) stage-based at the *surface learning*

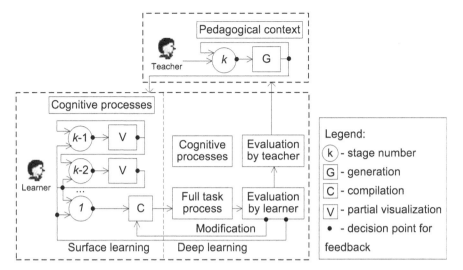

Fig. 8.10 A scenarios of LO adaptation and cognitive-based processes (© with kind permission from Baltic J. Modern Comp. [ŠBB+17])

phase, (ii) *technological* (i.e. intermediate) *phase* and (iii) *adaptation at the deep learning phase.*

What is the meaning of those scenarios? The surface learning and cognition process starts, when the learner gradually moves through stages (from k–1 to 1). At each stage, the learner introduces the parameter values via menu with a self-reflection on those values. Then the generation process with a possible partial visualization follows to represent the result of the *partial compilation*. The latter is possible because, after activating parameters at the adequate stage, a corresponding fragment of the target program (RobotC in our case) is created. In addition, the learner can see the fragment visually along with a remaining meta-code yet not being instantiated. The *complete compilation* (C in Fig. 8.10) is possible only after the full instance is generated in stage 1.

How the processes in surface learning are supported? The meta-language processor is the tool to support the *stage-based generation* and *partial compilation* of the adapted GLOs. The complete compilation differs from the partial compilation by the tool used and the product produced. The RobotC compiler performs the complete compilation, meaning the creation of an executable program (robot CP) to provide the learning task in the real setting.

Where is the technological scenario? When the learner uses the RobotC compiler to do the complete compilation, he/she *changes the* technological environment, because typically the learner uses a PC for managing the SB GLO specifications through the Internet and GLO library. This scenario also includes loading the robot CP into its memory. Therefore, we are able to treat the technological scenario as a bridge to link the surface and deep learning.

What is about deep learning? This scenario starts, when the learner observes the robot's operations. The task solving with the help of robots in the real setting has many technical aspects (such as visible characteristics related to sensors, motors used, their velocities, etc.) and social attributes (such as a curiosity to know whether or not everything is going as planned, etc.). Therefore, deep learning is concerned with self-reflecting on what is going on the screen, analysing, discussing, formulating questions and trying to improve the robot's actions. All these may require changes and some processes to repeat. The indicated multiple feedbacks serve in this role. Therefore, we define the active learning as the integration of the introduced scenarios using the feedback links.

8.11   Analysis of Capabilities of the SB Model

8.11.1   Designer's Perspective

The designer may focus on two aspects: (1) how the initial parameterized GLO and (2) how the SB GLO should be created. As already stated (see Sect. 8.5, definitions), the learning variability space is the main concept on which both models rely. In fact, the variability space is the *TEL domain model* to be created in advance through analysis and modelling. As the domain is highly heterogeneous, most likely the expert knowledge taken from different subdomains is needed in creating the domain model. For example, the most crucial knowledge might be required in defining the *interaction* among the pedagogical, social and content attributes. The creation of the semantically correct domain model is the responsibility of the domain expert. The designer should be aware that the domain model is correct or, otherwise, should address to the domain expert for advice and corrections. The designer's responsibility is to map the domain model onto the solution domain model in creating the initial GLO. That can be done manually or using the adequate tools [BBŠ13].

From the designer's perspective, the parameterized GLO along with the language processor, in which the parameter-language relationship is coded, is the *generator* of the LO components on demand. The task of creating SB GLO becomes extremely error-prone, when the number of stages is more than two. Therefore, the adequate tool is needed [BBŠ13].

From this viewpoint, SB GLO is the generator of the others narrower SB GLOs. The generation process is first implemented by the specific refactoring tool transforming the initial GLO into the stage-based one. Having the stage-based specification, the language processor stands for the meta-generator.

What is the experience of the designer (i.e. CS teacher) in using the model? At the beginning (in 2012), two-stage GLOs were created manually. Later (in 2013), the tool to design the SB GLOs was created [BBD+14, BBŠ13].

8.11.2   Teacher's Perspective

The teacher is a top-level user of both the initial and SB GLOs. How can the teacher interpret a single initial GLO? The specification can be seen as a full set of LO components to be generated from the predefined variability space by selecting all defined parameter values. The generated components are related and differ only in some aspects predefined by parameter variability. If we have, for example, five independent parameters each having four variants, the variability space is equal to $4 * 4 * 4 * 4 * 4 = 1024$, and the number of components is the same. The generated components as a learning resource can be located in a local library supplied by metadata for search. Therefore, it is possible to make juxtaposition between the library and the parameterized (preprogrammed) GLO specification. The following pairs of items (the first belongs to the library, the second to the GLO) are under the focus:

- Metadata – parameter.
- Search through metadata – generation through parameterization.
- Multiple explicit components – one specification with the multiple components specifically woven inside the specification.
- Typical case of the component-based reuse – typical case of generative reuse.
- The library scaling problem [Big94] may occur – no such a problem or its effect is highly reduced.
- Context is implicit (search errors may occur) – context is explicit, i.e. context awareness is at hand (erroneous generation is excluded).
- Library maintenance requires a substantial handwork – maintenance is easier.

How can the teacher interpret *a set of the initial GLO* in terms of the teaching process? The set may cover the whole course, perhaps with some specific examples of LOs taken from the digital libraries. Therefore, the teacher is able to create his/her own local library, containing mixed LOs, generative and component-based. What is the role of SB GLOs? Using the refactoring tool that transforms the initial GLO into SB GLO, it is possible to create *the generative local library* with the much capabilities for *adaptation on demand*. In addition, those capabilities can be expressed explicitly through the concrete context. For example, if the pedagogical context contains two teaching activities (e.g. *case study, practice*), then two GLOs, separated for each context, are generated. If the teacher wants to adapt this specification further to a particular group of students satisfying their specific learning interests, the teacher may move to the next (lower) stage and repeat the generation/adaptation process. For that, the teacher needs first to select from the menu the *context-aware* parameter values relevant to those interests and then initiate the run of the language processor. There is no need of knowing the internal structure of the SB GLO by the teacher. Always the teacher (if he/she has no knowledge to act as co-designer of the specification) works with the SB GLO as the black-box entity.

What is the experience of teacher in using the model? We have started creating and using the parameterized GLOs in 2011 and context-aware SB GLO in 2014 (see also Sect. 6.3).

8.11.3 Student's Perspective

Again, students work with the "narrowed parameter space" of GLO already adapted to their context through staging. The working mode is similar as the teacher's: students see the graphical interface and perform the parameter selection relevant to their needs. The student is able to create his/her personal library of GLOs (or LOs) specifically oriented to his/her profile.

We have created a questionnaire to assess the students' opinion on using GLOs (SB GLOs) in the learning process. The respondents (in total, 80 who used GLOs during 2014–2015 and 38 who used SB GLOs during 2015–2016) were secondary school students of the tenth grade (15–16 years old). Results are given in Table 8.1. Results are calculated taking into account the total number of answers (in the case of

Table 8.1 Results of the students' evaluation

Student choices	GLO		SB GLO	
1. At which extent the methodology was useful? (only one answer possible)				
Very useful	28	36%	17	45%
Useful	32	40%	21	55%
More useful than non-useful	16	20%	0	0%
More non-useful than useful	4	6%	0	0%
Non-useful	0	0%	0	0%
Totally non-useful	0	0%	0	0%
2. What was the most interesting within the methodology? (multiple answers possible)				
Interesting tasks	48	31%	24	28%
New learning way	39	25%	24	28%
Learning is easier and faster	22	14%	10	12%
Fault tolerance	16	10%	10	12%
Stimulate thinking	31	20%	17	20%
3. What knowledge and competence you were able to improve using GLOs? (multiple answers)				
Programming	58	38%	31	34%
Mathematics	27	18%	24	26%
Logic thinking and cognition	36	24%	33	33%
The practical evidence on how the task is solved	8	5%	4	4%
4. Where and when the use of GLOs should be targeted? (multiple answers possible)				
Always in each lesson on programming	30	27%	10	19%
In other courses (mathematics, physics)	21	19%	14	27%
Sometimes for lesson variation	51	46%	24	47%
For generalizing the topic	9	8%	4	7%
5. For what student's abilities the use of GLOs fits best? (multiple answers possible)				
Low abilities	12	8%	11	13%
Adequate abilities	46	31%	21	25%
High abilities	56	38%	35	42%
Very high abilities	34	23%	17	20%

multiple answers). Note that there was no specific intent to make a distinction between the parameterized initial GLO and its derivatives (i.e. SB GLOs).

We can conclude that students treat the methodology as a useful means for their active learning, because the methodology supports to some extent the interdisciplinary aspects of GLOs. Some students, however, have achieved the knowledge level of deep learning only, though that was not measured explicitly. One can find more on overall evaluation in [SBB+16, ŠBB+16].

8.12 Summary and Concluding Remarks

In this chapter, we have introduced a stage-based (SB) generative learning object (GLO) model to specify the learning content. Capabilities of the model are the content automatic generation and automated adaptation. We have discussed two kinds of the SB model. The first has a monolithic structure; however, we represent this structure specifically, i.e. as a multistage meta-program. We are able to build this representation, either manually (for the small number of stages, e.g. two or three) or using the refactoring tool that transforms the given context-aware original GLO (meaning one-staged) into the multistaged format without the loss of functionality. As the SB GLO is a meta-meta-program constructed with the context awareness in mind, firstly, it enables the automatic generation by moving through stages gradually so that the system (i.e. meta-language processor or compiler) provides narrowing of the search space for adaptation. As the user (learners) provides control over the process by selecting the adequate parameter values manually, we speak about the automated adaptation process (but not automatic). The second kind of the SB model has an *external hierarchical structure* that enables to aggregate STEM aspects explicitly through the attachment of various components taken from external sources. Those might be component-based LOs, GLOs or even the others SB GLOs. Therefore, this kind of the SB model has extended capabilities for adaptation and ways for introducing STEM knowledge. From the technological viewpoint, this model represents a meta-program of *Type 3* (in terms of the definitions given in Sect. 5.5).

We have also presented the stage-based processes and scenarios of their use in the classroom. We have evaluated the SB model of the first kind from different perspectives (designer, teacher and learner) using the relevant approaches. Though we have implemented both kinds of SB model, we have more results that are evident on the first model. The aggregative model requires the additional efforts of research. The following are topics we consider as research questions for future investigation: (1) How the adaptation should be distributed among the basic part of the SB model and its external components? (2) To clarify, to which extent it is reasonable to introduce STEM? (3) What are the capabilities and limitation of the model when the base part has more than two stages?

References

[AKB01]   Anderson LW, Krathwohl DR, Bloom BS (2001) A taxonomy for learning, teaching, and assessing: a revision of Bloom's taxonomy of educational objectives. Allyn and Bacon, Boston

[AT11]   Arai K, Tolle H (2011) Module based content adaptation of composite e-learning content for delivering to mobile learners. Int J Comput Theory Eng 3(3):382

[BBA06]   Berri J, Benlamri R, Atif Y. Ontology-based framework for context-aware mobile learning. In: Proceeding of the Int'l conference wireless communication and mobile computing. pp 1307–1310

[BBD+14] Burbaite R, Bespalova K, Damasevicius R, Stuikys V (2014) Context aware generative learning objects for teaching computer science. Int J Eng Educ 30(4):929–936

[BBŠ13]   Bespalova K, Burbaite R, Štuikys (2013) MP-ReTool tools. http://proin.ktu.lt/metaprogram/MP-ReTool/

[BD08]   Barnstable SB, Dart MA (2008) Developmental stages of the learner. In: S. Barnstable (Ed.) Nurse as educator: principles of teaching and learning practice, 3rd ed. Jones and Bartlett, Boston, pp 172–195

[Big94]   Biggerstaff T (1994) The library scaling problem and the limits of concrete component reuse. In: International conference on software reuse, Rio de Janeiro, November 1–4, 1994. pp 102–110

[BLA+08] Boyle T, Ljubojevic D, Agombar M, Baur E (2008) The conceptual structure of generative learning objects (GLOs). In: Proceedings of world conference on educational multimedia, hypermedia and telecommunications, Vienna, Austria: Association for the Advancement of Computing in Education (AACE), pp 4570–4579

[BLC04]   Boyle T Leeder D, Chase H (2004) To boldly GLO – towards the next generation of learning objects. In: World conference on eLearning in corporate, government, healthcare and higher education, Washington USA, Nov. 2004

[Blo56]   Bloom BS (1956) Taxonomy of educational objectives, Cognitive domain, vol 1. McKay, New York

[Boy03]   Boyle T (2003) Design principles for authoring dynamic, reusable learning objects. Aust J Educ Technol 19(1):46–58

[BR12]   Boyle T, Ravenscroft A (2012) Context and deep learning design. Comput Educ 59 (4):1224–1233

[BRH+15] Brinton CG, Rill R, Ha S, Chiang M, Smith R, Ju W (2015) Individualization for education at scale: Miic design and preliminary evaluation. IEEE Trans Learn Technol 8(1):136–148

[CAM+06] Convertini V, Albanese D, Marengo A, Marengo V, Scalera M (2006) The OSEL taxonomy for the classification of learning objects. Interdiscip J E-Learning Learn Objects 2(1):125–138

[CHE05]   Czarnecki K, Helsen S, Eisenecker U (2005) Staged configuration through specialization and multilevel configuration of feature models. Softw Process Improv Pract 10 (2):143–169

[DA06]   Desmoulins C, Azouaou F (2006) Using and modeling context with ontology in e-learning: the case of teacher's personal annotation. In: Proceedings of international workshop on applications of semantic web technologies for e-learning, Dublin, Ireland

[DAC+16] Dorca FA, Araujo RD, De Carvalho VC, Resende DT, Cattelan RG (2016) An automatic and dynamic approach for personalized recommendation of learning objects considering students learning styles: an experimental analysis. Inform Educ Int J 15 (1):45–62

[Dey01]   Dey AK (2001) Understanding and using context. Pers Ubiquit Comput 5(1):4–7

[Dij70]   Dijkstra EW (1970) Notes on structured programming

[Dou04]   Dourish P (2004) What we talk about when we talk about context. Personal Ubiquit Comput 8:19–30. Feb. 2004

[ECH+09] Ebraert P, Classen A, Heymans P, D'Hondt T (2009) Feature diagrams for change-oriented programming. In: Nakamura M, Reiff-Marganiec S (eds) Feature interactions in software and communication systems X. IOS Press, Amsterdam, pp 107–122

[FK05] Frakes WB, Kang K (2005) Software reuse research: status and future. IEEE Trans Softw Eng 31(7):529–536

[GAP+16] Gutiérrez I, Álvarez V, Paule M, Pérez-Pérez JR, de Freitas S (2016) Adaptation in e-learning content specifications with dynamic sharable objects. Systems 4(2):24

[Gre08] Greer D (2008) The art of separation of concerns. Web log post

[Hou04] Houghton W (2004) Engineering subject centre guide: learning and teaching theory for engineering academics. © Higher Education Academy Engineering Subject Centre, Loughborough University, Loughborough

[HP05] Huddlestone J, Pike J (2005) Learning object reuse-a four tier model. In: People and systems-who are we designing for, the IEE and MOD HFI DTC symposium on (Ref. No. 2005/11078), IET. pp 25–31

[KM09] Koehler MJ, Mishra P (2009) What is technological pedagogical content knowledge. Contemp Issues Technol Teach Educ 9(1):60–70

[Kra02] Krathwohl DR (2002) A revision of Bloom's taxonomy: an overview. Theory Pract 41(4):212–218

[Kru13] Krueger CW (2013) Multistage configuration trees for managing product family trees. In: Proceedings of the 17th international software product line conference, Tokyo, Japan, ACM, pp 188–197

[MJ10] Man H, Jin Q (2010) Putting adaptive granularity and rich context into learning objects. In: Information technology based higher education and training (ITHET), 2010 9th international conference on. pp 140–145

[MLB05] Morales R, Leeder D, Boyle T (2005) A case in the design of generative learning objects (GLOs): applied statistical methods. In: World conference on educational multimedia, hypermedia and telecommunications, vol 2005, No. 1. pp 2091–2097

[PG15] Premlatha KR, Geetha TV (2015) Learning content design and learner adaptation for adaptive e-learning environment: a survey. Artif Intell Rev 44(4):443–465

[Pol06] Polsani PR (2006) Use and abuse of reusable learning objects. Journal of Digital Information, 3(4). Retrieved from https://journals.tdl.org/jodi/index.php/jodi/article/view/89/88

[Pri88] Prieto-Diaz R (1988) Domain analysis for reusability. In: Software reuse: emerging technology. IEEE Computer Society Press, Los Alamitos, CA, USA, p 347–353

[RB00] Rajlich VT, Bennett KH (2000) A staged model for the software life cycle. Computer 33(7):66–71

[Red03] Redeker GH (2003) An educational taxonomy for learning objects. In: Advanced learning technologies, 2003, Athens, Greece. Proceedings of the 3rd IEEE international conference, IEEE, pp 250–251

[RJR+05] Rossano V, Joy MS, Roselli T, Sutinen E (2005) A taxonomy for definitions and applications of LOs: a metaanalysis of ICALT papers. Educ Technol Soc 8(4):148–160

[Sam97] Sametinger J (1997) Software engineering with reusable components. Springer, New York

[SAW94] Schilit B, Adams N, Want R (1994) Context-aware computing applications. In: Proceeding of the first workshop mobile computing systems and applications (WMCSA'94). pp 85–90

[SBB+16] Stuikys V, Burbaite R, Bespalova K, Drasute V, Ziberkas G, Venckauskas A (2016) Stage-based generative learning object model to support automatic content generation and adaptation. In: Computer Software and Applications Conference (COMPSAC), 2016 IEEE 40th Annual, Vol. 1, IEEE, pp 712–721

[ŠBB+17] Štuikys V, Burbaitė R, Bespalova K, Blažauskas T, Dominykas Barisas D (2017) Stage-based generative learning object model for automated content adaptation. Balt J Mod Comput 5(2):183–205

[ŠBB+16] Štuikys V, Burbaitė R, Bespalova K, Ziberkas G (2016) Model-driven processes and tools to design robot-based generative learning objects for computer science education. Sci Comput Program 129:48–71

[ŠD13]   Štuikys V, Damaševičius R (2013) Meta-programming and model-driven meta-program development: principles, processes and techniques. Springer, London/ Heidelberg/New York/Dordrecht

[Štu15]   Štuikys V (2015) Smart learning objects for smart education in computer science. Springer, New York

[Tah04]   Taha W (2004) A gentle introduction to multi-stage programming. In: Domain-specific program generation. Springer, Berlin/Heidelberg, pp 30–50

[Tah99]   Taha W (1999) Multi-stage programming: its theory and applications. Doctoral dissertation, Oregon Graduate Institute of Science and Technology

[UV09]   Urquiza-Fuentes J, Velázquez-Iturbide JÁ (2009) Pedagogical effectiveness of engagement levels–a survey of successful experiences. Electron Notes Theor Comput Sci 224:169–178

[VMO+12] Verbert K, Manouselis N, Xavier O, Wolpers M, Drachsler H, Bosnic I, Duval E (2012) Context-aware Recommender Systems for Learning: a Survey and Future Challenges. IEEE Transactions on Learning Technologies 5(4):318–335

[Wil00]   Wiley DA (2000) Learning object design and sequencing theory. Ph.D. dissertation. Brigham Young University, Utah

[Win01]   Winograd T (2001) Architectures for context. Hum Comput Interact 16(2):401–419

[Yan13]   Yang J (2013) Research guides: instructor college: instruction resources: instructional strategies

[ZLO07]   Zimmermann A, Lorenz A, Oppermann R (2007) An operational definition of context. In: Proceeding of the sixth int'l and interdisciplinary conference modeling and using context (CONTEXT '07). pp 558–572

Chapter 9
Agent-Based GLOs/SLOs for STEM

Abstract This chapter deals with the problem on how to enforce additionally the smart capabilities of the generative learning objects (GLOs) by connecting them with agent-based technology. We consider two aspects of this wide problem only. Firstly, we investigate similarities and differences among meta-programming-based GLOs and software agents. The result is that one can consider a GLO as a weak software agent without the autonomy in decision-making while selecting parameter values. Secondly, we introduce the technological agent enabling to replace the human's actions in selecting technological parameter values by the agent. The provided experiment showed that using this agent it is possible to achieve a higher robot's accuracy. The main contribution of this chapter is the agent-based architecture of the system and its partial implementation, enabling to solve the prescribed tasks more efficiently, i.e. with a less user's intervention and a higher robot's accuracy.

9.1 Introduction

With technology advances, the capabilities of technology-enhanced learning (TEL) are increasing adequately. The advanced technology enables to add more and more smart features to the educational content and environments to make them indeed smart. So far, we have defined smart learning objects (SLOs) as entities with enlarged capabilities for generative reuse and adaptation along with smart STEM-driven education in CS, using robots. It is also possible to add new features that make SLOs more intelligent. Typically, the agent-based approaches entail those capabilities.

Therefore, the aim of this chapter is first to analyse those GLOs (SLOs) with the agent technology in mind and then to enhance the existing distributed educational environment by introducing software agents for enforcing the intelligence capabilities of both the environment and GLOs (SLOs). In general, there are human beings as agents (HBAs), hardware agents (HWAs) and software agents (SWAs). Typical

© Springer International Publishing AG, part of Springer Nature 2018   217
V. Štuikys, R. Burbaitė, *Smart STEM-Driven Computer Science Education*,
https://doi.org/10.1007/978-3-319-78485-4_9

examples of HWAs are educational robots (ERs), the extremely active branch in educational research [Ali13, Ben12]. ERs are equipped with the sensor system to react to the changes in the working (educational) environment. Control programs ensure the robot's functionality. They specify the robot's actions to perform the physical task (such as obstacle finding and passing, line following, etc.). The robot control program, on the other hand, is the learning object (further LO) to be understood and learnt by students (e.g. for CS subjects). It is possible to understand that deeply only through the explorations of the robot's environment that, in this case, is a part of the educational environment. ER operates autonomously (to the extent of the control program capabilities), though the interaction with the HBA is not excluded. Therefore, one can consider the robot's environment with the embodied control program, possibly enriched with the additional feedback capabilities due to the adequate use of sensors, as a generic agent (meaning that it covers both the hardware and software notions). Sometimes, when the hardware and software agents are combined to solve a common task, they are also called hybrid agents.

There are two main possibilities to introduce agent-based technology into the STEM systems. The first possibility refers to integrating those features within the educational software *internally*, for example, within SLOs at the design time. The second possibility is introducing the SWAs *externally*. Of course, there might be some compromise between those approaches. In general, SWAs are defined as computer systems situated in an environment and being able to achieve the prescribed objectives by (1) *acting autonomously*, i.e. deciding themselves (fully or partially: the term semi-autonomy is also used) what to do, and (2) being sociable, i.e. interacting with other software agents or users. The attribute "autonomy" also means that after deciding what to do, the SWA performs actions automatically.

With respect to the interfacing and communicating capabilities of generative LOs (GLOs) or SLOs discussed so far, we can already consider them as simple SWAs (we provide the more extensive discussion on that later). However, also we are able to enforce their automomy in decision-making. For example, by introducing the technological agent, it is possible to replace the human's action in selecting values of some parameters by the agent actions. In this chapter, we consider the robot-oriented STEM-based GLOs enhanced with those capabilities.

The main contribution of this chapter is the agent-based architecture of the system and its partial implementation, enabling to solve the prescribed tasks more efficiently (with a less user's intervention and a higher robot's accuracy). Further, to keep a consistency of the terminology, we prefer the use of the term GLO because of its more popularity, meaning the agent-based GLO here.

The remaining part of this chapter includes the related work (Sect. 9.2), agent-based analysis of GLOs (Sect. 9.3), description of the extended architecture of the educational subsystem (Sect. 9.4), a case study describing the implementation of SWA (Sect. 9.5) and evaluation and conclusion (Sect. 9.6).

9.2 Related Work

We categorize the related work into three groups: (A) relevant to agent-based e-learning, (B) SWAs in the LOs domain and (C) educational robots as agent-based LOs.

(A) Researchers emphasize the definitions, goals and functionality of pedagogical agents [VR14], e-Learning agents [Gre07] and agent-based approaches in e-Learning paradigms and applications [IJ13]. The mentioned literature resources raise the main issues to use SWAs in the e-Learning domain, such as adaptability, personalization, effectiveness, etc. The paper [KB15] highlights the role of pedagogical agents and defines three categories of those: expert, motivator and mentor agents. The paper [VR14] emphasizes software engineering models and their applications in e-Learning. The paper [DET12] presents the intelligent ontology based on the using of SWAs. The papers [AB12, AVC +15] present a multi-agent-based architecture for secure and effective e-Learning and the conceptual design of a smart classroom based on multi-agent systems. The researchers [GCR13] focus on learners' characteristics and groups' formation principles purification (refinement) using agent-based approaches. This paper also highlights intelligent learning environments (ILE) with implemented SWAs.

(B) The researchers propose some denominations of LOs that are in the relations with software agents: agent-based LO [MM05], personalized LO [PV11], intelligent LO [SGV06] and intelligent learning resources [MS09]. The general properties of the intelligent LOs are *(i) to respond* to changes in its environment [MS09]; *(ii) to act* without the direct intervention of humans [MM05]; *(iii) to control* over their actions [MM05]; and *(iv) to be* self-contained, reusable, adaptable, flexible, customizable and contextualized [PV11, SGV06].

Therefore, the most important issues are related to integration LOs into ILEs and making them more intelligent from a viewpoint of adaptation and personalization aspects.

(C) The paper [Wer13] interprets educational robots as embodied teachable agents that open new possibilities as the social and educational tools. The paper [BKH13] discusses the issues of engaging learners into the process by using the robotic educational agent. Lin et al. [LCL+15] present the usage of the physical agent (robot) as interactive media integrated into the traditional e-book with the purpose to contextualize the content. The papers [CPC13, LKB+15] focus on the intelligent robotic tutor that can be treated as a physical educational agent. Therefore, ERs have a great potential and not well enough exploited capabilities for e-Learning such as those to increase learning motivation, to apply modern educational methods, to extend the learning environments facilities, etc.

Though the analysis is by no means comprehensive, we are able to conclude that both SWA-based and ER-based approaches cover many different aspects of e-Learning and gaining ground on it. Nevertheless, so far, little is known on the integrative aspects of LOs (GLOs), ERs and SWAs within educational systems.

9.3   GLOs and SW Agent Domains Analysis: Problem Statement

In this section, we introduce a series of definitions for both the GLOs and SW agent domains (because there is no unified view of them) and analyse the definitions aiming at the identification of similarities and differences of the two. Then, based on making the juxtaposition of relevant attributes, we formulate the problem to consider in this chapter.

Definition 1A Generative LO (GLO) is "an articulated and executable learning design that produces a class of learning objects" [LBM+04]. In this chapter, we consider those GLOs which are defined by Definitions 1B, 1C, and 1D.

Definition 1B GLO is the executable meta-level specification (meaning parameterized) to enable producing of concrete LOs on demand automatically according to the prespecified parameter values and the context of use. In this context, the meta-programming techniques [Štu15] are regarded as a relevant technology to develop the meta-specification. Note that LOs may be chunks of text, pictures, computer programs, etc.

Definition 1C Robot-oriented GLO is the executable meta-level specification to enable producing of concrete LOs being the robot control programs (CPs) generated on demand automatically according to the prespecified parameter values and the context of use.

Definition 1D Context-aware GLO is the executable meta-level specification (as defined by Definitions 1B and 1C) whose parameters are enriched by the pedagogical and technological context information to support the automatic content generation and adaptation. Context-aware robot-oriented GLO is also treated as smart LO [BBD+14].

By the context information, we mean the technological context (such as robot-specific attributes), pedagogical context (e.g. teaching goal, model, student's profile, age, etc.) or some combination thereof.

Property 1 GLO interface is the graphical representation of parameters (P) and their values (V). Parameters represent variants of either the context or content attributes. Parameter values define the GLO's semantics.

Property 2 Variability space for decision-making is expressed as $P \times V$.

Property 3 GLO's meta-body implements the variability space through the constructs of the meta-language and target language (see Sect. 5.5 in Chap. 5 and [ŠD13]).

Definition 2A Agents are "... programs that engage in dialogs and negotiate and coordinate transfer of information" (Michael Coen [BBB+11]).

Definition 2B Intelligent agents are defined as: "...software entities that carry out some set of operations on behalf of a user or another program with some degree of independence or autonomy, and in so doing, employ some knowledge or representation of the user's goals or desires" (IBM [BBB+11]).

Definition 2C Software agents are entities that "differ from conventional software in that they are long-lived, semi-autonomous, proactive, and adaptive" (Software Agents Group at MIT [BBB+11]).

Definition 2D An autonomous agent is "a system situated within and a part of an environment that senses that environment and acts on it, over time, in pursuit of its own agenda and so as to effect what it senses in the future" [FG97].

Definition 2E The agent is "a hardware or (more usually) software based computer system that enjoys the properties: *autonomy, social ability, reactivity,* and *proactiveness* [WJ95]."

Property 4 *Autonomy* is the property when agents operate without the direct intervention of humans or others and have some kind of control over their actions and internal state.

Property 5 *Social ability* is the property when agents interact with other agents (and possibly humans) via some kind of agent-communication language.

Property 6 *Reactivity* is the property when agents perceive their environment (which may be the physical world, a user via a graphical user interface, a collection of other agents, the Internet or perhaps all of these combined) and respond in a timely fashion to changes that occur in it.

Property 7 *Proactiveness* is the property when agents do not simply act in response to their environment; they are able to exhibit goal-directed behaviour by taking the initiative [WJ95].

Definition 3A *Environment* is a part of the agent-based system in which the agent is operating through communication.

Definition 3B *GLO environment* is the space where the interactions occur among the following entities: user and his/her PC, PC's operating system, meta-language processor and remote server where GLO resides.

Definition 3C *Educational robot's environment* is the robot itself and its working surrounding that typically holds the following properties. It is *observable* (new action can be based on the most recent percept), *deterministic* (predicting effects of actions are easy), *episodic* (there is no need to look ahead beyond the end of the previous episode) and *static* (there is no significant time restriction to make a decision).

Definition 3D   Combined environment is the distributed environment that includes the GLO environment, the robot's environment and the Internet (meaning the direct link "Robot-Server").

Based on the analysis of related work and provided definitions, as well as on the simplified functionality for both entities introduced in Fig. 9.1, we have made a juxtaposing of the entities trying to identify their similarity according to the coincidence range: *very poor*, *poor*, *moderate*, *good* and *excellent* (those are based on our and expert knowledge). We outline the results in Table 9.1.

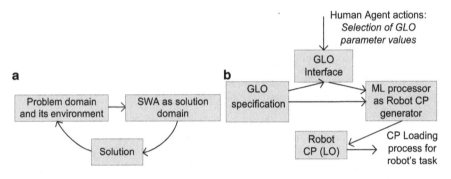

Fig. 9.1 SWA-based problem solving (**a**) and LO generation from GLO (see Definition 1C) (**b**) (© with kind permission from Springer [ŠBD+16])

Table 9.1 Juxtaposing of GLOs and SWA attributes as they are seen in the given definitions

Agent definition	Similarity: matching properties of GLO and SWA	Differences: non-matching properties of GLO and SWA	Explanation and evaluation
Definition 2A	"engage in dialogs and negotiate"	"coordinate transfer of information"	Poor (see Definition 1C)
Definition 2B	"carry out some set of operations on behalf of a user with some degree of independence"	"carry out some set of operations on behalf of another program"	Moderate (see Definition 1B and Definition 1C)
Definition 2C	"long-lived, semi-autonomous and adaptive"	"proactive", i.e. exhibit goal-directed behaviour by taking the initiative	Moderate (see Definition 1D)
Definition 2D	"situated within and a part of an environment and acts on it" through human intervention	"situated within and a part of an environment that senses that environment"	Poor
Definition 2E	"semi-autonomy, social ability, reactivity, and proactiveness"	"autonomy, proactiveness"	Poor

We formulate the main results of analysis as follows: both entities, SWAs and GLOs, are complex software specifications with different degrees of intelligence; though their functionality and structure differ significantly (the first is functioning on the fly dynamically; the second is functioning based on static predefined specification), however, both have also some similarity as it is defined by Property 8.

Property 8 The system that consists of GLO (as a specific small knowledge base for the robot's specific tasks) and meta-language processor (as a semi-autonomous tool for providing the solution automatically) is seen as a week specialized SW agent (meaning a very low level of intelligence) (see Fig. 9.1b). It is so, because the following properties hold *semi-autonomy*, partial *social ability* (both due to the human intervention) and *reactivity*.

The task we formulate is as follows: to propose the concept and its implementation to substitute (partially or fully) the *human actions* in the process of generating robot control programs (RCPs) *by the predefined system of SW agents*.

9.4 Robot-Oriented Agent-Based Educational Environment: Architecture and Processes

In Fig. 9.2, we outline the robot-oriented agent-based educational environment (ROABEE). We have developed it using the previous system as a basis [ŠB15, ŠBD+16]. Initially, we have extended the base system by adding the highlighted components. The "thin arrows" indicate the internal interaction among the components, while the "fat arrows" indicate the external processes.

In the GLO knowledge base (KB), there is the initial knowledge about the tasks to be accomplished by the robot. Again, this knowledge is relevant to the existing types of parameters within GLOs specification. Furthermore, there might be a specific knowledge inherent to a particular task (e.g. the initial technological knowledge of the robot's straightforward moving differs from the knowledge of the curved-line moving task). Some part of the initial knowledge resides within the GLO library (within of the GLO interface for each task). The remaining part of GLO KB is the dynamic knowledge representing the histories of the statistical data accumulated over time by using GLO in real teaching setting.

The GLOs library represents a set of GLOs, the predesigned and tested entities. From the pedagogy viewpoint, each entity covers a separate topic of the course (Introduction to Programming taught in the 9th–12th classes of the gymnasium, i.e. high school). From the functionality and capabilities viewpoint, GLO is the generator (meta-language (ML) processor accomplishes this task) of the content. The latter is the robot control program (RCP), here treated as LO to support the teaching task. In the former system, the user was fully responsible for selecting the parameter values from the GLO interface. In the enhanced system (i.e. ROABEE), this function (fully or partially) is given to the software agents (SWAs). As the GLO interface

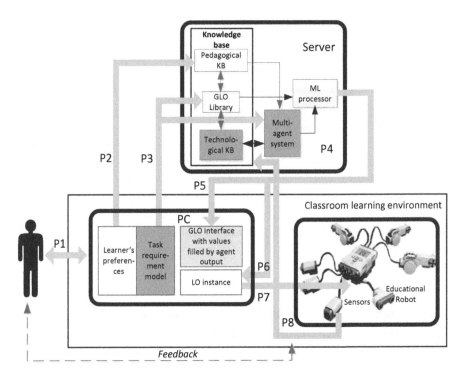

Fig. 9.2 Architecture of the extended system along with the functioning processes (© with kind permission from Springer [ŠBD+16])

contains different parameters (pedagogical-social context, technological, content), it is convenient to have a separate SWA for each group of parameters.

We present the functionality of the system ROABEE as a sequence of the cooperating processes indicated by adequate numbers (from 1 to 8, see Fig. 9.2). The user interacts with PC (P1) to send his/her current profile to the profile KB (P2). Then the task requirement model should be supplied (P3) to the agent-based system and GLOs library to initiate the processes (P4) in the server. The latter activity results in completing the GLO interface (fully or partially, depending on the agents' functionality) and generating LO. Both items are sent to the PC (P5) for possible checking. Then the system transfers the generated LO (P6) to the educational robot for accomplishing the task (P7). Finally, it is possible to transfer the sensor's data to the KB either directly (P8) or through the feedback and user connections.

We have continuously improved the ROABEE system. We have extended the GLO library. These improvements resulted in creating the personal generative library for STEM. In addition, we have added generative scenarios. We explain those improvements in detail in Chap. 12. In Sect. 9.5, we focus on the implementation of GLOs as technological software agents.

9.5 Implementation of Software Agent: A Case Study

As within the GLO interface, there are semantically different parameters (pedagogy-related, technological and content); it is convenient to have separate SW agents for managing selecting values for each kind of parameters. Therefore, we have a multi-agent system to communicate with the human agent, GLO library and GLO knowledge base (KB). With respect to the SW agent type and GLO KB, the most crucial issue is managing of the robot's technological data. That is so because, in many cases, technological parameters depend on the task specificity. Therefore, in our case study, we focus on the SW agent responsible to managing technological data and consider the following task: to pick up the object being in the initial location A and bring it to the target location B. The *distance* between A and B and the processing *time* are defined by the user. The function of the SWA is to identify the relevant straightforward algorithm and the adequate robot's velocity based on data taken from the technological part of the KB. Figure 9.3 presents the functionality of the SWA based on regression analysis and using the *if-then* techniques. Dependences of the technological data are taken from KB. Figure 9.4 shows the velocity-distance dependency when the robot moves 4 s, using the straightforward moving algorithms (A1, A2, A3).

Depending on the task requirements, SWA performs calculations to define the adequate algorithm and the relevant velocity to be transferred into GLO specification.

In Table 9.2, we present results of experiments to evaluate the SWA performance by measuring the real distances of moving as compared to the given requirements.

9.5.1 How to Integrate Technological Agent into Our Vision of STEM?

There are two visions of the problem. The first is how to create the technological agent (TA) by the teacher or even by students. The second is how to integrate the given TA (taken from external sources, created in the classroom by teacher or student) into the STEM content. Most likely, the TA is a part of Science (Physics) component, i.e. it dedicated to play a role of facility to enhance effectivity to provide the physical experiment. It is so, because the agent is able to suggest selecting of

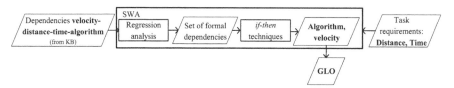

Fig. 9.3 SWA functioning algorithm (© with kind permission from Springer [ŠBD+16])

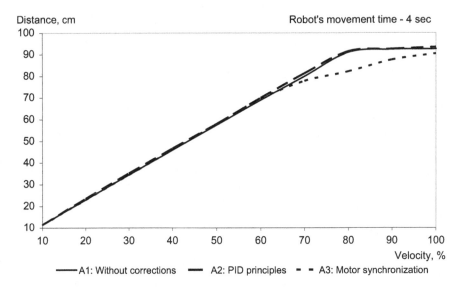

Fig. 9.4 A fragment of technological data taken from KB (© with kind permission from Springer [ŠBD+16])

Table 9.2 Experimental evaluation of SWA performance (© with kind permission from Springer [ŠBD+16])

Distance[a], cm	50	40	30	20	10
Time[b], s	Measured distance[c], cm				
1	–	–	29.3	19.8	10.0
2	46.5	39.0	29.4	20.3	10.0
3	48.6	39.5	29.5	20.3	10.0
4	48.2	39.5	29.5	20.5	10.0
5	48.6	39.5	29.5	20.5	10.3
6	48.6	39.5	30.0	20.5	10.3
7	49.0	40.0	30.0	20.5	10.0
8	49.4	39.5	30.0	20.5	10.3
9	49.6	39.5	31.0	20.5	10.0
10	49.6	40.5	31.0	20.3	10.2
Average	48.7	39.6	29.9	20.4	10.1
Standard deviation	1.0	0.4	0.6	0.2	0.1

Explanation:
[a]Distance is taken from task requirements
[b]Time is also taken from task requirements
[c]Measured distance is obtained by experiment

technological parameter values. Therefore, there are two problems: (1) creating the TA as an autonomous item and (2) integrating it with the GLO specification. The aim is to substitute the manual selection of technological parameters from the prespecified values by autonomous selection of those values by TA. The simplest way to integrate the TA into the GLO specification is as follows. We need to introduce a new parameter within the interface of the GLO. This parameter identifies the mode as a choice of two possibilities: (1) the user uses the agent; (2) the agent is not used. The user needs to tell to the system (1) what parameters and their values should be defined by the TA and (2) to indicate the location of the TA. Note that each GLO may have different agents depending on many factors, such as task type, parameter dependences, etc.

9.6 Evaluation and Conclusion

The robot-oriented GLOs are meta-specifications for generating control programs for educational robots. The human agent (teacher or student) is involved in the autonomous generation process through selecting or introducing parameter values via the graphical user interface of GLOs. In this chapter, we have identified (1) some similarity of GLOs to software agents (SWAs) and (2) proposed the structure to integrate the multi-agent system in the previous developed and used robot-based educational environment to enhance its and GLOs intelligence.

Currently we have developed and tested the SWA that is responsible for calculating or selecting values of technological parameters in managing GLOs. The remaining parameter values are yet to be defined by the human agent. We are able to conclude the following: (1) One can hardly consider the GLO as a typical SW agent; nevertheless, the GLO has some resemblance with SW agent and contains "hooks" (such as parameter variability space, partially covering the knowledge base), on which basis the true intellectual features can be introduced and integrated. (2) Due to the heterogeneity of the GLO parameter space, the multi-agent system is required. (3) The developed SWA excludes the tedious calculations of technological dependencies and ensures a higher accuracy. (4) The provided research should be also seen as a move towards the STEM-based learning. (5) The pedagogical agents are beyond the scope of this chapter.

References

[AB12]   Ahmad S, Bokhari MU (2012) A new approach to multi agent based architecture for secure and effective e-learning. Int J Comput Appl 46(22):26–29
[Ali13]   Alimisis D (2013) Educational robotics: open questions and new challenges. Themes Sci Technol Educ 6(1):63–71
[AVC+15] Aguilar J, Valdiviezo P, Cordero J, Sánchez M (2015) Conceptual design of a smart classroom based on multiagent systems. In: Proceedings on the international conference on artificial intelligence (ICAI), The Steering Committee of The World Congress in Computer Science, Computer Engineering and Applied Computing (WorldComp). p 471. (2015)

[BBB+11] Bădică C, Budimac Z, Burkhard HD, Ivanovic M (2011) Software agents: languages, tools, platforms. Comput Sci Inf Syst 8(2):255–298. (2011)

[BBD+14] Burbaite R, Bespalova K, Damaševičius R, Štuikys V (2014) Context aware generative learning objects for teaching computer science. Int J Eng Educ 30(4):929–936

[Ben12]   Benitti FBV (2012) Exploring the educational potential of robotics in schools: a systematic review. Comput Educ 58(3):978–988

[BKH13]   Brown L, Kerwin R, Howard AM (2013) Applying behavioral strategies for student engagement using a robotic educational agent. In: Systems, man, and cybernetics (SMC), 2013 I.E. international conference on, IEEE. pp 4360–4365

[CPC13]   Corrigan LJ, Peters C, Castellano G (2013) Identifying task engagement: towards personalised interactions with educational robots. In: Affective computing and intelligent interaction (ACII), 2013 humaine association conference on, IEEE. pp 655–658

[DET12]   Davidovsky M, Ermolayev V, Tolok V (2012) An implementation of agent-based ontology alignment. In: ICTERI. p 15. (2012)

[FG97]   Franklin S, Graesser A (1997) Is it an agent, or just a program? A taxonomy for autonomous agents. In: Intelligent agents III agent theories, architectures, and languages. Springer, pp 21–35

[GCR13]   Giuffra P, Cecilia E, Ricardo AS (2013) A multi-agent system model to integrate virtual learning environments and intelligent tutoring systems. IJIMAI 2(1):51–58

[Gre07]   Gregg DG (2007) E-learning agents. Learn Organ 14(4):300–312

[IJ13]   Ivanović M, Jain LC (2013) E-learning paradigms and applications: agent-based approach. SCI, vol. 528. Springer, Heidelberg

[KB15]   Kim Y, Baylor AL (2015) Research-based design of pedagogical agent roles: a review, progress, and recommendations. International Journal of Artificial Intelligence in Education 26(1):160–169

[LBM+04] Leeder D, Boyle T, Morales R, Wharrad H, Garrud P (2004) To boldly GLO-towards the next generation of learning objects. In: World conference on e-learning in corporate, government, healthcare, and higher education. pp 28–33

[LCL+15] Lin J-M, Chiou CW, Lee C-Y, Hsiao J-R (2015) Supporting physical agents in an interactive e-book. In: Genetic and evolutionary computing. Springer, pp 243–252

[LKB+15] Li J, Kizilcec R, Bailenson J, Ju W (2015) Social robots and virtual agents as lecturers for video instruction. Computers in Human Behavior 55:1222–1230

[MM05]   Mohammed P, Mohan P (2005) Agent based learning objects on the semantic web. SW-EL'05: Applications of semantic web technologies for E-learning. p 79

[MS09]   Mamud M, Stump S (2009) Development of an intelligent learning resource using computer simulation about optical communications. In: Education and training in optics and photonics. Optical Society of America, p EMB1

[PV11]   Pukkhem N, Vatanawood W (2011) Personalised learning object based on multi-agent model and learners' learning styles. Maejo Int J Sci Technol 5:3

[ŠB15]   Štuikys V, Burbaitė R (2015) Robot-based smart educational environments to teach CS: a case study. In: Štuikys V (ed) Smart educational smart learning objects for the smart education in computer science: theory, methodology and robot-based implementation. Springer, Cham, pp 265–285

[ŠBD+16] Štuikys V, Burbaitė R, Drąsutė V, Bespalova K (2016) Robot-oriented generative learning objects: an agent-based vision. In: Agent and multi-agent systems: technology and applications. Springer International Publishing, pp 247–257

[ŠD13]   Štuikys V, Damaševičius R (2013) Meta-programming and model-driven meta-program development: principles, processes and techniques. Springer Science & Business Media, Berlin

[SGV06]   Silveira RA, Gomes ER, Viccari RM (2006) Intelligent learning objects: an agent approach to create reusable intelligent learning environments with learning objects. In: Advances in artificial intelligence-IBERAMIA-SBIA 2006. Springer, pp 17–26

[Štu15]   Štuikys V (2015) Smart learning objects for the smart education in computer science: theory, methodology and robot-based implementation. Springer, Heidelberg

[VR14]   Veletsianos G, Russell GS (2014) Pedagogical agents. In: Handbook of research on educational communications and technology. Springer, pp 759–769

[Wer13]   Werfel J (2013) Embodied teachable agents: learning by teaching robots. In: Intelligent autonomous systems. The 13th international conference on

[WJ95]   Wooldridge M, Jennings NR (1995) Agent theories, architectures, and languages: a survey. In: Intelligent agents. Springer, pp 1–39

Part IV
Infrastructure to Support STEM-Driven CS Educational Practice

Part IV describes the infrastructure of our approach and the use of this infrastructure in practice, i.e. in the real educational setting. Here, by infrastructure, we mean the following components: STEM-driven personal generative library, STEM-driven generative scenario (GS), and smart STEM-driven educational environment (SEE). Part IV includes Chaps. 10, 11, 12, and 13. In Chap. 10, we introduce the concept *Personal Generative Library* (PGL) and discuss topics on how it can be created and adapted for STEM. The term "personal" has two meanings: either the teacher's library or the student's library. They differ in the mode of accessing and managing the resources, though the structure is the same. The term "generative" indicates on automated procedures to maintain the PGL. Firstly, we present the concept PGL as a separate topic having in mind its suitability for other contexts. Then, we provide adaptation of the PGL to the needs of STEM referring to PGL as the STEM library.

In Chap. 11, we describe STEM-driven GS. This description includes the methodology and tools to design STEM-driven GS. Again, the term "generative" means that the process of creating this component is automated. Furthermore, this chapter has a separate theoretical part for independent reading and a case study for evidence and approval. In Chap. 12, we present the SEE component in the following dimensions: (1) principles, requirements, and architectural aspects; (2) properties and features (characteristics); (3) usage and evaluation aspects. In Chap. 13, we summarize the practice and experience of using the proposed approach in the real setting. In this regard, we analyze and evaluate three typical case studies.

Chapter 10
Personal Generative Library for STEM-Driven Educational Resources

Abstract This chapter, we introduce a novel concept, called personal generative library (PGL), and analyse the approach build on this concept. We firstly discuss the approach in a wider context, i.e. for personalized learning, and then show how it can be applied to STEM-driven education. The term "generative" indicates two aspects. The first is that a large body of the library entities are generative (smart) learning objects. The second means that procedures to maintain the library itself are implemented as meta-programs to generate the instances of concrete programs on demand. In the context of STEM, we categorize PGL as a teacher's library for the general use and learner's library for the personalized use. This chapter includes the theoretical part representing a background in designing the PGL and the experimental part presenting results of the developed maintaining procedures. In addition, we provide an evaluation of the approach.

10.1 Introduction

Digital libraries (DLs) also known as learning object (LO) repositories play a significant role in providing educational resources for the huge e-Learning communities worldwide. The main objective of DLs is to support wide-scale reuse by systemizing the accumulated knowledge in order that it would be possible to share and reuse those resources in multiple contexts of use as efficiently as possible. Typically, the structure and functionality of the DLs are predefined by the metadata standards, such as IEEE LOM [IEEE00], Dublin Core and CanCore [RSG10]. Standards enable to systemize and create indeed the huge spaces of available resources within DLs. On the other hand, this also leads to serious difficulties and problems for users in searching the resources that fit best in each use case. This problem is known as *semantic interoperability*, meaning that any information given by the library creators should be understood in the same way correctly by the library users [DK07].

Another problem is the *incompleteness* of the metadata standards (e.g. LOs for game-based learning [HPD+12]). The internal structure of DLs (such as clustering of LOs) is not always relevant to the teacher's or learner's profile (such as knowledge

© Springer International Publishing AG, part of Springer Nature 2018   233
V. Štuikys, R. Burbaitė, *Smart STEM-Driven Computer Science Education*,
https://doi.org/10.1007/978-3-319-78485-4_10

level and learning style [SM12, DVN+12]), DLs for specialized LO collections (for teachers with limited computer skills) [F–PDL+11]. Therefore, the quality of LOs themselves within DLs is also a big issue [CO14, Och11].

With regard to DLs, the list of problems is by no means full. We will extend them later. As our literature review shows, there is the extremely intensive research to overcome the existing problems and difficulties in this field. Among other concepts and approaches, however, the personalization of educational resources and personalized education [ABB+16] is at the focus now. It is so, because the personal space encourages the reuse of learning materials, makes the adaptation easier and enables the construction of unique learning processes that suit the learner's needs best [CRS15]. In fact, personalization nominates the paradigm shift from teacher-centred learning to student-centred learning [ROD15]. This change also poses new problems. Among others, the report [ABB+16] emphasizes the tight relationship among personalization and STEM paradigm. A key challenge to personalized education is to foster a robust stream of diverse groups of students to STEM and related disciplines. Personalization can meet the demands of different backgrounds and a variety of learning styles and ensure engagement and retention.

Therefore, the aim of this chapter is to discuss the concept of the *personal generative library* (further PGL) and describe its implementation to support this paradigm change and respond to the existing challenges with regard to STEM and, to some extent, to personalized education. We start our discussion by explaining the concept itself.

10.2 A Concept of Personal Generative Library and More

The concept *library* is very old and very powerful and therefore is used in multiple contexts. Typically, a library serves for saving static data resources needed for multiple use (reuse) in the mode *use-as-is* (also known as component-based or component-from-the-shelf). Therefore, typically any advanced automated system (e.g. for modelling, design, etc.) is equipped with the internal library to support reuse. There are external DLs or *repositories* to support wide-scale reuse and *dedicated libraries*. In the first case, they represent independent systems. In the second case, they are integrated within a particular system. We consider the latter case and introduce the concept of the *personal generative* library (PGL) to support CS education on the STEM paradigm. No matter what library either for general use or dedicated purposes is, we can interpret it as a tool for saving resources for *a long-term* use.

A great deal of those resources is an *educational content* represented in various forms for easier search to respond to the particular needs. Though the educational content stands for a core resource, the *social content* plays a significant role in learning too. By the social content, we mean the information that enables to measure and evaluate learning outcomes in a longer perspective. There is a variety of social information that may be influential on how students retain the previous knowledge in case of STEM, what level of knowledge students are able to achieve over a durable learning process, what is the student's achievement curve over time, etc. Therefore, it is highly important to accumulate *histories* on the social behaviour and state of learners during the predefined period. The learning histories may affect, implicitly or explicitly, on personalized education and its possible improvement. Therefore, we assume that the personal library may include items for storing *learning histories* too. Those items may be implemented either as special components along with the content components or as a separate entity within the same educational environment where the library resides. In this chapter, we consider the latter case. Here, by learning histories, we mean a collection of *the pure social information* that describe the progress and achievements of an individual learner over a predefined period of learning. In our view, the learning history is *a systemized social feedback* for evaluating learning outcomes, for improving the processes itself by both teacher and student. In addition, the learning histories contain the initial data for building software agents, for example, responsible for making some pedagogical decisions automatically. Therefore, we treat learning histories as a beneficial instrument to support both STEM and personalized education.

In this context, therefore, the term "personal" firstly should be understood as the possibility to have the common and individual resources (more specifically, in a concrete situation, we call them LOs, smart LOs, generative LOs) for both the teacher and students for using, extending and sharing the educational material (i.e. STEM content) in the given context. The resources may be partially taken from the external repositories and, to a larger extent, created by the teacher in advance to support the course specificity (such as teaching programming using educational robots), as well as by the students themselves in the course of using PGL. Therefore, we categorize the personal library as the *teacher's personal library* for collective use and the *student's personal library* for individual use. Secondly, the term also means that the library also relates to *additional resources* such as *learning histories* to provide measures of a student's achievement and their progress over time. We assume that the learning history can be extracted partially from the student's personal library and partially from the teacher registered observations about a student's progress.

The term "generative" indicates three aspects of generative reuse here: (1) automated maintenance of the library using a generative technology (meta-programming in our case), (2) generative items themselves within the PGL and (3) library links with a generic (generative*)[1] scenario. The first aspect includes (i) the automated generation of annotations regarding a library item and (ii) automated generation of queries in searching items within the PGL. The second aspect is that a great deal of PGL resources is the smart generative LOs (SLOs for short) and the *history component* is also generative. We will discuss the third aspect in Chaps. 11 and 12.

The concept *personal library* to support CS education using robots (without implementation) was already proposed in [ŠB15]. However, later we have extended it by proposing the concept *personal generative library* (PGL) for the same purpose, i.e. robot-oriented CS (programming) education for secondary school students. We

---

[1]*means that the generative scenario is always the executable item in contrast to the generic scenario.

have implemented it and presented the approach (i.e. implementation methodology, and use cases) in [DBŠ+16]. The structure and capabilities of PGL do not depend on the items of the library. Therefore, it was possible to derive the core of the STEM-driven library from the PGL by changing the content only, i.e. by refactoring SLOs and other items to fit STEM needs. On the other hand, however, the STEM-driven PGL we discuss in this chapter has extended capabilities due to links with the other functional components such generic scenarios and agent-based subsystem (see Chap. 9). We discuss the remaining components in subsequent chapters.

Therefore, we present the material of this chapter as an adaptation and extension of the main concepts of the paper [DBŠ+16]. What is or might be the main contribution of PGL in general? Firstly, it enables, to some extent, to resolve the *library scaling problem* [Big94] at the component level. Secondly, it eliminates, partially or fully, the synonym problem in searching library items [ND02]. Finally, from the methodological perspective, it enables to extend the degree of automation by forwarding the generative reuse from the level of library items (i.e. separate GLOs/SLOs) to the system (i.e. the whole library) level, using the same technology, i.e. meta-programming [ŠD13]. Though so far there were attempts to automate the DL maintenance procedures (see, e.g. [LMS+12]), to our best knowledge, the meta-programming approach at the library level has been applied for the first time. It enables to achieve the high degree of automation and flexible content personalization. A summarized contribution of this chapter is the stated additional functionality towards the creation of STEM-driven PGL.

The remaining content of this chapter has the following structure. In Sect. 10.3, we analyse the related work. In Sect. 10.4, we formulate tasks considered in this chapter. In Sect. 10.5, we present the basic idea of the approach. In Sect. 10.6, we outline the background. In Sect. 10.7, we provide a detailed description of the approach. In Sect. 10.8, we present a case study and experiments. In Sect. 10.9, we provide adaptation of PGL for STEM. In Sect. 10.10, we summarize and evaluate the approach. Finally, in Sect. 10.11, we formulate conclusions.

10.3   Related Work

We categorize the related work into the following groups: (A) the general issues related to DLs (LO repositories) and (B) existing solutions to respond to the emerging DLs problems.

(A) The paper [Cer12] emphasizes the lack of social functionality (such as enabling user comments) in developing DLs for LOs. The paper [DK07] focuses on the semantic interoperability problem defining it as "an information given by one actor should be understood correctly by another actor". The paper [Jes13] discusses the properties and issues in sharing the educational content. The content is regarded to be shareable via the repository if it is validated against the standards and it is reusable in multiple contexts, editing tools, runtime environments and learning management systems. The paper [CRS15] emphasizes the need of the possibility and ability of personal expression in a shared open, global, and public space. Some papers discover the problems related to the metadata: (1) selection criteria and interoperability [PT10], (2) metadata modelling [CBS+11, CDR+13], (3) LO accessibility profiles in metadata models [GJP+06], (4) the need of semantic metadata [USB13] and (5) the incompleteness of the metadata standards (e.g. LOs for game-based learning) [HPD+12]. The other papers are related to the LOs quality problems in DLs [CO14, Och11]. Researchers propose the evaluation of the quality of LOs taking into account the opinion of the community [CCO+12], define relationships between metadata and LO quality metrics in repositories [PHP12], construct statistical profiles of highly rated learning objects [CSG11], and use LO analytics for collections, repositories and federations [SOS+13].

LOs discovery (searching, selecting) from the different DLs is also a big problem. In this regard, the paper [NFF+13] suggests "a theoretical approach that permits the use of a single LOR for classifying and enriching LOs according to domain-dependent information schemas, which can be dynamically changed after their definition". The paper [TN07] focuses on finding of the personalized learning paths, [BFG+14] offers a model for recommending LOs based on item response theory, [ZMP+11] suggests the hybrid recommendation method in the LO search system. The papers [BBR+11, BGF+12, NGF+12, and ZMP+11] describe the distributed LO metadata searching process and micro-context-based location process (two different possible contexts: micro-context of the LO in repository structure and micro-context in the curricular structure). The study [TCB+12] discusses the semantic search of LOs. The paper [Hsu12] proposes LO Finder and an intelligent LOM (LO metadata) shell based on semantic web technologies that enhance the semantics and knowledge representation of LOM. The paper [KFN+13] presents the strategies to gather heterogeneous learning objects from the web of data based on using linked data principles (these principles describe methods of publishing structured data so that it can be interlinked and become more useful through semantic queries).

(B) This research focuses on using recommendation strategies to select suitable LOs from DLs. That, for example, includes collaborative filtering recommendations inside DLs [CSS+13]. Also that covers an algorithm to recommend LOs for students satisfying their pedagogical needs and learning goals (algorithm is based on LOs dynamic weight and similarity between LOs calculating) [QB15]. Furthermore, the authoring tools based on the use of proactive context-aware recommender are also important [GBG+13] and evaluation and selection of group recommendation strategies for collaborative searching of learning objects [ZMP+15].

Researchers that work in the DLs problem domain suggest different solutions. Studies [RTD+12, VCP+11] propose a multi-agent model for searching, recovering, recommendation and evaluation of LOs from Repository Federations. The study [OOM+12] highlights that "most repositories are usually autonomous, that is, they work as portals that can be accessed through a Web-based interface, providing a search mechanism and a list of categories to conduct the search", and offer the possibility of making federated searches in distributed repositories from the original repository. A model [LPO+12] for multi-label classification and ranking of LOs offers a methodology that "illustrates the task of multi-label mapping of LOs into types queries through an emergent multi-label space, and that can improve the first choice of learners or teachers". The paper [LVO+12] presents an approach for the extraction and the annotation of the LO categories of the Universia DL that "has been transformed in a semantic LO repository following the principles of linked data".

The paper [PGM+14] proposes an architecture based on a cloud computing paradigm that "will permit the evolution of current learning resource repositories by means of the cloud computing paradigm and the integration of federated search system". The paper [SZ13] analyses the design and the implementation of DLs from the KMSs' (knowledge management systems) perspective with an intention to support the management of implicit and explicit knowledge. The study [BFG+14] describes an architecture of the semantic DLs based on using the ontology of all e-Learning artifacts and LOs, and on the representation of a domain through the logical language. The proposed architecture also includes the use of rules and concepts of semantic web services. Another paper [LMS+12] presents a comprehensive framework that consists of defining, retrieving and importing LOs for personalized courses. The suggested framework is partially implemented in the Moodle-based personalization system and support the retrieval of LOs in a personalization context. The study [ROD15] focuses on the student-centred educational recommender system that combines content-based, collaborative and knowledge-based approaches. The paper [TPB+11] deals with design and implementation of collaborative DLs based on the filing and retrieving distributed knowledge. The overview given in [TN07] discusses the general, content, technical and quality characteristics of the existing DLs.

We have not provided a more intensive review on technical aspects (such as feature-based modelling, meta-programming, domain-specific languages and robotics in teaching and GLOs) to implement the library items (GLOs). The reader can learn more on those issues, for example, from [ACL+13, MBC09, SBD13, TBK09].

Because of the analysis, we are able to conclude the following: (1) DLs are indeed the powerful instrument and therefore is a widely discussed topic to support the component-based reuse vision in the technology-enhanced learning. (2) Due to the complexity of this problem domain (in terms of its scope, interdependences among the separate subdomains, diversity of needs of different communities, etc.), there is a variety of issues and problems as well as approaches under intensive researching. (3) In the context of this chapter, it is possible to exclude the two problems: the *content personalization* and more *effective use of DL resources*. (4) Though the provided analysis by no means is exhaustive, nevertheless, it is possible to conclude:

(i) So far the potential of generative reuse within this domain is yet in the infancy stage.
(ii) There are few research efforts to introduce systematic studies to enforce more effective managing procedures of digital educational resources.

(iii) This chapter should be seen as our proposal for the explicit use of generative technology (such as meta-programming) and its benefits for STEM in this problem domain.

10.4 Tasks in Creating PGL for STEM-Driven Education

In this chapter, we discuss the so-called STEM library. Its function is to provide the basic educational resources needed to support robot-oriented CS education using the STEM-driven paradigm. Therefore, the STEM library is an essential part of the educational environment discussed in Chap. 12. This library is a derivative exemplar. It was derived from the personal generative library (PGL) [DBŠ+16]; however, in doing so, we have introduced some modifications. In essence, they regard to the implementation of the STEM library items. The modifications made include (1) separation of the pedagogical context from a separate GLO/SLO and its inclusion within the scenario description that is common for all library items; (2) STEM attributes that are also within scenario, but not within GLO/SLO body; and (3) STEM library that is directly connected with scenario automatically, but not through the user's manual actions. Therefore, the reader should be aware what the structure and capabilities of the PGL are and how it was created.

In the remaining sections, therefore, we deal with the following research tasks.

Task 1: analysis of the PGL concept, the background of its implementation, the PGL structure and the functionality

Task 2: the development of generic specifications using meta-programming techniques to support the PGL creation and maintenance

Task 3: adapting PGL to STEM needs

10.5 Basic Idea of the Approach

We start considering *Task 1* with the analysis of the basic idea to implement the personal generative library (PGL). Our aim is to present the *main processes* the designer needs to go through in creating PGL (Fig. 10.1). Here, by creating PGL, we mean the development not the library items themselves (that was discussed in Chap. 7) but the *generative facilities* to manage those items. The initial data is the IEEE LOM standard for metadata. As the list of metadata supports wide scale of reuse, we need to specialize the list for the personalization purposes. The result of the process (it is identified by the number 1 in Fig. 10.1) is the subset of metadata to be used in PGL. The next activity is the transformation process, converting the selected metadata into the formal model, using the feature-based notion [Bat05, TBK09]. The transformation process (denoted as 2*) is also applied to the user-oriented data

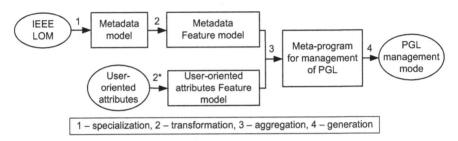

Fig. 10.1 Process-based framework to explain main activities of the approach (© with kind permission from Information Technology and Control [DBŠ+16])

needed for personalization. Therefore, we have two separate feature models that are to be combined into the one through aggregation (process denoted as 3 in Fig. 10.1).

The main requirement in constructing feature models is their consistency to be approved by using the adequate tools [ACL+13, MBC09]. The aggregation is to be performed on the correct models. The resulting feature model specifies the basic problem domain aspects (PDL just is treated as the problem domain in our case) needed in creating the meta-program for managing PGL. In fact, those aspects specify metadata variability implemented in the PGL. The external tool for managing the PGL variability is meta-programming techniques (we use heterogeneous meta-programming here) which are treated as the solution domain. To apply the techniques (see also Sect. 10.6), we need to introduce two languages (meta-language and target language). In our case, we use PHP in the role of the meta-language and MySQL as the target language. Note also that a large body of the library items are GLOs (or smart LOs) oriented to using robots in teaching. Those are implemented using RobotC as a target language. The meta-program is the specification that generalizes the possible modes and processes taken place in communicating with PGL. The external tool for managing the PGL variability is just the meta-program (meta-programs) we have developed along with the PGL. Finally, taking the concrete metadata values (they also treated as parameter values), it is possible to automatically generate PGL management mode on demand. In fact, this process (in Fig. 10.1 identified as generation numbered by 4) is the personalization process. We describe the result, i.e. the PGL modes, in more detail, in Sects. 10.6 and 10.7.

10.6 Background of the Approach

First, we define the basic terms and their relationships treated as the theoretical background here. Note that the background is not concerned with the problem on how PDL is to be created but rather on how it should be managed automatically as much as possible. More specifically, the background is concerned with the model-driven development of the meta-program for managing the PGL processes in order we could be able to achieve the prescribed aim of generative reuse. Next, we present more details (in Sects. 10.7 and 10.8) of the approach from the use perspective, focusing on the structural, functioning and manageable aspects of PGL.

10.6.1 Definitions of Basic Terms and Relationships

Definition 1 A digital learning library is the set of digital educational resources created to provide the access, using the adequate technology, to the resources to support wide-scale reuse for learning communities worldwide (adapted from [Hol03]).

Definition 2 Metadata is a data model, used to describe other data, such as an LO. The purpose of LO metadata is to support the reusability of LOs, to aid discoverability and to facilitate their interoperability (adapted [IEEE00, RSG10]).

Definition 3 LO is "any entity, digital or non-digital, which can be used, re-used or referenced during technology supported learning" [IEEE00]. In this paper, we consider digital entities. Therefore, LO is treated as an educational resource. It is also treated as component-based LO (CB LO).

Definition 4 Generative LO (GLO) is "an articulated and executable learning design that produces a class of learning objects" [BLA+08]. In addition, GLO is the metalevel specification (meaning parameterized) to enable producing of concrete LOs on demand automatically according to the prespecified parameter values and the context of use (definition used in this chapter).

Definition 5 Smart LO (SLO) is the robot-oriented GLO with extended generative features (e.g. multistaged, context-aware, agent-based, etc.) for adaptability and personalization.

Definition 6 Personal generative library (PGL) is the set of the entities organized so that it would be possible to provide the access and maintenance to the entities with regard to the personal needs, using the adequate generative tools (e.g. meta-program and meta-language processor).

PGL entities might be of the following types: (1) LO searched out from the external DL by the PGL user (typically teacher or knowledgeable student), (2) GLO created in advance by the teacher or designer, (3) smart GLO (meaning multistage GLO with the explicit parameter context for generating adapted GLOs [Štu15]; see Chap. 8), (4) LO derived by the teacher or student from the scratch or specifications (2) or (3) and (5) personal LO modified by the student after the derivation (generation) process.

Definition 7 Feature is a user-visible characteristic, qualitative property of the concept, or the functional requirement [CE01, KCH+90]. In the context of this chapter, feature is either the entity of PGL or an attribute of the entity.

Definition 8 Feature model (FM) is the specification to describe the commonality and variability aspects of a domain (in our case PGL) through the feature types, their relationships and constraints.

There are the mandatory, optional and alternative features. There are parent-child and AND, OR and XOR relationships. There are constraints of the type "requires" and "excludes" [Bat05, CHE04].

A feature model is abstract if its features can be further decomposed into the other "smaller" features. A feature model is concrete if its leaf features are atomic features (atomic feature is its value).

Definition 9 Transformation is the process of changing one model into another according to the predefined rules.

We consider the following types of transformations in this section:

Specialization (when the feature model A is transformed into the feature model B, which is a sub-model of the model A [TBK09]).

Aggregation (it is a composition of two or more models so that the resulting model that does not have the same parts [ACL+13]).

Mapping is the kind of transformation when input and output models are represented by different languages.

Definition 10 Meta-programming is the high-level programming paradigm aiming at creating generalized programs – meta-programs [ŠD13]. Here, it is also treated as the solution domain to implement the problem domain tasks.

Definition 11 Heterogeneous meta-program (further meta-program) is the executable generic program, described using at least two languages (meta-language and target language) in the same specification. Typically, the target (also domain) language serves for expressing aspects of the problem domain commonality. The meta-language serves for expressing aspects of the problem domain variability. In addition, meta-program is the generator to create program instances automatically on demand [ŠD13].

Definition 12 Parameter is a syntax-driven entity within the interface or meta-body of the meta-program, expressing domain variability independently from the semantics of the domain.

Definition 13 Interface of a meta-program is the set of parameters, their values and relationships among the values.

Definition 14 Meta-body is the specification to implement the functionality of the meta-program using a set of meta-language functions, where arguments of the functions are parameters, fragments of the target language (program) fragments, other functions of a combination thereof [ŠBB14].

Definition 15 Meta-language is the subset of the functions (e.g. to specify an operation, alternatives and loops used in the mode of structured programming) of the general-purpose programming language (PHP in our case) [ŠD13].

Definition 16 Meta-language processor is the tool to automatically generate an instance of a target program (in our case it is either the management program or the PGL item derived from the GLO specification).

Definition 17 Management & support meta-program (shortly M&S MP) is the specification of the aggregated meta-program to support management processes of the PGL by generating the program instances to manage the selected mode of use.

Definition 18 PGL management process (mode) is any process taken from the list: (1) LO adding into PGL and the annotation formation for an entity, (2) search of the entity, (3) delete of the entity and (4) change attributes of the PGL. Each item of the list is based on using generated queries.

Therefore, the defined terms fall into two categories, belonging either to the problem domain (PD) or to the solution domain (SD). However, the process of solving the prescribed task (such as the development and then the use of the M&S MP for PGL in our case) is not a straightforward mapping of the PD entities onto the SD entities. Rather, it is the multi-level transformation process that includes various forms of transformation (T1–T4), which in Fig. 10.2 are represented graphically using the set

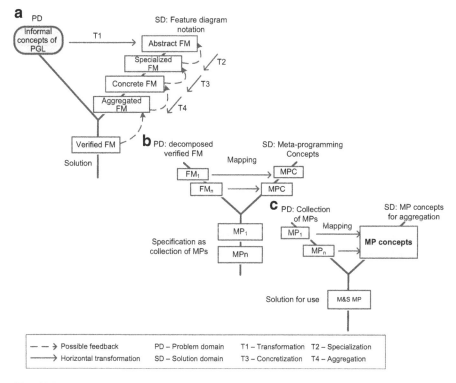

Fig. 10.2 Y-chart-based framework to outline the processes for implementing the approach (© with kind permission from Information Technology and Control [DBŠ+16])

of the Y-charts. We use Y-charts because they have three branches (left for PD, right for SD and vertical for the obtained solution) to visually express the essence of transformations. Note that Y-charts (a), (b) and (c) represent the whole meta-program development process through feature model transformations starting from the informal requirements statement for the PD (PGL in our case). The final solution is the M&S MP specification to automatically generate the needed management and support programs with regard to predefined parameter values.

10.7   A Detailed Description of the Approach

The personal library provides the educational and managerial support in storing, updating and searching the content to realize the Computer Science (CS) curriculum objectives and tasks within the smart environment [Štu15]. Currently, we treat the library as a personal internal database, because it was created by the CS teacher (second author of this book) to satisfy the local needs of the teaching institution only. However, we do not exclude the opportunity of extending the status of the library use in the future.

Currently, the creator of the library is also responsible for maintenance and updating tasks. The users of the library are both teachers (there might also be other teachers as library users within the institution) and students. However, the access mode is different for the teacher-administrator, teachers as users and students. The teacher-administrator holds the highest priority: all accessibility functions are allowable. The overall structure of the library is shown in Fig. 10.3.

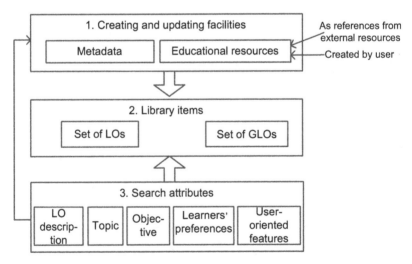

Fig. 10.3 Architecture of the personal generative library (PGL) (© with kind permission from Information Technology and Control [DBŠ+16])

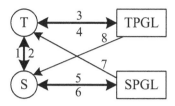

Fig. 10.4 Interaction between users and PGLs (*T* teacher, *S* student, *TPGL* teacher's PGL, *SPGL* student's PGL) (© with kind permission from Information Technology and Control [DBŠ+16])

The entities within the library are those as defined by Definition 5 (see Sect. 10.6). Among others, there are traditional learning objects to be obtained through linking to the external resources. They might be given in the form of text, pictures, video, etc. (e.g. to support the theoretical part of the topic, or it is the other additional material such as instructions to construct robots). Before the links being stored into the library, those links (LOs) first are enriched with metadata to enable their search procedure later, in the time of the use.

Note that Fig. 10.3 represents the common structure of the library. Using the structure, the user (i.e. teacher or student) can create his/her own PGLs. In Fig. 10.4, we show the interaction processes between users and PGLs. The processes 1 and 2 define the two-side interaction "teacher-student". The processes 3 and 4 (and also 5 and 6) define the two-side managing and supporting procedures "user-PGL". The procedures include the management processes (modes) as defined by Definition 18 (see Sect. 10.6). The processes 7 and 8 define the modes of use the adequate educational resources from another user's PGL.

As the focus of this proposal is the development of meta-programs to support the automated management of PGL processes, we explain in more detail parts (b) and (c) of our framework (see Fig. 10.2). The development goes through subsequent model transformations in the following way.

The specialized concrete PD FM is transformed into the concrete SD FM using the abstract SD FM through mapping of corresponding PD items (e.g. variation points and variants) onto SD items (i.e. meta-program interface and body) using Rules 1, 2, 3 and 4.

Rule 1 The variation points of PD FM correspond to parameters within the meta-program or its model, and variants of a variation point correspond to the parameter value.

Rule 2 The parameter and their values are to be specified in the interface of the meta-program. The dependencies between parameter values (if any) are to be specified in the interface and expressed through the constraints (requires, excludes) to be implemented by the alternative meta-function (see Rule 3).

Rule 3 The SD model (i.e. meta-program model) is transformed into the executable meta-program specification (MPS) by performing the following actions: (i) selecting the concrete meta-language (ML) constructs (such as if function of the meta-language, PHP in our case), (ii) choosing the relevant target language (TL) scenario or scenarios (that depends on the task complexity, MySQL in our case) and (iii) generalizing them using the ML constructs and PD variability model through coding and testing the specification.

Rule 4 The executable MPS is transformed into the application programs (such as those for PGL management in our case) via the following actions: (i) selecting a preprogrammed parameter values taken from the interface, (ii) processing (interpreting) MPS by the ML processor and generating the concrete target program and (iii) adapting it to the different use cases (if any) by the regeneration process.

We provide more details of our approach in Sect. 10.8.

10.8 A Methodology of Experiments and Case Study

We start describing our methodology of experiments assuming that the architecture of PGL is developed and its items (i.e. LO and GLOs) are loaded already. The experiments cover the development of meta-programs for solving the GLO managerial tasks only. Therefore, the methodology includes the following stages: (i) specification of the requirements of the tasks, using feature models; (ii) model-to-model transformation and verification; (iii) the development of meta-programs based on using transformation rules; (iv) generation of program instances from the meta-programs to solve managerial tasks; and (v) obtaining the solutions of the tasks. The tasks include (1) user-interface creation for all management modes (see Definition 18), (2) database table creation and (3) adding/deleting/selecting of the educational entities. This section contains two parts: Sects. 10.8.1 and 10.8.2. In Sect. 10.8.1, we explain the stages (i) and (ii) of our methodology. In Sect. 10.8.2, we present the remaining part of experiments we have carried out.

10.8.1 Results of Modelling

Here, we provide the characteristics of the verified aggregated FM (see Fig. 10.2b). Note that there are two versions of this model: one to support database creation (*Task 2*) and the other to support selecting and deleting of an entity (*Task 3*). Now we present the abstract metadata feature model (see Definition 8) based on the LOM IEEE standard (see Fig. 10.5). We have extracted from the standard only those attributes of metadata relevant to our purposes (see processes 1 and 2 in Fig. 10.1). For the model's detail, see Definitions 8 and 9 in Sect. 10.6 and Legend in Fig. 10.5.

In Fig. 10.6, we present also an abstract feature model to define the user-oriented attributes (see process 2* in Fig. 10.1 and also Definitions 8 and 9 in Sect. 10.6). In Table 10.1, we present the characteristics of those versions. We can conclude: there are a large number of features of different types (see Definition 8), a huge number of

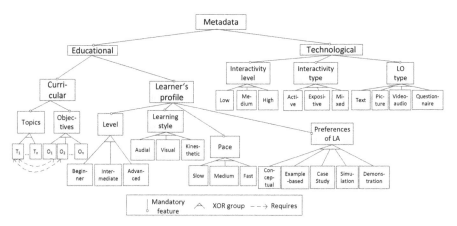

Fig. 10.5 Abstract feature-based metadata model (© with kind permission from Information Technology and Control [DBŠ+16])

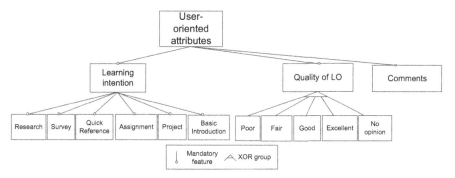

Fig. 10.6 User-oriented attributes abstract feature model (© with kind permission from Information Technology and Control [DBŠ+16])

valid configurations that defines the number of the possible implementations. In our approach, a valid configuration defines the annotation of an educational entity of the created PGL.

In Fig. 10.7, we present the modelling results obtained using the tool SPLOT [MBC09]. Note that these results are aggregated models derived from the abstract models given in Figs. 10.5 and 10.6.

10.8.2   A Case Study: Results Obtained by the Generated Programs

Now we present the second part of the experiments we have carried out so far. It covers the remaining stages (iii–v) of our methodology. At the current state of the

Table 10.1 Characteristics of aggregated FM obtained using FAMILIAR and SPLOT for the created PGL

Model metrics	Mode	
	DB creation, supplementing	Selection, deleting of the LO
# Features	94	94
# Mandatory features	14	14
# Optional features	10	10
# Core features	15	15
# XOR groups	24	28
# OR groups	4	0
#Cross-tree constraints	2	2
CTCR, %[a]	0.02	0.02
Tree depth	8	8
Valid configurations	1.23E12	624,490,560
Variability degree, %[b]	6.2085E-15	3.1529E-18
# Dead features	None	None
Consistency	Consistent	Consistent

[a]CTCR – constraints representativeness, number of variables in the CTC divided by the number of features in the feature diagram
[b]Variability degree is the number of valid configurations divided by $2n$, where n is a number of features in the model

research, we have developed three separate meta-programs to support management activities. They include cases representing our researching Tasks 1, 2 and 3 (see Sect. 10.4). Using those meta-programs, we are able to generate or derive the concrete programs automatically on demand for each task. In Fig. 10.8, we present the fragment of the interface for the meta-program (*Task 3*).

We have tested the tasks experimentally. The experiments have shown that the functionality of the meta-programs was as expected. The results given in Fig. 10.9 demonstrate the correct functioning of the meta-programs.

Therefore, the provided experiments (meta-program testing, generation of the managerial programs, the use of the programs to support the tasks and obtained results) have validated our approach.

10.9   Adaptation of PGL Concept to STEM Library

So far, in the context of considering *Task 1* and *Task 2*, we have discussed the personal generative library (PGL), i.e. its concept, design framework with background, implementation with case studies and experiments. We have presented the topics without the STEM context because, we believe, the PGL-based approach is applicable in many other contexts too. However, each new context of use may introduce extra requirements and the need of adaptation or extension and modification. Therefore, the topic of this section is on how the concept of PGL can be adapted for STEM, i.e. we consider *Task 3* here.

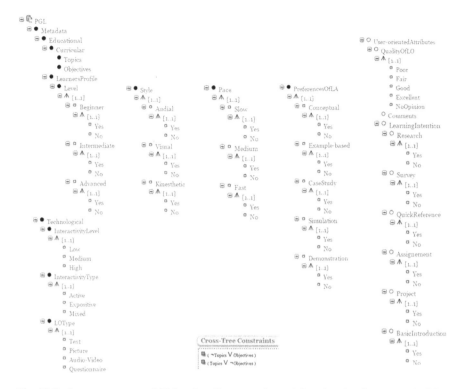

Fig. 10.7 Concrete aggregated FM to describe annotations of the educational resources in PGL (model created using SPLOT [MBC09]) (© with kind permission from Information Technology and Control [DBŠ+16])

Add Learning Object

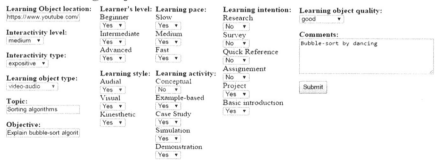

Fig. 10.8 A fragment of MP of the interface to add the new entity into PGL (see also the left branch in Fig. 10.2c) (© with kind permission from Information Technology and Control [DBŠ+16])

location	interactivity_level	interactivity_type	lo_type	name	objective	beginner	intermediate	advanced
https://www.youtube.com/watch?v=XaqR3G_NVoo	medium	expositive	video-audio	Sorting algorithms	Explain merge-sort algorithm	Yes	Yes	Yes
https://www.youtube.com/watch?v=Ns4TPTC8ahw	medium	expositive	video-audio	Sorting algorithms	Explain select-sort algorithm	Yes	Yes	Yes
https://www.youtube.com/watch?v=ROalU37i9U	medium	expositive	video-audio	Sorting algorithms	Explain insert-sort algorithm	Yes	Yes	Yes
https://www.youtube.com/watch?v=IyZQPjUT5B4	medium	expositive	video-audio	Sorting algorithms	Explain bubble-sort algorithm	Yes	Yes	Yes

audial	visual	kinesthetic	slow	medium	fast	conceptual	example_based	case_study	simulation	demonstration	quality	comment
Yes	Yes	Yes	Yes	Yes	Yes	No	Yes	Yes	Yes	Yes	Good	Merge-sort by dancing
Yes	Yes	Yes	Yes	Yes	Yes	No	Yes	Yes	Yes	Yes	Good	Select-sort by dancing
Yes	Yes	Yes	Yes	Yes	Yes	No	Yes	Yes	Yes	Yes	Good	Insert-sort by dancing
Yes	Yes	Yes	Yes	Yes	Yes	No	Yes	Yes	Yes	Yes	Good	Bubble-sort by dancing

research	survey	quick_reference	assignment	project	basic_introduction
No	No	No	No	Yes	Yes
No	No	No	No	Yes	Yes
No	No	No	No	Yes	Yes
No	No	No	No	Yes	Yes

Fig. 10.9 The obtained results (DB tables) by using meta-programs (© with kind permission from Information Technology and Control [DBŠ+16])

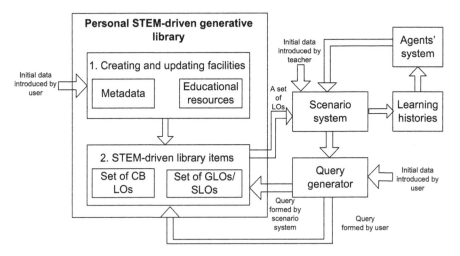

Fig. 10.10 Personal STEM-driven generative library and its use context

Figure 10.10 outlines the structure of the STEM library and its context of use. There are three aspects to stress: (*i*) changes in the internal structure of PGL considered so far, (*ii*) external relationships with the other components of the STEM educational environment and (*iii*) the status of use.

With regard to the internal structure (*i*), there are no essential changes as compared to the architecture of Fig. 10.3. The changes relate to the internal structure of the library items. Here the item's content is STEM related. For example, the metadata model includes also the information about the technology (robot platforms and other smart devices (see Chap. 3). Furthermore, the context information (i.e. pedagogical aspects) is not within the items for each SLO, but this context is within the STEM scenario. We have considered the previous architecture of the PGL

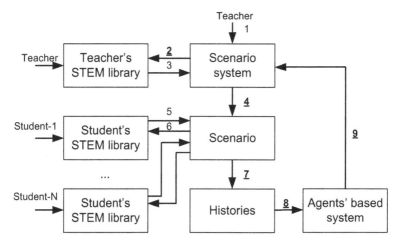

Fig. 10.11 Integrated processes among systems and components. (*1*) *Initial data* given by the teacher (objectives, type, topic, subtopic, expected results). (*2*) Query generation and transfer to teacher's STEM library. (*3*) Learning resources taken from the teacher's library. (*4*) Scenario instance generation for use by student. (*5*) The student takes resources from own library according to scenarios tasks. (*6*) Student uploads newly created resources to own library. (*7*) History formation. (*8*) History data transfer to agent-based system. (*9*) Solution as recommendations

as a stand-alone system. Now, with regard to the aspect (ii), the STEM library has a rich external context to communicate with other components or systems. They include the *scenario system* (note that it also is generative), *agent-based system*, *learning history component* and *query generator*. There are a few external links to be initiated by the user or teacher. Note that in case of the link "*Initial data introduced by user*" (they are the two; see Fig. 10.10) by the *user*, we mean either a student or teacher. Therefore, students are able to create queries for search the teaching content in the library independently (the right link) from the teacher or to create the library items for personal use (the left link). However, the responsibility of managing the scenario system fully belongs to the teacher.

With regard to the status of use (iii), there are the two. We identify them as purely teacher-oriented and student-oriented. The first is common for both the teacher and learners in terms of use. From the teacher's perspective, this library is treated as personal. In addition, therefore, the maintenance procedures of those resources are to be performed by the teacher only. The second is the student's personal STEM library. In this case, the student is free in manipulating with library items because of the *personal status* of the library. Figure 10.11 explains the interaction between the teacher's STEM library and the student's personal STEM library as related to the use. We describe the remaining components in more detail in other chapters (i.e. agent-based system in Chap. 9, scenario system in Chap. 11 and smart educational environment in Chap. 12).

Note that learners' histories are a part of the knowledge base and define the learning paths. We discuss that in Chap. 12.

Note that underlined numbers of the processes in Fig. 10.11 indicate on their description in other chapters as stated above.

10.10   Summary, Discussion and Evaluation

Digital libraries (DLs) are powerful instruments to support wide-scale reuse of the educational content. Typically, the basic item of DLs is the educational resource called learning object (LO). The resource stands for distribution, sharing, use and reuse. Though there is a variety of types and models to represent LOs, generative LOs (shortly GLOs) nominate a specific kind of LOs. The original concept of GLO is due to the contribution of Boyle, Leeder and Morales et al. [LBM+04], characterizing GLOs as "the next generation learning objects". The Center for Excellence in the design, development and use of LOs in the UK (shortly, RLO-CETL) defines GLO as "an articulated and executable learning design that produces a class of learning objects" [BLA+08]. In fact, the concept GLO means the shift from the component-based reuse model to the generative reuse model. The latter has far more possibilities for adaptation and personalization, especially in the case when meta-programming is used as a generative technology [ŠD13]. In this case, it is also possible to add new features for the meta-programming-based GLOs aiming at extending their capabilities for adaptation and personalization. Such features as preprogrammed context and staging of GLO parameters for adaptation combined with the advanced capabilities of educational robots enable us to recall GLOs and treat them as smart LOs [Štu15] (shortly SLO or SLOs). In the context of this book, the smartness is added by combining GLOs with the agent technology [ŠBD+16] and introducing hierarchical aggregated stage-based GLO/SLO model.

In this chapter, therefore, we have made a step from the concept GLO/SLO as an item in a traditional library towards the generative library. We have extended the use of meta-programming techniques for managing the variability issues at the library level by introducing the concept of a personal generative library (PGL) to investigate and support the new capabilities for personalization of the educational content. Firstly, those capabilities are supported by the diversity of LOs types the PGL contains. There are traditional LOs, for example, taken from the external repositories. There are one-stage meta-programming-based GLOs. There are context-aware multistage GLOs to support better adaptation and personalization. There are also aggregated stage-based GLOs. In addition, there are student created LOs derived from the all kinds of GLOs in the teaching process. The type diversity reflects the evolution of our approach.

Secondly, the capabilities are supported by the mode of use the items of PGL along with the adequate tools (such as meta-program to maintain PGL and meta-language processor). For example, the teacher is able to derive from the context-aware multistage GLO a "smaller" GLO being adapted for a particular group of students. Then each student of the group is able to derive from the smaller GLO a particular LO that fits to his/her context. The student is also able to repeat the process aiming to improve the content, if the generated result does not satisfy expectations, or even to modify the content manually.

Finally, the capabilities are also supported by the mode of maintaining the content within PGL. This is because of the dynamic nature of the maintaining procedure that has been implemented as a meta-program. The following modes of using this meta-program enable (1) automatic generation of LO (GLO) annotations in creating PGL, (2) automatic generation of queries in searching items within the PGL and (3) the items of PGL that can be changed, modified and added to the new ones using the adequate modes of the program.

Therefore, we summarize the contribution of this chapter as follows. There are two basic results: (1) the concept, the models of the PGL and its implementation that enables to resolve, to some extent, two scientific and practical problems known as a library scaling [Big94] and synonymy in searching items from libraries [ND02]. (2) The next is a novel maintaining procedure to support the PGL enabling automatic annotations and queries generation, as well as resulting in enhanced capabilities for personalization and adaptation of the PGL content.

The discussed approach has also some limitations. (1) There may arise the problem of "dead links" to resources of external libraries. (2) The students' fraction within PGL is yet little as compared to the whole DPL content, where the fraction created by the teacher dominates now. (3) Some difficulties may arise if the user wants to change the annotation system he/she previously introduced.

10.11 Conclusion

1. The personal educational space encourages reuse of learning materials and enables the construction of unique learning processes to support student-centred learning. The personal generative library (PGL) proposed in this chapter is regarded as a tool to implement the learning paradigm more effectively as compared to the conventional library. It is so, because we use meta-programming, the powerful generative technology for implementing PGL, enabling (1) automatic annotation generation of the library items and (2) automatic generation of queries in searching items within the PGL.

2. The benefits of PGL, however, are for both paradigms, i.e. teacher-centred learning and student-centred learning. It is so, because personalization and flexible content adaptation through automation are equally important in both cases, though the processes are different by objectives, scope and results.

3. The proposed models and their implementation in creating PGL nominate the generalization of the educational content at the higher level of abstraction as compared to the separate generative LO. Therefore, PGL can be thought of as a top-level content generator for managing and personalization of the content on demand.

4. The scientific and practical value of the PGL is as follows. The approach enables to eliminate the semantic interoperability problem in the whole (due to the

explicit metadata at both the PDL management and GLO representation levels in the case when the library creator and user is the same actor). In other cases, it enables to diminish a negative effect of the problem substantially (due to the explicit metadata and the capabilities of the rapid regeneration of queries if needed).

5. Though we have focused on the education-based application, the concepts, the models and the results obtained are also applicable and may be interesting for a much larger community, because the discussed problems are common in designing of many other systems.

References

[ABB+16]　Alur R, Baraniuk R, Bodik R, Drobnis A, Gulwani S, Hartmann B, Kafai Y, Karpicke J, Libeskind-Hadas R, Richardson D, Solar-Lezama A, Thille C, Vardi M (2016) Computer-aided personalized education. www.cis.upenn.edu/~alur/cape16.pdf

[ACL+13]　Acher M, Collet P, Lahire P, France RB (2013) Familiar: a domain-specific language for large scale management of feature models. Sci Comput Program 78(6):657–681

[Bat05]　Batory D (2005) Feature models, grammars, and propositional formulas. SPLC 3714:7–20

[BBR+11]　Baldiris SM, Bacca JL, Rojas AN, Guevara JC, Fabregat R (2011) LORSE: intelligent meta-searcher of learning objects over distributed educational repositories based on intelligent agents. In: Frontiers in Education Conference (FIE), 2011. IEEE, p F1E-1

[BFG+14]　Baldiris S, Fabregat R, Graf S, Tabares V, Duque N, Avila C (2014) Learning object recommendations based on quality and item response theory. In: Advanced Learning Technologies (ICALT), 2014 I.E. 14th international conference on. IEEE, pp 34–36

[BGF+12]　Baldiris S, Graf S, Fabregat R, Méndez NDD (2012) Looking for contextualized learning objects to support semi-automatic learning design generation. In: Workshop on Technology-Enhanced Learning and Living (TELL 2012), pp 43–49

[Big94]　Biggerstaff TJ (1994) The library scaling problem and the limits of concrete component reuse. In: Software reuse: advances in software reusability, 1994. Proceedings, Third International Conference on IEEE, pp 102–109

[BLA+08]　Boyle T, Ljubojevic D, Agombar M, Baur E (2008) The conceptual structure of generative learning objects (GLOs). In: EdMedia: world conference on educational media and technology. Association for the Advancement of Computing in Education (AACE), pp 4570–4579

[CBS+11]　Campos F, Braga R, Santos N, Souza AC, Rabello C (2011) Expanding access to distance learning using learning objects, education in a technological world: communicating current and emerging research and technological efforts, 1

[CCO+12]　Cechinel C, da Silva CS, Ochoa X, Sicilia MA, Sanchez-Alonso S (2012) Populating learning object repositories with hidden internal quality information. In: Manouselis N, Draschler H, Verber K, Santos OC (eds) Proceedings of the 2nd workshop on Recommender Systems for Technology Enhanced Learning (RecSysTEL 2012). Published by CEUR workshop proceedings, vol 896, pp 11–22

[CDR+13]　Casali A, Deco C, Romano A, Tomé G (2013) An assistant for loading learning object metadata: an ontology based approach. In: Proceedings of the informing science and information technology education conference, 2013, pp 77–87

[CE01]   Czarnecki K, Eisenecker U (2001) Generative programming: methods, tools and applications. Addison-Wesley, Boston

[Cer12]   Cervone HF (2012) Digital learning object repositories. OCLC Syst Serv: Int Digit Libr Perspect 28(1):14–16

[CHE04]   Czarnecki K, Helsen S, Eisenecker U (2004) Staged configuration using feature models. SPLC 3154:266–283

[CO14]   Cechinel C, Ochoa X (2014) A brief overview of quality inside learning object repositories. In: Proceedings of the XV international conference on human computer interaction. ACM, p 83

[CRS15]   Cohen A, Reisman S, Sperling BB (2015) Personal spaces in public repositories as a facilitator for open educational resource usage. Int Rev Res Open Distrib Learn 16(4)

[CSG11]   Cechinel C, Sánchez-Alonso S, García-Barriocanal E (2011) Statistical profiles of highly-rated learning objects. Comput Educ 57(1):1255–1269

[CSS+13]   Cechinel C, Sicilia MÁ, SáNchez-Alonso S, GarcíA-Barriocanal E (2013) Evaluating collaborative filtering recommendations inside large learning object repositories. Inf Process Manag 49(1):34–50

[DBŠ+16]   Drąsutė V, Burbaitė R, Štuikys V, Bespalova K, Drąsutis S, Ziberkas G (2016) Personal generative library of educational resources: a framework, model and implementation. Inf Technol Control 45(4):430–442

[DK07]   Dagienė V, Kurilovas E (2007) Design of Lithuanian digital library of educational resources and services: the problem of interoperability. Inf Technol Control 36(4)

[DVN+12]   Domazet D, Veljković D, Nikolić B, Jovev L (2012) Clustering of learning objects for different knowledge levels as an approach to adaptive e-learning based on SCORM AND DITA. In: The third international conference on e-learning (e-Learning-2012), pp 27–28

[F-PDL+11] Fernández-Pampillón A, Domínguez E, Lahoz JM, Romero D, De Armas I, Palmaz S, Arús J (2011) A strategy for the inductive generation of learning objects in low-Tech contexts. In: Proceedings of ECEL, pp 235–245

[GBG+13]   Gallego D, Barra E, Gordillo A, Huecas G (2013) Enhanced recommendations for e-Learning authoring tools based on a proactive context-aware recommender. In: Frontiers in education conference, 2013 IEEE. IEEE, pp 1393–1395

[GJP+06]   Green S, Jones R, Pearson E, Gkatzidou S (2006) Accessibility and adaptability of learning objects: responding to metadata, learning patterns and profiles of needs and preferences. ALT-J 14(1):117–129

[Hol03]   Holden C (2003) From local challenges to a global community: learning repositories and the global learning repositories summit. The Academic ADL Co-Lab

[HPD+12]   Hendrix M, Protopsaltis A, Dunwell I, de Freitas S, Arnab S, Petridis P, ..., Llanas J (2012) Defining a metadata schema for serious games as learning objects

[Hsu12]   Hsu IC (2012) Intelligent discovery for learning objects using semantic web technologies. J Educ Technol Soc 15(1):298

[IEEE00]   IEEE (2000) IEEE Learning Standards Committee, WG 12: learning object metadata. Available: https://ieee-sa.imeetcentral.com/ltsc/. Last accessed 13 Sept 2017

[Jes13]   Jesse R (2013) Mobile authoring of open educational resources as reusable learning objects. Int Rev Res Open Distrib Learn 14(2):28–52

[KCH+90]   Kang K, Cohen S, Hess J, Novak W, Peterson S (1990) Feature-Oriented Domain Analysis (FODA) feasibility study. TR CMU/SEI-90-TR-21, Software Engineering Institute, Carnegie Mellon University, November 1990

[KFN+13]   Kawase R, Fisichella M, Niemann K, Pitsilis V, Vidalis A, Holtkamp P, Nunes B (2013) Openscout: harvesting business and management learning objects from the web of data. In: Proceedings of the 22nd international conference on World Wide Web. ACM, pp 445–450

[LBM+04]   Leeder D, Boyle T, Morales R, Wharrad H, Garrud P (2004) To boldly GLO-towards the next generation of Learning Objects. In: E-learn: world conference on e-learning in corporate, government, healthcare, and higher education. Association for the Advancement of Computing in Education (AACE), pp 28–33

[LMS+12]   Limongelli C, Miola A, Sciarrone F, Temperini M (2012) Supporting teachers to retrieve and select learning objects for personalized courses in the Moodle_LS environment. In: Advanced Learning Technologies (ICALT), 2012 I.E. 12th international conference on. IEEE, pp 518–520

[LPO+12]   López VF, de La Prieta F, Ogihara M, Wong DD (2012) A model for multi-label classification and ranking of learning objects. Expert Syst Appl 39(10):8878–8884

[LVO+12]   Lama M, Vidal JC, Otero-García E, Bugarín A, Barro S (2012) Semantic linking of learning object repositories to DBpedia. Educ Technol Soc 15(4):47–61

[MBC09]   Mendonca M, Branco M, Cowan D (2009) SPLOT: software product lines online tools. In: Proceedings of the 24th ACM SIGPLAN conference companion on Object oriented programming systems languages and applications. ACM, pp 761–762

[ND02]   Neven F, Duval E (2002) Reusable learning objects: a survey of LOM-based repositories. In: Proceedings of the tenth ACM international conference on multimedia. ACM, pp 291–294

[NFF+13]   Navarro A, Fernández-Pampillón AM, Fernández-Chamizo C, Fernández-Valmayor A (2013) A meta-relational approach for the definition and management of hybrid learning objects. J Educ Technol Soc 16(4):258

[NGF+12]   Navarro SMB, Graf S, Fabregat R, Méndez NDD (2012) Searching for and positioning of contextualized learning objects. Int Rev Res Open Distrib Learn 13 (5):76–101

[Och11]   Ochoa X (2011) Learnometrics: metrics for learning objects. In: Proceedings of the 1st international conference on learning analytics and knowledge. ACM, pp 1–8

[OOM+12]   Otón S, Ortiz A, de Marcos L, de Dios SM, García A, García E, ..., Barchino R (2012) Developing distributed repositories of learning objects. In: Methodologies, tools and new developments for e-learning. InTech

[PGM+14]   De la Prieta F, Gil AB, Martín AJS, Zato C (2014) Learning object repositories with federated searcher over the cloud. In: Methodologies and intelligent systems for technology enhanced learning. Springer, Cham, pp 93–100

[PHP12]   Pons D, Hilera JR, Pagés C (2012) A set of quality metrics in learning object metadata. In: Proceedings of the 2012 international conference on e-learning, e-business, enterprise information systems, and e-government (Worldcomp 12)

[PT10]   Park JR, Tosaka Y (2010) Metadata creation practices in digital repositories and collections: schemata, selection criteria, and interoperability. Inf Technol Libr 29 (3):104

[QB15]   Qamar S, Bashir SR (2015) Towards the recommendation of highly relevant learning objects to the learners. VAWKUM Trans Comput Sci 5(2):19–23

[ROD15]   Rodríguez PA, Ovalle DA, Duque ND (2015) A student-centered hybrid recommender system to provide relevant learning objects from repositories. In: International conference on learning and collaboration technologies. Springer, Cham, pp 291–300

[RSG10]   Roy D, Sarkar S, Ghose S (2010) A comparative study of learning object metadata, learning material repositories, metadata annotation & an automatic metadata annotation tool. Adv Semant Comput 2(2010):103–126

[RTD+12]   Rodríguez P, Tabares V, Duque N, Ovalle D, Vicari RM (2012) Multi-agent model for searching, recovering, recommendation and evaluation of learning objects from repository federations. In: Ibero-American conference on artificial intelligence. Springer, Berlin, pp 631–640

[ŠB15]   Štuikys V, Burbaitė R (2015) Smart education in CS: a case study. In: Smart learning objects for the smart education in computer science: theory, methodology and robot-based implementation. pp 287–310

[ŠBB14]   Štuikys V, Bespalova K, Burbaitė R (2014) Refactoring of heterogeneous meta-program into k-stage meta-program. Inf Technol Control 43(1):14–27

[ŠBD+16]   Štuikys V, Burbaitė R, Drąsutė V, Bespalova K (2016) Robot-oriented generative learning objects: an agent-based vision. In: Agent and multi-agent systems: technology and applications. Springer, pp 247–257

[SBD13]   Stuikys V, Burbaite R, Damasevicius R (2013) Teaching of computer science topics using meta-programming-based GLOs and LEGO robots. Inf Educ 12(1):125

[ŠD13]   Štuikys V, Damaševičius R (2013) Meta-programming and model-driven meta-program development: principles, processes and techniques, vol 5. Springer

[SM12]   Sabitha AS, Mehrotra D (2012) User centric retrieval of learning objects in LMS. In: Computer and Communication Technology (ICCCT), 2012 third international conference on IEEE, pp 14–19

[SOS+13]   Sicilia MA, Ochoa X, Stoitsis G, Klerkx J (2013) Learning object analytics for collections, repositories & federations. In: Proceedings of the third international conference on learning analytics and knowledge. ACM, pp 285–286

[Štu15]   Štuikys V (2015) Smart learning objects for smart education in computer science. Springer, New York

[SZ13]   Sampson DG, Zervas P (2013) Learning object repositories as knowledge management systems. Knowl Manag E-Learn: Int J (KM&EL) 5(2):117–136

[TBK09]   Thum T, Batory D, Kastner C (2009) Reasoning about edits to feature models. In: Proceedings of the 31st international conference on software engineering. IEEE Computer Society, pp 254–264

[TCB+12]   Teixeira TN, Campos F, Braga R, Santos N, Mattos E (2012) Broad project: semantic search and application of learning objects. IEEE Technol Eng Educ (ITEE) 7 (3):23–32

[TN07]   Taylor Northrup P (2007) Learning objects for instruction: design and evaluation: design and evaluation. IGI Global

[TPB+11]   Tasso S, Pallottelli S, Bastianini R, Lagana A (2011) Federation of distributed and collaborative repositories and its application on science learning objects. Computational Science and Its Applications-ICCSA 2011, pp 466–478

[USB13]   Ullrich C, Shen R, Borau K (2013) Learning from learning objects and their repositories to create sustainable educational app environments. In: Advanced Learning Technologies (ICALT), 2013 I.E. 13th international conference on IEEE, pp 285–287

[VCP+11]   Vian J, Campos RLR, Palomino CEG, Silveira RA (2011) A multiagent model for searching learning objects in heterogeneous set of repositories. In: Advanced Learning Technologies (ICALT), 2011 11th IEEE international conference on IEEE, pp 48–52

[ZMP+11]   Zapata A, Menendez VH, Prieto ME, Romero C (2011) A hybrid recommender method for learning objects. IJCA proceedings on design and evaluation of digital content for education (DEDCE), 1, 1–7

[ZMP+15]   Zapata A, Menéndez VH, Prieto ME, Romero C (2015) Evaluation and selection of group recommendation strategies for collaborative searching of learning objects. Int J Hum-Comput Stud 76:22–23

Chapter 11
A Methodology and Tools for Creating Generative Scenario for STEM

Abstract In this chapter, we discuss the concept of generative scenario for STEM-driven CS education. This chapter introduces a framework and methodology that firstly identifies a generic scenario, and then, using it as a basis, we create a generative scenario for STEM. The generative scenario, in fact, is a tool to derive a concrete scenario on demand. As the generic scenario specification includes multiple aspects (socio-pedagogical, technological, content, etc.) and describes activities that support the entire cycle of educational processes, a variety of concrete scenarios is possible to derive from the generic specification. This process is time-consuming and error-prone, because it is dependent upon a variety of robot tasks. Therefore, the automation of the process, i.e. the creation of the generative scenario, is a relevant solution. To implement the generative scenario, we use heterogeneous meta-programming as generative technology. Structurally, the generative scenario is a system-level meta-program composed of a few meta-generators and generators. To our best knowledge, we have described the scenario specification based on using meta-programming techniques for the first time in the educational literature, though it requires additional efforts and a more thorough research work.

11.1 Introduction

Simply speaking, a learning scenario is a predefined plan on how to sequence and deliver the educational activities for learners. The content of the curriculum pre-determines those activities. Activities also relate to resources, tools and services. In Chap. 2, we have presented a vision for introducing STEM into CS education at school. The use of robotics to teach CS courses predefines our vision. Also in Chap. 2, we have defined four types of scenarios by connecting them with the STEM knowledge that it is possible to gain using robots. However, the main intention was not to discuss scenarios but rather to define the knowledge pieces related to STEM so that we could be able to outline the STEM-driven processes. Therefore, in this chapter, we return to the scenario problem and provide a more extensive discussion.

© Springer International Publishing AG, part of Springer Nature 2018
V. Štuikys, R. Burbaitė, *Smart STEM-Driven Computer Science Education*,
https://doi.org/10.1007/978-3-319-78485-4_11

Despite of the fact that the STEM paradigm exists two decades or so, it still has many challenges and issues imposed by the rapid technological advancements and ever-increasing demand for the economic growth and social well-being. With respect to CS education, those challenges may include (i) motivating and engaging students to participate in STEM-oriented learning [AEM+14, AMG+15, OOS+17] and (ii) integrating STEM-oriented aspects into the CS curriculum [GMB+14, Rob15]. There are also other challenges such as (iii) selecting adequate technological tools, pedagogical methods and activities [DHL+14, Rob15] and (iv) providing students' research and introducing real problem solving to enforce critical and computational thinking, to develop collaborative learning skill for modern work-force market [AEM+14, DGL+14, DHL+14, FMT14, GMB+14, Hol14, MBS15, NLS16, Rob15, SGW16]. We are able to manage those challenges, to some extent, by introducing the relevant scenarios based on using robotics in CS education. Therefore, the well-formed scenario is a big concern for the CS educator. Taking into account the following (the indicated challenges, the enlarged scope of knowl-edge learners needs to learn, the ever-growing technological and functional capabil-ities of educational robotics), the STEM scenarios become largely *not static* but *dynamic entities*. The manual managing of scenarios dynamicity is a big problem. In this chapter, therefore, we introduce the concept of the generative scenario. Its meaning is the same as in case of GLO/SLO or the generative library. The generative scenario is a tool that enables to generate a concrete scenario on demand, depending on the context of the situation.

In our vision, the generative scenario should be developed using some well-formed template, i.e. a generic scenario, perhaps with some adaptation. By the generic scenario, we mean the structure defining activities (socio-pedagogical, technological, content delivery) within the entire cycle of educational processes that were tested and probed elsewhere. We distinguish between two terms (generic and generative) here. Typically, the generic item (component, scenario), when used, does not rely on the tool support. Its managing is manual. On the contrary, the functionality of the generative item relies on using the adequate tool that generates a concrete instance on demand. Note that we have developed a set of generative scenarios specific to the types of tasks relevant to STEM education (e.g. movement programming task, sensor programming task, etc.; for more details, see Tables 13.2 and 13.3 in Chap. 13).

Both, the specification of the generative scenario and processor, are tools to generate the concrete instances for use. As the generic scenario relates to multiple aspects (socio-pedagogical, technological, content, etc.) and describes activities that support the entire cycle of educational processes, a variety of the concrete scenarios is possible to derive from the generic specification. This process is time-consuming and error-prone, because it is dependent upon robot tasks. Therefore, the automation of the process is a relevant solution.

The aim of this chapter is to introduce a framework and methodology that firstly identifies a generic scenario and then, using it as a basis, to build a generative scenario for STEM. The generative scenario, in fact, is a tool to derive a concrete scenario on demand. To implement the generative scenario, we use heterogeneous meta-programming as generative technology. Structurally, the generative scenario is a system-level meta-program composed of a few meta-generators and generators (i.e. meta-program of *Type 4*, see Sect. 5.5, Chap. 5). To our best knowledge, we have described the scenario specification based on using meta-programming techniques for the first time in the educational literature.

The structure of this chapter is as follows. In Sect. 11.2, we discuss the related work and motivate this research. In Sect. 11.3, we describe the basic idea of our approach that contains a conceptual model and framework providing more details on the model. In Sect. 11.4, we provide a process-based vision of our approach with the focus on the development of STEM-driven content and its use in CS education. In Sect. 11.5, we deliver a discussion and summarizing evaluation. Finally, in Sect. 11.6, we provide the conclusion and outline the future work.

11.2 Related Work

This section consists of two parts. **Part A** concerns with analysis of the context of the STEM scenario problem. **Part B** analyses two topics: general issues of STEM scenarios and the problem of the automated creation of those scenarios.

11.2.1 Part A: STEM Context Issues

We define the context to the STEM scenarios using two base terms, i.e. "integrated STEM experiences" and "knowledge transfer". We coined the first from [HPS14] and the second from [NRC12]. In our view, using those terms and some derivatives from them, it is possible to understand the essence of the scenario problem deeper. Indeed, the goal of STEM education is producing of the integrated knowledge for learners and by learners. For integrated STEM, it is important to determine how to help students both build the knowledge in individual disciplines and learn to make connections among them. The foundation of knowledge building and rebuilding is the learner's experience. All new knowledge builds on existing knowledge and involves making connections from previous experiences to the current context [NRC12]. On the other hand, transferring of the knowledge is one of the principal goals of learning in school. It is so, because students should be able to take the knowledge and skills learned in one context and apply them in another. Knowledge transferring, in fact, is about "deeper learning". The report [NRC12] defines *deeper learning* as "the process through which an individual becomes capable of taking what was learned in one situation and applying it to new situations (i.e. transfer)". Deeper learning often involves shared learning and interactions with others in a community that enable the individual to develop an expertise in a particular domain of knowledge and/or performance. The report also distinguishes between *transferable knowledge*, including content knowledge in a domain, and *knowledge of how*, *why and when* to apply this knowledge to answer questions and solve problems. In addition, the report refers to this blend of both knowledge and skills as "21st century competencies". The key conclusion in this regard is:

> The process of deeper learning is essential for the development of 21st century competencies (including both skills and knowledge), and the application of transferable 21st century competencies, in turn, supports the process of deeper learning in a recursive, mutually reinforcing cycle.

Typically, teaching for transfer aims to increase transfer within a discipline. Integrated STEM educational experiences, by design, ask students to engage in the transfer of the disciplinary knowledge and, ideally, enable the students to reliably transfer their knowledge to other areas and activities in the future.

As stated in [HPS14], integrated STEM experiences vary depending on whether they are designed to the target discipline-specific knowledge and skills or to support integration of knowledge across disciplines. In some cases, a context or activity incorporates the knowledge and requires the use of practices from more than one discipline, but students are expected to demonstrate learning gains in only one discipline. In other cases, experiences are designed to help students to advancing in more than one discipline, but students are not expected to demonstrate an ability to make connections across disciplines. In addition, a smaller number of integrated experiences are designed to help students make and demonstrate connections between ideas across disciplines. Depending on the outcomes of interest, an integrated learning experience should take into account of students' knowledge within individual disciplines as well as help them make connections among disciplines, drawing on the disciplinary knowledge they already possess.

A recent NRC report [NRC12] on transfer in the context of learning twenty-first-century skills also formulates the following observation: "there is little research on how to help learners transfer competencies learned in one discipline or topic area to another". The report identifies features of instruction that may support transfer [NRC12]:

- Using multiple and varied representations of concepts and tasks
- Encouraging elaboration, questioning and explanation
- Engaging learners in challenging tasks
- Teaching with examples and cases
- Priming student motivation
- Using formative assessment

Many of these features are present in integrated STEM programs, but research is needed to assess whether and how they support the development of both disciplinary competence and the ability to make connections across disciplines. All these, in our view, have a connection to the STEM scenario problem.

11.2.2 Part B: Educational Scenarios Review

In general, *scenario* is defined as "an account or synopsis of a possible course of action or events" (*www.merriam-webster.com/dictionary/scenario*). *Learning scenario* is defined as "an a priori description of a learning situation, independently of the underlying pedagogical approach. It describes its organization with the goal of ensuring the appropriation of a precise set of knowledge, competences or skills. It may specify roles, activities and required resources, tools and services" (*www.telthesaurus.net/wiki/*). The paper [LP04] proposes a conceptual framework, vocabulary and taxonomy of scenarios and focuses on relationships between activities and resources. This paper also gives some answers to questions linked with such approaches, particularly concerning the resource aggregation paradigm and new reusing strategies. The study [Bou12] provides the definition and analysis of educational scenarios in the context of *Discover the COSMOS*. It includes a template as the guidelines for "The Pedagogy of Inquiry Teaching: Strategies for Developing Inquiry as part of Science Education", as well as two examples of the filled-in template.

The paper [RSG09] deals with the problem on how to automate specifications in creating learning scenarios. One aspect of the problem is to create a catalogue of learning scenarios and technique to facilitate automated retrieval of stored specifications. The proposed technique uses ontology that is useful in the creation and validation of new scenarios as well as in the personalization of learning scenarios or their monitoring. An example of a concrete learning scenario illustrates some relevant concepts supported by this ontology in order to define the scenario in such a way that it could be easy to automate. The paper [Not06] proposes and discusses a typology of scenario methods. There are three "macro" characteristics (goals, design and content) and ten "micro" characteristics within these broad categories. This typology demonstrates the diversity of scenario approaches and the ways and contexts in which they are used, as well as the output they produce.

The study [DO01] focuses on problem-based learning scenarios and considers on how the scenarios used in a 10-week introductory course of a new 4-year undergraduate program in environmental science functioned in terms of the structure and content of the questions they evoked. The results are discussed in relation to the design of scenarios and in relation to students' approaches. The paper [EAJ+10] proposes an approach for personalization of learning scenarios based on two levels. The first one allows the personalization of learning scenarios according to a predefined personalization strategy. The second level enables teachers to select personalization parameters and combine them flexibly to define different personalization strategies according to the specifics of courses. The web service technology constitutes an operational solution for implementing that approach and for the interoperability with other e-Learning personalization systems.

The paper [VP03] presents the system COW (Cooperative Open Workflow) developed in the Trigone laboratory (France) which aims at enacting learning path in learning management systems (LMS). Educational modelling languages (EML) are treated as a common solution to express learning paths in LMS. The COW engine is dedicated for distant learning. The paper compares EML and workflow approach to know how to pass from a pedagogical modelization to a workflow modelization. The paper [BS07] discusses adaptation-oriented learning scenarios, where the full e-Learning cycle (design, publication, use and auditing) is considered. The approach focuses on dynamically generating learning design templates with the support of user modelling, planning and machine learning techniques.

The study [NHS+12] discusses the multiuser immersive learning scenarios that accordingly hold a strong potential for lifelong learning since they can support the acquisition of higher-order skills in a more efficient and attractive way. As existing virtual environments, game development platforms, etc. only partly suit for the proliferation of such scenarios, this study aims at identifying architectures that most effectively support the development of those scenarios. This study also outlines a method for defining and setting up such architectures by using experts and existing literature.

The [LMA+15] describes the efforts of adapting problem-based learning and collaborative problem solving to project-based learning and presents a framework and technology for such an adaptation.

The paper [CMB+15] examines the use of gamification to positively change learners' motivation and engagement. As that requires a deeper knowledge about game design and their impact on collaborative learning (CL), the paper suggests an ontology called OntoGaCLeS to provide a formal systematization of the knowledge about gamification and its correct application. We obtained only a few papers that directly consider STEM-oriented scenarios. The paper [GCV+13], for example, describes the Go-Lab project to motivate and orient students from an early age on to study STEM fields in their future educational path by applying inquiry learning using online labs. This paper presents an inquiry-learning portal where teachers can discover, use and enhance online labs appropriate for their courses and students can acquire scientific methodology skills while doing experiments using the labs.

The paper [KNS+17] states that scenario-based learning "has a positive impact on students' interest in computing, while engaging them in the real-world, multi-disciplinary content". The [KRM16] describes a scenario-based approach for designing educational robotics activities based on using co-creative problem solving. The [Cos14] uses scenario-based learning with robots with the aim to increase students' motivation to learn programming. Essalmi et al. [EAJ+13] highlight that the personalized learning scenarios are one of the most effective personalization strategies in e-Learning.

What is about the automated scenario design? The paper [ZLR+12] proposes an automated scenario generator that creates training scenarios for military purposes. The paper [GBB+12] involves the multi-agent scenario generation framework for simulations in preventive medicine education. [MSB+09] describes the automatic scenario generation through procedural modelling.

In summary, it is possible to state the following: one of the biggest challenges in STEM-driven CS education is the implementation of the most effective learning methods, resources and tools to achieve learning goals. Though there are many possible solutions, the use of educational robotics in schools should be the focus in this regard. Though the provided analysis covers multiple topics and a variety of approaches, there is still a big gap between the current technological capabilities and needs for the improvement of CS education on the STEM paradigm at school. This is especially true in terms of integrating the advanced technology with STEM-driven scenarios aiming at achieving a higher efficiency through systematization, integration and automation. We hope that our approach is able to bring the relevant contribution in this respect.

11.3   Research Tasks and Methodology

The aim of this section is to propose and describe a methodology for designing the STEM-driven *generative scenario* for CS education at secondary school using robots. By the generative scenario, we mean a software tool or system that *generates* a scenario instance for the concrete situation on demand. Further, we use the abbreviation STEM GS (or GS for short). Within the proposed methodology, we consider the following research questions (RQ) or tasks.

RQ1 The development of a *framework* to build GS. That motivates the problem domain and results in selecting the scenario template as an initial data for the remaining tasks.

RQ2 Analysis of the *architectural aspects* of the tool to be developed.

RQ3 The development *of process-based and model-based visions* of the system.

RQ4 Key aspects of theoretical background on which basis we have implemented the design processes.

11.3.1   A Framework for Creating Scenarios

The initial information to start describing the framework is a *structure* of the inquiry-based science education scenario taken from [Bou12, BPT08]. Here, we treat the selected specification as *a typical or generic* because its structure is common for many use cases, though the paper [Bou12] presents it as a *scenario template*. The content of the structure, however, needs to be adapted while used in a concrete situation. We do the same. Firstly, we introduce small structural modifications in the original scenario. We have left the two-level structure unchanged (in Fig. 11.1, we represent it as a *header* and *main part*); however, we have reduced the number of phases from five to four in the *main part* (identified as *phases*, shortly *F1÷F4* in Fig. 11.1). In addition, we have made some changes in the *header*, i.e. excluded the *student roles* because they are the same and combined *expected results* with *curriculum-related objectives*.

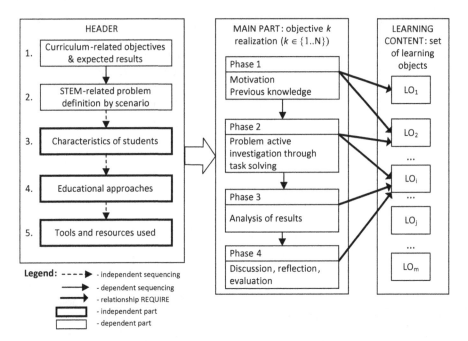

Fig. 11.1 Two-level framework for developing STEM-driven scenarios

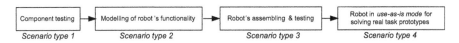

Fig. 11.2 Scenarios types and a possible sequence of their use (taken from Chap. 2)

Therefore, the *header* contains five items and the *main part* four items. The content of items within both parts is entirely specific and oriented to STEM-driven CS education using robotics. The specificity appears in the next process of our framework when we introduce the *scenario types* oriented to STEM-oriented objectives and context. In Fig. 11.2, we present the types of scenarios and a possible sequence of using them within the full cycle of education (meaning the duration of the year or half-year, i.e. semester). The adherence to the indicated sequence is not obligatory. Depending on objectives or other reasons, it is possible to omit some scenarios. However, the presented sequence supports not only problem-based learning but also inquiry-based learning. According to Barell [Bar10], the inquiry is "the driver of complex thinking during the problem solving". This approach depends on the student's previous knowledge to construct the new ones by themselves. Therefore, the indicated sequence promotes the gradual use of knowledge obtained by the previous use of the type of scenarios.

The types, in fact, indicate on the activities and the kinds of tasks without any details. By knowing and using these types, it is possible to focus on a particular portion of knowledge in education of a particular topic on the STEM paradigm. As

"STEM pedagogy is rooted in interdisciplinary application of knowledge" [GA13], from the methodological viewpoint, it is convenient to split the knowledge into the following portions: S-knowledge, T-knowledge, E-knowledge, M-knowledge and integrated knowledge (further for short SK, TK, EK MK and IK adequately). The use of robotics within the STEM paradigm, perhaps, brings the only IK; however, we are able to focus on the only one aspect at a time, depending on the objectives and tasks. This is possible even using the same type of scenario. For example, in case of using the scenario of type 1, students provide scientific experiment (inquiry) aiming at obtaining characteristics of robot's components such as motors (e.g. dependency between the applied voltage (V) and speed (S), or sensors, e.g. sensitivity analysis). The result of the inquiry is the SK. When students need to represent the obtained result formally as a functional relationship, they encounter with MK.

As our aim is automation, we need to analyse the domain aiming at the introduction more details into the framework. In the next section, we analyse the framework from the structural (architectural) viewpoint.

11.3.2 Architectural Aspects

We describe architectural aspects at two levels, i.e. the component and system. The introduced framework (Fig. 11.1), in fact, outlines those levels, though very abstractly. For example, the internal boxes (e.g. in the *header* they are enumerated from 1 to 5) represent the component level, while the large boxes represent the system level. To be more representative, however, the boxes should be described in more detail. Therefore, the aim of this section is to do that. We start with the component level.

11.3.2.1 Component Level

We accept the curriculum-related objectives and expected results (Component 1) as items delivered along with CS teaching topics. In Fig. 11.3, we outline the structure of this component and dependency of its subcomponents. The component consists of a hierarchical set of *attributes*. For example, *Subtopic 2* is the middle-level attribute

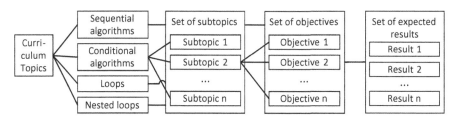

Fig. 11.3 Component 1 representing topics along with objectives and expected results

Fig. 11.4 Student
characteristics model

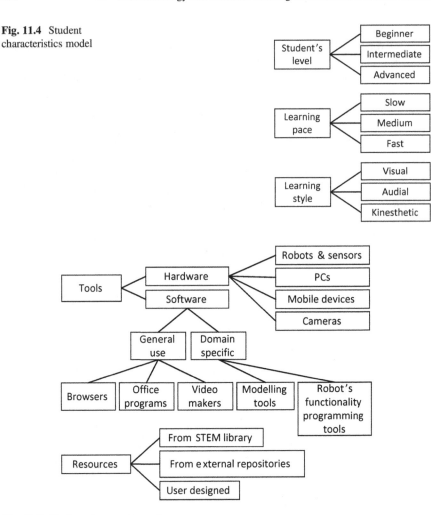

Fig. 11.5 Tools and resources used

of the component *conditional algorithms*, while the *set of expected results* is the lower-level attribute. Attributes have concrete values (they not shown here).

Here, we omit representing Component 2 (i.e. scenario types) in more details because Fig. 11.2, in fact, provides this information. Figure 11.4 explains the structure of Component 3. It has three learner's attributes (*level*, *pace* and *style*), each providing three values (e.g. *beginner*, *intermediate* and *advanced* are the values of the attribute *student's level*). We define the Component 4 (i.e. STEM educational approaches) by the following list: *project-based*, *problem-based*, *inquiry-based*, *design-based* and *others*. The list, in fact, represents the *values* of the attribute *educational approaches*). Finally, the Component 5 (Tools and resources) has many attributes, though we do not show their concrete values in Fig. 11.5. Note

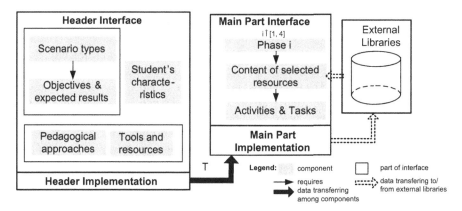

Fig. 11.6 System-level architecture

also that the STEM library contains content resources (i.e. smart learning objects (SLOs), component-based LOs designed by teacher or student) to support the scenarios.

11.3.2.2 System Level

Figure 11.6 outlines the system-level architecture. It includes the three top-level components: *header*, *main part* and *external libraries*. The header and main part, in turn, contain the middle-level components, identified as the *interface* and *implementation* in Fig. 11.6. The interface of each top-level component, in turn, consists of lower-level components. The *header interface* serves for transferring attribute values to other components. There are four transferring streams: (i) among the middle-level components that reside within the *header's interface* and (ii) transferring to the *header's implementation* part (for simplicity, we have not shown them in Fig. 11.6). The remaining transfers are between two top-level components: (iii) transferring T from *header* to *main part* (see Fig. 11.6). We specify the functionality of the *header implementation* in the next section.

The *main part* component has the same structure. It consists of the *main part interface* and *main part implementation*. The first covers all four phases (as defined on the right side in Fig. 11.3). Furthermore, this interface also has the concrete content resources taken from *external libraries* to perform the activities and task according to the selected scenario type. Finally, the third top-level component is the *external libraries*. As the architecture is generic and applicable in the other context, in general, the educational resources can be gained from different sources identified here as *external libraries*. Later we clarify the meaning of the term in our case. Here, the reader should interpret this component as a source of the needed resources for both the *main part interface* and m*ain part implementation*. We provide more details on the *main part implementation* in the next section.

11.3.3 Design Processes to Develop Generative Scenario

The system-level architecture enables us to define the entire functionality. It is convenient to express the latter using the process-based description. We present that vision in Fig. 11.7. The full process is a sequence of subprocesses. We represent the sequence by numbers from 1 to 14. There are *manual* and *automatic* subprocesses. In addition, we categorize subprocesses as the *scenario design* once (sequence 1–9) and the *scenario use mode* (sequence 10–14). The designer creates the *header* and *main part* specifications using the architecture described as a *problem domain* and the PHP language as a *solution domain*. Those specifications are high-level specifications. In fact, from the meta-programming viewpoint, they are *meta-programs* (for definitions, see Sect. 5.5). Therefore, the mode of using PHP differs from its conventional use. We use the language in the role of a meta-language, i.e. PHP functions (*if*, *while*, *read*, *write*, etc.) specify operations that manipulate either on itself constructs or on the constructs of target languages (HTML for representation + MySQL for query in our case). In general, when the PHP specification describes manipulations on the target language constructs, we have a *meta-program*. When the PHP specification describes manipulations on itself constructs, we have a *meta-meta-program*.

For example, the *header* specification developed in this way is the meta-program named as *high-level* one in Fig. 11.7. It sources the generation tool, i.e. the conventional PHP processor (see Fig. 11.7, among 3 and 4). The latter generates the

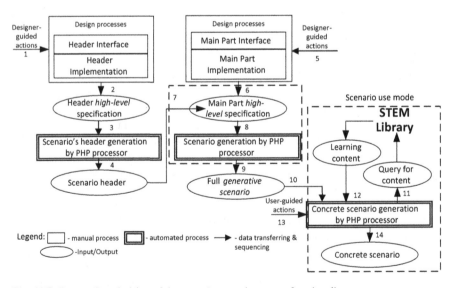

Fig. 11.7 Process-based vision of the *generic* scenario system functionality

scenario *header* automatically. The *generated header* is the HTML file, i.e. a target language program. Similarly, the designer develops the *main part* specification. However, it is a meta-meta-program because, additionally, it specifies operations on PHP constructs. In addition, this specification has the PHP function describing the inclusion of the previously generated file (this indicated by the bold arrow). Next, the main part specification, during its processing by the PHP processor again (see Fig. 11.7, among 8 and 9), inserts the *header* file and provides the aggregation of both files. Then, the PHP processor along with the aggregated file stands for the generator to produce the full specification. It is the meta-program, i.e. an executable specification named *generative scenario*. Here, by the generic scenario, we mean the aggregated parameterized specification ready for use. At this point the development process of the tools is over (here we neglect possible feedbacks needed, e.g. for testing).

Before using, the generative scenario has to pass the third-generation phase (among 13 and 14) in order to create a *concrete scenario* for a concrete situation and setting to support CS STEM-driven education. This process represents the scenario *use mode*, in which the library resources are included. The mechanism to do that is the same as in case of the *header* file inclusion, i.e. a dedicated function within the. generative scenario specification indicates on the link to the library resources. Here, by the library, we mean the personal generative library (see Chap. 10) adopted for STEM needs, where the content is represented in two forms: (i) as component-based learning objects (LOs; they may be also taken from external repositories) and as smart LOs (SLOs), meaning generative LOs adopted for STEM-driven CS course.

Therefore, we have discussed two processes: (1) the process for the development of tools that creates the generative scenario and (2) the process of using the developed tools to create the scenario instance on demand semiautomatically. Therefore, in our case, by the scenario (instance) development *tools*, we mean the generative scenario specification (it is a meta-program and, therefore, a tool because it generates other programs) and conventional PHP processor (compiler).

Before describing the methods and theoretical background used in developing the system, we need to introduce the model-based vision to represent the processes and the system itself. Due to the complexity issues, however, we are able to do that only fragmentally. We have selected the fragment that specifies the *header interface* (see Fig. 11.8). Typically, the model representation relies on the use of a specific notion and terms. We use the graphical notion whose semantics we explain in the **Legend**.

The model is hierarchical because of hierarchical relationships (*requires*). The data transfer specifies the attribute value transfer from the interface part to the implementation part. We represent the latter by a set of *attribute-function* relationships. Here, by the function, we mean a meta-language function. By the attribute-function relationship, we mean the attribute as a parameter of the function.

11.4   Methods Used

In this section, we outline the methods used to develop the generative scenario. We provide this description without details. Reasons in doing so are the three. Firstly, the essence of the background is the same as presented in previous chapters (see Chaps. 5, 7 and 10). We remind that here. At the conceptual level, the background includes the following stages:

(i)   Defining of the problem domain (PD)
(ii) Development of feature models for this domain
(iii) Transformation of feature models within PD
(iv) Defining of the solution domain (SD) feature models, i.e. meta-programming
(v)   Mapping of PD models onto SD models
(vi) Development of the executable meta-specifications

Secondly, the generative scenario as *the design object* is far more complex as compared to GLO/SLO discussed in Chap. 7 or STEM library components discussed in Chap. 10. Finally, the *Model 2* considered in Chap. 7 (see Figs. 7.5 and 7.6) has the *context components* that, in fact, are the same components within the generative scenario, though they are presented in the other form, i.e. as separate distributed components there (compare Fig. 11.8 and Fig. 7.6).

Note that, at the conceptual level (see stages (i–vi) above), the model-driven design methodology is independent upon the design object; however, at the implementation level for different design objects, the content of design stages differs significantly. This depends on the problem domain-specific attributes and the need to interpret them specifically. Specific attributes may include, for example, specific requirements, the list of concepts, relationships among the concepts and the mode of their separation, complexity and specificity of the design object. The mode of using approaches of the solution domain, i.e. meta-programming in our case, also may differ. For example, for implementing the PGL components, we have used meta-

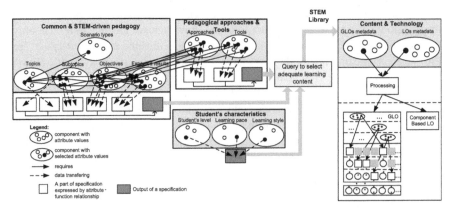

Fig. 11.8 A structural hierarchical model to specify the generative scenario

programs of *Type 1*. For implementing GLOs/SLOs, we have used meta-programs of *Type 1* and *Type 2* (see Sect. 5.5 and Chap. 7). For implementing generative scenario, we have used meta-programs of *Type 1*, *Type 3* and *Type 4*. The structure of generative scenario is quite different. It contains a hierarchical interface with specific interface links to transfer feature (parameter) values from the higher level to the lower level.

Now let us return to *Model 1* and *Model 2* introduced in Chap. 6 (see Sect. 6.3) and discussed in Chap. 7. Both represent the vision on how to design the generative content, i.e. GLO/SLO. What is the relationship between the *generative content* and scenario? In *Model 1*, the content specification also integrates *scenario*. It appears within the interface as a *prioritized sequence* of parameters. Not all activities are explicit. We represent the most important activities by explicit parameter values that have the highest priority such as of pedagogical and social-related ones. The remaining activities, e.g. the teacher's support, resource search, etc., are implicit. Furthermore, this scenario is an *internal simplified entity*. In *Model 2*, the generative scenario is the *external system*. When operating, it integrates much more learning activities, including those that require linking with the needed content (generative or component-based that reside in the STEM library). Therefore, the *generative scenario* and *Model 2* are the products developed to support STEM-driven CS education. What are capabilities of this approach, in terms of generative scenario and *Model 2*, one can learn from the next section.

11.5   Discussion and Summarizing Evaluation

In Table 11.1, we compare *Model 1* and *Model 2* (see Fig. 6.1, in Sect. 6.3) by metrics defined in [MBC09] and obtained using the tool SPLOT. Therefore, it is possible to conclude that *Model 2* (i) has much more features and (ii) the *variability space* of this model (expressed through the number of valid configurations) is much larger (this space is larger from 3 to 300 times, depending on the task).

With regard to the pedagogical evaluation (see Table 11.2), *Model 2* covers much more *cognitive process dimensions* as well as *knowledge dimensions* explicitly as compared to *Model 1*. Therefore, *Model 2* brings higher level of *metacognition*, especially in *evaluating* and *creating* cognitive processes.

We have proposed a hierarchical architecture that specifies the structure and functionality of the generic STEM-driven scenario. We have developed the architecture using the known generic scenario, which we have adapted for the needs of STEM education taking into account the possibilities of educational robotics. We have implemented the scenario specification using meta-programming approaches. At the top level, we represent the specification of the architecture as a *meta-meta-program*. The latter enables to generate the other meta-programs from which it is already possible to derive an instance of the scenario for the concrete use case. The generated meta-program, in turn, may have multiple links to external resources such as the personal STEM library or open content repositories. The STEM library

Table 11.1 Technological juxtaposition of *Model 1* and *Model 2* (see Fig. 6.1) at feature model level

| No. | Model metrics [MBC09] | GLOs (*Model 1*) [Bur14] | | | | | | | Scenario header part (*Model 2*) |
		Robot calibration	Line Follower	Ornaments design	Scrolling text on LCD	Light follower	Traffic light	Scenario header part (*Model 2*)
1.	# Features	38	44	51	27	41	44	87
2.	# Mandatory features	11	10	15	7	10	12	6
3.	# Core features	15	14	20	8	11	14	7
4.	# XOR groups	8	8	11	5	7	8	8
5.	# OR groups	1	1	2	2	1	2	14
6.	# Cross-tree constraints	18	12	21	12	7	14	0
7.	CTCR, %[a]	0.53	0.57	0.43	0.63	0.24	0.39	0
8.	Tree depth	3	3	3	3	3	5	4
9.	Valid configurations	1296	8640	62,208	1440	87,480	97,200	317,520
10.	Variability degree, %[b]	4.7148 E-7	4.9113 E-8	2.7626 E-9	1.0729 E-3	3.9781 E-6	5.5252 E-7	2.0519 E-21

[a]CTCR – constraints representativeness, number of variables in the CTC divided by the number of features in the feature diagram
[b]Variability degree is the number of valid configurations divided by 2^n, where n is a number of features in the model

Table 11.2 Comparison of *Model 1* (M1) and *Model 2* (M2) according to revised Bloom's taxonomy [AK01]

Cognitive process dimension		Knowledge dimension			
		Factual	Conceptual	Procedural	Meta-cognitive
Remembering	M1	E	I	I	I
	M2	E	E	E	E
Understanding	M1	E	I	I	I
	M2	E	E	E	E
Applying	M1	E	E	I	I
	M2	E	E	E	E
Analysing	M1	I	I	I	I
	M2	E	E	E	E
Evaluating	M1	I	I	I	N
	M2	E	E	E	E
Creating	M1	I	I	I	N
	M2	E	E	E	E

E expressed explicitly, *I* expressed implicitly, *N* no support

contains educational resources of two types (components, i.e. learning objects such as tutorials, quizzes and robot control programs represented as smart generative learning objects [Štu15]); however, here we were able to present the library as a black box only. Smart learning objects are also meta-programs realized by the same meta-language as the generic scenario itself. Therefore, the system is a set of distributed components, i.e. instances and smart generative components, managed by the top-level component that is by the meta-meta-program. When used, the system (i.e. the generic specification along with the meta-language processor) provides a multiphase user-guided process that generates the concrete scenario instances on demand semiautomatically to support STEM-driven computer science education based on using robots. Due to the diversity of STEM tasks, which require different pedagogical approaches, due to the diversity of choices for selecting individual learning paths and due to the diversity of content and its dependency on the context of use, the space of possible concrete scenarios is indeed huge. It would be impossible to perform a flexible and effective management of those scenarios without means of automation.

Our system does automation and ensures the effective management by the rapid redesign in creating scenarios. The user-friendly interfaces, the predesigned content and capabilities of meta-programming ensure that. Note that this system requires of using the system-level meta-programming. It represents a novel approach. As we use the general-purpose language processor (PHP in our case), there is no need to devise a specialized scenario generation tools. Furthermore, it can be integrated in any educational environment without efforts. The tool (the developed system), therefore, is highly applicable. However, its efficacy is dependent upon the use of the STEM library. The latter is domain-specific, i.e. oriented to the use of robots. If one wants to rely on external repositories for finding the relevant content, the usefulness of the tool will drop.

11.6   Conclusion

A concrete scenario is the objective-task dependent and, therefore, the STEM knowledge dependent. The choice of a task within the scenario enables to support gaining either the concrete STEM knowledge (in engineering, in science) or the integrated knowledge. Therefore, we need to create a set of scenarios in order to fulfil learning objectives. Our system ensures that semiautomatically under the guidance of the user. From the methodological viewpoint, learners are able to create multiple learning paths and regenerate them if some trial was not successful. With respect to automation capabilities, by using the tool, we are able to close the gap between the STEM library (meaning a generative multifunctional content) and efficacy in using this content in the real educational setting to educate CS using the STEM paradigm.

Though we have tested the generative scenario (as a tool to design concrete scenarios) in the real setting providing real activities for STEM-driven learning, we have yet accumulated a little amount of experimental data to reason about the effectiveness of the tool in a wider perspective. Therefore, we need to provide a more extensive research in both aspects, theoretical (i.e. modelling and system-level programming) and practical.

References

[AEM+14]   Arshavsky N, Edmunds J, Mooney K, Thrift B, Wynn L, Center S, Samonte K, Janda L (2014) Race to the Top STEM affinity network, 2014

[AMG+15]   Ardies J, De Maeyer S, Gijbels D, van Keulen H (2015) Students attitudes towards technology. Int J Technol Des Educ 25(1):43–65

[AK01]   Anderson LW, Krathwohl DR (2001) A taxonomy for learning, teaching, and assessing: a revision of Bloom's taxonomy of educational objectives. Longman, New York

[Bar10]   Barell J (2010) Problem-based learning: the foundation for 21st century skills. In: Bellanca J, Brandt R (eds) 21st century skills: rethinking how students learn. Solution Tree Press, Bloomington, pp 175–199

[Bou12]   Boudalis A (2012) Implementation scenarios definition and analysis. Discover the COSMOS deliverable

[BPT08]   Bybee RW, Powell JC, Trowbridge LW (2008) Teaching secondary school science –
            strategies for developing Scientific literacy, 9th edn, Pearson, Columbus OH 2008, pp
            60–64

[BS07]   Boticario JG, Santos OC (2007) A dynamic assistance approach to support the
            development and modelling of adaptive learning scenarios based on educational
            standards. In: Fifth international workshop on authoring of adaptive and adaptable
            hypermedia. International conference on user modeling

[Bur14]   Burbaitė R (2014) Advanced generative learning objects in informatics education: the
            concept, models and implementation. Summary of doctoral dissertation, physical
            sciences, informatics (09P), Kaunas University of Technology, Kaunas

[CMB+15]   Challco GC, Mizoguchi R, Bittencourt II, Isotani S (2015) Steps towards the
            gamification of collaborative learning scenarios supported by ontologies. In: Interna-
            tional conference on artificial intelligence in education. Springer International Publish-
            ing, pp 554–557

[Cos14]   Costa JM (2014) Using a scenario-based learning with robots to increase the program-
            ming interest. In: Proceedings of the second international conference on technological
            ecosystems for enhancing multiculturality. ACM, p 133–138

[DGL+14]   Dutta-Moscato J, Gopalakrishnan V, Lotze MT, Becich MJ (2014) Creating a pipeline
            of talent for informatics: STEM initiative for high school students in computer science,
            biology, and biomedical informatics. J Pathol Inf 5:2014

[DHL+14]   Duran M, Höft M, Lawson DB, Medjahed B, Orady EA (2014) Urban high school
            students'; IT/STEM learning: findings from a collaborative inquiry-and design-based
            afterschool program. J Sci Educ Technol 23(1):116–137

[DO01]   Dahlgren MA, Öberg G (2001) Questioning to learn and learning to question: structure
            and function of problem-based learning scenarios in environmental science education.
            High Educ 41(3):263–282

[EAJ+10]   Essalmi F, Ayed LJB, Jemni M, Graf S (2010) A fully personalization strategy of
            E-learning scenarios. Comput Hum Behav 26(4):581–591

[EAJ+13]   Essalmi F, Ayed LJB, Jemni M, Graf S (2013) Automating the E-learning personal-
            ization. In: Human-computer interaction and knowledge discovery in complex,
            unstructured, big data. Springer, Berlin, pp 342–349

[FMT14]   Freeman B, Marginson S, Tytler R (2014) Widening and deepening the STEM effect,
            The Age of STEM: educational policy and practice across the world in Science,
            Technology, Engineering and Mathematics, 2014, p 1

[GA13]   Gomez A, Albrecht B (2013) True stem education. Technol Eng Teach 73(4):8–16

[GBB+12]   Gupta M, Bertrand JW, Babu SV, Polgreen P, Segre AM (2012) An evolving multi-
            agent scenario generation framework for simulations in preventive medicine education.
            In: Proceedings of the 2nd ACM SIGHIT international health informatics symposium.
            ACM, pp 237–246

[GCV+13]   Govaerts S, Cao Y, Vozniuk A, Holzer A, Zutin DG, Ruiz ESC, ..., Tsourlidaki E
            (2013) Towards an online lab portal for inquiry-based stem learning at school. In:
            International conference on web-based learning. Springer, Berlin, pp 244–253

[GMB+14]   Gamse BC, Martinez A, Bozzi L, Didriksen H (2014) Defining a research agenda for
            STEM corps: working white paper. Abt Associates, Cambridge, MA. 2014

[Hol14]   Holmquist S (2014) A multi-case study of student interactions with educational robots
            and impact on Science, Technology, Engineering, and Math (STEM) learning and
            attitudes, 2014

[HPS14]   Honey M, Pearson G, Schweingruber H (eds) (2014) STEM integration in K-12
            education: status, prospects, and agenda for research. The National Academies Press,
            Washington, DC. www.nap.edu

[KNS+17] Kerven D, Nagel K, Smith S, Abraham S, Young L (2017) Scenario-based inquiry for engagement in general education computing. In: Proceedings of the 2017 ACM SIGCSE technical symposium on Computer Science Education. ACM, pp 303–308

[KRM16] Komis V, Romero M, Misirli A (2016) A scenario-based approach for designing educational robotics activities for co-creative problem solving. In: International conference EduRobotics 2016. Springer, Cham, pp 158–169

[LMA+15] Luckin R, Mavrikis M, Avramides K, Cukurova M (2015) Analysing project based learning scenarios to inform the design of learning analytics: learning from related concepts. Intelligent support in exploratory and open-ended learning environments learning analytics for project based and experiential learning scenarios, 25

[LP04] Lejeune A, Pernin JP (2004) A taxonomy for scenario-based engineering. In: CELDA. pp 249–256

[MBC09] Mendonca M, Branco M, Cowan D (2009) SPLOT: software product lines online tools. In: Proceedings of the 24th ACM SIGPLAN conference companion on Object oriented programming systems languages and applications. ACM, pp 761–762

[MBS15] Mentzer N, Becker K, Sutton M (2015) Engineering design thinking: high school students' performance and knowledge. J Eng Educ 104(4):417–432

[MSB+09] Martin G, Schatz S, Bowers C, Hughes CE, Fowlkes J, Nicholson D (2009) Automatic scenario generation through procedural modeling for scenario-based training. In: Proceedings of the human factors and ergonomics society annual meeting (Vol. 53, No. 26). SAGE Publications, pp 1949–1953

[NHS+12] Nadolski RJ, Hummel HG, Slootmaker A, Van der Vegt W (2012) Architectures for developing multiuser, immersive learning scenarios. Simul Gaming 1046878112443323

[NLS16] Nelson TH, Lesseig K, Slavit D (2016) Making Sense of "STEM Education" in K-12 Context. NARST International Conference Baltimore (USA)

[Not06] Van Notten P (2006) Scenario development: a typology of approaches. Think scenario, rethink education. OECD Publishing, Paris, pp 69–84

[NRC12] National Research Council (2012) Education for life and work: developing transferable knowledge and skills in the 21st century. The National Academies Press, Washington, DC

[OOS+17] Ohkuma K, Osogami M, Shiori N, Sugihara K (2017) Motivation effects of using actual robots controlled by the scratch programming language in introductory programming courses. Int J Eng Educ 33(2A):575–587

[Rob15] Robertson C (2015) Restructuring high school science curriculum: a program evaluation, 2015

[RSG09] Rius À, Sicilia MA, García-Barriocanal E (2009) An ontology to automate learning scenarios? An approach to its knowledge domain. Int J Doctoral Stud 4:151–165

[SGW16] Sochacka NW, Guyotte K, Walther J (2016) Learning together: a collaborative autoethnographic exploration of STEAM (STEM+ the arts) education. J Eng Educ 105(1):15–42

[Štu15] Štuikys V (2015) Smart learning objects for smart education in computer science. Springer, New York

[VP03] Vantroys T, Peter Y (2003) COW, a flexible platform for the enactment of learning scenarios. In: International conference on collaboration and technology. Springer, Berlin, pp 168–182

[ZLR+12] Zook A, Lee-Urban S, Riedl MO, Holden HK, Sottilare RA, Brawner KW (2012) Automated scenario generation: toward tailored and optimized military training in virtual environments. In: Proceedings of the international conference on the foundations of digital games. ACM, pp 164–171

Chapter 12
Smart STEM-Driven Educational Environment for CS Education: A Case Study

Abstract In this chapter, we firstly discuss some aspects of known smart educational environments (SEEs). Those aspects include a framework in creating SEEs, as well as the architectural and functional aspects. Knowing that, we introduce our SEE. One should treat it as a case study connected to our vision for STEM-driven CS education. We present the architecture and functionality of this SEE. The architecture integrates all smart components discussed so far, i.e. generative (smart) learning objects (GLOs/SLOs), generative scenario and personal generative libraries, educational robot-based workplaces and additional entities, such as knowledge base, to support managing of the whole system. We describe the functionality of the SEE by the communicating processes among indicated components. We also provide an evaluation through the juxtaposition of qualitative features proposed by Hwang and those of our system.

12.1 Introduction

First, we define the term "smart educational environment". There are *standard* educational environments that use the Internet-based technology along with some e-Learning-oriented systems such as Moodle. Typically, the word "environment" means the overall infrastructure, i.e. technological support (hardware, software and networking with remote terminals) and the methodological support, including databases or digital libraries with the teaching content, management facilities and teaching instructions (for teachers and students) to support e-Learning. Human beings working within the infrastructure, i.e. students, teachers and technical or methodological personnel ensuring the maintenance procedures, either are components of the environment too or could be viewed as the components. In a *narrow sense*, by the educational environment, we mean the facilities that ensure the functionality of e-Learning processes to achieve teaching goals within the teaching organization.

© Springer International Publishing AG, part of Springer Nature 2018   279
V. Štuikys, R. Burbaitė, *Smart STEM-Driven Computer Science Education*,
https://doi.org/10.1007/978-3-319-78485-4_12

Nowadays we use the word "smart" very often in a spoken language as well as the scientific term. In previous chapters, we have used it multiple times (e.g. smart learning object, smart learning scenario and smart education). Though there is a slightly different understanding of the term (see, e.g. the papers [BEK+14, GSK16]), the word "smart", as applied to some object, means the extended functional capabilities of the object through applying an advanced technology such as knowledge-based, automation-based, etc. As technology advances extremely rapidly, the object to which we add the property "smart" evolves towards a higher-level of "smartness". Therefore, Brusilovsky et al. [BEK+14] introduce the term "level of smartness" (see also Chap. 6).

According to Hwang, a smart learning environment means "a technology-enhanced learning system that is capable of advising learners to learn in the real-world with access to the digital world resources" [Hwa14]. On the other hand, however, Hwang extends that by saying: "It is more than merely incorporating an intelligent tutoring system into a context-aware ubiquitous learning environment. There are several features that make such an innovative notion of learning go beyond the combination of the two" [Hwa14]. Koper [Kop14] defines smart learning environments "as physical environments that are enriched with digital, context-aware and adaptive devices, to promote better and faster learning".

In Chap. 6, we have discussed the evolution curve of meta-programming-based generative learning objects (from a simple model to the smart model). Similarly, educational environments evolve too. Previously (see Chapter 12 in the book [Štu15]), we have defined the smart educational environment (SEE) as the infrastructure containing "smart" educational robotic facilities, smart learning objects integrated along with standard computing facilities.

In the context of this book, the term SEE means much more: we have extended the level of smartness significantly. We have done that in all dimensions, i.e. pedagogy, content and technology. In terms of pedagogy, we have integrated new STEM-driven educational models such as inquiry-based. In terms of content, we have integrated the generative scenario (Chap. 11) with smart LOs (SLOs) and implemented personal generative library (PGL) (Chap. 10). In terms of technology, we have introduced the knowledge-based module within the infrastructure and extended the physical environments of educational robotics.

The aim of this chapter is to analyse SEEs and present the STEM-driven robot-based SEE as a case study to support smart STEM-driven CS education at a high school. The structure of this chapter includes the following topics. In Sect. 12.2, we analyse the related work. In Sect. 12.3, we outline a framework in creating SEEs. In Sect. 12.4, we discuss the architectural and functional aspects of SEEs. In Sect. 12.5, we present main features of the STEM-driven SEE for CS education. In Sect. 12.6, we summarize and evaluate our project. In Sect. 12.7, we provide discussion and conclusion and indicate on how the proposal might evolve.

12.2 Related Work

We categorize the related work into three streams, though they are interrelated: (A) robotics for education, (B) STEM and computer science (CS) education and (C) smart environments to teach CS.

Stream A Robotics is an exciting multidisciplinary area that is going to dominate in the twenty-first century. The robotics industry is entering a new period of rapid growth [SS12]. The paper [IFR12] indicates that the year 2011 was the most successful year for industrial robots since 1961. The current high school and university students will live in a highly technologized society surrounded by industrial and service robots at work, educational robots at educational institutions, assistive robots at hospitals and care facilities and domestic/entertainment robots at home. With a continuous expanding of the digital world and robotics, the educational priorities must shift towards teaching students how to manipulate all digital devices (computers, robots, smart TVs, high-tech gadgets, etc.) that surround them for their own needs [Ben12, Bri11].

On the other hand, one can view robots as specialized computers with both computing and mechanical facilities to perform physical movement-oriented tasks. Robots allow demonstrating the capabilities of electronics technology and providing students with opportunities for project-based learning. In the context of e-Learning, robots are increasingly seen as a means for enforcing engagement, excitement and fun in learning, promoting interest in mathematics, engineering and science career [PR04], increasing student achievement scores [BA07], encouraging problem solving [Mau01] and promoting cooperative learning [BCD99].

The study [SB16a] shows that robotics offers a playful and tangible way for children to engage with both T (technology) and E (engineering) concepts during their early childhood years. This study looks at 60 children in prekindergarten through second grade who completed an 8-week robotics curriculum in their classrooms using the KIWI robotics kit combined with a tangible programming language. Children were assessed on their knowledge of foundational robotics and programming concepts upon completion of the curriculum. Results show that beginning in prekindergarten, the children were able to master basic robotics and programming skills, while the older children were able to master increasingly complex concepts using the same robotics kit in the same amount of time.

One population that could benefit from early instruction in computing is students with autism spectrum disorders (ASD). Unfortunately, many individuals with ASD lack the social competencies to navigate a work environment successfully. The paper [SB16] therefore proposes a digital game-based learning intervention for youth with ASD to learn computational thinking and social skills. Dubbed *Virtuoso*, the intervention targets youth with ASD to gain social skills while working together to solve introductory computer programming problems with virtual, programmable robots.

With the advance of technology, new technology-based models of teaching and learning are becoming more popular. Currently learning is being transformed from traditional classroom-centred to education based on using various forms. They include (i) e-Learning-based on web resources and mobile devices (m-learning) [HTK02], (ii) immersive learning in a context-aware ubiquitous learning environment (u-learning) [JJ04]. A context-aware environment able to offer ubiquitous personalized content (i-learning) [KSY11]. The same is with a context-aware system that overlays virtual educational information on the real world based on the learner's location and needs (augmented learning) [Klo08, TKS14].

Stream B In the last two decades, educational robots offer new benefits by implementing the most effective active learning methods and supporting tools for the teaching of science, technology, engineering and mathematics (STEM).

As it is stated in [Ben12], researchers deal with problems of the field such as ones: (a) the use robotics as an educational tool, (b) empirical testing of the effectiveness of robots and (c) defining future perspectives of the use of robots. The paper also summarizes the educational potential of robotics in schools and concludes the following issues. (1) Most of the studies are concentrated in areas related to pure robotics, meaning robot construction, mechatronics and robot programming. (2) There is a predominance of the use of LEGO robots (90%). (3) With regard to the STEM concept, robotics tend to increase the learning achievements, especially in schools; a great deal of applications is "descriptive in nature, based on reports of teachers achieving positive outcomes with individual initiatives".

The other publications consider the following topics. The paper [FP09] discusses a learner-centred robotic enhanced environment based on the constructivist approach and a methodology to involve students in knowledge construction. The paper [CFW +06] presents a simple programming environment AiboConnect for robotics. The paper [Has08] introduces an introductory programming environment based on the use of Lego Mindstorms robots designed for CS learning to program in C++. The paper [CLL+11] focuses on a game-based learning system using robots, which enhances students' learning motivation and effectiveness.

The paper [MSR+14] describes a project that includes single-session workshops using the Thymio-II (a small, self-contained robot designed for young students) and VPL (a graphical software development environment based upon event handling). The aim was to investigate if the students could learn core CS concepts while enjoying themselves in the robotics context. The authors have developed a visual questionnaire based upon the combined Bloom and SOLO taxonomies, although it proved difficult to construct a questionnaire appropriate for young students. The findings are all, but the youngest students achieved the cognitive level of unistructural understanding, while some students achieved higher levels of unistructural applying and Multistructural Understanding and Applying.

The paper [IDD14] discusses gamification in non-game settings to engage participants and encourage desired behaviours. This study evaluated the learning effectiveness and engagement appeal of a gamified learning activity targeted at the learning of the programming language C. The results of the evaluation show positive effects on the engagement of students towards the gamified learning activities and a moderate improvement in learning outcomes. Students reported different motivations for continuing and stopping activities once they completed the mandatory assignment.

The papers [FME+15, MEF+16] describe the project EarSketch developed and conducted at Georgia Institute of Technology (USA). EarSketch is an authentic STEAM (STEM + Arts) environment for teaching and learning programming (i.e. where learners are engaged in authentic practices both in computing and in the aesthetics of music remixing) aimed at increasing and broadening participation in computing. In the EarSketch environment, students write code to manipulate, or remix, musical samples. It is an integrated programming environment, digital audio workstation, curriculum and an audio loop library.

The paper [MZJ+16] describes an interesting project aiming to use projection-augmented reality to add design studio learning models to a classroom for an introductory media computation computer science class. "Students do classwork using an enhanced version of Pythy, a web IDE for Python and Jython that captures the students' work and displays it around the room". Using pairs of projectors and depth cameras, the Microsoft RoomAlive Toolkit constructs a room-scale augmented reality. "The system "pins" students' work to the walls, where teachers and students can see and discuss the work". The authors hope that "by seeing each other's work, the system will foster collaboration and support the creation of STEM learning experiences that encourage creativity, innovation, and help build strong peer learning environments".

The paper [LLV+15] studies STEM education, explores it with the creative and experiential activity and suggests applying STEM education by designing technical toys for the middle school students. This study uses a qualitative approach to carry out teaching integration for STEM education. The implementation of the practical model suggests the possibility in using the integrated approach to STEM education through designing technical toys for middle school students in Vietnam.

Stream C The paper [Gro16] discusses the key characteristics of smart learning and the main challenges that need to overcome in designing smart educational environments to support personalization. This study describes the main characteristics of smart learning (SL) and smart learning environments (SLEs) and sustains the relevance of taking the participation of future users into account during the design process to increase knowledge of the design and the implementation of new pedagogical approaches in SLEs.

According to Boulanger et al. [BSK+15], a new concept of "Education as a Service" is emerging as an approach to deal with the challenges of global and open markets. Educational resources in this approach are made easily accessible to global learners by delivering them as a service. From this perspective, one can expect organizational structures of traditional education and teaching processes to undergo great changes.

The paper [BSK+15] also considers SLE from the perspective of smart learning analytics, i.e. SLE is characterized by the key provision of personalized learning experiences. This study also presents a framework that tracks finer level learning experiences and translates them into opportunities for a custom feedback. It was possible to track the habits of novice programmers in teaching the first-year engineering students, using a prototype version of the scale system. Note that learning analytics is a research area that combines different disciplines such as computer science, statistics, psychology and pedagogy to achieve its intended objectives. The main goals illustrate in creating convenient interventions on learning as well as its environment and the final optimization about learning domain's stakeholders [KE16].

The paper [Pri16] illustrates the key considerations and challenges related to technology integration, policy recommendations and sustainable resources in the context of the Intel initiatives to transform education towards the smart learning environment. The paper states: "Transforming education systems and supporting national competitiveness are challenging, long-term endeavours and require a holistic multidimensional approach. On-going support embedded monitoring and visionary leadership can inform policies, teaching and learning processes and professional development to enable reform efforts that support real change".

The paper [Kop14] presents the definition of SLE (see also Sect. 12.1) aiming to promote "better and faster learning". Taking into account that, this paper presents the idea of Human Learning Interfaces (HLI), i.e. the set of learning-related interaction mechanisms that humans expose to the outside world and can use to control, to stimulate and to facilitate their learning processes. The paper identifies three basic HLIs that represent three distinct types of learning: (i) learning to deal with new situations (*identification*), (ii) learning to behave in a social group (*socialization*) and (iii) learning by creating something (*creation*). As these HLIs involve a change in cognitive representations and behaviour, the provided study enables to identify the conditions for the development of effective smart learning environments (SLEs) and their research agenda.

In the context of Smart City research, the paper [YKS16] considers smart learning and education as key areas. Measuring the effectiveness of smart education depends on measuring the desired learning outcomes. This paper suggests major key features one needs to take into consideration while developing learning the analytics tool to measure and assess any learning outcome. The paper also demonstrates the relationship between smart learning environments, learning outcomes and learning analytics.

This short analysis confirms the prediction that the constructing, testing and using of the robot-based environments are the focus in the case of interdisciplinary-oriented teaching such as STEM. On the other hand, there is a lack of publications about the smart learning environments associated with the use of robots for advanced STEM-driven CS education. Therefore, our research aims at fulfilling this gap to some extent. Therefore, we consider the robot-based smart learning environments in the context of smart CS education along with SLOs as an important area of research.

12.3   A Framework for Creating Smart Educational Environments: Principles and Requirements

The smart educational environment (SEE), if it properly constructed or chosen, helps to achieve learning objectives of smart education. According to [YKS16], SEE is a technology-enhanced learning environment that integrates the criteria and functions of intelligent learning systems and context-aware ubiquitous learning. SEE therefore is for smart learning, while the smart education is the educational system that allows students to learn by using up-to-date technologies, and it enables them to learn at anytime and anywhere through the technologies offered in their SEE [Jan14]. Those capabilities do not come free – one needs to use many efforts and resources. Therefore, constructing the smart environment is not an easy task. It requires the use of a systematic approach. Hwang [Hwa14] indicates three key characteristics inherent to SEE and 13 key features. Those characteristics are:

1. *Context awareness*: the system must be able to provide learning support based on learners' online and real-world status.
2. *Adaptive support*: the system must offer instant and adaptive support to learners based on their individual needs from different perspectives (learning performance, learning behaviours, profiles, personal factors, etc.), as well as the online and real-world contexts in which they are situated.
3. *Adaptive interface*: the system must be able to adapt the interface to the user (ways of presenting information, learning preferences, learning performance, etc.) The user interface can be any mobile device (smartphones, tablet computers, etc.), wearable device (a digital wristwatch) or even ubiquitous computing systems embedded in everyday objects.

A SEE must have the following features [Hwa14]:

  (i) Detect and take into account the real-world contexts.
 (ii) Situate learners in real-world scenarios.
(iii) Adapt learning interfaces for individual learners.
 (iv) Adapt learning tasks for individual learners.
  (v) Provide personalized feedback or guidance.
 (vi) Provide learning guidance or support across disciplines.
(vii) Provide learning guidance or support across contexts.
(viii) Recommend learning tools or strategies.
 (ix) Consider the learners' online learning status. Consider learners' real-world learning status.
  (x) Facilitate both formal and informal learning.
 (xi) Take into account the multiple personal and environmental factors.
(xii) Interact with users via multiple channels.
(xiii) Provide learners with support in advance, across real and virtual contexts.

We will use those features for evaluating our SEE presented in Sect. 12.6.

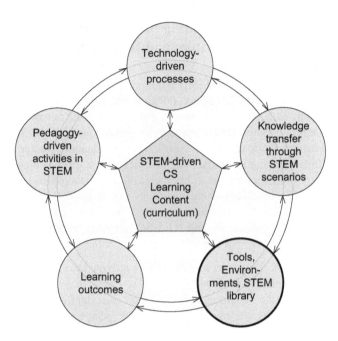

Fig. 12.1 A framework to implement STEM-driven conceptual model in the CS curriculum

Here, we formulate some principles and requirements to construct SEE dedicated to STEM-driven CS education. However, to do that, we first need to know the context. We treat our conceptual model (see Fig. 2.1 in Chap. 2) and the framework to implement the model (see Fig. 2.3 in Chap. 2) as the context to formulate requirements. In Fig. 12.1, we outline the context by introducing our slightly modified conceptual model (see Fig. 2.3 in Chap. 2). In our case, smart LOs are treated as the root of the CS learning and teaching conceptual model. Under the use of adequate tools, it is possible to ensure the interaction of SLOs with pedagogical activities, technological processes, knowledge transfer channels, tools and pedagogical outcomes.

This context has some resemblance to the one described in [ŠB15] (see Chapter 12). Indeed pedagogical activities closely relate to learning objectives, content, teaching model, selection of the tools, formulation of the task and evaluation of the pedagogical outcomes. Technological processes start with choosing the task. Those processes allow creating SLO, but they depend on tools, programming languages and algorithms that cover topics of the course. After the creation or selection of SLOs from the library, the parameters' selecting and content generating processes occur. The user compiles and executes the generated program and performs the control of the task's solution. However, the context we consider in this book has two essential differences. If the driver of processes was SLO in former case, the main driver of the processes is *the scenario* in STEM-driven case. This is the first difference. The second difference is that all processes performed are STEM oriented. Therefore, the knowledge transfer channels connect STEM-driven peda-gogical activities and STEM-driven technological processes (see Chap. 2). The feedbacks among components ensure the flexibility of the content regeneration, modification and knowledge extraction through learning scenarios. The implemen-tation of SEEs goes beyond the application of smart technology. The SEE not only enables learners to access digital resources and interacts with learning systems in any place and at any time, "it also actively provides the necessary learning guidance, hints, supportive tools or learning suggestions in the right place, at the right time and in the right form".

According to Pons et al. ([PCJ15], p. 511), "it is unlikely that developers can come up with systems capable of discovering the user's contextual preferences with a high degree of accuracy in all cases without any input from users themselves. The user's preferences should therefore form the key knowledge to be identified during the initial stages of the configuration."

Now, taking into account the presented context, we are able to formulate the basic principles and requirements to develop the smart learning environment. Those principles and requirements, we have defined on both the approved knowledge (extracted through the thorough literature analysis in the domain) and our practical experience, are as follows:

(a) *Analyse* main components of the smart learning environment (the audience, goals, resources and tools, relationships and networks, training and education, the company and supervisor support aspects [Lom08]).
(b) *Consider* the possibility of incorporating all necessary components.
(c) *Treat* SLO as the obligatory component of the smart learning environment.
(d) *Apply* the verified teaching and learning methods and models [LY11, CAL12, Had09, Sch02, SHL+13].
(e) *Ensure* an individualized learning as much as possible.
(f) *Support* the formal learning activities and active interpersonal connections with respect to the learning context.
(g) *Define* the roles of actors in the ongoing feedback and coaching.
(h) *Use* collaborative technologies and other rapid development techniques [Lom08].
(i) *Identify* priorities of each type of components.
(j) *Identify* specificity of using robotics facilities (including their capabilities for STEM) in creating a smart educational environment
(k) *Use a prototype (if any)* in developing the environment.
(l) *Evaluate* the smart learning environment as a whole using technological [KD09] and pedagogical [KSV04] evaluation criteria.

12.4 Part 1: Architectural and Functional Aspects of STEM-Driven SEE

A Generalized Framework In this section, we discuss the STEM-driven smart learning environment (STEM SLE or SLE for short) as a case study. We have developed this environment to support smart STEM-driven CS education at the high school. We have created this environment not from scratch but using an initial prototype described in [ŠB15] (see Chaps. 12 and 13). The aim of this section is to show the evolutionary process in creating the SLE and to discuss its structural and functional aspects as well as to present some evaluation. The framework we propose in order to make the discussion more systematic includes three parts. In Part 1, we outline the structure and functionality of the prototype. In Part 2, we discuss the current state of SLE, i.e. its architecture, functionality and capabilities. In Part 3, we provide a comparative study to evaluate main characteristics of the SLE in comparison to those taken from the literature.

Part 1: Main Features of the Prototype System We have developed the system in early 2014 to support CS education based on using robots and smart learning objects. Here, we call it the prototype system. The prototype system was also smart in terms of smart tools to develop smart learning objects (SLOs), but its "level of smartness" was low as compared to the newly developed system we discuss in Sect. 12.5. Nevertheless, the prototype has played a significant role in constructing components for the new system. Therefore, we consider the structure and functionality of the prototype below. The prototype includes three interrelated parts: teacher's component, learner's component and server (see Fig. 12.2). The teacher's component (in fact, the teacher's computer) serves as a tool for the development of SLOs. The teacher's computer among other facilities contains both software of general use and specific tools. The software of general use includes the PHP language processor and facilities for communication with the server (see Fig. 12.2). Software of specific use includes feature-based modelling tools (such as FAMILIAR, SPLOT [ACL+13]) and SLO development tools (such as, MePAG, MP-ReTool) [ŠB15].

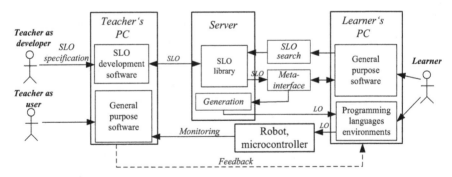

Fig. 12.2 The generalized structure of SEE prototype: a behavioural model [ŠB15]

Note that the SLO design process provided by the teacher and the use process provided by learners are separate processes in time. The teacher applies the model-driven methodology to design SLOs in advance. The methodology results in creating firstly feature models (we have outlined this methodology in the STEM context in Chap. 5). Then those models serve as input information for tools to develop SLOs. The teacher performs transferring of the created SLOs to the SLOs repository located in the server. We install software of general use on the learner's computer to enable to generate the LO according to the user's needs. Moreover, programming language processor that resides in the learner's PC enables to generate an executable specification, i.e. robot control programs for transferring to the educational robot or microcontroller.

Figure 12.2, to some extent, also presents a behavioural model of the previously developed system. Firstly, the CS teacher (acting as a designer) creates the original SLO's specification and transfers it to the local library. The teacher, in the course of using SLO, can modify it according to the accumulated feedback. The design tool MePAG is helpful in this case. Furthermore, the teacher is able to change the internal structure of the initial SLO without changing its functionality using the refactoring tool MP-ReTool. This tool transforms the original SLO specification into the multi-staged format (see Chap. 8). The latter is helpful to provide a semiautomatic adaptation of the SLO to the teacher or learner's context. In fact, this transformation enforces the context awareness of SLOs.

The learner can find the original SLO or transformed (i.e. stage-based one) in the library by using software of general use. He/she selects the values of parameters in the user's meta-interface (SLO interface) and generates learning object (LO) on demand. In fact, the generated LO is a robot control program representing the CS teaching content. Later, the learner uploads it to the robot language environment (typically RobotC, ArduinoC) and creates executable specification and after that transfers it into the robot or a microcontroller. The teacher ensures monitoring and a flexible feedback. Using this simple system as a prototype and adding requirements for STEM, we have developed the indeed advanced system that we call STEM-driven smart educational environment (SEE).

12.5   Part 2: Main Features of the STEM-Driven SEE for CS Education

In this section, we present the architecture and functionality of the STEM-driven smart environment for CS education we use at the high school. We have developed this environment not from scratch but taken into account the structure of the prototype we have outlined in Sect. 12.4 and the experience accumulated by using the prototype in real teaching setting. The development process has taken a few years. We have gradually added new features that needed for the STEM education. One needs to look at the SLO evolution curve, because this environment has evolved

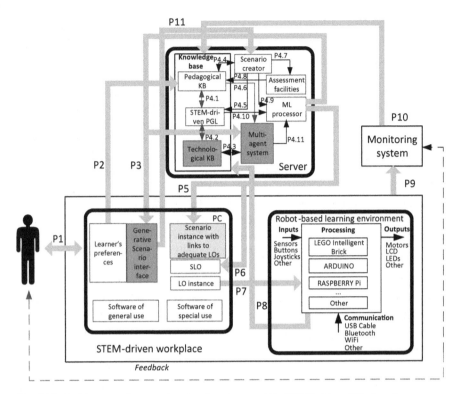

Fig. 12.3 Architecture of smart educational environment for STEM-driven CS education

along with the involvement of SLOs (see Fig. 6.2, in Chap. 6). In Fig. 12.3, we outline the architecture, i.e. the current state of the system (we mean the state of the system at the time of writing the book, i.e. the first half of 2017). In describing the architecture, we focus on communication processes among the external and internal components. There are 11 external processes denoted from P1 to P11. The internal process P4 within the server part contains also 11 subprocesses indicated as P4.1÷P4.11. Here, we do not explain the role and functionality of internal components (with some exception to be discussed later), because we have presented them previously in the adequate chapters in detail.

Note also that each of them is complex entities and, when considered separately, are in fact systems, such as the personal generative library (PGL; see Chap. 10), scenario creator (see Chap. 11) or multi-agent system (see Chap. 9). Figure 12.3 presents the architecture taken into account the only one workplace. In the classroom, there is a set of identical workplaces. Furthermore, we represent the architecture from the user's perspective and focuses on the most common scenario (identified as Scenario *type 4* in Chap. 2) when the robot is functioning and ready to solve a physical task.

Therefore, the SEE consists of two large parts: server part and STEM-driven workplace (WP). The role of server part is to provide two services: tool-based and information-based. The role of STEM-driven WP is to provide facilities to enable smart learning processes. The structure of STEM-driven WP includes two interrelated components, i.e. PC- and robot-based learning environment (RBLE). The user PC serves for communicating with the server part and RBLE. In addition, PC accumulates data resulting from learning processes and then performs data analysis. Therefore, the PC contains the SW of general use and SW of special use. The second component, i.e. RBLE, consists of a set of the possible alternatives to select the adequate robotics facilities, including mechanical parts to construct real things. Those facilities perform four functions: accept data (input), data processing (processing), communication with other components (communication) and output data after processing (output).

12.5.1   Communication Processes: A User Perspective

Below we describe the communication processes P1-P11 from the perspective of *why-what-how* attributes. The *why attribute* specifies the role and intension of the adequate process. The *what attribute* describes INPUT/OUTPUT of the process. The *how attribute* defines by what means, i.e. how we realize the process indicating on tools needed.

P1 ensures the initial communication process "user PC" (*why*); INPUT is an extended user interface; OUTPUTS are processes **P2**, **P7**, **P9** (*what*); communication is ensured through communication protocols, using software tools (both of general and special use) (*how*).

P2 indicates on learner's preferences for transferring data to pedagogical knowledge base (PKB) (*why*); INPUT is a learner's preferences (learner's context); OUTPUT generates queries to PKB (*what*); communication is ensured through communication protocols, using software tools (both of general and special use) (*how*).

P3 ensures the communication between the meta-language (ML) processor and generative scenario interface (*why*); INPUT is **P4.9** and the process initiated by the ML processor; OUTPUT is a generative scenario interface (*what*); again, communication is ensured through communication protocols, using software tools (both of general and special use) (*how*).

P4 is the internal process of the server part. Subprocesses of this process are as follows:

P4.1: Communication *PKB – STEM-driven PGL* (*why*); INPUT-OUTPUT are queries between those components (*what*); server SW tools ensure the communication (*how*).

P4.2: Communication *technological KB – STEM-driven PGL* (*why*); INPUT-OUTPUT are queries between those components (*what*); server SW tools ensure the communication (*how*).

P4.3: Communication *technological KB – multi-agent system* (*why*); INPUT-OUTPUT data transfer between those components (*what*); server SW tools ensure the communication (*how*).

P4.4: Communication *PKB – scenario creator* (*why*); INPUT-OUTPUT are queries between those components (*what*); server SW tools ensure the communication (*how*).

P4.5: Communication *STEM-driven PGL – scenario creator* (*why*); INPUT are parameter values from the generative scenario interface; OUTPUT is the query from the scenario creator (*what*); communication is ensured through communication protocols, using software tools (both of general and special use) plus server SW tools (*how*).

P4.6: Communication *PKB – multi-agent system* (*why*); INPUT are learner's preferences (learner context); OUTPUT are parameter values from PKB (*what*); communications are ensured through communication protocols, using software tools (both of general and special use) plus server SW tools (*how*).

P4.7: Communication *scenario creator – assessment tools* (*why*); INPUT is a set of parameter values from **P11**; OUTPUT is learner's knowledge level (*what*); communications are ensured through communication protocols, using software tools (both of general and special use) plus server SW tools (*how*).

P4.8: Communication *PKB – assessment tools* (*why*); INPUT is learner's knowledge level; OUTPUT are records to be written into PKB (*what*); server SW tools (*how*).

P4.9: Communication *scenario creator – ML processor* (*why*); INPUT is the generative scenario in the form of a meta-program; OUTPUT is a scenario instance derived from the generative scenario. The ML processor performs this generation (derivation) (*what*). Communication is ensured through communication protocols, using software tools (of both general and special use) (*how*).

P4.10: Communication *STEM-driven PGL – ML processor* (*why*). INPUT is PGL as a meta-program (in terms of PGL creation) and as a query from scenario creator-formed links to content resources (SLOs) (in terms of use). OUTPUT is enriched scenario by links to learning resources (*what*). ML processor performs the insertion of links (*how*).

P4.11: Communication *multi-agent system – ML processor* (*why*). INPUT – parameter values recommended by multi-agent system; OUTPUT – LO instance (instances) (*what*); server SW tools ensure the communication (*how*).

P5 is the process between the meta-language (ML) processor and scenario instance with links to the adequate LOs (*why*). INPUT – generative learning scenario as a meta-program; OUTPUT – scenario instance with links to the adequate LOs (*what*). Communication is ensured through communication protocols and using software tools (both of general and special use) plus server SW tools (*how*).

P6 is the generation process and data transferring between ML processor and SLO (*Why*). INPUT – SLO; OUTPUT – generated instance (instances) (*what*). Communication is ensured through communication protocols and using software tools (both of general and special use) plus server SW tools (*how*).

P7 is the process of data transfer between the learning instance (content) and robotic facilities (RF) (*why*). INPUT – generated instance; OUTPUT- task solving in real time (visualization in real time, i.e. the robot stands for physical LO) (*what*). SW of special use and communication protocols (*how*).

P8 is the process between RF and Knowledge Base (KB) (*why*). INPUT – data from the robot's environment; OUTPUT – Records into KB (*what*). SW of special use and communication protocols ensure the communication (*how*).

P9 is the process between the STEM-driven workplace and monitoring system (*why*). INPUT – accumulated data from the STEM-driven workplace; OUTPUT – accumulated data from the monitoring system to form records into KB (*what*). Communication is ensured through communication protocols and using software tools (both of general and special use) plus server SW tools (*how*).

P10 is the process between the monitoring system and server (*why*). INPUT – accumulated data from the monitoring system to form records into the KB. OUTPUT – records of KB (*what*). Communication is ensured through communication protocols and using software tools (both of general and special use) plus server SW tools (*how*).

P11 is the process between the generative scenario interface and scenario creator (*why*). INPUT – a set of scenario parameter values taken by the user; OUTPUT – generative learning scenario in the form of meta-program (*what*). SW of general and special use ensures the communication (*how*).

12.5.2   Structure of the Server Part

The server part is the top-level component that ensures the service of the entire system to make it functioning. This part provides learners with pedagogical and technological data needed to start and support the learning processes over the whole learning cycle. With regard to the previous system (prototype), we have changed this part significantly by adding a set of new components that really made the system smarter. Those components include the scenario creator, assessment tools, multi-agent system and knowledge base. We have significantly extended the local library by adding new features such as automatic generation of query and other supporting procedures, the possibility for each student to have a personal library. Therefore, we now treat the STEM-driven library as a personal generative library (PGL). Furthermore, we have changed the structure of PGL. The STEM-driven library currently has two parts. One part is for creation. The remaining part is within the knowledge base. What we preserved unchanged is the meta-language processor (i.e. PHP compiler), because we use PHP as a meta-language in both cases, i.e. in old (prototype) and new systems.

Therefore, the structure of server part has two functional components, i.e. information-based and operational-based. The first, in fact, is the knowledge base (KB) consisting of pedagogical KB, technological KB and a part of STEM-driven PGL interpreted as content KB. Pedagogical KB is a database that accumulates learner's profile dynamically. The latter consists of two parts: general learning preferences (level, style, pace, etc.) and specific part. The latter includes learning paths, i.e. the processes performed by the learner, the content used, time, sequence of activities, self-assessment, partial assessment, etc.

We have extended the server part with the assessment facilities too. There are two types of the facilities. The first type represents conventional quizzes. The second type represents the so-called assessment lists. There is a set of lists different for each task. A list includes a set of evaluating criteria along with the range of possible values expressed by points. Note that we are able to generate sets of assessment list from some template using meta-programming techniques. Furthermore, each list is a part of the SLO description of a given task.

The architecture of the SEE also contains the monitoring system. Though this system is a separate component within the classroom, we discuss it in the server part. The monitoring system provides facilities for monitoring what is going in the classroom during the learning session in order to react and provide the feedback by the teacher. There are automatic monitoring facilities, such as cameras and teacher's PC. In addition, it is possible to use smart phones by both actors, students and teacher. A student may send messages to the other student or teacher. The teacher has a possibility to block the communication if it does not concern the teaching context. Of course, the teacher provides also a natural observation of the situation and provide the feedback (if any) without using automatic facilities. Typically, the automatic monitoring is more useful when there are four or more learners' groups.

One can learn more on separate components of the server part by reading the previous chapters, i.e. Chap. 9 (about agent-based system), Chap. 10 (about personal generative library (PGL)) and Chap. 11 (about creator of generative scenario).

12.6   Part 3: Evaluation of Smart Educational Environments

In this section, we provide some evaluation of smart educational environment (SEE) we have developed. The evaluation, basically, includes the qualitative aspects. Below we compare the features of the newly developed SEE against the features proposed in [Hwa14]. Next, we outline the technological and pedagogical evaluation of the old and new systems, using the criteria taken from the literature. Furthermore, we provide a comparative study of the influence of SEEs with regard to learning paradigm changes.

Qualitative Evaluation of SEEs with Regard to Other Proposals. As stated previously, there are many features to define the functionality of SEEs. However, it is very difficult to express those features quantitatively because of the lack of adequate measures and relevant measuring methodologies, though there are efforts to evaluate pedagogical and technological aspects of learning environments to some

Table 12.1 Juxtaposition of qualitative features proposed by Hwang and those in our system

#	Required features of SEE according to [Hwa14]	How those features are supported by our new SEE
(i)	Detect and take into account the real-world contexts	Through real-world tasks (prototypes)
		Using smart technologies
(ii)	Situate learners in real-world scenarios	Through tasks solving scenarios
(iii)	Adapt learning interfaces for individual learners	Through management of parameter space for given tasks
(iv)	Adapt learning tasks for individual learners	Through management of parameter space for given tasks
(v)	Provide personalized feedback or guidance	Through communication procedures and personal scenarios
(vi)	Provide learning guidance or support across disciplines	Through scenario creator and concrete scenario produced
(vii)	Provide learning guidance or support across contexts	Through scenario creator and concrete scenario produced
(viii)	Recommend learning tools or strategies	Through scenario creator and concrete scenario produced
(ix)	Consider learners' online learning status consider learners' real-world learning status	Through accumulated data analysis
(x)	Facilitate both formal and informal learning	Through incorporated tools
(xi)	Take into account the multiple personal and environmental factors	Through accumulated data analysis
(xii)	Interact with users via multiple channels	Through a variety of communication protocols and special SW
(xiii)	Provide learners with support in advance, across real and virtual contexts	Through a set of scenarios

extent quantitative [KD09, KSV04]. Furthermore, SEEs are quite different in their structure. Therefore, firstly, we try to evaluate our system qualitatively with regard to the criteria taken from the literature. We have selected a set of features taken from [Hwa14] that are inherent to SEEs. In Table 12.1, we have explained how our system supports the indicated features; however, it is difficult to say to which extent we are able to provide this support. Therefore, this evaluation is indicative on technological capabilities only.

As we have created the new system applying an evolutionary approach by the gradual extending the capabilities of the old system, it is reasonable to evaluate the achieved enhancement in the new system against the qualitative features of the old system.

Qualitative Evaluation of the Developed SEEs Here, we present an evaluation of the quality of the developed environments using the quantitative criteria. We have selected and adapted the quality criteria of technological evaluation taken from [KD09]. Table 12.2 presents those criteria and their values. The rate range is $0 \div 4$ (0, no support; 1, poor support; 2, fair support; 3, good support; 4, excellent support).

Table 12.2 Learning environments' technological evaluation

	Environments	
	Old	New
Criteria	SEE	SEE
Scalability	3	4
Modularity	2–3	3–4
Reasonable performance optimizations	3	4
Robustness and stability	3	2
Reusability and portability	2–3	4
Localizable user interface	4	4
Localization to relevant languages	4	4
Facilities to customize for the educational institution's needs	2–3	3
Automatic adaptation to the individual user's needs	3	3–4
Automatically adapted content	3	3–4
Additive utility function of technological criteria	29–32	34–37

We obtained the figures though continuous monitoring over 5 years (for old SEE) and over 1–2 years (for new system) along with the needed improvements (if any).

In Table 12.3, we present a pedagogical evaluation of both systems. We have adapted the criteria taken from [KSV04].

Finally, we discuss yet another vision to evaluate the educational environments. Namely, we focus on the role of the environments to the learning paradigm change in CS education. With regard to the introduction of STEM into CS education, there are evident signs of the emphasis on the learner-centred learning rather than on teacher-centred learning. Therefore, in Table 12.4, we summarize an evaluation of the created SEEs in relation to this change of learning paradigms. The evaluation criteria are a taken from [HB00, All04].

By analysing and comparing the roles of the teacher (T) and learner (L) in both systems, one can see that the new system better supports the paradigm change, i.e. there are much more features related to learner's personalization.

12.7   Discussion, Summary and Conclusion

Our research has confirmed the importance of using smart educational environments (SEEs) for teaching and education that was known so far in the literature on e-Learning. In this summarizing chapter, we have discussed the vision, the role, the structure and the capabilities of SEEs partially taken from the literature, as well as those capabilities we have integrated and tested into our SEE. There is no a commonly agreed definition on what the *smart* environment means. However, it is possible to exclude the features that are relevant in defining the existing and future smart environments. These features relate to the use of smart technologies in educational   systems   such   as   knowledge-based   for   decision-making,

Table 12.3 Pedagogical evaluation of SEEs

Criteria	Environment	
	Old SEE	New SEE
Knowledge of learning content	Content generated from SLO	Content generated from SLO+ component-based LOs
Knowledge of learning process	Intuitive through selecting parameter values	Activities predefined by scenario
Cognitive learning skills	Scope of gained skills covers only content generated from the SLO and executed by the robot (fragmented skills)	Scope of gained skills covers not only content, but also a variety of tools used, a variety of activities (integrated STEM skills)
Affective learning skills	Motivation of using robot as physical learning object, solving of real-world tasks	Additionally, stronger motivation through a partial assessment (within processes) and a various aspects of the given task (modelling, constructing, programming, etc.); receiving of stimuli due to the use of scenario
Social learning skills	Intuitive communication	More communication and group work using tools
Transfer skills	Narrow possibilities (focus on robot control programs)	Extended possibilities in terms of modelling, designing, programming using inquiry models
Preparatory learning functions	C, A,	C, A,
	M at lower level	M at higher level
Executive learning functions	C, A,	C, A,
	M at lower level	M at higher level
Closing learning functions	C, A,	C, A,
	M at lower level	M at higher level
Learning theory	Constructivism	Plus the focus on inquiry-based learning
Learners' roles	Cp, Cm, I	Cp, Cm, I, mentoring

C cognitive, *A* affective, *M* metacognitive, *Cn* constructivism, *Cp* cooperative, *Cm* competitive, *I* individual

communication-based for ubiquitous learning at any time, representation-based (i.e. visualization, automated adaptation) for better acceptance of knowledge and context-awareness support (i.e. smart things such as sensors, smart phones, smart robots) to name a few. As smart technologies evolve extremely rapidly, so should do smart applications such as SEEs. Therefore, we have proposed and discussed an evolutionary-based vision in dealing with the design and usage of SEEs.

Table 12.4 Evaluation of smart learning environments in respect to the teacher-centred (T) and learner-centred (L) paradigms

Criterion # and name [HB00, All04]	Old SEE	New SEE
1. Teaching goals	**T1** Cover the subject	**T1** Cover STEM subjects
	L1.1 How to use subject	**L1.1** How to use subjects
	L1.2 How to integrate subjects	**L1.2** How to integrate subjects
	L1.3 Core learning objectives: communication and information literacy skills	**L1.3** Core learning objectives: communication and STEM literacy skills
2. Organization of curriculum	**L2** Cohesive program with opportunities to synthesize, practice and develop new ideas and skills	**L2** Extended cohesive program with opportunities to synthesize, practice and develop new ideas and skills
3. How students learn	**T3.1** Listening	**T3.1** Listening
	T3.2 Reading	**T3.2** Reading
	T3.3 Independent learning	**T3.3** Independent learning
	L3.1 Learners construct knowledge by integrating new learning into what they already know	**L3.1** Learners construct *new* knowledge in *a personalized way* by integrating *new items* of learning along with those they already know
	L3.2 Learning is a cognitive and social act	**L3.2** Learning is a cognitive and social act
4. Pedagogy	**L4** Based on the engagement of students	**L4.1** Based on the engagement of students
		L4.2 Based on STEM pedagogy
5. Course delivery	**L5.1** Active learning	**L5.1** Active learning
	L5.3 Collaborative learning	**L5.3** Collaborative learning
	L5.5 Cooperative learning	**L5.4** Community service learning
	L5.6 Self-directed learning	**L5.5** Cooperative learning
	L5.7 Problem-based learning	**L5.6** Self-directed learning
		L5.7 Learning-by-doing methods:
		Consequential
		Side-by-side
		Inquiry-based
		Design-based
		Game-based
		Project-based
		Problem-based

(continued)

Table 12.4 (continued)

Criterion # and name [HB00, All04]	Old SEE	New SEE
6. Faculty role	**L6** Designer of learning environments	**L6** Designer of learning environments
7. Knowledge transmission	**T7** From teacher to learners	**T7** From teacher to learners, *from external sources*
	L7 Learners construct knowledge through gathering and synthesizing information and integrating it with the general skills of inquiry, communication, critical thinking, problem solving	**L7** Learners construct knowledge through gathering and synthesizing information and integrating it with the general skills of inquiry, communication, critical thinking, problem solving, *advice coming from pedagogical KB*
8. Learner's role	**L8** Are actively involved	**L8.1** Are actively involved
		L8.2 *Are engaged in self-adaptation and responsibility*
9. Teacher's role	**L9.1** To be the coach and consultant	**L9.1** To be the coach and consultant
	L9.2 To be the team to evaluate learning together	**L9.2** To be the team to evaluate learning together
10. Context role	**L10** Using the communicating knowledge to address enduring and emerging issues and problems in real-life contexts	**L10** Using the communicating knowledge to address enduring and emerging issues and problems in *advanced* real-life contexts
11. Teaching and assessing	**L11** Are intertwined	**L11.1** Are intertwined
		L11.2 *Self-assessment*
		L11.3 *Accumulated assessment*
12. Assessment's role	**T12** To monitor learning	**T12** To monitor learning
	L12 To promote and diagnose learning	**L12** To promote and diagnose learning
13. Emphasis	**L13** Generating better questions and learning from errors	**L13.1** Generating better questions and learning from errors
		L13.2 *Learning outcomes from inquiry*
		L13.3 *Personalized learning*
14. Focus	**L14** Interdisciplinary learning	**L14** Interdisciplinary *STEM* learning

Over 5 years or so of the intensive research and practice in the field, we have developed two systems called as old (prototype) and new ones here. We have developed the new system (SEE) using the old system as a prototype by introducing continuing extensions and improvements. Those include a few essential features: (i) STEM orientation based on using educational robots, (ii) the use of generic scenario that integrates smart learning objects and other resources, (iii) the capabilities for automation (a variety of supporting tools, including the personal generative library) and (iv) explicit knowledge-based aspects (i.e. pedagogical and technological knowledge base). The gradual enhancements have served for getting the need feedback to provide a smooth integration of advanced features and make functioning of those features to support smart learning on STEM paradigm to educate students in CS.

We have identified that the robot-based SEE due to smart constituents highly extends the *constructivist model* of learning and teaching and fits well for STEM-driven CS education. In addition, this enriched environment supports *collaborative learning* and provides the interdisciplinary aspects of teaching because many considered tasks and the mode of their delivery include the knowledge that directly relates to mechanics, physics, mathematics and computer science. The developed smart environment increases the level of student *engagement in learning* and largely provides the possibility for *personalized learning*. In addition, such the environment develops student abilities to critically analyse and compare a variety different problem-solving algorithms taken from the real world (e.g. line-following algorithms, carrying objects, etc.). From the STEM perspective, applying the inquiry model of teaching contributes to foundations of research and presentation research results.

We have also identified some difficulties to implement the approach in practice in a wider context. The main social barrier is the teacher's determination and the need of changing the mind in using the approach and lack of previous knowledge. We have obtained those features through discussions with other CS teachers providing CS in other schools. The other challenges include (1) the need of the flexible communication infrastructure for groups of mobile robots and (2) the complexity of specifying collaborative behaviour. The future work will focus on the extension of the architecture of the discussed environment with the multi-master/multi-slave model to allow using a larger number of communicating robots for learning at the same time and thus allowing to deliver teaching of more complex CS topics. One can treat the developed environment as the specific architecture of the Internet-of-Things in the context of STEM.

References

[ACL+13]	Acher M, Collet P, Lahire P, France RB (2013) FAMILIAR: a domain-specific language for large scale management of feature models. Sci Comput Program 78 (6):657–681

[All04]   Allen MJ (2004) Publishing assessing academic programs. Anker, Boston

[BA07]   Barker BS, Ansorge J (2007) Robotics as means to increase achievement scores in an informal learning environment. J Res Technol Educ 39(3):229–243

[BCD99]   Beer RD, Chiel HJ, Drushel RF (1999) Using autonomous robotics to teach science and engineering. Commun ACM 42(6):85–92

[BEK+14] Brusilovsky P, Edwards S, Kumar A, Malmi L, Benotti L, Buck D, ... Urquiza J (2014) Increasing adoption of smart learning content for computer science education. In: Proceedings of the working group reports of the 2014 on innovation & technology in computer science education conference. ACM, pp 31–57

[Ben12]   Benitti FBV (2012) Exploring the educational potential of robotics in schools: a systematic review. Comput Educ 58(3):978–988

[Bri11]   Brittain N (2011) IT education remains mired in uncertainty. Computing, 20

[BSK+15] Boulanger D, Seanosky J, Kumar V, Panneerselvam K, Somasundaram TS (2015) Smart learning analytics. In: Chen G, Kumar V, Kinshuk HR, Kong S (eds) Emerging issues in smart learning. Lecture notes in educational technology. Springer, Berlin

[CAL12]   Livingstone DECampos AM, Alvarez-Gonzalez LA, (2012) Analyzing effectiveness of pedagogical scenarios for learning programming a learning path data model. Editor: Ion Mierluş-Mazilu, 51

[CFW+06] Chown E, Foil GT, Work H, Zhuang Y (2006) AiboConnect: a simple programming environment for robotics. In: FLAIRS Conference, pp 192–197

[CLL+11] Chou LD, Liu TC, Li DC, Chen YS, Leong MT, Lee PH, Lin YC (2011) Development of a game-based learning system using toy robots. In: Advanced Learning Technologies (ICALT), 2011 11th IEEE International Conference, pp 202–204

[FME+15] Freeman J, Magerko B, Edwards D, Moore R, McKlin T, Xambo A (2015, August) EarSketch: a STEAM approach to broadening participation in computer science principles. In Research in Equity and Sustained Participation in Engineering, Computing, and Technology (RESPECT), 2015, IEEE, pp 1–2

[FP09]   Frangou S, Papanikolaou KA (2009) On the development of robotic enhanced learning environments. In: Kinshuk DGS, Spector JM, Ifenthaler D (Eds.), Proc. of the IADIS International Conference on Cognition and Exploratory Learning in Digital Age, pp 18–25

[Gro16]   Gros B (2016) The design of smart educational environments. Smart Educ Environ., Springer 3:15

[GSK16]   Giannakos MN, Sampson DG, Kidziński L (2016) Introduction to smart learning analytics: foundations and developments in video-based learning. Smart Educ Environ., Springer 3:12

[Had09]   Hadjerrouit S (2009) Teaching and learning school informatics: a concept-based pedagogical approach. Inform Educ-Int J 8(2):227–250

[Has08]   Hasker RW (2006) An introductory programming environment for LEGO® MindStorms™ robots. In: Proceedings of the 2006 ASCUE Conference

[HB00]   Huba ME, Freed JE (2000) Learner centered assessment on college campuses: shifting the focus from teaching to learning. Community Coll J Res Pract 24(9):759–766

[HTK02]   Houser C, Thornton P, Kluge D (2002) Mobile learning: cell phones and PDAs for education. In: Computers in education, International Conference, IEEE Computer Society, pp 1149–1149

[Hwa14]   Hwang G-J (2014) Definition, framework and research issues of smart learning environments – a context-aware ubiquitous learning perspective. Springer Smart Educ Environ 1:4

[IDD14]   Ibáñez MB, Di-Serio A, Delgado-Kloos C (2014) Gamification for engaging computer science students in learning activities: a case study. IEEE Trans Learn Technol 7 (3):291–301

[IFR12]   International Federation of Robotics (IFR) (2012) World robotics 2012 industrial robots. Executive summary. [Online]. Available http://www.ifr.org/industrial-robots/statistics/

[Jan14]   Jang S (2014) Study on service models of digital textbooks in cloud computing environment for SMART education. Int J U- E-Serv Sci Technol 7(1):73–82

[JJ04]   Jones V, Jo JH (2004) Ubiquitous learning environment: an adaptive teaching system using ubiquitous technology. In: Beyond the comfort zone: Proceedings of the 21st ASCILITE conference, p 474

[KD09]   Kurilovas E, Dagienė V (2009) Multiple criteria comparative evaluation of e-learning systems and components. Informatica 20(4):499–518

[KE16]   Khalil M, Ebner M (2016) What is learning analytics about? A survey of different methods https://arxiv.org/pdf/1606.02878

[Klo08]   Klopfer E (2008) Augmented learning: research and design of mobile educational games. MIT Press, Cambridge, MA

[Kop14]   Koper R (2014) Conditions for effective smart learning environments. Smart Educ Environ 1:5. http://www.slejournal.com/content/1/1/5

[KSV04]   De Kock A, Sleegers P, Voeten MJ (2004) New learning and the classification of learning environments in secondary education. Rev Educ Res 74(2):141–170

[KSY11]   Kim S, Song SM, Yoon YI (2011) Smart learning services based on smart cloud computing. Sensors 11(8):7835–7850

[LLV+15]   Le QX, Le HH, Vu CD, Nguyen NH, Nguyen ATT, Vu NTH (2015) Integrated Science, Technology, Engineering and Mathematics (STEM) Education through active experience of designing technical toys in Vietnamese Schools

[Lom08]   Lombardozzi C (2008) Learning environment design. E-learning guild's leading solutions e-magazine

[LY11]   Lau WW, Yuen AH (2011) Modelling programming performance: beyond the influence of learner characteristics. Comput Educ 57(1):1202–1213

[Mau01]   Mauch E (2001) Using technological innovation to improve the problem-solving skills of middle school students: educators' experiences with the LEGO mindstorms robotic invention system. Clear House 74(4):211–213

[MEF+16]   Moore R, Edwards D, Freeman J, Magerko B, McKlin T, Xambó A (2016) EarSketch: an authentic, STEAM-based approach to computing education. Proceedings of the 2016 American Society for Engineering Education Annual Conference & Expo, New Orleans, Louisiana

[MSR+14]   Magnenat S, Shin J, Riedo F, Siegwart R, Ben-Ari M (2014) Teaching a core CS concept through robotics. In: Proceedings of the 2014 conference on innovation & technology in computer science education, ACM, pp 315–320

[MZJ+16]   MacIntyre B, Zhang D, Jones R, Solomon A, Disalvo E, Guzdial M (2016, March) Using projection AR to add design studio pedagogy to a CS classroom. In Virtual Reality (VR), 2016 IEEE, pp 227–228

[PCJ15]   Pons P, Catala A, Jaen J (2015) Customizing smart environments: a tabletop approach. J Ambient Intell Smart Environ 7(4):511–533

[PR04]   Portsmore M, Rogers C (2004) Bringing engineering to elementary school. J STEM Educ 5(3&4):17–28

[Pri16]   Price JK (2016) Transforming learning for the smart learning environment: lessons learned from the Intel education initiatives. Smart Educ Environ., Springer 2:15

[ŠB15]   Štuikys V, Burbaitė R (2015) Robot-based smart educational environments to teach CS: a case study. In: Štuikys V (ed) Smart educational smart learning objects for the smart education in computer science: theory, methodology and robot-based implementation. Springer, Cham, pp 265–285

[SB16]   Schmidt M, Beck D (2016, June) Computational thinking and social skills in Virtuoso: an immersive, digital game-based learning environment for youth with autism spectrum disorder. In International Conference on Immersive Learning. Springer International Publishing, pp 113–121

[SB16a] Sullivan A, Bers MU (2016) Robotics in the early childhood classroom: learning outcomes from an 8-week robotics curriculum in pre-kindergarten through second grade. Int J Technol Des Educ 26(1):3–20

[Sch02] Schulte C (2002) Towards a pedagogical framework for teaching programming and object-oriented modelling in secondary education. In: Proceedings of SECIII 2002, pp 22–26

[SHL+13] Schäfer A, Holz J, Leonhardt T, Schroeder U, Brauner P, Ziefle M (2013) From boring to scoring–a collaborative serious game for learning and practicing mathematical logic for computer science education. Comput Sci Educ 23(2):87–111

[SS12] Shukla M, Shukla AN (2012) Growth of robotics industry early in 21st century. Int J Comput Eng Res (IJCER) 2(5):1554–1558

[Štu15] Štuikys V (2015) Smart learning objects for smart education in computer science: theory, methodology and robot-based implementation. Springer, Berlin

[TKS14] Tanner P, Karas C, Schofield D (2014) Augmenting a child's reality: using educational tablet technology. J Inf Technol Educ: Innov Pract 13:45–54

[YKS16] Yassine S, Kadry S and Sicilia M-A (2016) Measuring learning outcomes effectively in smart learning environments. Conference: 2016 smart solutions for future cities, Year: 2016, Page 1, https://doi.org/10.1109/SSFC.2016.7447877

Chapter 13
Practice of Smart STEM-Driven CS Education at High School

Abstract This chapter, we focus on a series of case studies that represent a sequenced combination of processes and outcomes of the discussed approach from the perspective of the practical use and value. The aim is to show the functionality, the capabilities and the progress of achievements gained by students in solving real-world tasks (or their prototypes) to support STEM-driven CS education. We have proposed the following methodology to represent the content of this chapter. Firstly, we introduce the CS (i.e. Programming Basics) curriculum in association with the real-world tasks to support STEM. This enables us to discover the most relevant case studies. We restrict and analyse three case studies and provide examples of learning paths related to each introduced case study. Next, we compare evolutional aspects of those case studies within the capabilities of evolutional models (*M1* and *M2* introduced in Chap. 6). Finally, we provide the assessment of the approach from the pedagogical viewpoint using known methodologies.

13.1 Introduction

In previous chapters, we have described the most essential aspects, i.e. theoretical and methodological of our approach. Those aspects have covered a list of topics ranging from the motivation and conceptual representation of the approach to high-level modelling of the educational scenario and the content of the domain (i.e. STEM-driven CS education), the adequate model transformations and the implementation in practice in the real setting of the high (secondary) school. Though in presenting those aspects we try to illustrate the practicality of a particular topic (where it was appropriate and possible) by providing some practical examples and case studies, however, this is not enough for combined overall understanding of practical issues and value of our approach. Therefore, in this chapter, we focus on series case studies that represent a sequenced combination of processes and outcomes of different stages of the approach from the perspective of practical use and value. The aim is to show the functionality, the capabilities and the progress of achievements gained by students in solving real-world tasks (or their prototypes) to

© Springer International Publishing AG, part of Springer Nature 2018   305
V. Štuikys, R. Burbaitė, *Smart STEM-Driven Computer Science Education*,
https://doi.org/10.1007/978-3-319-78485-4_13

support STEM-driven CS education. We have proposed the following methodology to represent the content of this chapter.

Firstly, we introduce the CS (Programming Basics) curriculum associated with the real-world tasks to support STEM. This enables us to discover the most relevant case studies. We restrict and analyse three case studies and provide examples of learning paths related to each introduced case study. Next, we compare evolutional aspects of those case studies within the capabilities of evolutional models (Model 1 and Model 2 introduced in Chap. 6; see Sect. 6.3). Finally, we provide the assessment of the approach from the pedagogical viewpoint using methodologies [AK01, DF05, EN13, LN07].

The remaining content of this chapter includes the related work (Sect. 13.2), curriculum of *Programming Basics* module to support our approach (Sect. 13.3), case studies (Sect. 13.4), evaluation (Sect. 13.5) and conclusion (Sect. 13.6).

13.2 Related Work

The related work includes only a few selected papers that, in our view, are most relevant to this context. The selected works focus (A) on the existing CS education practices related to STEM-driven education with the aim to highlight the variety of pedagogical, technological and content aspects and (B) on the main aspects of revised Bloom's taxonomy we use for the evaluation of our approach.

(A). Park and Ko [PK12] define basic concepts to realize STEM in education. They include (1) systematic connection between different STEM areas, (2) variability of applications and activities, (3) usage of various creative tools and methods, (4) ability to see the generalized picture, (5) rapid response to the technological and scientific changes, (6) practicality and reality and (7) integrative design concept which should be an important spirit in STEM education. The paper [RBC+10] compares engineering design processes and scientific inquiry processes and states that "incorporating engineering principles and design concepts into science curricula... requires new knowledge and changes in classroom instruction" where robotics as a vehicle is a tool that brings engineering concepts and principles into the science classroom. The authors present Medibotics curriculum that enables "to design robots to perform simulated computer-assisted surgeries" using principles of mathematics, applied physics, CS and computational thinking (CT).

Sengupta et al. [SKB+13] propose a set of guidelines that helps to develop CT with scientific expertise. CT includes problem representation, abstraction, decomposition, simulation, verification and prediction practices. "Integrating CT with science and mathematics... requires the design of coherent curricula in which CT, programming, and modelling are not as taught as separate topics, but are interwoven with learning in science domains". The researchers present a framework, which can be applied to develop CTSiM (Computational Thinking in Simulation and

Modelling) learning environment. A framework consists of four components: (1) relationship between CT and scientific expertise, (2) selection of a programming paradigm, (3) selection of curricula of science topics and (4) principles for system design. The authors have developed two curricular modules in the CTSiM environment: (1) a kinematics unit and (2) an ecology unit.

The paper [RKK17] motivates the role of robotics in education under the TPACK (Technological, Pedagogical and Content Knowledge) framework and formulates requirements to effectively teach math and science using robotics. It states that "integration of robotics for teaching science and math under TPACK framework has the potential to advance the technological components, yield rich pedagogical strategies, render novel and effective representations of disciplinary content, and thus produce a novel instantiation of the TPACK methodology".

(B). The revised Bloom's taxonomy proposed by Anderson and Krathwohl [AK01] focuses on the fact that any learning objective is represented in two dimensions, i.e. *knowledge* and *cognitive process*. The first dimension consists of (1) *factual* knowledge, (2) *conceptual* knowledge, (3) *procedural* knowledge and (4) *metacognitive* knowledge. *Factual* knowledge includes the terminology and specific details and elements. *Conceptual* knowledge covers classifications and categories, principles and generalizations, theories, models and structures. *Procedural* knowledge defines subject-specific skills and algorithms, techniques and methods and criteria for using appropriate procedures. *Metacognitive* knowledge "is the knowledge of one's own cognition and about oneself in relation to various subject matters" [AK01]. The listed knowledge types range from *concrete* to *abstract*.

The *cognitive process* dimension introduces a continuous sequence of cognitive complexity. Cognitive processes are divided into six categories – from the lower-order to the upper-order (thinking) skills (see Table 13.1).

This taxonomy outlines psychological aspects of education. We use it along with other methodologies to evaluate the educational processes. With regard to the aim of this chapter, we use the following scheme of our discussion. The starting point is the content of curriculum to educate Programming Basics. Next, we show how we introduce STEM aspects into the module. After that, three case studies of varying complexity demonstrate the educational practice. Finally, we provide an evaluation of our approach from different perspectives.

13.3 Curriculum of Programming Basics to Support Our Approach

The *Programming Basics* module is one of optional CS modules in the ninth or tenth grade (15–16 years). The aim of this module is (1) to introduce students to the basics of programming technology, (2) to increase the choice of learning opportunities and

Table 13.1 Bloom's revised taxonomy: the cognitive processes dimension

	Category	Cognitive processes
Lower-order thinking skills	*Remembering* – retrieving relevant knowledge from long-term memory	Recognizing
		Recalling
	Understanding – determining the meaning of instructional messages, including oral, written and graphic communication	Interpreting
		Exemplifying
		Classifying
		Summarizing
		Inferring
		Comparing
		Explaining
Upper-order thinking skills	*Applying* – carrying out or using a procedure in a given situation	Executing
		Implementing
	Analysing – breaking material into its constituent parts and detecting how the parts relate to one another and to an overall structure or purpose	Differentiating
		Organizing
		Attributing
	Evaluating – making a judgement based on criteria and standards	Checking
		Critiquing
	Creating – putting elements together to form a novel, coherent whole or make an original product	Generating
		Planning
		Producing

Adapted from [AK01]

(3) to help assess their inclinations and learning abilities and decide on further learning of CS and IT. The tasks include (1) to provide the opportunity for all students to develop the ability to consistently, structurally and algorithmically think, (2) to get the knowledge on the basic algorithm structures and concepts, (3) to create simple programs to solve the problem, (4) to go deeply into programming technology and (5) to help students understand the practical benefits of algorithms and programming. The curriculum covers (1) the connections between algorithms and computer programs; (2) the fundamental structural elements of computer programs; (3) the basic data types and operations; (4) the main structures, such as a sequence of operations, conditional algorithms, loops and nested loops; and (5) the development and execution of a computer program.

In Table 13.2, we summarize the objectives and consequences of the course delivery for students. That includes the expected skills, knowledge and understanding of the basic programming concepts.

The skills defined in Table 13.2 closely relate to the use of principles and methodologies that enable the development of the computational thinking skills, such as (1) abstraction, (2) pattern recognition, (3) algorithm design, (4) decomposition, (5) data representation, (6) coding and (7) digital information system usage [Cum16]. We have enriched *Programming Basics* module with STEM-driven aspects by including real-world tasks students have to solve through the processes

Table 13.2 Programming Basics: the expected skills, knowledge and understanding

#	Skills	Knowledge and understanding
1.	Explain the concept of an algorithm and associate it with programming	1.1. Define the concept "algorithm" by giving examples
		1.2. Define the concept "computer program", explain relationship "algorithm-computer program"
		1.3. Explain the concepts "programming language" and "programming environment" and indicate their purpose
		1.4. Describe the purpose of a compiler
2.	Perform operations with different forms of data; describe the program's arguments and results	2.1. Define the concepts "data", "variable", "variable value"
		2.2. Explain the concepts "initial data" and "results" of a computer program
		2.3. Explain the structure of an assignment by giving examples
		2.4. Use operations with different types of data in computer programs
3.	Apply the main algorithms and write them in a programming language	3.1. Describe the sequence of operations – sequential algorithms by giving examples
		3.2. Describe the choice of operations – conditional algorithms by giving examples
		3.3. Describe the repetition of operations – loops and nested loops by giving examples
4.	Create computer programs for uncomplicated tasks and problems	4.1. Create programs to solve problems using known algorithms and formulas
		4.2. Execute computer programs
5.	Follow the rules of the development of computer programs	5.1. Use the principle of decomposition
		5.2. Define the main stages of a program's development, such as code writing, debugging and testing
		5.3. Explain the importance of control data for the program
6.	Follow the rules of programming style	6.1. Define the concept "programming style" accompanied by examples
		6.2. Choose meaningful variable names, visual appearance of the source code, with the aim of readability
		6.3. Use comments to describe the main operations

of *creating* (*generating*), *testing* and *executing* robot control programs. We have borrowed some tasks from the well-known educational websites http://www. teachengineering.org, http://www.nxtprograms.com, http://www.education.rec.ri. cmu.edu, http://robotc.net/ and http://www.tik.ee.ethz.ch. However, we have extended and adapted those tasks to our educational context. In Table 13.3, we

Table 13.3 Real-world STEM-oriented tasks integrated into course "Programming Basics"

Real-world task	CS topic	Science	Technology	Engineering	Mathematics
1. Robot sensors' testing	Loop-based algorithms	Physics – sensors' operating principles and properties / CS – sensors' programming principles	Different robotic platforms with sensors	Modelling and designing of environment for experimental research	Interdependencies of variables
2. Robot calibration	Sequential algorithms	Physics – different forms of movement, physical motors properties / CS – different movement algorithms	Different robotic platforms with motors	Robot vehicle designing and constructing	Time-speed dependencies
3. Baseball batter	Conditional and loop-based algorithms	Physics – different forms of movement, physical motors' and ultrasonic sensor's properties / CS – ultrasonic sensors' and motors' movement programming principles	NXT robot platform	Baseball batter constructing, according to the provided guide	Calculation of the correct values of parameters
4. Obstacle detection	Conditional and loop-based algorithms	Physics – different forms of movement, physical motors' and ultrasonic sensor's properties / CS – ultrasonic sensor's and motors' movement programming principles	NXT robot platform	Robot vehicle with ultrasonic sensor designing and constructing	Calculating optimal values of robot speed depending on the characteristics of the ultrasonic sensor
5. Wall detection	Conditional and loop-based algorithms	Physics – different forms of movement, physical motors' and touch and ultrasonic sensors' properties / CS – touch and ultrasonic sensors' and motors' movement programming principles	NXT robot platform	Robot vehicle with a touch and ultrasonic sensors designing and constructing	Environment map creating from the recorded data

6. Help system	Conditional and loop-based algorithms	CS – touch sensors' programming principles, the use of the task into smaller part (decomposition) principle, different ways to represent data	NXT robot platform	Help system constructing	–
7. Light meter	Conditional and loop-based algorithms	Physics – light and colour sensor operating principles, reflected light from different surface measuring CS – different ways to represent data, programming principles of light and colour sensors	NXT platform	Light meter constructing, according to the provided guide	Reflected light – different surface dependencies
8. Line following	Conditional and loop-based algorithms	Physics – light and colour sensor operating principle, light and colour physical properties CS – different lines following algorithms	Different robotic platforms with motors and sensors	Line follower designing and constructing	Line following accuracy calculation
9. Traffic light	Conditional and loop-based algorithms	Physics – LED working principle CS – different traffic light controls algorithms	Different robotic platforms with LEDs	Traffic light designing and constructing	Traffic light working accuracy measurement
10. Ornament drawing	Loops and nested loops	Physics – different forms of movement, physical motors' properties CS – different movement algorithms	Different robotic platforms with motors	Drawbot designing and constructing	Calculating optimal values of ornament parameters

present some examples of the real-world tasks (more precisely prototypes) by indicating their relevance to CS topics and STEM components.

Note that the enrichment of the module with the real-world tasks extends the possibility for developing computational thinking skills listed above. For example, students are able to get skills in data visualization, coding and robotics.

In the next section, we introduce case studies of STEM paradigm in CS education that cover different thinking skills and knowledge types according to revised Bloom's taxonomy [AK01].

13.4 Case Studies

We present three case studies to demonstrate the gaining of the STEM-based knowledge according to Model 2 (see Fig. 6.1 in Chap. 6). The aim of Case Study 1 is to explain the functionality and programming principles of the ultrasonic sensor (see Tables 13.2 and 13.3). Case Study 1 covers *factual* and some aspects of *conceptual* and *procedural* knowledge and involves cognitive processes, such as *remembering*, *understanding* and *applying* (see Sect. 13.2). The aim of Case Study 2 is to introduce different ways of representation and visualization of data and algorithms. It includes the same knowledge types as described in Case Study 1; however, there cognitive processes are enlarged by adding the *analysing* process. Note that the concrete learning scenarios for Case Study 1 and Case Study 2 are derived from the generative scenario. We remind that we have discussed the comprehensive methodology of the generative scenario tool in Chap. 11. Here (see Fig. 13.1), we present a generalized model on how to create a concrete scenario from generative one. Note that learning resources are taken from the STEM-driven personal generative library (PGL, Chap. 10).

The aim of Case Study 3 is specific. It aims at demonstrating the process of gaining an integrative STEM knowledge and skills by students. Some highly motivated students want to choose additional projects to implement them in after-school (informal) activities. For example, the projects may include "Braille printer", "Robot task virtual model transformation into real environment", "LED-matrix based video games console", "Virtual reality games for rehabilitation", etc. Note

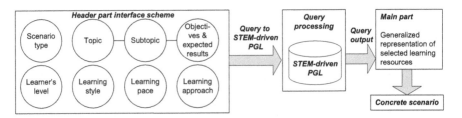

Fig. 13.1 A generalized model to generate concrete scenario from generative scenario

that those projects are real and were implemented, presented and defended in school workshops and various contests as students' personal research findings.

As an illustration, we provide the project "Educational robot task virtual model transformation into real environment" carried out by student A. Paulauskas (under supervising by R. Burbaitė) from scratch and published in the open-access *IOSR Journal of Computer Engineering* [Pau16]. The latter example covers all aspects of gaining knowledge according to revised Bloom's taxonomy, using the STEM paradigm in CS education.

13.4.1 Case Study 1

The concrete scenario for Case Study 1 is derived from generative one named as "Functionality and programming principles of sensors" (see Sect. 11.5 in Chap. 11). The user (in most cases the user is a teacher) chooses adequate values of parameters in the Header part interface (see Figs. 13.1 and 13.2). Then the query to STEM-driven library is generated, and the query output (i.e. extracted learning resources from the library) goes to the main part generator that generates the concrete scenario "Functionality and programming principles of ultrasonic sensor" (see Figs. 13.1 and 13.3).

As a student (or a small group (2–3) of students) gets a main part of the concrete scenario, he/she provides self-learning, aiming to acquire physical principles of functioning of the ultrasonic sensor (S-knowledge, i.e. physics). That is a *factual knowledge* and covers cognitive categories such as *remembering* and *understanding*. The learning resource is a component-based LO (CB LO) given as the illustrated text. Then the learner deals with the program code by carrying it out. By doing so, the learner obtains also S-knowledge, but in CS. In addition, the learner is able to get the *conceptual knowledge*, and, in addition, it is possible to extend the cognition to the *applying category*. In this stage, the learner uses CB LO and the generative learning object (GLO) named as "Ultrasonic sensor properties". Finally, the learner makes a practice. It includes solving practical tasks (see Fig. 13.3). This activity, in fact, provides with mixed science knowledge (physics and CS), leading to gaining the *procedural knowledge*. At this stage, the learner uses the previous learning resources and creates new ones. In this aspect, the learner is a creator of the learning resources to extend his/her own personal library. This is a very important aspect of learner-centred learning, because this activity opens the way for accumulating knowledge, for integrating it into new knowledge.

This case study is yet important from the other perspective. It stands for as a basis in solving complex tasks, such as tasks 3–5 in Table 13.3.

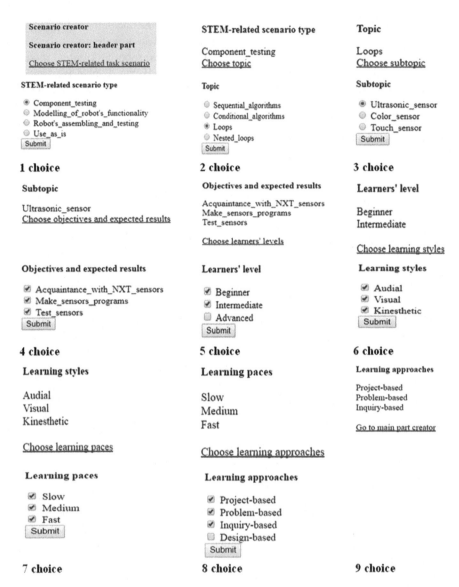

Fig. 13.2 The header part of the generative scenario "Functionality and programming principles of sensors"

13.4.2 Case Study 2

Case Study 2 introduces different ways of representation and visualization of data and algorithms. The ornament drawing task has chosen to explain the topic "Loops and nested loops". The concrete scenario consists of three independent

Objectives: Acquaintance_with_NXT_sensors

Large sized objects with hard surfaces return the best readings. Objects made of soft fabric or that are curved [like a ball] or are very thin or small can be difficult for the sensor to detect.

* Note that two or more Ultrasonic Sensors operating in the same room may interrupt each other's readings.

Source: **https://www.teachengineering.org/lessons/view/umo_sensorswork_lesson06**

1. Sensor has two main parts. A transmitter sends out a signal (an ultrasonic wave) that humans cannot hear. And a receiver receives the signal after it has reflected off nearby objects. The sensor times how long it takes for its signals to come back and relays that information to the LEGO brick/computer, which calculates how far away objects are.

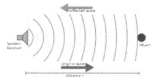

Objectives: Make_sensors_programs

```
while(SensorValue[sonarSensor] > distance_in_cm)
{
  nxtDisplayCenteredTextLine(4, "Bye Bye");
  nxtDisplayClearTextLine(4);
}
}
return;
}
```

2. **Analysis of program code**

- `#pragma config(Sensor, S1, sonarSensor, sensorSONAR)` defines that ultrasonic sensor is connected to the NXT through 1 (S1) input.

- Loop `while(true){...}` covers a group of code lines that will describe the program's actions. It is needed for our program to function as long as the robot is enabled (i.e., actions are repeated until the robot is turned on).

Objectives: Test_sensors

Practice

Task 1. Modify the program so that the distance to the obstacle will be 20, 30, 50 cm. Make sure you have the sensor reacts to the obstacle (or change the text on the screen).

Task 2. What result will be displayed on the screen if the distance to the obstacle is equal 20 cm, and the line cleaning sentence
`nxtDisplayClearTextLine (4);`
would be commented using //?

Task 3. What result will be displayed on the screen if the distance to the obstacle is equal 30 cm, and the line's item would be changed?

Fig. 13.3 Fragments of a concrete scenario "Functionality and programming principles of ultrasonic sensor"

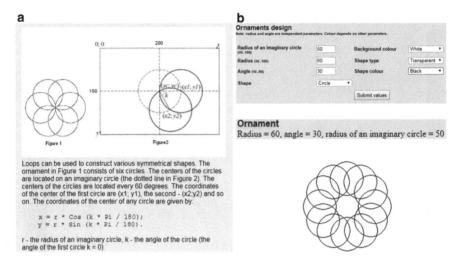

Fig. 13.4 Ornament drawing on computer screen. (**a**) The fragments of explanation part. (**b**) Ornaments design part

sub-scenarios: (1) ornament drawing on the computer screen, (2) ornament drawing on the NXT Intelligent Brick screen and (3) ornament drawing by the real drawbot (i.e. drawing robot). The sub-scenario "Ornament drawing on computer screen" explains the subtopic *while loop*. The learning objective is to introduce students to the *while loop* construct in programming and to provide a graphical visualization of the concepts in the form of ornaments in order to increase student understanding and engagement with the topic. In Fig. 13.4a, we explain ornament drawing principles. In Fig. 13.4b, we present the task visualization-related parameters (radius and angle of the shape as well as the shape type, shape colour and background colour) and their values (radius in pixels and angle in degrees). Using all possible combinations of the parameter values, the student can derive a large number of ornaments from the given specification.

This sub-scenario opens the possibility to obtain S-knowledge (CS), T-knowledge (data representation on the computer screen), M-knowledge (mathematical model of the pieces of the ornament) completely and A-knowledge (meaning art) partially. The used resources include illustrated text (i.e. CB LO) and GLO (see the top part of Fig. 13.4b). The second sub-scenario explains the subtopic *nested loops*. The learning objective is to develop the student's abilities to transfer the already acquired knowledge and skills into another context – to draw similar ornaments on NXT Intelligent Brick screen. Figure 13.5 shows some possible variants of the task solving results.

It is worth to note that in the second sub-scenario, the students may face the challenge, because the domain-specific language RobotC does not have a circle

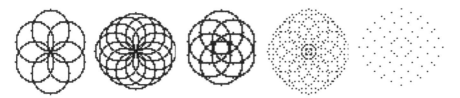

Fig. 13.5 Variants of tasks for the topic *nested loops*

drawing procedure. The third sub-scenario aims at transferring the ornament shown on the screen of the Intelligent Brick into a real drawbot, which will draw an ornament on a sheet of the paper. The advantage of the second and third sub-scenarios is that ornament drawings are animated and students can follow the process in real time.

In summary, from the pedagogy viewpoint, this study covers the *factual, conceptual*, and *procedural knowledge*, and, with regard to cognition categories, it covers *remembering, understanding, applying* and *analysing*.

13.4.3 Case Study 3

The aim of the project is to develop the real robot control programs using robot's behaviour modelling results received from the virtual system. The idea of this project came from the following researches: (1) robot control program's development using online and offline programming methods [PPL+12], (2) real virtual environment for robotic system analysis and testing [SMC+05] and (3) modelling of the virtual robot path in an unknown environment [OCN06].

The experimental environment consists of educational LEGO NXT robot [BSM12] and computer with the software for the modelling and robot programming environment (Fig. 13.6). A virtual modelling environment has been developed using the Unity game engine (https://unity3d.com/). In this environment, the user can create the movement of the robot, and data is transferred to the data transformation program for processing.

The data transformation program has been created as a separate module of the environment in C++ language using CodeBlocks environment (http://www. codeblocks.org/). The latter transforms data transferred from virtual model real robot calibration to the robot control program. Robot control programs have been developed using RobotC environment and transferred to the robot and tested. If the trajectory of robot's movement is not satisfied with the user requirements, the robot calibration should be repeated, and transformation rules should be revised.

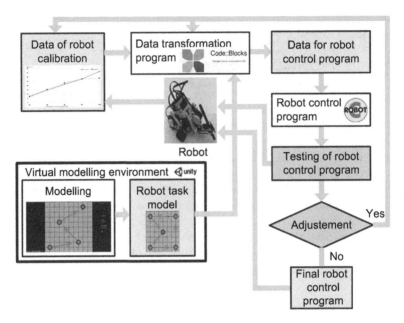

Fig. 13.6 The architecture of experimental environment. (Adapted from [Pau16])

The student formulates two generalized rules to describe the movement of the drawbot. The rules are as follows:

1. The time (t_s) of the drawbot straight-line movement forward and backward is defined by (13.1):

$$t_s = \frac{a_s \cdot k_{ch} \cdot 1000}{v_r \cdot k_s} \qquad (13.1)$$

where a_s, the distance travelled by the robot forward/backward; v_r, robot's speed; k_s, coefficient obtained from the robot calibration data when the robot moves straight forward/backward; and k_{ch}, coefficient which modifies the virtual model's space into the real space.

2. The time (t_r) of the drawbot rotational movement in a clockwise/anticlockwise direction

$$t_r = \frac{a_r \cdot 1000}{v_r \cdot k_r}, \qquad (13.2)$$

where a_r, the rotation angle; v_r, robot's speed; and k_r, coefficient obtained from the robot calibration data when the robot rotates in a clockwise/anticlockwise direction.

The coefficients k_s and k_r are obtained from the drawbot's calibration data (see Fig. 13.7a, b).

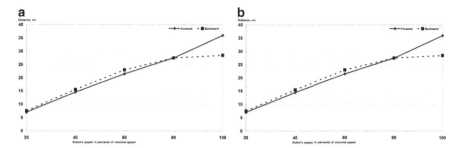

Fig. 13.7 The drawbot's calibration data: (**a**) distance, speed dependency (movement time $t = 1000$ ms); (**b**) robot's rotation angle, speed dependency (movement time $t = 1000$ ms). (Taken from [Pau16])

Fig. 13.8 Drawbot's straight-line movement: (**a**) virtual model; (**b**) real path; (**c**) corrected real path. (Taken from [Pau16])

Table 13.4 The comparison of model and real path of the drawbot

Parameter	Model	Real path: initial transformation rules	Real path: corrected transformation rules
Distance 1–2	8.52	64	70
Distance 2–3	6.27	42	58
Angle 2, radians	0.75	1.48	0.87

The modelled path of the drawbot consists of two parts: 1–2 and 2–3 (see Fig. 13.8a). After creating of the model, the coordinates of each point are stored in a text file and transferred to the data transformation program. The control program of the drawbot was created using transformed calibration and the virtual model data. Figure 13.8b presents the real path using initial transformation rules. Since there is an inadequacy between the model and the real path, a correction is needed. Figure 13.8c shows the result after correction of transformation rules.

The measurement results of distances among points 1–2 and 2–3 and values of the angle 2 are presented in Table 13.4.

The student also performed the experiments modelling the movement of the drawbot's in square, rectangular and equilateral triangle shapes. The speed of the

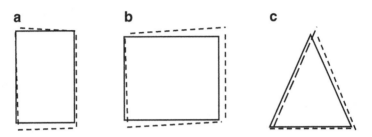

Fig. 13.9 Model (the solid line) and real path (the dotted line): (**a**) *rectangle* (21 × 30 cm); (**b**) square (50 × 50 cm); (**c**) equilateral triangle (40 cm). (Taken from [Pau16])

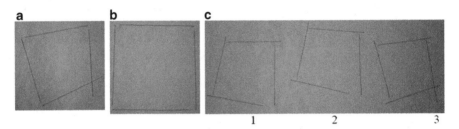

Fig. 13.10 Paths of the drawbot (square 50 × 50 cm): (**a**) without corrections of the coefficients; (**b**) with corrections of the coefficients; (**c**) maximal possible speed: 1 and 2 – with corrections of the coefficients; 3, without corrections of the coefficients. (Taken from [Pau16])

drawbot is 50% of the maximal speed. The results of the measurements are shown in Fig. 13.9a–c.

Figure 13.10 presents the movement of the drawbot in the square shape path without (Fig. 13.10a) and with (Fig. 13.10b) corrections of the coefficients (see Eqs. 13.1 and 13.2). If the speed of the drawbot is maximal, the movement path is inaccurate (see Fig. 13.10c). After correction of the coefficients, the path is more similar to the model's one but due to the inertia differs from them.

The created system can be successfully used to simulate the path of the robot according to the user needs, when the path is without obstacles. The developed program of the adjustment of robot's calibration coefficients allows the user to revise the real path flexibly. In the classroom, we use this experimental environment for optimal path searching tasks. The main improvements of the developed system include (1) the increased functionality by adding different sensors and (2) the possibility for adjusting calibration coefficients remotely.

Therefore, we have discussed three case studies to illustrate integrated aspects of STEM-driven CS education using Model 2. From the viewpoint of the organization of the educational processes, we are able to introduce STEM aspects into CS education differently. We have approved two variants for delivery educational processes. The first covers a situation when, firstly, students learn the basic data types and algorithms and solve problems using the general-purpose programming language, and then they create robot control programs using domain-specific languages, such as RobotC, ArduinoC, etc. The second variant focuses on students' *parallel learning* to program using general-purpose and domain-specific languages. In practice, the first one has been more successful because of a larger set of real-world tasks.

13.5 Evaluation

Now our aim is to compare two models (Model 1 and Model 2, see Section 6.3). We remind that we refer to Model 1 as the use of STEM attributes in the following way: CS plus technology explicitly while the remaining components without explicit specification of adequate parameters, i.e. the STEM knowledge was delivered in the indirect way. We refer to Model 2 as a concept to provide the integrated STEM knowledge explicitly according to the formulated objectives (see Chap. 1).

We provide the comparison using different methodologies and metrics. We compare the models, i.e. *Model 1* (M1) and *Model 2* (M2), in various aspects. We have adapted some metrics from LO quality frameworks [DF05, LN07]. Those metrics focus on the content properties. The other group of metrics we use focuses on pedagogical aspects entirely [AK01, EN13]. Table 13.5 presents the results of models' comparison, according to the learning objects' quality metrics proposed by [DF05] and adapted to our context.

It is possible to conclude that Model 2 is more complex with enhanced capabilities to provide integrative education of CS on the STEM paradigm. To deal with the complex issues, however, we apply concern separation implemented through hierarchies and the structure of generative scenarios.

Table 13.6 shows models' comparison results according to LORI (Learning Object Review Instrument) methodology [LN07]. We evaluate models using the adequate values of fuzzy variables taken from [Štu15]. The set of fuzzy variables includes {H, I, L, H-I, I-L, U} (see legend below Table 13.6). It was difficult to

Table 13.5 Comparison of *M1* and *M2* according to LO quality metrics

#	Metrics	Evaluation criterions	Model 1	Model 2
1.	Content quality	# of parameters	3..9	≥6
2.	Student need assessment	# of parameters for assessing the student's needs	3	9
3.	Metadata description quality	# of pedagogical parameters	3	9
4.	Reusability	# of variants	1296..97200	≥5184
5.	Structural complexity	# of stages	1..4	≥2
6.	Adaptability	# of the most commonly used variants	≥12	≥64

Table 13.6 Comparison of M1 and M2 according to the LORI methodology [LN07]

#	Item	Brief description	Model 1	Model 2
1.	Content quality	Veracity, accuracy, balanced presentation of ideas and appropriate level of detail	H-I	H
2.	Learning goal alignment	Alignment between learning goals, activities, assessments and learner characteristics	H-I	H
3.	Feedback and adaptation	Adaptive content or feedback driven by differential learner input or learner modelling	I	H-I
4.	Motivation	Ability to motivate and interest an identified population of learners	H-I	H
5.	Presentation design	Design of visual and auditory information for enhanced learning and efficient mental processing	I	H
6.	Interaction usability	Ease of navigation, predictability of the user interface and the quality of the interface help features	I	H
7.	Accessibility	Design of controls and presentation formats to accommodate disabled and mobile learners	I	I
8.	Reusability	Ability to use in varying learning contexts and with learners from different backgrounds	I	H
9.	Standards compliance	Adherence to international standards and specifications	I	H-I

Legend. Level measures: *H* high, *I* intermediate, *L* low, *H–I* between high and intermediate, *I–L* between intermediate and low, *U* undefined

obtain the external evaluation by experts. Therefore, we have defined the values on our personal experience and intuition. Nevertheless, they provide a systemized vision of our approach.

In summary, as *Model 2* is derivative from *Model 1* (in the sense of evolution), the first prevails in the following aspects: presentation design, interaction usability and reusability. With regard to the pedagogical evaluation (see Table 11.2), *Model 2* covers much more *cognitive process dimensions* as well as *knowledge dimensions* explicitly as compared to *Model 1*. Therefore, *Model 2* brings higher-level of *metacognition*, especially in *evaluating* and *creating* cognitive processes.

In Table 13.7, we have summarized the relevance of our models to the learning theories. We have identified the relevance by the *level of relevance* with respect to questions related to the known learning theories [EN13]. We have measured the level using the adequate values of fuzzy variables {H, I, L, H–I, I–L, U} again (see legend below Table 13.7). Note that we have evaluated *Model 1* in our previous book [Štu15].

In this regard, *Model 2* extends *Model 1* in transferring and memorizing aspects.

Table 13.7 Relationships between proposed models and learning theories [EN13]

	What is supported? To which level?	
Question/learning theory	Model 1	Model 2
How does learning occur?		
Behaviourism: black box – observable behaviour main focus	Black box: H	Black box: H
Cognitivism: structured, computational	Both: H–I	Both: H
Constructivism: social, meaning created by each learner (personal)	Social: H, H–I dependent on social group	Social: H
What factors influence learning?		
Behaviourism: nature of reward, punishment, stimuli	Stimuli: H, H-I	Stimuli: H
Cognitivism: existing schema, previous experiences	Both: H, H–I	Both: H
Constructivism: engagement (E), participation (P), social (S), cultural (C)	E, P, S: H	E, P, S: H
What is the role of memory?		
Behaviourism: influential	Influential: U	Influential: H–I
Cognitivism: retrieval	Retrieval: U	Retrieval: H-I
Constructivism: to current context	Context: H, H–I	Context: H, H–I
How does transfer occur?		
Behaviourism: Stimulus, response	Both: I, I-L	Both: H-I
Cognitivism: duplicating knowledge constructs of "knower"	U	I
Constructivism: socialization	I	H-I
What types of learning this theory explains best?		
Behaviourism: task-based learning	H	H
Cognitivism: reasoning, clear objectives, problem solving	H	H
Constructivism: social, vague ("ill defined")	Social: I	Social: H–I

Legend. Level of measures: *H* high, *I* intermediate, *L* low, *H–I* between high and intermediate, *I–L* between intermediate and low, *U* undefined

13.6 Conclusion

In this chapter, we have discussed some results related to the practice of using our approach in the real education setting. We have selected three case studies that, in our view, are relevant to illustrate the STEM integration possibilities in CS education at school. We have evaluated our educational practice by comparing the two models. *Model 1* covers our efforts to introduce STEM concepts partially and implicitly in CS education over the years 2013–2015. *Model 2* reflects our recent educational practice in the years 2015–2017. The latter covers our efforts to introduce the integrative STEM knowledge explicitly into CS education and in a broader context. By the extended context, we mean the extension of the list of real-world tasks relevant to robotics and STEM, the enlargement of the functionality of the educational scenarios and the increase of the "smartness level" of both the educational content and educational environment.

References

[AK01]   Anderson LW, Krathwohl DR (2001) A taxonomy for learning, teaching, and assessing: a revision of bloom's taxonomy of educational objectives. Longman, New York

[BSM12]   Burbaite R, Stuikys V, Marcinkevicius R (2012) The LEGO NXT robot-based e-learning environment to teach computer science topics. Elektronika ir Elektrotechnika 18 (9):113–116

[Cum16]   Cummins K (2016) Teaching digital technologies & STEM: computational thinking, coding and robotics in the classroom. Retrieved from Amazon.com

[DF05]   Defude B, Farhat R (2005) A framework to design quality-based learning objects. In: Advanced learning technologies, 2005. ICALT 2005. Fifth IEEE international conference on IEEE, pp 23–27

[EN13]   Ertmer PA, Newby TJ (2013) Behaviorism, cognitivism, constructivism: comparing critical features from an instructional design perspective. Perform Improv Q 26 (2):43–71

[LN07]   Leacock TL, Nesbit JC (2007) A framework for evaluating the quality of multimedia learning resources. J Educ Technol Soc 10(2)

[OCN06]   Ong SK, Chong JWS, Nee AY (2006) Methodologies for immersive robot programming in an augmented reality environment. In: Proceedings of the 4th international conference on computer graphics and interactive techniques in Australasia and Southeast Asia, ACM, pp 237–244

[Pau16]   Paulauskas A (2016) Educational robot task virtual model transformation into real environment. IOSR J Comput Eng 18:80–85

[PK12]   Park N, Ko Y (2012) Computer education's teaching-learning methods using educational programming language based on STEAM education. NPC 7513:320–327

[PPL+12]   Pan Z, Polden J, Larkin N, Van Duin S, Norrish J (2012) Recent progress on programming methods for industrial robots. Robot Comput Integr Manuf 28(2):87–94

[RBC+10]   Rockland R, Bloom DS, Carpinelli J, Burr-Alexander L, Hirsch LS, Kimmel H (2010) Advancing the "E" in K-12 STEM education

[RKK17]   Rahman SM, Krishnan VJ, Kapila V (2017) Exploring the dynamic nature of TPACK framework in teaching STEM using robotics in middle school classrooms

[SKB+13]   Sengupta P, Kinnebrew JS, Basu S, Biswas G, Clark D (2013) Integrating computational thinking with K-12 science education using agent-based computation: a theoretical framework. Educ Inf Technol 18(2):351–380

[SMC+05]   Stilman M, Michel P, Chestnutt J, Nishiwaki K, Kagami S, Kuffner J (2005) Augmented reality for robot development and experimentation. Robotics Institute, Carnegie Mellon University, Pittsburgh, PA, Tech. Rep. CMU-RI-TR-05-55, 2(3)

[Štu15]   Štuikys V (2015) Smart learning objects for smart education in computer science. Springer, New York

Part V
An Extended Vision to STEM-Driven CS Education

Part V is the concluding part of the book. It consists of two chapters, i.e. Chaps. 14 and 15. The aim of this part is twofold. The first aim is to provide readers with an introductory knowledge on how the discussed so far approach can evolve in the future. The second aim is to provide the extended summary along with the extended evaluation and analyses of extra capabilities of the approach. To demonstrate the possible evolution, we have selected only one topic, i.e. the Internet-of-Things (IoT). In Chap. 14, we have identified this topic as a new vision for STEM and CS education. Readers should accept this vision as the only starting point toward more extensive studies. Nevertheless, readers will find here architecture of the IoT system to provide STEM-driven CS education. We illustrate the applicability of the system by a case study. In Chap. 15, we summarize the capabilities of smart content and smart scenario indicating on some drawbacks of the approach. The essential part of this summarizing discussion is the analysis of how the described approach supports the computational thinking in learning. In addition, we present some indication on how one can interpret and apply the discussed approach at the university level. Finally, we indicate some links and possible applicability of the approach to the MOOC paradigm.

Chapter 14
Internet-of-Things: A New Vision for STEM and CS Education

Abstract In this chapter, we analyse new possibilities for STEM and CS education with regard to the *Internet-of-Things* (IoT). Typically, researchers define the IoT as an emerging networked infrastructure penetrated by embedded smart devices, *called things*, which have identities, sensing-actuating and computing capabilities, are connected via the Internet, can communicate with each other and with humans and can provide semantics of some useful services such as education. With this chapter, we aim to achieve two objectives: (i) to introduce the terminology of IoT for the book readers to start more thorough studies and (ii) to show the relevance of this topic to the ones we have discussed so far in the previous chapters. We present the architecture for considering tasks relevant to the IoT and CS education. We discuss a framework for solving some IoT tasks and a case study and experiments with these tasks.

14.1 Introduction

This chapter is about the new possibilities for STEM and CS education. A new vision in technology advancing known as the *Internet-of-Things* (IoT) brings those possibilities. Typically, researchers define the IoT as an emerging networked infrastructure penetrated by embedded smart devices, *called things*, which have identities, sensing-actuating and computing capabilities, are connected via the Internet, can communicate with each other and with humans and can provide semantics of some useful services [AGM+15, SMC11]. Therefore, embedded computing, sensors and ubiquitous technologies will define the "Internet-of-Things" era, in contrast to the previous era that was defined by PCs and the "Internet of People".

This technological leap is a great challenge for the information-communication technology (ICT) workers, scientists and society in the whole [AIM10]. This new technology directly concerns with the educational community, especially that part, which relates to teaching and researching in ICT, STEM and CS fields. Many recent reports announce on the start of educating students using the IoT paradigm. Examples are the MIT (USA) courses with the IoT programs [MIT17], CS master level courses on IoT at Malmö University (Sweden) [CSM17] and ten IoT degree courses

© Springer International Publishing AG, part of Springer Nature 2018   327
V. Štuikys, R. Burbaitė, *Smart STEM-Driven Computer Science Education*,
https://doi.org/10.1007/978-3-319-78485-4_14

in the UK [CBR17] to name a few. On the other hand, the research work is also on the agenda in this field. For example, the Carnegie Mellon University (USA) is teaming up with researchers at Stanford University, the University of Illinois and Google to create an IoT platform called GIoTTO [Hen16]. It will include inexpensive and easy-to-deploy sensors, new middleware to facilitate app development and manage privacy and security and new tools to help users create their own IoT experiences. Sirkka Freigang, an educational expert and PhD student, wrote in this account:

> My very personal IoT dream as an education expert is a fully connected study room: We spend so much time in conference rooms, in auditoriums or at school. I am convinced that the Internet of Things could make our information exchange and learning experiences much more efficient – and more fun.

What is the relationship between STEM and IoT in terms of CS education? As defined previously (see Chaps. 1 and 2), STEM focuses on providing the integrative (interdisciplinary) knowledge from many fields at once. The IoT educational courses are from the same shelf; however, they should be delivered with respect to the most crucial requirements for the IoT in terms of security, privacy and energy [VSD +16]. Therefore, the new aspects of interdisciplinary relationships arise. STEM focuses also on solving the real-world tasks. The IoT does the same, because *smart things* are real entities. The role of robotics is similar or just the same in both fields. The robot may have within smart things (sensors, actuators, cameras) and communicating capabilities. Furthermore, the robot itself may stand for the unit of the IoT in a wider context for many applications. Both fields (STEM and IoT) are either "consumers" or "sparklers" of the fundamental knowledge considered by CS. The list of stated similarities is by no means full. That is enough, however, to understand the reason why we have included this topic in our book, though our aim is very modest here. With this chapter, we aim to achieve two objectives: (i) to introduce the terminology of IoT for the book readers and (ii) to show the relevance of this topic to the ones we have discussed so far in the previous chapters. The remaining part of this chapter includes the following topics. In Sect. 14.2, we analyse the related work. In Sect. 14.3, we present the architecture for considering tasks relevant to IoT education. In Sect. 14.4, we discuss a framework for solving IoT tasks. In Sect. 14.5, we analyse a case study and experiments of the IoT tasks. In Sect. 14.6, we provide a summary and conclusion.

14.2   Related Work

We categorize the related work into streams A and B. The first brings the introductive knowledge in the field of the IoT. The second relates to educational aspects of the IoT, STEM and CS with the focus on their relationship.

14.2.1 Stream A

At the top level, researchers analyse the emerging challenges and methodologies to identify a roadmap for the future IoT research. At the application level, researching focuses on gaining a real evidence of the IoT benefits. The survey papers [Dru15, PZC+14, SEC+13, STJ14] analyse new visions and challenges on the basis of lessons learnt from the past Internet in order it would be possible to foresee future research directions for the IoT. IoT, in fact, is the integration of several technologies because of "synergetic activities conducted in different fields of knowledge, such as telecommunications, informatics, electronics and social science" [AIM10, WWR +12].

From a conceptual standpoint, the IoT builds on three pillars, related to the ability of smart objects to: (i) be identifiable (anything identifies itself), (ii) to communicate (anything communicates) and (iii) to interact (anything interacts) – either among themselves to build networks of interconnected objects, or with end-users or other entities in the network. Developing technologies and solutions for enabling such a vision is the main challenge [MSP+12].

Therefore, at the single component level, the basic concept in the IoT is "smart objects" or things. The papers [KKS+10, MSP+12] define smart objects as physical entities with the following capabilities. (i) They can communicate, i.e. to accept messages and respond to them. (ii) They have a unique identifier associated with at least one name and one address. (iii) They have some computing capabilities and means (sensors) to sense a physical environment and its phenomena or to trigger actions having an effect on the physical reality (actuators). Therefore, smart objects can analyse the data coming from their sensors and can use recognition facilities to detect activities and events [KKS+10]. On this basis, the smart objects obtain *social* features, i.e. they are able to share their data, to learn about each other, to perform intelligent actions based upon each other's state and to provide services to both humans and robots in real-world environments. In other words, smart objects are indeed *context-aware entities*.

From a system-level perspective, the IoT can be viewed as a highly dynamic and radically distributed networked system, composed of a very large number of smart objects producing and consuming information. The ability to interface with the physical realm is achieved through the presence of devices able to sense physical phenomena and translate them into a stream of information data. In this regard, the scalability may become a major issue due to the extremely large scale of the resulting system and considering also the high level of dynamism in the network [MSP +12]. Therefore, the quest for inclusion of self-management and autonomic capabilities may become a major driver in the development of a set of enabling solutions.

From a service-level perspective, the main issue relates to how to integrate (or compose) the functionalities and/or resources provided by smart objects (in many cases in forms of data streams generated) into services. This requires the definition of (i) architectures and methods for "virtualizing" objects by creating a standardized representation of smart objects in the digital domain, able to hinder the heterogeneity of devices/resources, and (ii) methods for seamlessly integrating and composing the resources/services of smart objects into value-added services for end-users. The vision of IoT provides a large set of opportunities to users and will find a wide applicability in many sectors (e.g. environmental monitoring, healthcare, inventory and product management, workplace and home support, security and surveillance [GBM+13, MSP+12]).

From a user point of view, the IoT will enable a large amount of new always-responsive services, which shall answer to users' needs and support them in every-day activities. The arising of IoT will provide a shift in service provisioning, moving from the current vision of always on services, typical of the web era, to always-responsive situated services, built and composed at runtime to respond to a specific need and able to account for the user's context.

At the system level, IoT needs to support (i) devices heterogeneity, (ii) scalability, (iii) ubiquitous data exchange through proximity wireless technologies, (iv) energy-optimized solutions, (v) localization and tracking capabilities, (vi) self-organization capabilities, (vii) semantic interoperability and data management and (viii) embed-ded security and privacy-preserving mechanisms.

The proliferation of devices with communicating-actuating capabilities is bring-ing closer the vision of the IoT, where the sensing and actuation functions seamlessly blend into the background and new capabilities are made possible through access of rich new information sources. IoT is an ideal emerging technology to influence the mobile communication domain by providing new evolving data and the required computational resources for creating revolutionary apps [GBM+13, MRT15].

During the last two decades, researchers and engineers have developed a signif-icant amount of prototypes, systems and solutions using context-aware computing techniques. Therefore, context awareness will play a critical role in deciding what data needs to be processed and much more in the IoT era with billions of interconnected sensors [PZC+14].

When large numbers of sensors are deployed and start generating data, the traditional application-based approach (i.e. sensors connected directly to applica-tions individually and manually) becomes infeasible. In order to address this ineffi-ciency, researchers introduced significant amounts of middleware solutions. Each solution focuses on different aspects in the IoT, such as device management, interoperability, platform portability, context awareness, security and privacy and many more. Even though some solutions address multiple aspects, an ideal middleware solution that addresses all the aspects required by the IoT is yet to be designed [PZC+14].

14.2.2   Stream B

The paper [CL16] presents a new visual programming language and its development environment (ASU VIPLE) for programming IoT devices and robots. ASU VIPLE extends the discontinued Microsoft VPL to help the community with their VPL projects. ASU VIPLE supports LEGO EV3 and all IoT devices based on an open architecture. The report [Aug16] deals with IoT education at schools, with the focus on connectivity, i.e. "Connectivity must be used creatively". The report writes:

> The truth is connectivity in schools is about far more than making lives "easier." Technology is often touted as doing more, faster, ultimately saving teachers time. This is fabulous, but utilizing technology in and of itself does not mean a better education. Real changes will come from fostering a better – not faster – learning climate. Thus far, better-connected computers have mostly been making the work of teachers easier. Teachers save time finding, connecting and implementing new resources, thanks to their connected technologies. But that is only the beginning. (the author had in mind IoT capabilities)

The report [Meo16] compiles a list of IoT education examples in the USA, including the uses of the IoT in higher education, the future of the Internet in education and examples of companies that are using the IoT to enter the education space. The foremost example of a tech company that has invaded schools is SMART. It pioneered the world's first interactive whiteboard in 1991. The others include IPEVO, IdeaPaint and IBM. For example, IBM has announced that it would invest $3 billion into the IoT over the next few years, and a significant portion of that money will go towards education. The paper [KBS+13], for example, shares an experience of having almost 2000 students in the first presentation of the course that includes collaborative and collective programming of real-world sensing applications. The paper [VM15] analyses the influence and application of IoT technologies on teaching system in engineering education through practical and methodological approach. The results of the research have shown that the introduction of new methods and strategies of teaching and learning may raise the quality level of the entire engineering educational process and guarantee the delivery of long-lasting knowledge and skills that are applicable to real-world problem solving.

Therefore, a greater connectivity and technological advancement introduced by the IoT have enriched and expanded possibilities in education, brightening its promise for personal growth and discovery, satisfying career possibilities and potential financial success. In this regard, the CISCO white paper [CISCO16] provides the extended definition of the IoT, i.e. treats the latter as the *Internet of Everything* (IoE). CISCO launched an extensive cooperative program on IoE with many organizations (NYAS (the NY Academy of Science), Udacity, Xerox and MIT) aiming at "fuelling educational innovation". One chapter, i.e. "NYAS Turns to Cisco Collaborative Knowledge to Address STEM Skills Gap" writes:

> In 2013, NYAS launched the Global STEM Alliance, an effort to scale STEM mentoring programs developed at NYAS and to galvanize support from industry, government, and non-profits to work together to address the problem of a mounting global STEM skills gap. Through a partnership with Cisco, NYAS will aim to reach one million students in 100 countries by 2020.

The paper [PAF15] presents a study how mobile learning and IoT technology can be designed for students in underprivileged areas of Northern Thailand. This paper also describes observation learning system, which targets primary science education. This system consists of (i) a sensor device, developed with low-cost open-source single-board computer Raspberry Pi, housed in a 3D printed case, (ii) a mobile device-friendly graphical interface displaying visualizations of the sensor data and (iii) a self-contained DIY Wi-Fi network which allows the system to operate in an environment with inadequate ICT infrastructure.

The paper [BSS16] explores a constructivist learning model to implement a weeklong workshop to encourage preuniversity teenagers to pursue careers in STEM, with a particular emphasis on computer science. Twenty-one students participated in the workshop completed pre- and post-surveys and a free word association exercise in the areas of computing and careers in computing. Analysis revealed that students' motivation to learn about the design process, programming, inputs and outputs and wearable technology (wearables)/Internet-of-Things (IoT) increased following participation. There were also increases in confidence in inputs and outputs and wearables/IoT following participation, as well as changes in the computing word associations, with students associating computing more with computer programming terms rather than general terms such as the Internet. The findings suggest that a learning model can be effective in motivating and increasing the self-efficacy of preuniversity teenagers in a number of emerging technological contexts such as IoT and wearables.

The paper [HLX+16] proposes the idea of transforming STEM core courses by integrating IoT-based learning framework into their corresponding lab projects. This paper also (i) presents a case study by incorporating IoT-based learning framework into a software engineering (SWE)-embedded system analysis and design course and (ii) introduces a lab development kit composed of Raspberry Pi/Arduino boards and a set of sensors with Zigbee supporting to provide wireless communication in the class lab section. The developed labware is evaluated through survey questions. The majority of the students provided positive feedback and enjoyed the IoT-based lab development kit.

The paper [PD14] presents a vision of using educational robots as smart mobile "things" of the IoT. Those robots, besides their primary mission to support learning, are able to communicate, to provide computing, to sense due to embedded sensors and actuators and to change their physical context. Robots serve both (i) as the educational service that allows visualizing knowledge through explicit actions and behaviour and (ii) as the enabler of learning and providing student engagement through immersion and instant feedback. The vision relies on the principles of contextualization, physicality and immersion. The pedagogical background is the proposed Internet-of-Things Supported Collaborative Learning (IoTSCL) paradigm based on constructivism, which provides a highly motivating learning environment in university, promoting collaboration among students and achieving the creation of new knowledge in a reflexive process directed by the teacher. The authors demonstrate the implementation of the paradigm in the project-based setting of the university course and evaluate it using the Four-Phased Model of Interest Development.

The other paper [UPB+16] discusses up-to-date findings and outcomes of the research, design and development project that aims at identifying the ontology of Internet-of-Things applications in smart engineering education. The ontology includes concepts, levels of "smartness", components, features and functions.

The study [Ray17] surveys 13 visual programming languages (VPLs) as applied to the application development, especially for the IoT. Those languages extracted from several popular research-electronic databases (e.g. IEEE Xplore, ScienceDirect, Springer Link, etc.) are compared under four key attributes such as a programming environment, license, project repository and platform supports. Grouped into two segments, open source and proprietary platform, VPLs pertain a few crucial challenges elaborated in this literature. The main goal of this paper is to present existing VPLs per their parametric proforma to enable naïve developers and researchers in the field of the IoT to choose an appropriate variant of VPL for a particular type of an application.

This paper [ChR16] analyses the possibility of using commercial off-the-shelf IoT devices to teach a cybersecurity course. The authors argue that the current level of the IoT device security makes testing them an excellent exercise for students. The developed course teaches students basic penetration testing techniques and then sets two rounds of group assignments in which they get hands-on experience with performing a security analysis of an IoT device. In the first round, the students get devices, which are vulnerable. In the second round, the groups are mixed, and they get devices with no previously known vulnerabilities. This approach enables educators to provide for students enough guidance in the first round to get the experience needed to perform the analysis independently in the second round. This seems to have been successful because those student teams found previously unknown vulnerabilities in five devices in the second round of tests.

The study [OR13] discusses an experiment with teaching IoTs as a common red thread across three courses, which ran in parallel during fall semester 2012 at Lulea University of Technology in Sweden. The discussion includes the teaching methodology, the technology blocks, which laid the ground for proposed teaching philosophy as well as the experiences and lessons learned.

In summary, the technology known as *Internet-of-Things* highly extends the capabilities of old approaches related to the "Internet of People". It also poses new challenges for research and opens a new way in constructing systems for many applications. The new capabilities of this technology enlarge the interest for many stakeholders to test it, to research it and to apply it. Therefore, it is not surprising that the educational community, among many others, moves towards the acceptance and adoption of this technology in real settings. In the context of this book, this technology widens the learning variability space in multiple dimensions. That covers pedagogical approaches (new courses, new learning scenarios), robotics (e.g. the robot may serve as a node of the IoT), CS topics (such as energy consumption and security for IoT) and STEM topics (the enlargement of interdisciplinary and heterogeneity nature among all components). Therefore, this technology opens new research possibilities and topics to enforce and to extend the approach we discussed throughout the book.

14.3   An Architecture of IoT System for STEM-Driven CS Education

Here, we discuss new educational tasks in relation to the IoT or new aspects of the tasks considered so far. This may occur if one (we mean CS educators) intends to extend the scope of interdisciplinary STEM and CS knowledge at a high school. To achieve this aim, we need to start from the essence, i.e. definition of the IoT itself. Then we need to look at the initiatives taken by the educational community in this regard (see Stream B in Sect. 14.2). As stated before, researchers define the IoT as an emerging networked infrastructure penetrated by embedded smart devices, *called things*, which have identities, sensing-actuating and computing capabilities, are connected via the Internet, can communicate with each other and with humans and can provide some useful services [SMC11]. This definition, to some degree, defines the structure of the IoT. In general, the IoT application consists of the three-level networked infrastructure. Typically, at the top level, there is the infrastructure of a particular service or application (e.g. healthcare, smart home, smart learning, etc.). At the intermediate level, there is the standard Internet, including the cloud facilities. At the bottom level, there are networks of sensors along with other devices. Note that this architecture model correlates to the smart educational environment we have discussed in Chap. 12. Indeed, the server part (see Fig. 12.3) corresponds to the application layer, intermediate layer corresponds to the user's PC, and the bottom layer corresponds to the robot's environment.

In Fig. 14.1, we present the IoT architecture model as applied to our context. We have devised it using the three-layered architecture taken from [AGM+15]. The architecture includes the *application layer*, the *network layer* and the *perception layer*. The latter aims to collect data needed for the solution of a given STEM-driven

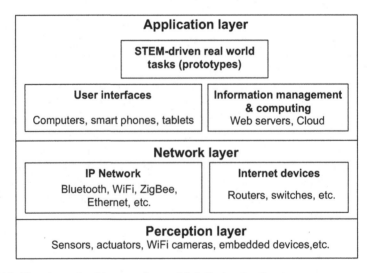

Fig. 14.1 Three-layered architecture of a possible IoT educational system

real-world task. This layer consists of highly heterogeneous sensors, actuators and embedded devices, which implement different functionalities such as querying distance to the obstacle, colour, temperature, humidity, lighting level, etc.

The network layer aims to transfer the obtained data to the application layer. The various wired and wireless communication protocols such as Ethernet, Bluetooth, Wi-Fi, etc. enable data transferring. The application layer provides the services and devices needed for the user and performs information management and computing in solving the STEM-driven tasks (prototypes). There are multiple real-world tasks, even within the classroom, which are indeed IoT-oriented ones. For example, it is possible to build a system responsible for maintaining the needed level of the temperature and humidity for plants at classrooms. The following scenarios are helpful to build the system. There are sensors as nodes of the IoT that measure the humidity of plants and temperature within the classroom. The measured data are transferred to the middle level through the Bluetooth connection. To implement the system, we need to provide the following actions: (i) observation of temperature and humidity, (ii) observation of the capacity of a robot's battery over time to prevent the interruption of the process and (iii) a prototype of the traffic system modelling using robots as autonomous vehicles and things of the IoT.

The task covers *the physical aspects* (obtaining physical characteristics of the sensors); *biological aspects* (sensors measure the soil humidity of plants); *mathematical aspects* to analyse, evaluate and represent the results of measurement; and *CS aspects* (control, observation and monitoring). We are able to modify the following tasks considered so far with regard to the IoT concept: (i) help system, (ii) monitoring and observing unknown surroundings and (iii) Raspberry Pi as server. There is also a set of real task prototypes suitable to explain the IoT concepts in education CS on the STEM paradigm. Examples are the humidity control for the classroom plants, traffic control, etc. We discuss the latter in more detail in Fig. 14.2.

We interpret the IoT as an interconnected set of things, i.e. as nodes of different types. There are three types of nodes:

- Node of *Type* 1 serves as a traffic light and consists of three sub-nodes: LED1 (red), LED2 (yellow) and LED3 (green).
- Node of *Type* 2 serves as a vehicle and consists of following sub-nodes:

    - Sub-node S1 is an ultrasonic sensor for obtaining obstacles.
    - Sub-node S2 is a colour sensor for recognizing colours.
    - Sub-nodes S3 and S4 are light sensors for following the road.
    - Sub-nodes M1 and M2 are motors for ensuring the movement of vehicles.

- Node of *Type 3* is the Wi-Fi camera that serves for registering possible accidents.

Note that each node has a specific functionality to solve a particular part (i.e. subtasks) of the *traffic control* task. Note also that we have realized those subtasks as *independent tasks* in the form of smart learning objects (SLOs/GLOs) in our previous research. For example, the node of *Type 1* is responsible for the traffic light controlling subtask. We have presented its implementation as a case

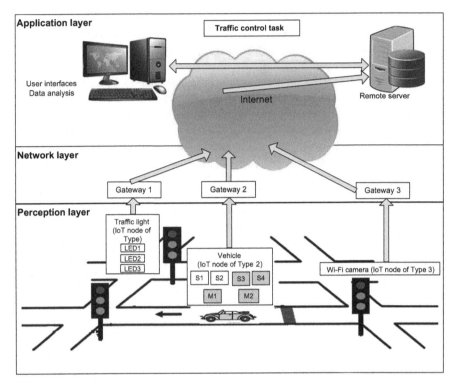

Fig. 14.2 Architectural view to define *traffic control* as educational task

study in [BBD+14]. The node of *Type 2* specifies functionality that is much more complex and covers four subtasks. They are as follows:

1. Obstacles obtaining in the context of positioning of the vehicles (published in [ŠBB+16] as a case study)
2. Colour recognition in the context of choosing the correct traffic light colour (published in [ŠBB+16] as a case study)
3. Line following task in the context of moving on the road (published in [ŠB15, BSD13] as case studies)
4. Robot's movement task to ensure the relevant movement (adequate velocity, stability of the movement, etc.) of the vehicle (published in [BSM12] as a case study)

The node of *Type 3* corresponds partially to a monitoring task described in [BSD13] (however, in the other context).

Note that we have considered all these tasks previously in another context having other aims. There our aim was to illustrate the relevance of the discussed approaches to the topics of CS education. There was no explicit intent on STEM and IoT in those published papers. Now, in terms of the IoT application for education, we have developed a SLO that integrates (1), (3) and (4) subtasks [ŠBB+17].

Therefore, by introducing the architecture (Fig. 14.2), we have shown the way on how it is possible to combine and adapt the ideas of previously researched tasks to the needs of the IoT context. Taking into account the smart educational environment (see Chap. 12), smart devices (Chap. 3) and presented architecture in this section, we are able to formulate a few research questions (RQ) posed by the IoT context.

RQ1 Investigate characteristics of smart devices, including educational robots, as nodes of IoT used in solving the adequate tasks such as *traffic control* or its subtasks such as *line follower, etc.*

RQ2 Develop a *remote smart environment* by extending the mode of the created (see in terms of the IoT) ideology

RQ3 Investigate pedagogical aspects and new capabilities of this remote mode for CS, STEM and IoT education

Those questions require intensive researching efforts. We are not able to consider them fully due to the accepted format of the book and aims of this chapter. Instead, we provide a restricted analysis focusing on specific task aspects relevant to the IoT and STEM (i.e. energy and accuracy aspects) only. Firstly, in Sect. 14.4, we discuss a framework related to new tasks. Next, in Sect. 14.5, we apply an inquiry-based (i.e. relevant to STEM) approach and others in our case study to deal with those specific tasks.

14.4   A Framework to Consider Educational Tasks in Relation to IoT

In creating the IoT-based systems, context plays the essential role, because smart devices that collect data from the environment rely on the contextual information coming from other devices to process this information collectively [Che12]. This paper defines that as a *connected context* of computing. From the perspective of STEM-driven CS education, we argue that the IoT extends this paradigm in this regard. There are a few possibilities to obtain the contextual information, i.e. explicitly and implicitly, through inferring or modelling. In the first case, it is possible to access and extract data directly. In the second case, we may obtain the needed data through approaching to the relevant people, e.g. by asking direct questions or through other sources. Inferring the context is possible using statistical or data mining methods [AT11]. However, the most powerful approaches rely on context modelling.

There are many approaches and solutions to model the IoT context. The paper [AAF12], for example, relies on agents with the self-configuration of their internal architecture in order to use different communication protocols taking into account the context and the needs of the application. The paper [VCV+12] presents an interaction model which is nonintrusive from the point of view of the "user-intelligent system" relationship. This model permits a user to accomplish IoT tasks without

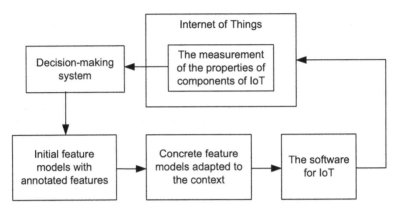

Fig. 14.3 Framework 1 to adapt IoT to a certain context

the need of a composition environment, i.e. screen editors. [ABC+12] proposes the multi-scale framework based on three aspects, i.e. (i) distributed context management with the integration of imperative, deductive and multi-agent-based managers; (ii) dynamic adaptation and privacy requirements from the consumer and the producer points of view, respectively; and (iii) autonomous deployment and reconfiguration of context management software components in the multi-scale environment. [WDT+12] proposes the description ontology that integrates the existing semantic web approaches for modelling the IoT domain concepts and is extended with essential concepts such as testing to ensure correct functionality of IoT services at both design and runtime stages. [KRM13] introduces the four-layer context-aware conceptual framework systematizing the IoT infrastructure to receive e-services out of raw data captured by physical devices.

The discussed models confirm the need of the dynamic modelling of the IoT variability. That is so, because IoT is a highly dynamic and radically distributed networked system composed of a very large number of smart objects producing and consuming information. Below we propose two frameworks to model the IoT context variability using the feature-modelling notion.

Framework 1 (Fig. 14.3) Initially, the designer creates the initial static feature model with annotated features. It evolves over time, depending on the context. The designer adds the context features and develops IoT components. The created static IoT models are supplemented with properties that define the value of the feature. The properties of the IoT components are measured and transferred to the decision-making system. The latter computes the received data (i.e. the properties of the IoT components) and forms a set of rules. Then it is possible to adapt the concrete feature models to the context using those rules. Finally, concrete feature models are transformed into the software for the IoT.

We have realized Framework 1 partially in our case study in Chap. 9, though there was no explicit reference to the IoT. Here, we present the use of this framework explicitly in our case study (Sect. 14.6).

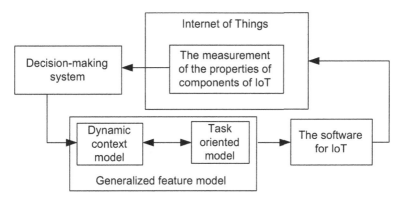

Fig. 14.4 Framework 2 to adapt IoT to a certain context

Framework 2 (Fig. 14.4) The context model is dynamic, and it is composed of collaborative features that will exchange data and control information at runtime.

The properties of the IoT components are measured and transferred to the decision-making system that computes the received data and forms sets of rules that define the values of the context features. The dynamic context model is related to the task-oriented model through collaborative features.

We have yet not implemented Framework 2 because of the difficulty of extracting data at runtime.

14.5   Case Study: Line Following Task

This case study implements Framework 1. The aim is to define some characteristics (such as availability and battery energy level) relevant to the IoT context in dealing with the adequate robot task. We treat the robot as a mobile component of the IoT in this case study. The task of the robot is to follow the black line (given on some background) using different algorithms. Therefore, the robot is a *line follower*. It represents the *base system*. We consider the base system from the very beginning, i.e. from the statement of requirements and taking into account needs for IoT. These represent *the context* of the base system. It is convenient to represent the base system and its context semiformally, using the feature-based notion (see Fig. 14.5 and Chap. 5, for more details). As the model (Fig. 14.5) is abstract, we need to introduce more details, i.e. concrete features, for the relevant entities of the task (base system). Note that, for the simplicity reasons, we consider two aspects of the IoT context, i.e. availability and the level of battery energy. By availability, we mean the correct use of physical nodes (motors and sensors). In the model, we represent them by the collaborative links (see Fig. 14.5). The feature "battery energy level" collaborates with the features "speed" and "algorithm".

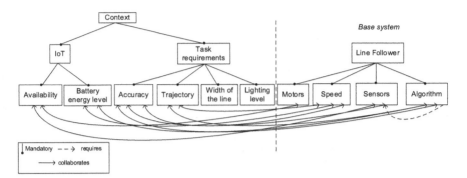

Fig. 14.5 Abstract feature model of the entire system with collaborative features

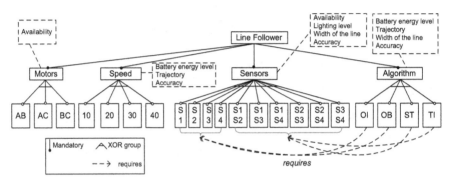

Fig. 14.6 Initial feature model of *line follower* with annotated features (annotations are in dotted boxes)

In Fig. 14.6, we present the concrete feature model with annotation. This model includes LF algorithm types (OI, One Inside; OB, One Bounce; ST, Straddle; TI, Two Inside [Gra03]), names of motor outputs (A, B, C of the Lego NXT Robot), a possible speed of the motors and light (colour) sensor inputs (S1, S2, S3 and S4) used. We use the programming language RobotC to specify robot's actions. There is some specificity in expressing the robot's speed in RobotC named by *power level*. *Power levels* range from -100 to $+100$.

Negative values indicate on a reverse direction, and positive values indicate on a forward direction. For example, to move the motor A forward at 30% of full power, we should use the following statement: *motor [motorA]* $= 30$. The distance driven by the robot per time depends on the motor's *power level*.

Experiment 1 The aim of Experiment 1 is to obtain the dependencies of the preprogrammed motor speed that expressed the power level and the real speed with regard to the three different battery energy levels (7 V, 8 V, 9 V). We present the results of measurements in Table 14.1 and Fig. 14.7. We have not obtained an evident difference in real speeds when preprogrammed speed is within 20–60% of the maximal power. However, when the preprogrammed speed was between

Table 14.1 Motor speed-battery energy level-real speed dependencies

Motor speed expressed by power level, %	Real speed (m/s)		
	Battery energy level 7 V	Battery energy level 8 V	Battery energy level 9 V
20	0.07	0.07	0.07
40	0.15	0.15	0.15
60	0.22	0.22	0.22
80	0.26	0.28	0.30
100	0.26	0.29	0.31

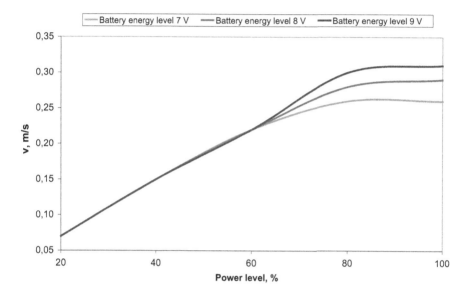

Fig. 14.7 Dependencies between the preprogrammed speed (power level) and measured real speed (v) when the battery power level is equal to 7 V, 8 V and 9 V (top curve)

80 and100%, the real speed varies significantly and depends on the battery energy level.

In terms of the IoT, the essence of the task is to obtain the level of battery voltage when the robot follows the line and at the same time to send the message to a PC. The user accepts the decision regarding this message.

Experiment 2 The aim of *Experiment 2* is to obtain the accuracy of the line following. A dotted line (Fig. 14.8) presents the real path of the *line follower* obtained experimentally. When the robot's speed is 10–30% of full power, the robot trajectory coincides with the black line. When the robot's speed is larger than 40% of full power, it is unable to follow the black line exactly, and the real path consequently deviates from the black line.

Fig. 14.8 Elliptical and rectangular routes followed by line follower (© with kind permission from Springer [Štu15])

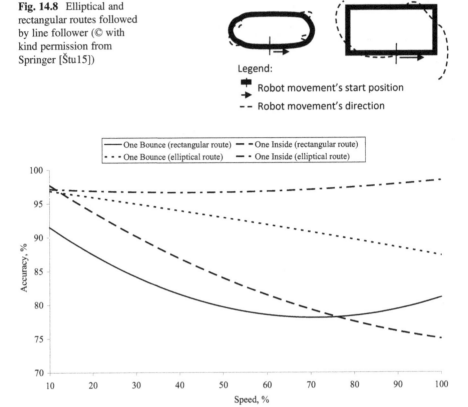

Legend:

▬ Robot movement's start position

‑‑ Robot movement's direction

Fig. 14.9 Results of research on the line following algorithm using elliptical and rectangular routes (© with kind permission from Springer [Štu15])

In Fig. 14.9, we present the results of the accuracy comparison of the line following when different algorithms are used. The accuracy is calculated by estimating what part of the robot path overcomes without leaving the black line while following the routes of different shape and driving at the different speed (speed is expressed as a percentage of max power level of servomotors controlling the rotation of the robot wheels).

14.6 Summary and Conclusion

In this chapter, we have introduced a basic terminology of the technology known as *Internet-of-Things*. It highly extends the capabilities of old approaches related to the "Internet of People" or "Internet of Computers". The Internet-of-Things (IoT) also poses new challenges for research and opens a new way in constructing systems for many applications. The new capabilities of this technology enlarge the interest for many stakeholders to test it, to research it and to apply it. Therefore, it is not surprising that the educational community, among many others, moves towards the acceptance and adoption of this technology in real educational settings. There are many announcements on this technological shift in education. In the context of this book, this technology widens the learning variability space in multiple dimensions. That covers pedagogical approaches (new courses, new learning scenarios, inquiry-based learning), robotics (e.g. the robot may serve as a node of the IoT), CS topics (e.g. complex task decomposition/composition and new aspects within robot control programs) and STEM aspects (such as energy consumption, accuracy, the enlargement of interdisciplinary and heterogeneity nature among all STEM components). Therefore, this technology opens new research possibilities and topics to enforce and extend the approach we discussed throughout the book. We have proposed the architecture and framework to deal with tasks related to IoT education. We have showed on how it is possible to combine the previously researched tasks (in our case studies with the focus on STEM and CS topics) aiming to solve much more complex tasks that indeed are relevant to IoT education. Therefore, the latter educational paradigm also supports STEM-driven CS education, even to a larger extent. As the IoT is a complex system and its tasks too, not all of them are relevant to teaching at the school level. For example, analysis of security aspects, communication and managing aspects of the middle and top layers are more relevant to the university level. Nevertheless, even at the upper layer there is a huge space for researching STEM-related tasks.

References

[AAF12]   Ayala I, Amor M, Fuentes L (2012) An agent platform for self-configuring agents in the internet of things. In: Third international workshop on infrastructures and tools for multiagent systems, ITMAS, pp 65–78
[ABC+12]   Arcangeli JP, Bouzeghoub A, Camps V, Canut MF, Chabridon S, Conan D, ..., Zaraté P (2012) INCOME–multi-scale context management for the internet of things. In: Ambient intelligence. Springer, Berlin, pp 338–347
[AGM+15]   Al-Fuqaha A, Guizani M, Mohammadi M, Aledhari M, Ayyash M (2015) Internet of things: a survey on enabling technologies, protocols, and applications. IEEE Commun Surv Tutor 17(4):2347–2376
[AIM10]   Atzori L, Iera A, Morabito G (2010) The internet of things: a survey. Comput Netw 54 (15):2787–2805
[AT11]   Adomavicius G, Tuzhilin A (2011) Context-aware recommender systems. In: Recommender systems handbook. Springer, pp 217–253
[Aug16]   Augur H (2016) IoT in education: the internet of school things. https://www.ibm.com/blogs/internet-of-things/iot-education/
[BBD+14]   Burbaitė R, Bespalova K, Damaševičius R, Štuikys V (2014) Context-aware generative learning objects for teaching computer science. Int J Eng Educ 30(4):929–936
[BSD13]   Burbaite R, Stuikys V, Damasevicius R (2013) Educational robots as collaborative learning objects for teaching Computer Science. In: System Science and Engineering (ICSSE), 2013 international conference IEEE, pp 211–216

[BSM12]		Burbaite R, Stuikys V, Marcinkevicius R (2012) The LEGO NXT robot-based e-learning environment to teach computer science topics. Elektronika Elektrotechnika 18(9):113–116

[BSS16]		Byrne JR, O'Sullivan K, Sullivan K (2016) An IoT and wearable technology hackathon for promoting careers in computer science. IEEE Trans Educ

[CBR17]		Computer Business Review 10 UK IoT degree courses covering UI, AI & machine learning			http://www.cbronline.com/news/internet-of-things/10-uk-iot-degree-courses-covering-ui-ai-machine-learning-4874100/

[Che12]		Chen YK (2012) Challenges and opportunities of internet of things. In: Design automation conference (ASP-DAC), 2012 17th Asia and South Pacific. IEEE, pp 383–388

[ChR16]		Chothia T, de Ruiter J (2016) Learning from others' mistakes: penetration testing IoT devices in the classroom. In: 2016 USENIX workshop on Advances in Security Education (ASE 16). USENIX Association

[CISCO16]	The Internet of Everything—A $19 Trillion Opportunity (2016) CISCO consulting services. http://www.cisco.com/c/dam/en_us/services/portfolio/consulting-services/documents/consulting-services-capturing-ioe-value-aag.pdf

[CL16]		Chen Y, De Luca G (2016) VIPLE: visual IoT/robotics programming language environment for computer science education. In: Parallel and distributed processing symposium workshops, 2016 I.E. International. IEEE, pp 963–971

[CSM17]		Computer Science Internet of things, master's course. Malmo University. http://edu.mah.se/en/Course/DA650A

[Dru15]		Drucker PF (2015) Internet of things. http://www.internet-of-things-research.eu/pdf/IERC_Position_Paper_IoT_Standardization_Final.pdf view on 30/05/2015

[GBM+13]	Gubbi J, Buyya R, Marusic S, Palaniswami M (2013) Internet of Things (IoT): a vision, architectural elements, and future directions. Futur Gener Comput Syst 29 (7):1645–1660

[Gra03]		Gray JA (2003) Toeing the line: experiments with line-following algorithms

[Hen16]		Hennick C (2016) Internet of things: coming to your campus soon. http://www.edtechmagazine.com/higher/article/2016/08/internet-things-coming-your-campus-sooner-you-think

[HLX+16]	He J, Lo DCT, Xie Y, Lartigue J (2016) Integrating Internet of Things (IoT) into STEM undergraduate education: case study of a modern technology infused courseware for embedded system course. In: Frontiers in Education conference (FIE), 2016 IEEE. IEEE, pp 1–9

[KBS+13]	Kortuem G, Bandara A, Smith N, Richards M, Petre M (2013) Educating the internet-of-things generation. Computer 46(2):53–61

[KKS+10]	Kortuem G, Kawsar F, Sundramoorthy V, Fitton D (2010) Smart objects as building blocks for the internet of things. IEEE Internet Comput 14(1):44–51

[KRM13]		Kanter T, Rahmani R, Mahmud A (2013) Conceptual framework for internet of things' virtualization via OpenFlow in context-aware networks. IJCSI Int J Comp Sci Issues 10(Issue 6., No 1):16–27

[Meo16]		Meola A (2016) How IoT in education is changing the way we learn. www.businessinsider.com/internet-of-things-education-2016-9

[MIT17]		MIT courses on IoT. http://web.mit.edu/professional/digital-programs/courses/IoT/

[MRT15]		Madakam S, Ramaswamy R, Tripathi S (2015) Internet of things (IoT): a literature review. J Comp Commun 3(05):164

[MSP+12]	Miorandi D, Sicari S, De Pellegrini F, Chlamtac I (2012) Internet of things: vision, applications and research challenges. Ad Hoc Netw 10(7):1497–1516

[OR13]		Osipov E, Riliskis L (2013) Educating innovators of future internet of things. In: Frontiers in Education conference, 2013 IEEE. IEEE, pp 1352–1358

[PAF15]   Putjorn P, Ang CS, Farzin D (2015) Learning IoT without the I-educational internet of things in a developing context. In: Proceedings of the 2015 workshop on do-it-yourself networking: an interdisciplinary approach. ACM, pp 11–13

[PD14]   Plauska I, Damaševičius R (2014) Educational robots for Internet-of-Things supported collaborative learning. In: International conference on information and software technologies. Springer, pp 346–358

[PZC+14]   Perera C, Zaslavsky A, Christen P, Georgakopoulos D (2014) Context aware computing for the internet of things: a survey. Commun Surv Tutor IEEE 16(1):414–454

[Ray17]   Ray PP (2017) A survey on visual programming languages in internet of things. Scientific Programming, 2017

[ŠB15]   Štuikys V, Burbaitė R (2015) Smart educational environments to teach topics in CS: a case study. In: Smart learning objects for the smart education in CS (Theory, methodology and robot-based implementation). Springer

[ŠBB+16]   Štuikys V, Burbaitė R, Bespalova K, Ziberkas G (2016) Model-driven processes and tools to design robot-based generative learning objects for computer science education. Sci Comput Program 129:48–71

[ŠBB+17]   Štuikys V, Burbaitė R, Bespalova K, Blažauskas T, Barisas D (2017) Stage – based generative learning object model for automated content adaptation. Baltic J Mod Comput 5(2):183–205

[SEC+13]   Schirner G, Erdogmus D, Chowdhury K, Padir T (2013) The future of human-in-the-loop cyber-physical systems. IEEE Comput 46(1):36–45

[SMC11]   Serbanati A, Medaglia CM, Ceipidor UB (2011) Building blocks of the internet of things: state of the art and beyond. In: Turcu C (ed) Deploying RFID – challenges, solutions, and open issues. In Tech (2011)

[STJ14]   Singh D, Tripathi G, Jara AJ (2014) A survey of Internet-of-things: future vision, architecture, challenges and services. In: Internet of things (WF-IoT), 2014 I.E. World Forum on IEEE, pp 287–292

[UPB+16]   Uskov V, Pandey A, Bakken J P, Margapuri VS (2016) Smart engineering education: the ontology of Internet-of-Things applications. In: Global engineering education conference (EDUCON), 2016 IEEE. IEEE, pp 476–481

[VCV+12]   Vega-Barbas M, Casado-Mansilla D, Valero M, López-de-Ipina D, Bravo J, Flórez F (2012) Smart spaces and smart objects interoperability architecture (S3OiA). In: Innovative Mobile and Internet Services in Ubiquitous Computing (IMIS), 2012 sixth international conference on IEEE, pp 725–730

[VM15]   Vujović V, Maksimović M (2015) The impact of the 'Internet of Things' on engineering education. The second International Conference on Open and Flexible Education (ICOFE 2015), Hong Kong, pp 135–144

[VSD+16]   Venckauskas A, Stuikys V, Damasevicius R, Jusas N (2016) Modelling of internet of things units for estimating security-energy-performance relationships for quality of service and environment awareness. Secur Commun Netw 9(16):3324–3339

[WDT+12]   Wang W, De S, Toenjes R, Reetz E, Moessner K (2012) A comprehensive ontology for knowledge representation in the internet of things. In: Trust, Security and Privacy in Computing and Communications (TrustCom), 2012 I.E. 11th international conference on IEEE, pp 1793–1798

[WWR+12]   Walczak D, Wrzos M, Radziuk A, Lewandowski B, Mazurek C (2012) Machine-to-machine communication and data processing approach in future internet applications. In: Communication Systems, Networks & Digital Signal Processing (CSNDSP), 2012 8th international symposium on IEEE, pp 1–5

Chapter 15
A Finalizing Discussion and Open Issues

Abstract In this finalizing chapter, we firstly summarize our discussions taken in previous chapters by presenting the essential features and capabilities as well as focusing on limitations of our approach. One important aspect is the analysis of capabilities of the approach to promote computational thinking in CS education on the STEM paradigm. We present the capabilities and limitations of the approach from the viewpoint of a common sense and from the learner and teacher perspectives. Analysis of limitations is helpful for foreseeing the way on how the approach could or might evolve in the future. This analysis enables us to formulate the open issues too. Secondly, we present some ideas on the applicability of the approach for STEM-driven CS education at the university level, as well as on STEM in industry. Finally, we close the discussion with our vision on how the proposed approach may be beneficial for introducing the MOOC paradigm.

15.1 Introduction

This is a finalizing chapter. Firstly, its aim is to summarize our discussion taken in previous chapters by presenting the essential features of the approach we have identified as STEM-driven CS education at the high school. In doing so, we focus on the essential capabilities as well as on the limitations of our approach. We present those issues from the viewpoint of common sense and from the learner and teacher perspectives. Analysis of limitations is helpful for foreseeing the way on how the approach could or might evolve in the future. This analysis enables us also to formulate the open issues. Secondly, our aim is to present some ideas on the applicability of the approach for STEM-driven CS education at the university level. Again, we discuss those ideas taking into account the new possibilities and drawbacks of the approach. Finally, we could not be able to close our discussion without presenting our vision on CS and STEM integrated education using the MOOC paradigm with regard to the proposed approach.

Therefore, the content of this chapter includes three topics. The first is about an evaluation of the approach from the pure practice with the focus on the essential new capabilities and difficulties that might be encountered by the other users who do not

© Springer International Publishing AG, part of Springer Nature 2018   347
V. Štuikys, R. Burbaitė, *Smart STEM-Driven Computer Science Education*,
https://doi.org/10.1007/978-3-319-78485-4_15

yet test the proposed ideas in some way. One important aspect of the evaluation is an analysis of the capabilities of the approach to promote *computational thinking* in learning on STEM paradigm. This is extremely important, because the computer science concepts continuously migrate in multiple "non-technological" disciplines such as statistics, biology, social sciences, etc. The second topic emphasizes those aspects of the approach that might be relevant to CS and STEM education at universities. Here, we take our emphasis on the development and researching aspects. In presenting the third topic, we focus on the possibility and issues to connect the approach with the MOOC paradigm.

15.2 A Summary and Evaluation of the Proposed Approach

Firstly, we summarize the most common aspects that could be interesting to a majority of readers, including those who might identify themselves as education policymakers, educational software designers and researchers. Our approach deals with the way on how to integrate the STEM paradigm into CS, i.e. programming courses, using robots as educational tools at the high school. Note that the high school is the same name known in some countries as a secondary school or gymnasium. Integration is, in fact, a complex heterogeneous process. It covers all the pedagogical, the social, the technological and the content aspects, including those that are specific for STEM, such as the interdisciplinary knowledge to be delivered or the inquiry method used among others. The integration focuses on two top-level concepts. The first is from the methodological rank. The second is pure technological.

From the methodological viewpoint, the central idea of our approach is *STEM learning variability*. The learning variability covers the most frequently used variants that represent the pedagogy (by this, we also mean social aspects), technology and content. We have borrowed the term variability from software engineering. The power of this term is that we are able to express the essential attributes of any domain through its feature variability [AK09]. Therefore, the use of learning variability is relevant to the educational domain too. By introducing this term, firstly we are able, using adequate methods such as domain analysis and modelling, to identify possible variants for each learning components separately. Then we are able to integrate all ingredients, including STEM aspects, to identify interrelationships and to form the entire STEM learning variability. Expressed explicitly, it represents the *STEM-driven CS education model*. In terms of the content variability, we create this model not for the entire domain but for a separate topic or topics. In other words, STEM-driven pedagogy aspects and robotics technology are common for all topics.

The second concept relates to the implementation technology to implement this educational model. By doing so, we seek the enhancement of generative reuse, i.e. ensuring the level of automation as highly as possible. It was possible to bring this idea due to our previous experience in designing and exploring smart generative learning objects and using them in the real setting for more than 5 years to teach CS robot-oriented topics (see [ŠB15, Štu15] and also Sect 6.3 in Chap. 6). We were able to achieve the adequate level of automation in the previous and the current research because we use at the implementation stage the structured heterogeneous meta-programming. It is a powerful implementation methodology or technology in terms of automation and adaptation. One can see this power, for example, from the fact that its application does not depend on the complexity of the object to which we need to apply this technology. We apply it to smart learning objects, to generative STEM scenarios, and to creating managing procedures to support a personal generative STEM library. However, the mode of using this technology in each case is quite different. We have expressed this difference by meta-program types (*Type 1*, *Type 2*, *Type 3* and *Type 4*).

The automation in our approach covers not only the items mentioned above but also the processes of developing the meta-programming-based specifications. Those automation capabilities are due to the formal or semi-formal representation of STEM variability models and the use of adequate tools. We use feature models to represent STEM learning variability. Those models and their supporting tools ensure correct high-level specifications and open the way for introducing systematization, reuse and automation.

The important issue is the flexible internal models of such objects as smart learning objects. They directly relate to the capabilities of meta-programming to perform transformations through refactoring of one model to another without the loss of functionality. This kind of transformation enables to perform automated adaptation to the context of use. We are able to ensure a possibility for automated adaptation due to that the internal structure of smart learning objects that also contains some context information. On the other hand, automation also opens the way of a much broader view for learners to systemize, generalize and analyse the content to extend the computational thinking aspects. Therefore, we summarize the most essential properties of our approach as follows in presented sub-sections.

From the methodological viewpoint, we are able to present our approach as an adequate interaction of the following key components: *smart learning objects, generative STEM-driven learning scenarios, a personal generative library* to stor-age learning content and *smart educational environment.* Our approach also covers the design and usage aspects of the components in two modes: as separate entities and entities integrated into the smart educational environment. The latter is smart in terms of using smart devices (robots, camera, etc.) and smart approaches and tools.

15.2.1   Capabilities of Smart Learning Objects

Smart learning objects (further SLO, meaning generative LO with enhanced functionality) represent the STEM-driven CS learning variability content, meaning generalized content that integrates also *pedagogical*[1], *social* and *technological attributes*. When implemented, this generalized content stands for the input to the standard processor (i.e. meta-language compiler). The latter is the generator of the concrete content for the use in a given learning situation. Typically, a smart learning object is a black-box entity to the user (teacher or learner). He/she sees only the interface boxes for selecting parameter values. Parameters are concepts that reside within implemented specifications to describe SLOs. In terms of the implementation, parameters and their values specify the STEM learning variability features. Therefore, the user does not extract the needed (concrete) teaching content from the library as it is in a standard case (the extracted item is a smart learning object itself), but the user guides the automatic process of the content generation with regard to his/her preferences. The context awareness implemented within the generic smart specification ensures a flexible managing process to deal with the user preferences. SLOs are not static but rather dynamic entities. Dynamicity appears in two ways: (1) as predesigned attributes to implement learning variability for STEM, for context awareness, etc. with possibly minor changes, and (2) as evolutionary major changes, including structural changes. The first case refers to those dynamic features that we are able to foresee in advance, to express through variability feature variants and implement statically. However, it is possible to introduce minor changes, for example, to change parameter values without redesign of the entire specification. The second case relates to the evolution of SLO over a longer time. The accumulated experience in using SLOs may cause the need to introduce enhanced functionality (as it is in the case with STEM). The latter requires of introducing structural changes of the SLO format. In this regard, we have defined two SLO models, identified as *Model 1* (where STEM features are implicit with *restricted functionality*) and *Model 2* (where STEM features are explicit with *enhanced functionality*). The term *restricted functionality* also means that this model implements the learning scenario within the SLO specification implicitly, i.e. the sequence of choice of predefined parameter values in fact predefines the learning scenario. The term *enhanced functionality* defines the structure of the external generative scenario as a separate tool developed to support STEM-driven education. Its capabilities deserve a separate evaluation.

In summary, smart learning objects (SLOs) are generative entities, in fact, meta-programs enabling to generate the robot program instances or call the component-based LO to support the STEM paradigm on demand. From the pure technological viewpoint, one can treat the SLOs specification coded in the meta-language (PHP in our case) as a generator of the educational content (i.e. robot control programs in our case). The conventional PHP processor serves as a generating tool. From the

---

[1]Note that in the recent SLO, the top pedagogical attributes are within the generative scenario.

methodological viewpoint, one can consider the SLO specification as a STEM learning variability space restricted for the concrete topic. By the term STEM learning variability, we describe and represent uniformly, through *features* or *parameters*, the following attributes: pedagogical, social, technological and content. These attributes may also contain the contextual information, such as priority-based fuzzy variables. Their role is to make easier the selection of parameter values in case of the manual content adaptation (one-stage SLOs) or automated content adaptation (multistage SLOs). Note that we are able to transform original one-stage SLOs into multistage ones. Multistage SLOs are meta-meta-programs. It is possible also to enhance the capabilities of SLOs by combining them with software agents. Therefore, SLOs have a capability to evolve from static generative entities towards autonomous knowledge-based entities.

15.2.2   Capabilities of Generative Learning Scenario

Generative learning scenario is the tool to generate *a concrete scenario on demand* by the user (teacher or learner) flexibly (i.e. depending on the task, using different types of learning resources, etc.). We implemented it using the same methodology as for designing SLOs. At the top level of the methodology are processes to discover a model of the generative scenario. The developed model predefines the structure (explicitly) and functionality (implicitly) of this scenario. The model is hierarchic and contains three levels: top, intermediate and low. At the top level, the model presents common and STEM-driven pedagogy (i.e. scenario types, topics as tasks, subtopics, learning objectives, expected outcomes) and pedagogical approaches and tools. At the intermediate level, the model presents the student characteristics (student's level, learning pace, learning style, etc.). As those attributes are available and visible through the user-friendly interface, the user is able to form a query (for the personal generative library) to select the adequate learning content. The latter part of the model forms the remaining level (i.e. low). Therefore, this level describes the technology and content. The learning content is of two types: component-based (i.e. video, instructions to construct/use smart devices, descriptions of scenario types, etc.) and smart (generative) learning objects.

Therefore, the implemented model provides links with other key components (e.g. *personal generative library* directly and *smart educational environment* indirectly). The essential property of the generative scenario is the possibility to form individual learning paths flexibly, meaning the capabilities of selecting adequate variants and automated processes to support needed activities. The reader is able to learn more details about those capabilities by reading and analysing case studies given in Chap. 13.

As a summary, we are able to outline and evaluate the benefits of our approach in three dimensions: (1) *what it is in large, (2) what it is in small,* and *(3) how it contributes and supports the formation and development of computational thinking in learning.*

In terms of the first dimension, our approach focuses on the following topics and issues related to the topics:

(i) Smart learning object (SLO) models and their implementation.

(ii) A set of implemented SLOs as the *use-as-is* library entities developed for different types of the models.

(iii) The processes of creating SLOs, i.e. robot-oriented STEM-driven entities for CS education.

(iv) Processes of using SLOs as educational content to educate high school students in STEM-driven CS courses.

(v) Generative scenario (GS) to generate a scenario instance on demand depending on the used context.

(vi) Personal generative library (PGL) of the educational content such as SLOs.

(vii) Smart educational environment (SEE) to support the educational processes. It contains a variety of tools, including hardware (robots, server, computers, cameras, etc.), software of general use and dedicated software to support STEM-driven CS education.

(viii) Practical aspects and capabilities of the approach to develop computational thinking of learners.

The presented constituents are different in their rank, role and functionality. With regard to the educational process, one needs to consider three items (SLOs, GS and PGL) as basic ones if we ignore integrative aspects to form a smart educational environment on this basis. Indeed SLOs represent the content, i.e. STEM learning variability specifically woven with STEM-driven attributes and some aspects of STEM pedagogy. GS implements the sequence of actions for extracting the adequate SLO and component-based LOs and then using those items according to the predefined attributes of STEM pedagogy. One can consider PGL as a part of *the knowledge base* of the educational environment. One can understand the functionality of those items through two processes. The first includes the *internal interaction* of a given item with the adequate supporting tools. The second includes the *external interaction* within the educational environment. Therefore, we categorize the educational process as a three-phase activity initiated by the user (teacher or student): (i) external interaction to gain the needed resource (GS and SLO); (ii) internal interaction to prepare the resource for use; and (iii) learner's activities and actions using the ready-for-use resources to gain the expected knowledge, i.e. achieving the prescribed learning objectives.

In terms of the second dimension, our approach focuses on the following SLO properties:

(i) A set of SLOs covers the CS curriculum topics for different student grades (from 9 to 12).

(ii) The set represents robot-oriented tasks implemented as *generative robot control programs plus component-based LO* (guides, tutorials, quizzes, etc.)

(iii) Semantically, the tasks represent prototypes of the real-world tasks, ensuring the delivery of STEM-driven knowledge that also includes CS knowledge.

(iv) From the implementation viewpoint, SLOs are domain-specific meta-programs (i.e. robot-oriented meta-programs).

(v) From the methodological viewpoint, (a) SLOs implement the STEM-driven CS-oriented learning variability, and (b) SLO is a software product or tool, i.e. generator producing a robot control program or programs on demand managed by the user (teacher or student) through parameter value selection and using the meta-language processor.

(vi) Though the SLO implementation is independent upon the meta-language, all variants of SLOs (we mean different structural models) are implemented using PHP in the role of the meta-language.

(vii) A large body of SLOs is implemented using three models, identified as *Model 0*, *Model 1* and *Model 2*. *Model 1* has two modifications (represented as one-stage or multistage). As *Model 0* represents the initial one-stage GLO/SLO, we do not treat it as a separate entity.

(viii) Multistage SLO is derivable from the one-stage SLO using a refactoring tool. For the same task, one-stage SLO and its derivative multistage SLO have the same functionality, but they have different structures to support an automated adaptation.

We consider the third dimension separately in the next sub-section.

15.2.3 How Does Our Approach Support Computational Thinking?

Computational thinking is a fundamental skill for everyone, not just for computer scientists. To reading, writing, and arithmetic, we should add computational thinking to every child's analytical ability. Computational thinking involves solving problems, designing systems, and understanding human behavior, by drawing on the concepts fundamental to computer science. Computational thinking includes a range of mental tools that reflect the breadth of the field of computer science, says Jeannette M. Wing [Win06].

We accept some narrative statements of this paper as the basis of a framework to outline the capabilities of our approach in this regard. Typically, computational thinking involves many things related to either problem solving by human or machine (i.e. computer, robot). Among others, they include thinking recursively. It is parallel processing. It is "interpreting code as data and data as code". Computational thinking is *using abstraction and decomposition* when attacking a large complex task or designing a large complex system. It is *separation of concerns*. It is choosing an *appropriate representation for a problem* or modelling the relevant aspects of a problem to make it tractable. It is using invariants to describe a system's behaviour succinctly and declaratively. In other words, it is using *computational models of various types* to specify algorithms of the tasks we intend to solve.

How does all the stated relate to the separate topics discussed throughout the previous chapters? We have chosen the key criteria to evaluate the approach in its possibility to support computational thinking:

- *Chain of abstractions used in our approach*
- *Level of separation of concerns*
- *Representation of data* (models, algorithms) for problem solving
- *Types of computational models used*

We present the chain of abstractions moving from more abstract to more concrete. The chain includes (i) *feature models*, (ii) *transformation processes*, (iii) *high-level executable specifications*, (iv) *algorithms and low-level robot control programs* for various STEM-related tasks and (v*) visualization of the problem-solving process* in the real setting. Each ingredient of the chain has a list of relevant abstractions. For example, feature models represent STEM learning variability as a problem domain and meta-programming abstractions as a solution domain. Transformation processes include *model-to-model* (i.e. various manipulations within feature models such as splitting, aggregation, verification, etc.) and model-to-code transformation (i.e. feature model transformation to meta-program in designing, redesigning and maintaining SLOs largely, generative scenario or generative library partially). High-level executable specifications of any type (i.e. smart learning objects, generative scenario and generative libraries) contain within indeed a very rich repertoire of abstractions (i.e. meta-language constructs, target language constructs, meta-program model, meta-interface, meta-body, types of parameters and their relation-ships). Algorithms to define STEM-oriented tasks and low-level robot control pro-grams are typical abstractions to explain CS fundamentals using our approach.

Separation of concerns is a key term in CS and beyond. It refers to the process of breaking a design (program, meta-program or other items such as learning object) into distinct parts that overlap in functionality as little as possible (note that researchers use two terms *concepts* and *concerns* interchangeably as synonyms in the literature). The levels of separation of concerns include among domains (problem domain, i.e. STEM learning variability, and solution domain, i.e. meta-programming), within a domain (separation of concerns of meta-language and target language, etc.), within a model (e.g. meta-interface and meta-body, i.e. implementation) and within a process (i.e. transformation, generation, execu-tion). There is a variety of representation forms of data to specify models (scenarios, smart learning objects) or algorithms to define robot-oriented STEM-driven tasks. Finally, there are a series of computational models relevant to indicated abstractions, data and processes, i.e. for model processing, for high-level specifications processing and for robot control program processing.

How do the all stated can achieve the learners' understanding and affect their minds? In our view, there are two general approaches (i.e. implicit and explicit ones). The first resides within the learning scenarios and processes considered in detail in different chapters. The second requires more efforts and specific preparation. For example, the teacher is able to design slides on explicit representations of abstrac-tions used, separation of concerns aside. The other possibility is to design a specific document such as a narrative story in simple terms (examples) about all this. In addition, it is possible to create a film illustrating on how those things look like in an abstract mode and in reality. This way perhaps is the most influential and powerful.

15.2.4   Drawbacks of the Proposed Approach

Despite of the capabilities discussed so far (they are treated as advantages and novelty), our approach suffers also from some difficulties we have identified here as drawbacks. Indeed the approach is a result of the intensive researching and experimentation work along with testing of the discovered results in the educational practice. Perhaps it is reasonable to consider drawbacks from different perspectives, i.e. designer, teacher and learner. However, the most important is the user's opinion and vision. Therefore, we formulate drawbacks from the learner's perspective separately. Firstly, we identify the following issues as common. However, we need to clarify to which constituent the provided issues relate. They include:

 (i) Complexity issues
 (ii) Maintainability issues (documentation, tools, changes)
 (iii) Maturity level
 (iv) Restricted scope of practice
 (v) Restricted statistical data accumulated
 (vi) Restricted evaluation of the competent external experts

All the enlisted issues are related. An external observer, for example, could evaluate the approach as complex enough. There are, however, well-defined metrics to evaluate the complexity of heterogeneous meta-programs, i.e. smart LOs and other generic specifications. Those metrics relate to multiple dimensions and, in fact, are issues of a designer, but not the user (teacher or student). They include *information dimension* known as the relative Kolmogorov complexity; *meta-language dimension*, i.e. meta-language richness; *the graph dimension*, i.e. cyclomatic complexity; *algorithmic complexity*; and *cognitive complexity* [ŠD13].

Maintainability issues include the clearness, completeness, quality and number of supporting documents. The documents lack of an external expertise and, in fact, are for the internal use in the local language. Though we apply this approach for more than 5 years, however, its maturity level, its scope of practice and collected data for the overall evaluation are restricted.

15.2.5   Difficulties from Teacher's Perspective

There are two views: (1) CS teacher is not a new resource creator but the consumer of personal generative library (PGL) resources or others without changes and (2) the smart teacher who is using principles of our approach but seeking for adaptation to his/her context. In case 1, there should not be many issues. In case 2, a series of challenges may occur. They could or might include the following: (i) deep understanding of the STEM-driven CS educational domain in order to be able to model (modify) the needed smart environment and formulate requirements for the designer; (ii) the PGL modification (adaptation) to fit to the needed context; (iii) problems related to acceptance of STEM-driven pedagogy, such as inquiry-based methods; and (iv) ensuring a qualitative monitoring and feedback. The stated is a part of open issues we discuss later in the ending section.

15.2.6 Drawbacks from Learner Perspective

Typically, the learner is a consumer of all components (i.e. SLOs, CB LOs, GS, PGL, SEE and other supporting tools) to be presented in the right place and at the right time. In the learning process, the teacher presents the components in the *black-box mode*, i.e. without the implementation details. This mode typically includes two possibilities of assisting and helping by the teacher. We identify them as teacher guiding here, i.e. as *high guiding* (case 1) and *low guiding* (case 2). In case 1, there are no difficulties for most students to accept the approach and perform the required activities. In case 2, especially when the student works online in the remote mode (this possibility also exists, but this is beyond the scope of topics we discuss in this book), there might arise some difficulties because of the lack of an adequate instructive material or its right interpretation, lack of self-motivation and other reasons. In both cases, the less motivated students evaluate the approach or some aspects (components) as complex enough.

The GS itself does not ensure the effective learning, i.e. there is no means to monitor and fix chaotic actions of the learner (if any) by choosing learning paths. The number of items the learner needs to select from the scenario interfaces may largely overpass the magic number "7". Therefore, selecting and understanding of a new portion of information may fall down significantly. The GS is very useful until the learner reaches the cognitive level of *Applying* and *Analysing* (according to Bloom's taxonomy). However, when the learner achieves highest levels of cognition, the GS may become an obstacle. For example, if the learner formulates a problem on his/her own or the teacher delivers a problem without the evident solution, in this case the scenario is not helpful. In this case, the PGL is more helpful.

The resources of PGLs are restricted. When the need to enrich PGLs by new resources from external repositories or created by teacher or student, the reliability issues may arise. This requires additional time and efforts. With extending the scope of the PGLs, maintainability of the resources also becomes an issue.

15.3   Applicability of the Approach at the University Level

We have discussed our approach in two modes, i.e. *design perspective* and *use perspective*. Both perspectives are applicable at the university level to teach CS or related disciplines. The design-related topics we discussed here, in fact, also are teaching themes of several programs provided at universities. In large, those themes include domain analysis methods, feature-based high-level modelling, the development tools for model transformation for both the application (educational software) and solution domain (high-level programming, domain-specific programming for robotics and educational software). For example, the development of the personal generative library might be a specific case study for database courses. The methodology to design the generative scenario is a relevant topic in designing complex systems. In our book, all the themes were the concern of the designer or CS teacher. At the university level, those themes become, largely, the concern of students too.

With regard to the use perspective, the university students are able to use the learning content in the black-box mode too. However, there might be the need to make some enhancements of capabilities of introduced items. One possibility is to enrich the considered tasks with additional functionality to make the same task more complex. The real candidates to do that could be tasks related to artificial intelligence [Pau17]. Solving, for example, tasks related to usage of artificial intelligence algorithms requires deeper insights into modelling and big data [Cao17] as compared to the school audience. The other possibility is to focus on the *white-box model* more intensively to enhance students' ability to modify and change systems. Furthermore, there is no doubt the modern concepts discussed so far are transferable to university teaching programs, however, most likely with some adaptation and enlargement.

15.4   STEM in Industry: A New Way

So far, we have discussed topics that belong to the educational paradigm one can call as "STEM in School". We did that from two perspectives, i.e. STEM-driven research and CS educational practice at school. Education in large is not a one-way activity. With regard to STEM, education is an extremely strong bidirectional activity. One way is the *school-industry* relationship and collaborative activities around that where school in a broader context is *master* and industry is *slave*. In other words, school authorities and academics are responsible for developing educational STEM programs, assigning resources for executing those programs with possible feedback from industry, as well as providing broad-scale research on various aspects. Industry plays the role of social ordering in this case. The other way is the inverse relationship, i.e. *industry-school* relationship, where industry is *master* and school (i.e. learners and teachers in a narrow sense) is *slave*. Today, as never before, industry has an extremely great interest in the STEM success at schools. Therefore, industry supports the "STEM in School" paradigm, i.e. school-industry relationship in a variety of ways. This paradigm has a long pre-history lasting at least two decades. Now however, there are evident signs of emerging of the paradigm that we call "STEM in industry" in which industry plays the role of master.

We have called this section "STEM in industry", aiming to outline what industry initiatives already have started with regard to STEM education and research. It is not our intention, however, to present a comprehensive analysis on this topic, but rather to pay attention on new possibilities. Here, we have identified them as "a new way". Those possibilities may include, for example, the interaction between the two paradigms enriching each other at least in two dimensions, i.e. STEM education practice and STEM education research. By STEM education research, we mean in the first place activities that lead to the development of more effective methodologies and finally the more advanced environments and tools than existing ones.

Currently, there is a myriad of government/industry initiatives known worldwide in the USA, Europe, Australia and other countries. To illustrate that, we have selected a few, in our view, of the representative initiatives as follows: (1) government initiatives; (2) industry-school (university) collaboration initiatives; (3) industry courses to support the STEM professional development of teachers; and (4) others, such as frameworks, tools and environments developed by industry for school.

1. In January 2017, the British Government published its Industrial Green Paper. The report [InS17] covers two themes, i.e. "Science, research and innovations" and "Developing skills" (meaning in STEM). It aims at feeding the Government's consultation exercise on its Green Paper. Among other issues, the report emphasizes the following

   The school curriculum must be kept relevant for students' STEM skills needs as they enter a continually evolving workplace. Continuing reforms will need to be evidence-based, however, to reflect not just what employers need but also the evidence on what initiatives are most effective in increasing and sustaining young people's interest in science and what really influences their study subject choices.

   For other governmental or responsible bodies initiatives, see Chap. 1.

2. The Microsoft initiative [MST17] focuses on strengthening K–12 education worldwide through a series of programs that support students, teachers and school leaders. The programs are indeed diverse and rich. We have selected only those that directly concern with STEM education. They include *Washington STEM initiative*, *Robotics* and *Games for learning*. For example, Microsoft External Research has sponsored a dozen robotics research and education projects at universities around the United States. In these projects, educators and learners have used Microsoft Robotics Developer Studio, an advanced general-purpose software toolkit enabling to run everything ranging from educational toys to industrial robots. Now, predominantly supported by the National Science

Foundation, Institute for Personal Robots in Education, uses personal robots to make introductory computer science instruction more relevant and engaging for both students and professors. The project's mission is to employ robots in STEM education at all levels, i.e. from middle school to graduate school.

3. In addition, Microsoft provides STEM professional development courses (https://education.microsoft.com/courses-and-resources/resources/STEM-resources) on the Microsoft Educator Community ("Teach Creative Coding through Games and Apps"). This video on-demand course prepares teachers for "providing an overview of course materials with suggestions how to use them, providing strategies for preparing to teach, and providing pedagogical tips for working with students in a collaborative, inquiry-based classroom".

4. The report [RY16] presents a view of Yaskawa Motoman needs for STEM education. It includes a comprehensive model for schools education on how to enforce the industrial workforce development. The model encompasses skill-based curricula, student-centric STEM robotic equipment, programming and virtualization software tools, and certification/credentialing programs to deliver real-world industrial experiences in a classroom environment. The report [And17] introduces the *SaaS digital platform* (developed by *GreenApple)*. The platform aims to enable educators and entrepreneurs to bring STEM education courses to their classrooms, camps, after school programs, workshops and organizations. The platform empowers students of all ages "to become STEM-proficient through rich multimedia offering hands-on activities, a virtual coaching tool for additional support, and game-based assessment".

At this end, yet another issue is important to speak. We mean re-education or requalification of currently existing workforce towards STEM. This topic is likely the internal business, and, no doubt, corporations are working on that. However, there are little direct announcements on this topic. It is most likely that this burden is left for individual self-learning, corporation learning, long-life learning or perhaps learning STEM using the MOOC paradigm.

15.5   MOOC and STEM-Driven CS Education

The acronym MOOC (MOOCs) stands for Massive Open Online Course(s). The learning paradigm based on MOOCs is the latest trend in higher education and research and perhaps the most significant one. Currently there is an evident hype on MOOCs and the extremely broad streams of research and practical activities on those issues. Therefore, we could not be able to close our discussion without presenting our vision on MOOCs in the context of what we discussed so far. Here, our aim is very modest. We aim in common vocabulary to outline (1) *what* are the key attributes of the MOOCs paradigm and (2) *what* concepts and ideas of our approach might be beneficial for this paradigm. The *how* aspects remain as open issues.

Researchers characterize MOOCs as the student-centred self-motivated learning aiming at gathering participants who are willing to jointly exchange the information of interest and collaboratively enhance their knowledge [CY14]. This paradigm represents a new generation of online education, freely accessible on the Internet and involving a huge number of students worldwide. A MOOC provides a new way of connecting distributed instructors and learners across a common topic or field of discourse. The *positive learning experience* is at the core of these learning activities. Those activities allow a single instructor to teach a huge number of students (e.g. tens or even hundreds of thousands). Participation in a MOOC is free; however, some MOOCs may charge a fee in the form of tuition if the participant seeks some form of accreditation [GS13]. MOOC is constructed using several principles stemming from connectivist pedagogy [Dow11, Kop11]:

(i)   The first principle is *aggregation.*
(ii) The second principle is *remixing*, that is, associating materials created within the course with each other and with materials elsewhere.
(iii) The third principle is *re-purposing* of aggregated and remixed materials.
(iv) The fourth principle is *feeding forward*, i.e. sharing of repurposed ideas and content with other participants and the rest of the world.

Below we summarize the key attributes taken from the literature [GMS13, Gar15, DOS15]:

- High flexibility (the participant can move beyond time zones and physical boundaries)
- High accessibility (you can connect across disciplines)
- Enhancement of the personal learning environment (MOOCs add to your own personal learning environment)
- Low cost and free tools (MOOCs are free for all who are interested)
- Effective guidance (it can be launched as quickly as you can inform the participants)
- Contribution to the paperless education environment (MOOCs can contribute heavily towards the paperless education environment)
- No obligation in receiving a degree (you do not need a degree to follow the course, only the willingness to learn)
- Learning occurs in an informal setting (instead of classroom)
- Digital skill development (students are often afforded a wide variety of assignments to choose)

However, this paradigm also poses many challenges. They include:

- Overcoming online cheating.
- Minor interaction with the course instructor.
- Difficulty in assessing complex learning.
- Chaotic nature in creating own content.
- More efforts and time are required from the participants.
- Need for self-regulation in learning.

- MOOC demands digital literacy and critical literacy.
- Need to be more active and higher level of creativity.
- Need for innovative thinking.

On this basis, we are able to identify the key problems with regard to the MOOC content design and delivery.

1. *Localization*
2. *Personalization*
3. *Adaptation and self-adaptation*
4. *Representation to enabling feedback for better understanding*
5. *Feedback for assessment and self-assessment*
6. *Technological support*

The stated MOOC attributes, challenges and problems is a context for the possible introduction of some ideas taken from our approach. Firstly, there are many efforts to deliver CS courses on this paradigm [CSM17]. Secondly, this context implicitly or explicitly tells about a huge variability space within the MOOC domain. Finally, as STEM-driven learning variability is the methodological background of our approach, similarly this concept is applicable in case of MOCC too, perhaps with a different interpretation. In terms of course design and delivery, for example, we can deal with a variety of variabilities, such as localization variability, personalization variability, adaptation and self-adaptation variability, representation variability, feedback and technological support variability. Those types of variability are applicable on both sides, i.e. design and delivery of the MOOC content and the user side. All these, however, are separate research topics.

15.6 Open Issues

Based on the discussion given in the previous sections, we are able to outline (of course, to some extent) open issues of the approach. They relate either to a separate component as a part of the approach or to the whole approach. On the other hand, one can deal with the approach from two perspectives, i.e. *design* and *use*. Therefore, we identify two groups of open issues, i.e. the *design-related* and *application-related* ones. The approach requires many design and predesign procedures in order to achieve the prescribed objectives (e.g. automation, reuse, adaptation, flexibility, practicality and other aspects) and to be efficient and applicable in learning practice. Those procedures focus on creating *domain-specific software (i.e. components of the approach) to support STEM-driven CS education.* Typically, those components represent educational tools, which are known in the scientific literature under the general term such as *educational software.*

In general, to create educational software, designers try to apply approaches borrowed from software engineering. One stream of those methodologies uses feature-based modelling. Our approach, at the top level, belongs just to that stream.

Though there are evident signs and efforts to introduce the feature-based design methodology in creating educational software, however, those efforts are still lack of a wider recognition and acceptance within the huge e-Learning community. As our application domain is extremely heterogeneous, has a dynamic nature and therefore is complex in terms of stated requirements, the static feature models are not sufficient to represent the domain requirements. *Dynamic feature models* are still in the infancy stage in software engineering research [CBT14]. The use of those models (they also cover static feature models) in creating educational software is a general open problem. It covers many other open issues such as a better understanding of *static learning variability, dynamic learning variability, identification of their boundaries* and *scope*. We remind readers that those abstractions stand at the centre of our approach. We believe in soundness of those abstractions and their applicability in many other educational paradigms (STEM, STEAM, MOOC, Smart learning eco-systems and contexts, etc.). That forms, however, the by-product issues.

The indicated issues relate to the *problem domain*. In addition, design-related open issues also cover the *solution domain* (i.e. meta-programming at the top level, agent-based methodology). We have applied meta-programming at two levels, i.e. component (we mean smart learning objects, or generative components that are a part of the generative library itself) and system (we mean the generative scenario for STEM). System-level meta-programming is indeed a big open problem that requires a specific attention and intensive research as a separate theme. The use of agent-based technology in our approach is still fragmental. This yet requires extensive research. With regard to the designed separate components, such as a personal generative library for student, we require to collect more statistical data for further investigation. The integrative aspects of the approach, such as smart STEM-driven educational environment, require investigation that is more extensive in efforts, resources and durability.

With regard to the application-level, we identify open issues as mixed *technical* and *non-technical* for the ready-to-use components of our approach. Technical issues relate to maintenance and evolution efforts of the key components. Practically, the designer (or CS teacher as a designer) is able to provide this activity and introduce changes (if any). If the CS teacher is also a designer as in our case, she has an explicit feedback and may want to introduce improvements into the functionality of a particular component. This requires additional efforts and resources and may reduce the quality and cause additional problems. On the other hand, the created components are indeed a valuable intellectual property. It needs to be protectable in a right way. In addition, this property should be accessible to as many interested parts (users, i.e. CS teachers) as possible. This requires a financial support and causes social problems such as either creation of the new adequate communities or entering into already existing communities. Therefore, the dissemination of this intellectual property has barriers such as the quality of the documentation, localization and financial issues. With respect to CS teachers who are not yet ready to play the role of designers or redesigners (e.g. to support a possible adaptation of our approach to personal needs), among others, there are open issues of teachers' preparation or requalification.

In summary, the discussed capabilities, the indicated difficulties and the outlined issues of our approach open a wide space for the further research in terms of each novel component proposed and in terms of the multiple methodological aspects we have introduced in this book.

References

[AK09]   Apel S, Kästner C (2009) An overview of feature-oriented software development. J Object Technol 8(2009):49–84
[And17]   Andringa P (2017) New STEM edtech platform provides training for coveted and in-demand jobs https://sociable.co/technology/edtech-stem-saas/
[Cao17]   Cao L (2017) Data science: a comprehensive overview. ACM Comput Surv (CSUR) 50(3):43
[CBT14]   Capilla R, Bosch J, Trinidad P, Ruiz-Cortés A, Hinchey M (2014) An overview of dynamic software product line architectures and techniques: observations from research and industry. J Syst Softw 91(5):3–23
[CSM17]   How to get a computer science education with 20 MOOCs for Free, http://www.computersciencezone.org/computer-science-education-free-with-moocs/
[CY14]   Chai Y, Yang LS (2014) A literature review of MOOC. In: 3rd International Conference on Science and Social Research (ICSSR 2014). Atlantis Press
[DOS15]   Drake JR, O'Hara M, Seeman E (2015) Five principles for MOOC design: with a case study. J Inf Technol Educ Innov Pract 14:125–143
[Dow11]   Downes S (2011) Connectivism and connective knowledge. Huffpost Education
[Gar15]   García I (2015) Massive Open Online Courses (MOOC): theoretical education and pedagogical foundation. In: CONGRESO CAFVIR2015
[GMS13]   Guàrdia L, Maina M, Sangrà A (2013) MOOC design principles: a pedagogical approach from the learner's perspective. eLearning Pap 33
[GS13]   Gupta R, Sambyal N (2013) An understanding approach towards MOOCs. Int J Emerg Technol Adv Eng 3(6):312–315
[InS17]   Industrial strategy: science and STEM skills. House of Commons, Science and Technology Committee, 29, March 2017
[Kop11]   Kop R (2011) The challenges to connectivist learning on open online networks: learning experiences during a massive open online course. Int Rev Res Open Dist Learn 12(3):2011
[MST17]   (2017) STEM: a foundation for the future: improving student skills in science, technology, engineering, and math. Microsoft
[Pau17]   Paulauskas A (2017) Virtual reality games for rehabilitation. Int J Comp Eng Inf Technol 9(10., October 2017):246–253
[RY16]   Roger C, Yaskawa M (2016) STEM education is critical to a vibrant manufacturing future, industry week
[ŠB15]   Štuikys V, Burbaitė R (2015) Smart education in CS: a case study. In: Štuikys V (ed) Smart learning objects for smart education in computer science: theory, methodology and robot-based implementation. Springer, New York, pp 287–310
[ŠD13]   Štuikys V, Damaševičius R (2013) Meta-programming and model-driven meta-program development: principles processes and techniques. Springer, London
[Štu15]   Štuikys V (2015) Smart learning objects for smart education in computer science: theory, methodology and robot-based implementation. Springer, New York
[Win06]   Wing JM (2006) Computational thinking. Commun ACM 49(3):33

Glossary

AB GLO	Agent-based generative learning object
AFM	Abstract feature model
ASM	Abstract state machine
CB LO	Component-based learning object
CC	Content context
CFM	Concrete feature model
CLV	STEM CS learning variability
CPACK	Computational, Pedagogical and Content Knowledge
CS	Computer science
CT	Computational thinking
DA	Domain analysis
DL	Domain language
DLs	Digital libraries
DSL	Domain-specific language
EEE	Effective educational environment
EML	Educational Modelling Language
ER	Educational robot
FAMILIAR	FeAture Model scrIpt Language for manIpulation and Automatic Reasoning
FBM	Feature-based modelling
FD	Feature diagram
FM	Feature model
FODA	Feature-oriented domain analysis
GLO	Generative learning object
GPPL	General-purpose programming language
GS	Generative scenario
HBA	Human being agent
HP	High priority
HWA	Hardware agent
IoT	Internet-of-Things

© Springer International Publishing AG, part of Springer Nature 2018   365
V. Štuikys, R. Burbaitė, *Smart STEM-Driven Computer Science Education*,
https://doi.org/10.1007/978-3-319-78485-4

IP	Intermediate priority
KB	Knowledge base
LO	Learning object
LP	Low priority
LV	Learning variability
M&S MP	Management and support meta-program
MB	Meta-body
MDA	Model-driven architecture
MePAG	Meta-program Automatic Generator
ML	Meta-language
MOOC	Massive Open Online Course
MP	Meta-program
MPG	Heterogeneous meta-programming
MP-ReTool	Meta-program refactoring tool
PC	Pedagogical context
PD	Problem domain
PGL	Personal generative library
PLE	Product Line Engineering
PLO	Physical learning object
RCP	Robot control program
ROABEE	Robot-oriented agent-based educational environment
SB GLO	Stage-based generative learning object
SCV	Scope-Commonality-Variability
SD	Solution domain
SEE	Smart educational environment
SLE	Smart learning environment
SLO	Smart learning object/smart generative learning object
SOLO	Structure of the Observed Learning Outcome (Taxonomy)
SPL	Software product lines
SPLOT	Software Product Lines Online Tools
STEAM	Science, Technology, Engineering, Arts and Mathematics
STEM	Science, Technology, Engineering and Mathematics
SWA	Software agent
SWE	Software engineering
TA	Technological agent
TC	Technological context
TEL	Technology-enhanced learning
TL	Target language
TPACK	Technological, Pedagogical and Content Knowledge

Index

A

Adaptation, vi, 9, 13, 21, 35, 72, 87, 88, 105, 114, 119, 121, 122, 128, 136, 140, 149, 153, 162, 163, 165, 168, 189–191, 193–201, 204–206, 208, 209, 211, 213, 217, 219, 220, 234, 236, 248, 252, 253, 260, 264, 289, 296, 297, 299, 322, 338, 349, 353, 355, 357, 361, 362

C

Component-based LO, 241, 313, 352
Computational thinking, 4, 13, 32, 34, 35, 60, 260, 281, 306, 308, 312, 348, 349, 351–354
Computer science (CS) education, vii
Content context (CC), 38, 49, 166, 168
Context, viii, 13, 167, 168, 281, 282, 286, 287, 323
Context-aware, 282
Context variability, 15, 76, 89, 93, 114, 172, 338

D

Domain analysis, 37, 42, 44, 73–75, 89, 104, 108, 109, 138, 160, 169, 348, 357
Dynamic variability, 75, 76, 93, 94, 102, 112, 123, 124

E

Educational robotics, v–vii, 21, 22, 33, 35, 38, 51, 58, 60, 66, 260, 264, 265, 273, 280

F

Feature model, 47, 48, 74, 79, 83, 84, 89, 92, 102, 109–112, 115, 124, 158, 164, 170–173, 175, 176, 178–181, 185, 240, 242, 244, 246, 274, 338, 340, 354
Feature modelling, vi, 102, 108, 109, 114, 158
Feature model script language for manipulation and automatic reasoning (FAMILIAR), 288, 365
Fuzzy variables, 321, 322

G

Generative component, 100, 119, 128, 365
Generative learning object (GLO), 136, 162
Generative scenario, 20, 21, 119, 183, 260, 265, 271, 272, 294, 312, 314, 350, 351, 354, 357, 362
Generic architecture, 58, 59, 64, 66

H

Hardware agent (HWA), 365
Heterogeneous meta-programming, vii, 107, 116, 117, 127, 138, 148, 166, 179, 180, 182, 190, 240, 260, 349

I

Inquiry-based learning (IBL), vi, 183, 266, 297, 343
Instructional design, 5, 159
Internet of Things (IoT), vii, 15–17, 22, 58, 183, 327–339, 341, 342, 365

© Springer International Publishing AG, part of Springer Nature 2018
V. Štuikys, R. Burbaitė, *Smart STEM-Driven Computer Science Education*,
https://doi.org/10.1007/978-3-319-78485-4

L
Learning, viii, 14, 167, 279, 281, 282, 284–287,
    296–299, 322, 323
Learning content, vi, 13, 42, 43, 79, 85, 89, 116,
    117, 135, 136, 140–142, 151, 159, 182,
    193, 213, 349, 351, 357
Learning object (LO), viii, 289, 298, 366
Learning process (LP), vi, 41, 48, 149, 192,
    197, 212, 235, 279, 297, 356
Learning scenario, 149, 151, 152, 159, 259,
    263, 280, 292, 293, 350, 351
Learning variability, vii, 21, 22, 71, 73, 81, 82,
    84, 87–89, 93, 95, 101, 104, 127, 138,
    144, 145, 148, 149, 151–153, 158, 163,
    164, 169–171, 173, 178–183, 185, 198,
    210, 333, 343, 348–350, 352–354, 361,
    362, 365

M
Massive Open Online Course (MOOC), vii, 22,
    78, 80, 101, 348, 359–362, 366
MePAG, 288, 366
Meta-body (MB), 366
Metadata, 37, 118, 119, 144, 145, 194, 195,
    198, 211, 233, 237, 239–241, 245–247,
    250, 254
Meta-language, 126, 175, 242, 243, 292, 293
Meta-meta-program, 121, 213, 270, 271, 273
Meta-program, 116, 119, 163
Meta-programming techniques, vi, 104, 106,
    153, 158, 161, 190, 220, 239, 240, 252,
    261, 294
MP-ReTool, 366

P
Pedagogical context (PC), 168
Personal generative library (PGL), vii, 20, 148,
    205, 224, 233–254, 271, 280, 293, 300,
    312, 366

R
Robot-based environment, 284, 296

Robot control program (RCP), 65, 142, 206,
    208, 218, 223, 289, 317, 353
Robot-oriented agent-based educational
    environment (ROABEE), 223, 224, 366

S
SB GLO, 190, 195–198, 205, 206, 209–213,
    366
Scenario design, 264, 270
Smart educational environment (SEE), 352
Smart learning environment (SLE), 279, 280,
    284, 287, 298
Smart learning object (SLO), 45, 47, 48, 50,
    116, 119, 120, 126, 135, 136, 138–153,
    157, 158, 161–164, 166–182, 184, 185,
    190, 239, 241, 250, 252, 260, 280,
    286–289, 292, 294, 297, 336, 350, 352,
    353, 366
Social context, 72, 224
Software agent (SWA), 218, 220, 222,
    224–227, 366
Software Product Lines Online Tools (SPLOT),
    288, 366
Static variability, 75, 93, 112, 119
STEM-driven CS education, vii, 5, 9, 10,
    20–23, 33, 35, 38, 39, 48, 50, 58, 61, 65,
    66, 71, 87–89, 140, 158, 165, 166, 168,
    170, 172, 182, 190, 264, 266, 280, 284,
    286, 288, 290, 300, 305, 320, 337, 343,
    347, 348, 352, 361

T
Target language (TL), 147, 175
Teaching model, 286
Technological context (TC), 38, 49, 168, 173,
    220

V
Variability space, 75, 86, 142, 144, 149, 195,
    197, 198, 201, 210, 211, 221, 227, 273,
    361

Printed in the United States
By Bookmasters